MIKHAIL BAKHTIN

MIKHAIL BAKHTIN

An Aesthetic for Democracy

KEN HIRSCHKOP

OXFORD
UNIVERSITY PRESS

OXFORD
UNIVERSITY PRESS

Great Clarendon Street, Oxford OX2 6DP

Oxford University Press is a department of the University of Oxford.
It furthers the University's objective of excellence in research, scholarship,
and education by publishing worldwide in

Oxford New York

Athens Auckland Bangkok Bogotá Buenos Aires Calcutta
Cape Town Chennai Dar es Salaam Delhi Florence Hong Kong Istanbul
Karachi Kuala Lumpur Madrid Melbourne Mexico City Mumbai
Nairobi Paris São Paulo Singapore Taipei Tokyo Toronto Warsaw

with associated companies in Berlin Ibadan

Oxford is a registered trade mark of Oxford University Press
in the UK and in certain other countries

Published in the United States
by Oxford University Press Inc., New York

British Library Cataloguing in Publication Data

Data available

Library of Congress Cataloging in Publication Data
Hirschkop, Ken.
Mikhail Bakhtin: an aesthetic for democracy / Ken Hirschkop.
Includes bibliographical references and index.
1. Bakhtin, M. M. (Mikhail Mikhailovich), 1895–1975.
2. Literature—History and criticism—Theory, etc. 3. Criticism—
Political aspects. 4. Language and languages—Philosophy.
I. Title.
PN75.B25H57 1999 801'.95'092—dc21 99-16106
ISBN 0-19-815961-7
ISBN 0-19-815960-9 (pbk.)

1 3 5 7 9 10 8 6 4 2

Typeset by Regent Typesetting, London
Printed in Great Britain on acid-free paper by
Bookcraft (Bath) Ltd.,
Midsomer Norton, Somerset

To the memory of my mother

PHYLLIS ABADZOGLOU (1931–1979)

Preface

No doubt some will think the subtitle of this book is forced or inappropriate. After all, they will probably say, Bakhtin mentions the word 'democratic' or 'democratized' only a few times in all of his work, and by all accounts he was neither convinced of the value of politics nor democratic in whatever political sympathies he had. All of which is true. If, nevertheless, I think democracy should be central to any study of Bakhtin's work, it is because I have become convinced that the last thing we should worry about these days is whether or not we are capturing the spirit of Bakhtin's work. For capturing its spirit has not got us very far. It has left us not with a knowledge of his work, but with a series of Bakhtin-figures or totems, each equally ambitious, equally insightful, equally dogmatic, and absolutely different from every other figure. The spirit of Bakhtin's enterprise usually turns out to be something global, impressive, fairly vague, and uncannily familiar, which makes me think that the letter of his work is what we should be looking at. In the detail of his texts— wherein God dwells, of course—lie the problems, the sources, the un-acknowledged debts, the historical negotiations and tensions, which may or may not add up to something whole. Bakhtin has been a heroic figure with a few brilliant insights; we need to make him a man caught in his circumstances, and struggling to make sense of them. We need a more technical, more difficult, less inspiring Bakhtin, and this book is an attempt to find one.

It might be better to say: we need a more 'historical' Bakhtin. A Bakhtin who does not deliver philosophical verities about dialogue, or a new ontology of language, but something more modest and more pointed. When Bakhtin wrote about dialogism, it was in the context of the culture around him; when he wrote of heteroglot language, it was as a creature of modern Europe. The crises he faced were distinctly of his time, the ethical pressures and confusions the historical fate of twentieth-century Europe. If we fail to see this (as Bakhtin himself sometimes did), we use his words not as a bridge between our world and his, but as a way to fill in the river itself. In that flat expanse we will find not a particular con-ception of dialogue, a specific model of language, an argument for novel-istic prose which makes historical sense, but language as such, dialogue as such, novelness as such, as if these were metaphysical substances travelling effortlessly over historical terrain. Which is to say, we will find only those ideas we are sure of already.

Bakhtin is distant from us, but not, of course, irrelevant; we have *reasons* for attending to him. In a typically arresting passage, Walter Benjamin once suggested that 'historical knowledge' could be represented as a weighing scale, one pan 'weighed down by the past, the other by knowledge of the present'. 'The facts assembled in the former', he remarked, 'can never be too numerous or too insignificant. The latter, however, may contain only a few massive, heavy weights.'[1] I am no historian (as I will make abundantly clear in the course of this book), but I have supplied plenty of facts, textual and biographical, and have spared no effort to ensure that the pan containing the past is well supplied. At the same time, my weight is clear and unambiguous and, to my mind, entirely appropriate, despite Bakhtin's aversion to politics in general and political democracy in particular. Why democracy?

One could justify this on tactical grounds alone, for democracy already lies below the surface of current passions for Bakhtin, which go far beyond the admiration one would expect even for a brilliant contributor to literary theory. No one doubts that Bakhtin may be inspiring as a critic, but 'dialogism' has not acquired its current aura on the basis of literary-critical merit alone; its extraordinary popularity depends upon a convenient marriage of literary to socio-political value. We rarely hear that a dialogical or carnivalesque text is a more beautiful one, more often that it incarnates moral responsibility, represents subordinate social voices, or idealizes the give-and-take which characterizes the perfect speech community. In Anglo-American discussion, dialogism is invoked as an ideal of communication from a political point of view, and disagreements over its meaning or shape are disagreements about the kind of communication we deem necessary to democratic life.

But there is more than a tactical question at stake, and I think it is no accident that democracy is the subtext of so much current discussion. For the problem Bakhtin articulates is that of a society in which democratizing culture and politics has destroyed traditional authority. Bakhtin does not write about language and culture *sub specie aeternitatis* but language and culture which have decisively broken with traditional forms: a vernacular language, in which all have a right to speak, in which no speaker holds absolute authority, and where subjects should adhere to a moral code they elaborate together. The struggles he recounts are struggles between

---

[1] Benjamin, from Notebook 'N' (Re the Theory of Knowledge, Theory of Progress) of the *Passagenwerk*, *Gesammelte Schriften*, vol. v, 1, ed. Rolf Tiedemann (Frankfurt: Suhrkamp, 1982), 585; quoted from Irving Wohlfarth, 'The Measure of the Possible, the Weight of the Real and the Heat of the Moment: Benjamin's Actuality Today', New Formations, 20 (1993), 11.

forms of language on this already transformed historical ground; they are struggles about the direction a distinctively modern language should take, and by extension, the direction modern social relationships, or the ethical life of modern societies, should take. Bakhtin does not think that political democracy has much to do with this, and this is why democracy turns out to be a paradox for him. As I argue below, much of what he wants a dialogical culture to achieve depends on the very kind of politics he regards as irrelevant. To understand his purely cultural conception of a dialogical, novelistic world, we will need political concepts he would rather do without.

But if Bakhtin tries to imagine a democratic culture without democratic politics, this is not something we should seek merely to correct. The massive weight of democracy bears down not just on him, but on us, too, and it is what compels us to look back on him with interest. For while there are plenty of political democracies today, there is far less in the way of democratic politics, and the reasons for this are cultural as much as political. Democracy must mean more than procedure; it needs the depth culture has to offer. An emancipated society has to mean not only control over economic life, but satisfying relationships, everyday dignity and solidarity, and narratives which make one's life not only prosperous but also meaningful. An account of democracy distant from the realities of capitalist cultural life forgets that the task of a socialist movement is, as Raymond Williams put it, 'one of feeling and imagination quite as much as one of fact and organization'.[2]

We can turn to Bakhtin for reflection on these questions because in the Russia where he lived and worked democracy existed *only* as culture, never having established itself as a set of observed political procedures. In the wake of 1917 'democracy' meant not polling booths and campaigns, but education, confidence amongst new sectors of the population, urbanization, electronic culture, literacy, and mass mobilizations: a partial democratization, one might say, of feeling and imagination though not of fact and institution, which told in the end. Bakhtin tangled with these changes, and their equivalents across Europe, in a way which was both intensive and blinkered. The intensity we see; the blinkers we often fail to notice. If we grasp them together, we have a striking account of the problems of a democratic culture. Bakhtin can still speak to us, but we have to ask him the right questions.

Weighing scales imply a rather classical, balanced architecture; alas, this is not the case with the present text, which has a somewhat unusual structure. Part I comprises a basic statement of aims and the fundamentals

[2] Raymond Williams, 'You're a Marxist, Aren't You?', in *Resources of Hope*, ed. Robin Gable (London: Verso, 1989), 76.

of my reading of Bakhtin. Its introduction argues that, first appearances notwithstanding, there can and should be an intimate relation between language and democracy. In this way I hope to justify at some length the terms in which I examine Bakhtin's work. The chapter which follows it demonstrates that to take this relation seriously, we have to acknowledge the specificity of 'dialogism' and its difference from what we think of as dialogue; we have to interpret it as a response to the historical problem of democratic culture. I do this through a comparative reading of two of Bakhtin's major works, 'Discourse in the Novel' and 'Author and Hero in Aesthetic Activity', which together reveal something neither of them can on their own. Having set out the basic case, I then provide a lengthy biographical excursus, which describes the chronology of Bakhtin's life and the historical logic of his writing. The final part of the book is composed of four shorter chapters, each of which investigates how Bakhtin worked through a particular theme. The first of these examines Bakhtin's theory of language, its relation to the idea of personality, and his assimilation of Saussure; the second discusses the theory of the novel as an attempt to mediate the idea of dialogue and the idea of narrative; the third focuses on the concepts of the public square and heteroglossia, as a way of bringing discussions of 'discourse in art' back to the question of 'discourse in life'; the final chapter discusses the theory of carnival and the relation of democracy to fear and laughter. The book's chapters constitute a consecutive argument, but they also provide a comprehensive and coherent account of Bakhtin's work. Only the reader, of course, can decide whether the scale finally balances.

K. H.
Manchester, England

Acknowledgements

I'll be blunt—this book has become something of an embarrassment to me. It should have been finished a long time ago, and as its seemingly endless revision dragged on through the years, loved ones and colleagues alike became increasingly emboldened to tell me so. So I am pleased—you cannot possibly imagine how much—to have put that awkwardness behind me, and to have rewarded, in however disappointing a way, the patience of all those who waited, cajoled, helped, and even reprimanded me. Writing in the humanities always involves a lopsided collectivism, in which the author depends on the support of dozens of people who are nevertheless powerless when it comes to making the sentences up. The longer the work takes, the more people become involved in this frustrating arrangement. Now the reader must be patient, for I have accumulated many debts in the writing of this book, and I am determined to recount as many of them as possible.

First and most patient was Terry Eagleton, for he supervised the doctoral dissertation on which the book is based, and encouraged my work on it for many years afterwards. Being something of a speed merchant amongst writers, he must have been puzzled by the time I took, but to his great credit he never showed it, and his enthusiasm for this project remained strangely undulled even to the very end. Paul Hamilton, Patrizia Nanz, and Bruce Robbins read the manuscript in whole or part and provided, across the years, not only intellectual advice of the highest calibre, but also encouragement that the project was worth sustaining. Tony Pinkney and Maria Lauret were constant friends and intellectual companions, and equally adept in each role. Jane Grayson was a brilliant and selfless teacher to me at the beginning, and a brilliant and selfless friend afterwards. Robin Gable, to whom patience and warmth come as easily as breathing, has done so much for me since my arrival in England, and has provided so much in the way of food for thought (and to be fair, food of the ordinary sort as well), that the book bears his imprint on every page.

Much of this text was researched and written while I worked in the English Department of the University of Southampton. I owe special thanks to the entire department past and present for their continuous warmth, support, and friendship, and in particular I want to thank Southampton colleagues Erica Carter, Bill Marshall, Robert Young, Peter

Middleton, and Jonathan Sawday. Tony Crowley, whom I've now known in three different academic contexts, has been an intellectual compatriot in every sense, and the present work owes a great deal to our many conversations and a few of our wagers (all of which, I will confess publicly, I have lost). To my colleagues at the University of Manchester I owe thanks for the generous grant of a sabbatical which allowed me to complete the text and for so generously supporting the research efforts of a newcomer in their midst. Through the generous support of the British Academy I have been able to conduct research in Moscow, Leningrad (as was), and the United States. And like every work of scholarship, this one depended on the help and expertise offered by countless library staff, in this case, from the British Library, the Russian State Library (formerly Lenin Library) in Moscow, the library at Pushkinskii Dom in Leningrad (again, as was), the Slavonic Section of the Taylorian Library at Oxford, the Sterling Library at Yale University, the Widener Library at Harvard University, the Hartley Library at the University of Southampton, the John Rylands University Library at Manchester, and, last but certainly not least, the New York Public Library. All of which would not have resulted in a book, of course, but for the efforts of my editors at Oxford University Press, Sophie Goldsworthy and Matthew Hollis, and the painstaking work of the copy-editor, Janet Moth. Together they turned a long, unwieldy manuscript into a printed book someone might actually read.

The world of Bakhtin scholarship has sometimes been described as an industry. If most industries were like it, the world would be a far better place and socialists like myself would be out of a job. For generous support of and help with my research, expressed in gestures large and small, I wish to thank Ann Jefferson, Ann Shukman, Clive Thomson, Anthony Wall, Craig Brandist, and Michael Holquist. Many Russian friends and colleagues have been welcoming, helpful, and generous in a way which does credit to the ideal of an intellectual community—for this I want to thank Vitaly Makhlin, Iudif Kagan, Iuri Medvedev, Nikolai Pan'kov, Viktoria Tsybulskaia, Olga Vainshtein, and Aydin Djzhebrailov. Brian Poole, who may someday revolutionize Bakhtin scholarship, has been extremely generous with the material he has accumulated on Kagan and Bakhtin, and has offered me invaluable advice. Graham Pechey would deserve a medal merely for having read in their entirety both the typescript of this book and the dissertation which preceded it; but I want to thank him most for the constant intellectual stimulation he has provided and for the example which his own exceptional work on Bakhtin has set. But most of all I should like to thank my friend David Shepherd for the innumerable times he has sent me an article or done me a favour, for the enormous labour of advising me on the translations, for the suggestions he offered after reading the typescript, and, most importantly, for being my partner in crime in the world of Bakhtin scholarship.

There are friends who have helped immeasureably simply by being friends. Although Clair Wills and I discussed much that found its way into the book, I need to thank her most of all for selfless and unacknowledged support at an early stage of the research, and for being a supportive and encouraging co-parent (or whatever the term should be) since. Peter Dews generously commented on two chapters, and is, as far as I can tell, the world's greatest stepfather (excepting, of course, my own). Francis Mulhern has been understanding and supportive with a series of typically last-minute requests. Several of my American friends—Michael Herz, Stephen Belsky, Jenny Connolly, Mark Risk—have helped me over the years in a variety of ways, though they have regarded this, being the people they are, as the natural course of friendship.

I want finally to acknowledge the help of my family, some of whom have had to communicate their support over long distances for almost two decades. To my father and stepfather I can only say thank you for decades of kindness and love; to my sister, a truly extraordinary person, thanks for a lifetime of warmth and support, but also for reminding me what democracy looks like in action; to Morty and Gilbert (uncles, since you ask) thank you both for support and a boundless faith in the virtues of being educated. My two children—Jacob, Roisin—haven't done much to help me write this; in fact, they have done more to distract me from it than anything else, but I have enjoyed every minute of not writing this more than they can imagine. I have to thank Joanne Hurley for changing my life utterly, for trying to make love and politics fit together in one house, and for being the wonderful person with whom I can share the bits and pieces of our lives.

And finally there is the one to whom this book is dedicated. A debt to a deceased parent needs no explanation, but a book which has an ethical and political case to make should acknowledge those who inspired its passions. The spectacle of human misery, the trials of an ordinarily difficult life, can lead to a sense of resignation or a lack of faith in the force of moral judgement. My mother never lost that faith, or the ability to extract from life the good humour and decency which are its essential complement. These qualities, too, are necessary to humanistic writing worthy of the name, and they can't be learned from books alone. To my greatest teacher and example, therefore, I dedicate a work which is overdue in more senses than one.

Contents

A Note on Sources, References, and Transliteration   xvi

List of Abbreviations   xviii

PART I. AN ARGUMENT ABOUT DIALOGUE

1. Introduction: Language and Democracy   3

2. Dialogue with History   50

PART II. THE MATTER OF HISTORY

3. Bakhtin Myths and Bakhtin History   111
   On the 'Accursed Question'—Childhood and Education, 1895–1917—
   Philosophy in Nevel' and Vitebsk, 1918–1924—Leningrad and the
   Turn to Science, 1924–1929—Work on the Novel, 1930–1946—
   Philosophy of Language and Saransk, 1945–1961—Rediscovery
   and Late Philosophy, 1961–1975

PART III. REFINEMENTS

4. Language   197

5. The Novel   225

6. The Public Square as Public Sphere   249

7. Fear and Democracy   272

Bibliography   299

Index   325

A Note on Sources, References, and Transliteration

Bakhtin is not the kind of writer who leaves you with a string of finished texts and the odd letter or sketch. The great majority of his work was published posthumously, and most of it consists of rough drafts for essays or notebooks. In the difficult conditions of the late USSR, many texts were put together by assiduous and dedicated editors, who were anxious to put material into the public domain and who did not have the luxury of providing a detailed editorial apparatus explaining their procedures. As a consequence, some of the essays central to Bakhtin's reputation exist only in censored form, some are in fact editorial inventions, and in many—in fact, most—cases we simply do not know the relation between the printed text and the manuscript materials. Add to this the fact that the English translations are inconsistent among themselves and often work from outdated versions, and the philological nightmare is more or less complete.

In these conditions, a fluent system of reference is hard to organize. Even though some of Bakhtin's 'works' are no more than a sequence of entries in a notebook, I have decided to treat all materials, from preparatory notes to formally edited books, as of equivalent status in my arguments. One could hardly do otherwise: we have no means for establishing a pecking order amongst the texts and no sequence of authorial revisions to rely on. It is a sad but irreversible fact of history that Bakhtin was to be a creator of notebooks rather than books. I therefore refer to all 'texts' by Bakhtin, as well as those of Medvedev and Voloshinov, whatever their form and origin, by means of the convention-ally used titles below, which I have turned into a set of abbreviations for use in parenthetical in-text references. In each case I have used either the most authoritative or else the most inclusive Russian version of the text to hand. The translations into English are my own, though I have of course greatly benefited from the earlier efforts of others (and from the invaluable advice of David Shepherd). On the assumption that many readers of this book will want to know where to find the relevant quotation in English, most of the references will consist of two sets of page-numbers, the first referring to the Russian text and the second to the existing English trans-lation. So, for example, a reference such as DN 72/263 means the passage is taken from page 72 of *Voprosy literatury i estetiki*, the collection in which the essay 'Discourse in the Novel' appeared in Russian, and page 263 of the relevant collection in English, in this case, *The Dialogic Imagination*. Where no English translation exists, naturally only one page reference is given.

As if this weren't bad enough, I need to warn readers in advance about three exceptional cases. (1) The book *Problems of Dostoevsky's Art*, published in 1929, was heavily revised for republication in 1963 as *Problems of Dostoevsky's Poetics*, and the English translation is of the revised edition, with some of the passages revised out included as appendices. When I am quoting from the 1929 edition, the second page reference is either to the English translation of the later edition or the appendices of that edition, when the passage in question is found there. (2) The essay 'The Problem of the Text in Linguistics, Philology and the other Human Sciences' was published in 1979 in Russian and translated into English in 1986. In the new *Collected Works*, the editors have revealed that this essay was created by putting together the contents of two distinct sets of notes, the latter of which should have been published with the notes known as 'Towards a Reworking of the Dostoevsky Book'. In the *Collected Works*, whose practice I have followed, the first half of the old essay continues life as 'The Problem of the Text'; the second half has now been reunited with the old 'Towards a Reworking of the Dostoevsky Book' and has been re-christened 'Notes from 1961', and I refer to it as such in my text (in English it still lives on as the second half of the original version of 'Problem of the Text'). (3) The opening section of 'Author and Hero in Aesthetic Activity', or rather what remains of it, was published in Russian seven years after the body of the work. I refer to it as 'Author and Hero: Fragment of the First Chapter'; in English it has appeared as a 'Supplementary Section' following 'Author and Hero' itself.

Russian terms and names have been transliterated using the Library of Congress system, but without diacritical marks. I have also retained the familiar practice of using -y to transliterate the Russian -*ii* or -*yi* when found at the end of proper names (e.g. Dostoevsky). The mark ⟨?⟩ is used in Russian editions of Bakhtin's work to indicate a section of manuscript text which the editors were unable to decipher. In the interest of accuracy, I've reproduced this editorial sign whenever appropriate.

List of Abbreviations

Note: Where full publishing details are not given, they can be found in the section headed 'Collections of Essays in Russian and English' in the Bibliography.

AddAmR   'Additions and Amendments to "Rabelais"' ['Dopolneniia i izmeneniia k "Rable"', 1944]. In *SS5*, 80–129

AH   'Author and Hero in Aesthetic Activity' ['Avtor i geroi v esteticheskoi deiat'elnosti', *c.*1924–27]. In *Estetika slovesnogo tvorchestva*, 9–191; English translation in *Art and Answerability*, 4–208

AH: FC   'Author and Hero in Aesthetic Activity (Fragment of the First Chapter)' ['Avtor i geroi v esteticheskoi deiat'elnosti (Fragment pervoi glavy)', *c.*1924–27]. In *Filosofiia i sotsiologiia nauki i tekhniki* (Moscow: Nauka, 1986), 138–57; English translation in *Art and Answerability*, 208–31

AR   'Art and Responsibility' ['Isskustvo i otvetstvennost"', 1919]. In *Estetika slovesnogo tvorchestva*, 7–8; English translation in *Art and Answerability*, 1–3

Archive   Material from the Bakhtin Archive which has been published in the notes and commentary of Volume 5 of the Russian *Collected Works*: see under *SS5* below

Bil.   'The *Bildungsroman* and its Significance in the History of Realism' ['Roman vospitaniia i ego znachenie v istorii realizma', 1936–38]. In *Estetika slovesnogo tvorchestva*, 199–249; English translation in *Speech Genres and Other Late Essays*, 10–59

Con.   *Conversations between V. D. Duvakin and M. M. Bakhtin* [*Besedy V. D. Duvakina s M. M. Bakhtinym*]. Transcript of 1973 interviews; Russian edition: ed. V. B. Kuznetsova, M. B. Radzishevskaia, and V. F. Teider (Moscow: Progress, 1996)

D-II   'Dialogue II' ['Dialog II', 1952]. In *SS5*, 218–40

DN   'Discourse in the Novel' ['Slovo v romane', 1934–35]. In *Voprosy literatury i estetiki*, 72–233; English translation in *The Dialogic Imagination*, 259–422

Dos61   'Dostoevsky 1961' ['Dostoevsky. 1961g.']. In *SS5*, 364–74

EN   'Epic and Novel' ['Epos i roman: O metodologii issledovaniia romana', 1941]. In *Voprosy literatury i estetiki*, 447–83; English translation in *The Dialogic Imagination*, 3–40

Flau.   'On Flaubert' ['O Flobere', *c.*1944–45]. In *SS5*, 130–7

FM   P. N. Medvedev, *The Formal Method in Literary Scholarship*

	[*Formal'nyi metod v literaturovedenii*, 1928]. English translation by Albert J. Wehrle (Cambridge, Mass. and London: Harvard University Press, 1985)
FPND	'From the Prehistory of Novelistic Discourse' ['Iz predystorii romannogo slova', 1940). In *Voprosy literatury i estetiki*, 408–46; English translation in *The Dialogic Imagination*, 41–83
Fr.	V. N. Voloshinov, *Freudianism: A Critical Sketch* [*Freidizm: Kriticheskii ocherk*, 1927]. English translation: *Freudianism: A Marxist Critique*, ed. and trans. I. R. Titunik with Neal H. Bruss (New York: Academic Press, 1976)
FTC	'Forms of Time and of the Chronotope in the Novel' ['Formy vremeni i khronotopa v romana', 1937–38]. In *Voprosy literatury i estetiki*, 234–407; English translation in *The Dialogic Imagination*, 84–258
HisType	'On the History of the Type (Generic Variety) of the Novel of Dostoevsky' ['K istorii tipa (zhanrovoi raznovidnosti) romana Dostoevskogo', *c.*1940–41]. In *SS*5, 42–4
LArtLit.	'Language in Artistic Literature' ['Iazyk v khudozhestvennoi literature', 1954–55]. In *SS*5, 287–97
Lec.	'Lectures and Interventions by M. M. Bakhtin in 1924–1925, from notes by L. V. Pumpiansky' ['Lektsii i vystupleniia M. M. Bakhtina 1924–1925 gg. v zapisiakh L. V. Pumpianskogo']. Ed. N. I. Nikolaev, in L. A. Gogotishvili and P. S. Gurevich (eds.), *M. M. Bakhtin kak filosof* (Moscow: Nauka, 1992), 221–52
Mayak.	'On Mayakovsky' ['O Maiakovskom', *c.*1940–45]. In *SS*5, 50–62
MPL	V. N. Voloshinov, *Marxism and the Philosophy of Language* [*Marksizm i filosofiia iazyka*, 1929]. English translation by Ladislav Matejka and I. R. Titunik (Cambridge, Mass. and London: Harvard University Press, 1986)
Mult.	'Multilanguagedness as a Precondition of the Development of Novelistic Discourse' ['Mnogoiazychie, kak predposylka razvitiia romannogo slova', *c.*1940). In *SS*5, 157–8
N61	'Notes from 1961' ['1961 god. Zametki 1961-62']. In *SS*5, 329–63; English translation: first section in *Speech Genres and Other Late Essays*, 118–28; second section as appendix to *Problems of Dostoevsky's Poetics*, 283–302: see under *PDP* below
N70–71	'From the Notes of 1970–71' ['Iz zapisei 1970–1971 godov']. In *Estetika slovesnogo tvorchestva*, 355–80; English translation in *Speech Genres and Other Late Essays*, 132–58
PCMF	'The Problem of Content, Material, and Form in Verbal Artistic Creation' ['Problema soderzhaniia, materiala i formy v slovesnom khudozhestvennom tvorchestve', *c.*1924]. In *Voprosy literatury i estetiki*, 6–71; English translation in *Art and Answerability*, 257–325
PDA	*Problems of Dostoevsky's Art* [*Problemy tvorchestva Dostoevskogo*, 1929]. English translation: the 1963 revised text was published in transla-

	tion in 1984 (see *PDP* below); this translation includes as an appendix three fragments of the 1929 text not included in the 1963 edition
PDP	*Problems of Dostoevsky's Poetics* [*Problemy poetiki Dostoevskogo*, 1963]. English translation by Caryl Emerson (Manchester: Manchester University Press, 1984)
PrepMat.	'Preparatory Materials' (for 'The Problem of Speech Genres') ['Podgotovitel'nye materialy', 1952–53]. In *SS5*, 240–86
PSG	'The Problem of Speech Genres' ['Problema rechevykh zhanrov', 1953]. In *SS5*, 159–206; English translation in *Speech Genres and Other Late Essays*, 60–102
QuLaugh.	'On Questions of the Theory of Laughter' ['K voprosam teorii smekha', *c*.1940–45]. In *SS5*, 49–50
QuSelf	'On Questions of Self-Consciousness and Self-Evaluation' ['K voprosam samosoznaniia i samootsenki', *c*.1943–46]. In *SS5*, 72–9
QuThNov.	'On Questions of the Theory of the Novel' ['K voprosam teorii romana', *c*.1940-45]. In *SS5*, 48–9
Rab.	*The Art of François Rabelais and the Popular Culture of the Middle Ages and the Renaissance* [*Tvorchestvo Fransua Rable i narodnaia kul'tura srednevekov'ia i renessansa*, 1965 (a revision of the text composed in 1940–46); new edn. 1990]. Citations are from the 1990 edition (Moscow: Khudozhestvennaia literatura); English translation: *Rabelais and His World*, trans. Hélène Iswolsky (Cambridge, Mass.: MIT Press, 1968)
Rhet.	'Rhetoric, to the extent that it is something false . . . ' ['Ritorika, meru svoei lzhivosti . . .', 1943]. In *SS5*, 63–70
Sat.	'Satire' ['Satira', 1940]. In *SS5*, 11–38
SS5	*Sobranie sochinenii, tom 5: Raboty 1940-kh—nachala 1960-kh godov* [*Collected Works in Seven Volumes*, vol. 5: *Works from the 1940s to the Beginning of the 1960s*], ed. S. G. Bocharov and L. A. Gogotishvili (Moscow: Russkie slovari, 1996)
StyN	'On the Stylistics of the Novel' ['K stilistike romana', *c*.1944–45]. In *SS5*, 138–40
TMHum.	'Towards a Methodology of the Human Sciences' ['K metodologii gumanitarnykh nauk', 1974]. In *Estetika slovesnogo tvorchestva*, 381–93; English translation in *Speech Genres and Other Late Essays*, 159–72
TPA	'Towards a Philosophy of the Act' ['K filosofii postupka', *c*.1920–27]. In *Filosofiia i sotsiologiia nauki i tekhniki* (Moscow: Nauka, 1986), 80–138; English translation: *Towards a Philosophy of the Act*, trans. Vadim Liapunov (Austin, Tex.: University of Texas Press, 1994)
TPBHum.	'Towards Philosophical Bases of the Human Sciences' ['K filosofskim osnovam gumanitarnykh nauk', *c*.1940–43]. In *SS5*, 7–10

PART I

An Argument about Dialogue

CHAPTER ONE

Introduction: Language and Democracy

'Someone who writes about communication', said Raymond Williams, 'becomes, in a sense without ever intending to have become, a social critic.'[1] This describes the fate of Mikhail Bakhtin, who wrote critically, not about politics and society, but about the history of the European novel, the epistemology of the human sciences, ethics, and the philosophy of language. True, he once promised a chapter on the 'ethics of politics', but the work was apparently never completed. No matter: had Bakhtin written directly on politics, it would have surely been less interesting than when he stumbled onto it unintentionally via the side-roads of language and culture. Distrustful of what he saw as the vulgar routine of political struggle and manoeuvre, Bakhtin examined the communication of his day and of the past with a careful eye and critical intent, thinking that *there* was where he would find the fundamental patterns of social relationship.

Or one could simply say, as many have done, that Bakhtin's work is social criticism because where others saw expressions, statements, or signs, Bakhtin looked for, and inevitably found, 'dialogues', precisely acts of communication, with multiple actors or participants. One could simply say that, and one would be wrong, for things are not so simple. Social critique does not flow from the mere recognition that there are lots of us about, neither is politics what one person does to another. Williams, very shrewdly, did not claim that one who wrote about communication became, instantaneously, a social critic, but that one would work one's way through to social criticism: that a detailed confrontation with the objects of modern culture would lead us not to 'people' in the abstract, but to the facts of cultural production, to the social divisions which structure texts and their interpretation, to the changing patterns and means of political and cultural power, and to the varied forms of modern social action and conflict. That what we experience as meaningful, we experience dialogically, as an event of communication, was Bakhtin's starting-point; it was only the elaboration of this precept on the material of modern European culture which led him beyond aesthetics and philosophy towards social criticism. While the idea of dialogue dominated his work

---

[1] Williams, 'Communications and Community', in *Resources of Hope*, 23. The quotation begins 'This is why, now, someone who writes about communication . . .'.

from the 1920s until his death in 1975, it did so precisely as an idea, a principle to be applied in cultural analysis, and not as a love of conversation or a belief in the restorative powers of everyday discourse. To have pinned one's hopes for the redemption of a scarred and discredited Europe on the latter would have been a moving, but ineffectual gesture in the wake of the First World War and the European revolutions of 1917–23. Bakhtin did not do so. Not content with simple dialogue, he sought to grasp the historical transformations which made a new kind of dialogue—'dialogism'—both possible and, to his mind, necessary.

In a lifetime of writing Bakhtin argued for the redemptive potential not of simple dialogue, but of the culture embodied in works of modern verbal art, and in particular in the modern European novel and its antecedents; works of great complexity to be sure, but not dialogues in the ordinary sense of the term. It would be far more accurate to claim that Bakhtin made a case for 'the novel' or 'artistic prose' *in the name of* dialogue—far more accurate, and far more difficult, for to put matters that way makes it immediately clear that the appeal to dialogue was never straightforward, but something crabbed, equivocal, and contradictory. Examine Bakhtin's texts: there is hardly any analysis of two-sided conversation or everyday dialogue, and this from the scholar heralded as its greatest champion; instead, constant analysis of works of prose art. There, in the style of the novel, Bakhtin thought he would uncover both the decisive social relationships of modern Europe and the norms and standards by which they could be judged. And this conviction that the novel held the key to modernity turned out to have consequences for the idea of dialogue itself. For if Bakhtin suggested that language, novels, or societies themselves could be thought of as dialogues, it was at the price of making it less clear why dialogues could be thought of as dialogues. To insist that the novel or the aesthetic work was the necessary medium of communicative experience was to admit that dialogues themselves were not up to the job, and that something new was required.

Our starting-point, therefore, is that Bakhtin's concept of dialogism is not a description of actual speech, even very good actual speech, but a philosophical idea, a characterization of our experiences of meaning and a shorthand answer to the question: what happens when one understands something expressed? And, as the language of this clipped account implies —'experiences of meaning'—it is an idea drawn initially from phenomenology, from a philosophical analysis of the 'thing' called meaning. Dialogism is indeed about the two-sided aspect of meanings, but not in any sense necessarily about two people. Rather it refers to what other writers would call the intersubjective quality of all meaning: the fact that it is always found in the space between expression and understanding, and that this space—the 'inter' separating subjects—is not a limitation but the very condition of meaningful utterance. And while this may sound dramatic, it is no more than the philosophical working out of the idea of communication, and a guide to making sure that one analyses communication precisely as communication, as a social act rather than the monological expression of a solitary individual. For implicit in the very idea of communication, despite its etymology (implying the sharing, and hence the production of a meaning), is the sense of an event which is not so much reproduction as response.

And to make the leap from philosophy to social critique? One then has not only to have a concept of communication, but to write about it, which is precisely what Bakhtin did, writing about the specific form of communication, the very modern intersubjectivity embodied in the form of the European novel. Novels, of course, are not just representations of people talking, they have a history, traditional and inherited forms, techniques which are developed and modified, and a social function and role, itself reflected in their composition. To disclose within them a distinctive form of intersubjectivity, a unique and unprecedented communicative structure, is to describe, analyse, and criticize the historical shape of a particular kind of social life. Not every philosopher interested in dialogue—and there were many in the 1920s—thought of novels as its natural embodiment. Those keen to award Bakhtin a patent on the concept should remember that the first work entitled *The Dialogical Principle* was not Todorov's study of Bakhtin but a collection of essays by Martin Buber, whose *I and Thou* had put intersubjectivity centre stage in 1923.[2] The distinguishing mark of Bakhtin's work was not an interest in intersubjectivity, but the conviction that one could reinterpret the public achievements of European culture through its prism.

But this bold move rendered the idea of dialogism liable to misinterpretation, even by—especially by—its most enthusiastic advocates. If taken literally the dialogism of the novel is just too good to be true, the happy coincidence of a great moral value and great aesthetic works. We might therefore illustrate its complexities by looking briefly at two characteristic and telling misreadings of it in contemporary commentary on Bakhtin's work, misreadings which it will only be a little unfair to call 'Russian-religious' and 'American-liberal' respectively. Both preserve the centrality of the concept of dialogue and the redemptive, world-historical force Bakhtin invests in it; both leave out the history with which it is burdened.

[2] A comprehensive account of the emergence of a philosophy of dialogue out of the weaknesses of Husserl's phenomenology is found in Michael Theunissen, *The Other: Studies in the Social Ontology of Husserl, Heidegger, Sartre and Buber*, trans. Christopher Macann (Cambridge, Mass. and London: MIT Press, 1986).

Both, therefore, make of dialogue a kind of magical substance or activity which will transform society from without. In the Russian misreading, which I will discuss first, this entails a mystical inflation of its power; in the American misreading, a sentimental one.

Thus, for the religiously guided interpretations of Bakhtin now current (but by no means exclusive) in Russia, dialogue is endowed with redemptive force only in so far as the model for all such interchange is conversation (in the form of prayer and confession) with the divine Himself.[3] For critics like N. K. Bonetskaia, L. A. Gogotishvili, I. L. Popova, and N. I. Nikolaev (to name the most interesting and rigorous of Bakhtin's religious interpreters) the inwardness of dialogue, its remoteness from the mundane cares of social life, guarantees access to that metaphysical sphere which alone holds the key to salvation. Bonetskaia, for example, has recently praised Bakhtin for focusing our attention on the 'high dialogue' of Dostoevsky, which made it possible for the latter to represent 'the "idea" of the person, the "ultimate semantic position" in relation to which the circumstances of one's life are to some degree accidental, inessential'.[4] In a similar vein, Popova, in her commentary on one of Bakhtin's notebooks from the 1940s, insists that the apparently cultural-historical concept of 'Menippean satire' is, in the context of Bakhtin's work, a 'euphemistic concept', allowing Bakhtin to discuss his real interest: 'the history of the forms of dialogue of the person with God'.[5] For such readings the meaning and effectiveness of 'dialogue' depends above all on its unworldliness, and the purer the dialogue, the freer from ordinary convention and social life, the more potent it becomes. Their explicit model is Bakhtin's account of the pure dialogical encounters staged in the works of Dostoevsky:

The exceptionally sharp sense of the other person as 'other' and of one's own 'I' as a naked 'I' presupposes that all the determinations which envelop the 'I' and the 'other' in socially-concrete flesh—familial, social group, class, and all the other forms of these determinations—have lost their authority and form-giving force. It is as if the human being senses himself immediately in the world as a whole, without any intermediate moments, apart from any social collective to which he might belong. And the communion of this 'I' with the other and with others takes place

---

[3] A significant exception is found in the work of Vladimir Bibler, who interprets Bakhtin's writings as a decisive contribution to the secular philosophical tradition. See his *Myshlenie kak tvorchestvo: Vvedenie k logiku myshlennogo dialoga* (Moscow: Izd. politicheskoi literatury, 1975); and *M. M. Bakhtin, ili poetika kul'tury* (Moscow: Progress-Gnozis, 1991); see also Daniel Alexandrov and Anton Struchkov, 'Bakhtin's Legacy and the History of Science and Culture: An Interview with Anatolii Akhutin and Vladimir Bibler', *Configurations*, 1: 3 (1993), 335–86.

[4] N. K. Bonetskaia, 'K sopostavleniiu dvukh redaktsii knigi M. Bakhtina o Dostoevskom', in *Bakhtinskie chteniia*, vol. i (Vitebsk: N. A. Pan'kov, 1996), 27.

[5] I. L. Popova, editorial commentary to 'Ritorika, v meru svoei lzhivosti . . .', in *SS5*, 461.

squarely on the terrain of ultimate questions, bypassing all intermediate and local forms. (*PDA* 240–1/280)

To reach this terrain of 'ultimate questions', where dialogue has maximal force, it is necessary to divest oneself of the roles and identities which flow from human institutions. Here history has no place: every act of earthly dialogue is at best a reasonable facsimile of relations between God and his subjects. At its extreme—in, for example, the writing of Gogotishvili—the 'creaturely world' itself is no more than the '*indirect* or *quasi-direct speech* of God'.[6] Such accounts cannot survive the profane social and historical concerns of the novels Bakhtin analysed, and the degree to which the concept of dialogue becomes infected by their necessary entanglement with European history. Not surprisingly, religious interpreters of Bakhtin have tended to throw up their hands when confronted with Bakhtin's essays on the novel.[7]

To have been consigned to the ranks of religious metaphysicians might have been a kinder fate, however, than the secular one Bakhtin has some-times endured in the United States, where 'dialogue' is often invested with a force only faintly less miraculous than in Russia. Here, too, the privacy and inwardness of dialogue is a condition of both its effectiveness and its value. An extreme example would be Gary Saul Morson's and Caryl Emerson's critical study of Bakhtin, which declares that Bakhtin is radical, and his mode of thought revolutionary, precisely to the extent that he guides our attention to the everyday, ordinary, and quotidian events 'that in principle elude reduction to "underlying" laws or systems'.[8] On this account the theory of dialogism enjoins us to particularize speech inter-actions, in the belief that the closer one gets to the particulars, the more one may 'appreciate the overlooked richness, complexity, and power of the most intimate and most ordinary exchanges'.[9] Here, too, one evades any sense of the historical transformation of dialogue itself, not by floating above the mundane but by getting so close to it that one does not notice the history which shapes it. Yet at the same time, Morson and Emerson,

---

[6] L. A. Gogotishvili, note to 'K filosofskim osnovam gumanitarnykh nauk', in *SS*5, 398 n. 8.

[7] In her 'Bakhtin's Aesthetics as a Logic of Form', Bonetskaia takes up the philosophical texts, the Dostoevsky book, and the Rabelais book, arguing in her defence that 'From the point of view of a theory of form, Bakhtin's other works are to my mind unrepresentative . . .' (p. 84), so leaving out the essays of the 1930s (in David Shepherd (ed.), *The Contexts of Bakhtin: Philosophy, Authorship, Aesthetics* (New York: Harwood Academic Press, 1998), 83–94). In her excellent article, 'Varianty i invarianty M. M. Bakhtina', *Voprosy filosofii*, 1 (1992), 115–33, L. A. Gogotishvili discloses the 'unified general conceptual basis' of Bakhtin's work at the cost of a similar leap from *Dostoevsky* (1929) to *Rabelais*. But the most usual strategy for dealing with works too secular in conception is Popova's: treat the historical discussions as essentially 'euphemistic'.

[8] Gary Saul Morson and Caryl Emerson, *Mikhail Bakhtin: Creation of a Prosaics* (Stanford, Ca.: Stanford University Press, 1990), 33.

[9] Ibid. 34.

unlike Bonetskaia, do not promote their 'philosophy of the ordinary' as a
Stoic alternative to public and political life, but as a source of significant
(and significantly anti-Marxist) moral guidance for it.[10] In the interstices of
their 'ordinary' conversation one finds familiar moral values:

Only dialogue reveals potentials. It does so by addressing them, by provoking a
specific answer that actualizes the potential, albeit in a particular and incomplete
way. At the same time, the questioner necessarily undergoes the same process,
which helps him comprehend unsuspected potentials in his own culture. The
process, then, is multiply enriching: it educates each side about itself and about the
other, and it not only discovers but activates potentials. Indeed, the process of
dialogue may itself create new potentials, realizable only through future activity
and dialogue.[11]

If the model for dialogue is the local—perhaps provincial would be a
better word—conversation, then the 'dialogism' which gives it force is
merely the playing out of this conversation on ever larger stages—a work
of literature, a culture, a political system. We are therefore asked to believe
that from the lineaments of the ideal conversation one can derive norms
for the conduct of social life more generally; conventions governing 'ordinary' linguistic practice are expected to serve as models for a desirable
political and ethical community. This move is, however, characteristic not
only of relatively conservative commentators like Morson and Emerson
(who espouse a familiar right-liberal belief in the overarching importance
of personal responsibility), but of left-liberal critics as well, whenever they
use 'dialogue' as the keystone for a case about the virtues of cultural
difference.

That Bakhtin's 'radical revolution in the fates of human discourse' (DN
178/367) should take its bearings from the self-understanding of a certain,
undoubtedly limited variety of American speech should give us pause. Yet
American interpreters derive models of social life from supposedly
unadorned linguistic reality so effortlessly because in their context 'dialogue' is *already* freighted with social and political meaning. In American
public life dialogue stands for that scene of negotiative give-and-take,
of debate aimed at compromise, so central to the identity of liberal
democracy. In conflicts of varying scale (we should bear in mind that
Washington and Moscow may enter into dialogue, however empirically
unlikely or philosophically bizarre that may seem) a commitment to

---

[10] Their assumption that attention to the everyday and mundane will provide an antidote to
Marxist 'systems' ignores the fact that the strongest claims for the everyday in the 20th century
have been made precisely by Marxist writers: see Henri Lefebvre, *The Critique of Everyday Life*,
vol. i: *Introduction*, trans. John Moore (London: Verso, 1991); Karel Kosik, 'Metaphysics of
Everyday Life', in *Dialectics of the Concrete*, trans. K. Kovanda and J. Schmidt (Dordrecht: D.
Reidel, 1976); and Agnes Heller, *Everyday Life* (London: Routledge & Kegan Paul, 1984).

[11] Morson and Emerson, *Mikhail Bakhtin*, 55.

dialogue means more than an interest in speaking; it signifies an agreement to observe certain procedures when resolving disputes. One talks with colleagues, friends, taxi drivers; one engages in dialogue with the police, elements of the welfare state, schools, or government agencies. And dialogue is not an innocent or open procedure, either: it is the search for that great white whale of the liberal imagination, compromise, a search which rules out certain kinds of solution in advance. Like the term 'democracy' itself, 'dialogue' sanctions a strategic call for specific procedures under the rubric of abstract principle.[12]

To stumble upon a theorist who claims that language itself is inherently 'dialogical' and that 'a living utterance cannot avoid becoming a participant in social dialogue' (DN 90/276) is therefore an irresistible windfall for the liberal consciousness. A theorist who detects in the European novel—a valued genre whose historical rise and plateau, of course, is linked with the fortunes of European and North American liberalism—a unique 'deepening, broadening and making subtle' (DN 113/300) of this natural dialogism seems not only to legitimate existing structures of power but to ornament them with the fine drapery of the aesthetic as well. The discovery that this much-cherished dialogue is both the essence of language itself and the defining characteristic of the aesthetic masterworks of Western culture has made it possible for literary critics in the West to endow a variety of canonical texts with a new political lustre and, *mutatis mutandis*, their own activity with a sense of generalized social purpose. All this, of course, at the price of not enquiring too deeply into the concept of dialogue or of dialogism itself, the political substance of which becomes no more than the reflected image of the self-understanding of American liberalism.

Such a 'relevant' Bakhtin has a lot to say about politics, but nothing new. The recent division of theoretical opinion in the West reflects this fact: the 'discovery' of dialogism with which Bakhtin is credited by devotees is regarded by others, quite rightly, as a circular adventure, in which the new continent is really an already known one made more glamorous by the exertion of the voyage itself.[13] Affirmations that dialogue is hidden in the recesses of every utterance amount to little more than wish-fulfilment in pseudo-philosophical form when the substance of that

---

[12] It may be worth pointing out that the antithesis of dialogue in this context is not violence but 'disruption' of agreed or enforced procedures for the resolution of conflict. It makes perfect sense, for example, to demand recourse to 'dialogue' in the midst of an industrial dispute prosecuted by entirely peaceful means.

[13] Lionel Gossman was an early sceptic of claims for Bakhtin's originality. See his review of the Clark–Holquist biography, 'Mikhail Bakhtin', *Comparative Literature*, 38: 4 (1986), 337–49. Edward Said has even cavilled at the use of the term 'dialogical' due to the 'cult of Bakhtin': see Raymond Williams and Edward Said, 'Media, Margins and Modernity', in Raymond Williams, *The Politics of Modernism: Against the New Conformists* (London: Verso, 1989), 181.

dialogue turns out to be the unfulfilled norms of American liberalism. While the religious-existential aura which envelops dialogue in Russia would have to be dispersed for anything worldlier to emerge, in the West the problem is nearly the reverse: dialogue is too worldly or, in the philosophical sense of the term, 'positive', a simple and uncritical reflection of institutionalized norms. For all the pathos-ridden affirmation of its centrality, in a great deal of American commentary dialogue functions strictly as a leftover concept, designating the arena in which differences are patched up once we accept the priority of liberal individualism or the unbridgeable boundaries of cultural difference. There are, of course, dialogues, and they are important, but their meaning and purpose has already been determined by beliefs in the priority of individual will or cultural tradition. The latter call the philosophical tune to which dialogue must dance.

The failure common to these interpretations, Russian-religious and American-liberal, is that they hypostasize and reify dialogue, the former concretizing it as metaphysical event, the latter as something tellingly close to academic conversation. Their dealings with Bakhtin are therefore marked by a symptomatic one-sidedness: fascinated by the dazzle of dialogue, they ignore the other great emphasis of Bakhtin's work—an insistent and ceaseless interest in the 'generic', as the textual form in which the dialogical is embodied.[14] For it is within these forms that inter-subjectivity finds itself worked out in historically concrete shapes. 'Genres', in Bakhtin's parlance, are not the options set out by the trinity of epic, tragic, and lyric (or some more recent variation thereof), but the historical forms which discourse assumes, and the novel is the form which marks the shift to European modernity. Ignore this, and all the works Bakhtin analyses appear as no more than expansions of a metaphysical dialogical substance, while the analysis itself loses its historical point. What poses as admiration for Bakhtin and his extraordinary powers of insight (it was there, dialogue, all along, but only Bakhtin heard the voices) is in fact an effort to transform historical insights into eternal verities. But it is his devotees who demonstrate an almost wilful lack of concern with the historical landscape which backs any form of intersubjectivity; in Bakhtin history presses its claims as incessantly as dialogue.

To be fair, it sometimes presses them rather discreetly. In a shrewd

---

[14] Brian Poole has rightly pointed out that the concept of genre keeps Bakhtin connected to the tradition of philosophical aesthetics. See 'Mikhail Bakhtin i teoriia romana vospitaniia', in V. L. Makhlin (ed.), *M. M. Bakhtin i perspektivy gumanitarnykh nauk* (Vitebsk: N. A. Pan'kov: 1994), 68–9. There he comments on 'The Problem of Speech Genres': 'In this work it is possible to recognize the one concept which Bakhtin did not want to sacrifice to literary scholarship for the sake of some more integral specialist science—whether linguistics, semiology, structural analysis or some other kind of art analysis. This is the concept of genre' (p. 68).

remark, Tzvetan Todorov has claimed that Bakhtin looks on the novel as simply the expression of the innate tendencies of language.[15] He is half right, in so far as Bakhtin never shakes off the desire to portray the most impressive and difficult achievements of modern culture as the setting loose of dialogical powers stored up in the structures of ordinary discourse, as if only this would justify them. He is half wrong, however, in so far as he fails to see that the fit between the conception of language and the properties of the novel is so neat because Bakhtin has incorporated 'novelness' into his theory of language to begin with. What poses as a pure philosophy of language in Bakhtin comes already historicized, for Bakhtin assimilates the historical experience stored up in whatever genre he is writing about into the account of language which accompanies it. Though dialogue is what Bakhtin claims to find throughout his life, he finds it in revealingly different *kinds* of places as he expounds it: first, in the aesthetic work as such; then, not in every aesthetic work, but uniquely in Dostoevsky's fiction; then, not just in the work of a particular writer, but in a genre—the novel; after this, not just in literature, but in popular culture—carnival; finally, not in the objects of humanistic interpretation, but in the process itself—the human sciences. In the interpretation of Bakhtin's work which follows, I have tried to understand these changes and their implications for the idea of dialogism, but the first conclusion to draw from them is that they are driven by Bakhtin's need to adjust his philosophy of language to his understanding of particular historical phenomena and vice versa. This seeming inability to commit himself to a single explanation of the aesthetic work is one of Bakhtin's greatest virtues, for without the constant desire for philosophical reflection, history can freeze into mere positive 'fact', where it fits into conceptual schemes sorted out in advance, filling them out but never shaking their outlines.

The conventional assumption that Bakhtin began by writing pure philosophy and gradually shifted to literary and historical issues is therefore inaccurate and misleading, and not only because his recently published notebooks from 1940 to 1946 juxtapose philosophical themes with discussions of carnival and reconstructions of the cultural history of the novel. Philosophical and historical concerns compete for space even in the flagship of his philosophical efforts, the lengthy essay-fragment on verbal art, 'Author and Hero in Aesthetic Activity'. True, the essay presents itself as a work in philosophical aesthetics, and its first two lengthy sections imply that the relationship between author and hero (which is not yet described as 'dialogical') we find in art merely actualizes possibilities inherent in a timeless everyday life. But even by the third section of the

---

[15] Tzvetan Todorov, *Mikhail Bakhtin: The Dialogical Principle*, trans. Wlad Godzich (Manchester: Manchester University Press, 1984), 90–1.

essay, 'The Whole of the Hero as a Whole of Meaning', Bakhtin is describing the *historical* development of the intersubjectivity he had apparently derived phenomenologically, as if this had not always been available, but had to wait on the patient labours of humanity, and in particular its prose writers. In fact, it turns out that the aesthetic consciousness Bakhtin pins his hopes on has still not quite yet arrived, for his literary history ends with a comparison of the complementary weaknesses of the Classical and the Romantic hero, each of which is not quite dialogical enough (one has too much author, the other too much hero), and an evocation of a current 'crisis of authorship', in evidence, 'above all in prose from Dostoevsky to Bely' (AH 186/203). The solution to that crisis would be the perfectly 'dialogical' aesthetic work, but it remains a phantom solution, without historical realization—unless, of course, one imagines that the book *Problems of Dostoevsky's Art*, published soon afterwards, is its delayed settling of accounts. There Dostoevsky is presented as an aesthetic revolutionary, whose formal achievements mark out a historically innovative dialogical—now the term appears in its own right—path for artistic discourse. The Dostoevsky book makes clear what was implied by the very form of the earlier essay: that the dialogism which ought to have been second nature was in fact a creature of modern Europe.[16]

In the essays on the novel which followed, the historical meaning of this new aesthetic is thematized. As the genre which incarnates 'contemporaneity' the novel cannot remain just one genre among others, but becomes the modern form of the aesthetic as such, as all literature becomes 'novelized':

The novel is the only genre which is in a state of becoming, therefore it more profoundly, essentially, sensitively and rapidly reflects the becoming of actuality itself . . . The novel became the leading hero of the drama of the literary development of modernity precisely because it best of all reflects the tendency of the modern world to become; it is, after all, the only genre born of this modern world and in every respect of a piece with it. The novel in many respects has anticipated and continues to anticipate the future development of all literature. (EN 451/7)

This is an argument reflected in the form taken by all of Bakhtin's works in the 1930s, each of which isolates the specifically modern features of the novel by comparing it either with some genre it has supposedly left behind (e.g. the epic) or with precursors which are partly, but not ultimately

---

[16] When precisely Bakhtin wrote his study of Dostoevsky is not clear. The imminent completion of *a* book on Dostoevsky by Bakhtin was announced in the journal *Zhizn' isskustva* (22–8 Aug. 1922), 4. According to the testimony of S. N. Broitman, Bakhtin claimed that the book on Dostoevsky was written four to five years before its publication; see S. N. Broitman, 'Dve besedy s Bakhtinym', in S. N. Broitman and N. Gorbanov (eds.), *Khronotop* (Dagestan: Dagestanskii gosudarstvennyi universitet, 1990), 112.

'novelistic'. In these texts, dialogism, the realistic chronotope, and grotesque (carnivalesque) realism are historical achievements, which decisively alter the rules of the cultural game. And as for 'popular-festive culture'—its resurrection by Bakhtin is intended to compel us to rethink our very conception of modernity and the meaning of its historical consciousness. For with the triumph of the novel and 'novelization', history has become an internal rather than merely external fact of genre. While Bakhtin may claim that 'the fates of genres' embody the 'great historical fates of artistic discourse' (DN 72/259), the novel, as the genre embodying modernity itself, replaces the very idea of fate with the modern 'tendency to become', that is, with a self-consciously historical culture. And in this respect it places demands on any philosophy which claims to comprehend it. For a philosophy attuned to modernity must, as Jürgen Habermas has argued, grasp the historical character of modernity as a challenge to the received methods and role of philosophy itself.[17] Modernity cannot be just the latest era, and the novel cannot be just the most recent genre.

What we encounter in most commentary on Bakhtin, however, is history or philosophy in isolation. Literary-critical readings understand and appreciate the histories of prose forms, but refuse to entertain the philosophical questions raised by what appears to be a chronology of literary styles and genres; philosophical readings understand the larger stakes but refuse to acknowledge the historical dimension so evident to the literary historian. While for the literary interpreter Bakhtin charts not changes in social relations mediated by language, but changes in the language of literature, for the philosopher, though Bakhtin reveals the communicative basis of every artwork, the intersubjectivity he uncovers is an anthropological or religious rather than historical fact. Bakhtin appears to have foreseen this problem: he claims that his newly discovered objects, dialogism and the novel, require a new method to interpret or even recognize them. His writing will therefore be a critique not only of existing language but also of the positive science which allows us to speak of language and its properties

---

[17] See Jürgen Habermas, 'Modernity's Consciousness of Time and its Need for Self-Reassurance', in *The Philosophical Discourse of Modernity*, trans. Frederick Lawrence (Cambridge: Polity Press, 1987). The Russian term Bakhtin uses for modernity is *novoe vremia*, literally 'new time' and, I assume, a calque of the German *Neuzeit*. Bakhtin uses the term to refer to a historical epoch beginning with the later Renaissance, and, in particular, with the displacement of the authority of Latin by the European vernaculars. In this respect it appears close to *Neuzeit*, which refers to European history following the Renaissance, and at the same time, to a distinctive form of historical consciousness. See Reinhart Koselleck, '"Neuzeit": Remarks on the Semantics of the Modern Concept of Movement', in *Futures Past: On the Semantics of Historical Time*, trans. Keith Tribe (Cambridge, Mass. and London: MIT Press, 1985). In Bakhtin that form of consciousness is registered by the term *sovremennost'*, which means literally—and is translated in this book as—'contemporaneity'. It is nonetheless clear that this contemporaneity is the consciousness of modern times, and that it therefore serves as the Russian equivalent for the Western European historico-philosophical concept of modernity.

in the first place. The 'stylistics of genre' with which he proposes to assess the novel presents itself as the only method willing to draw the necessary philosophical conclusions from the unprecedented historical experience manifest in the genre of contemporaneity and 'becoming'. The dialogical consciousness adequate to modernity may depend on the historically accumulated resources of artistic prose, on techniques and stylistic innovations built up over the course of its development and reflecting its role in a rapidly transforming society, but it will take a philosophical perspective to understand the significance and value of these radically new forms. To every attempt to confine the interpretation of language or art within the boundaries of established positive 'science' Bakhtin replies with an appeal to philosophical criticism, for the latter alone will not shrink from the degree of self-reflection necessary in the face of new historical evidence. To see in the aesthetic work or the novel a revolution in intersubjectivity requires a degree of philosophical boldness unavailable to those who work by settled parameters of scientific enquiry; the historians of literature 'do not see, behind the surface colour and commotion of the literary process, the great and essential fates of literature and language, the leading heroes of which are above all genres, while tendencies and schools are heroes of the second and third order' (EN 451/7–8). The human sciences, at least in the 1920s and 1930s, have to be pushed by philosophy to open up a question about intersubjectivity which they consider settled; settled by, it will turn out, the existing disciplines of natural law, political economy, scientific psychology, and the social sciences.

Bakhtin's discussions of Western literary tradition are therefore distinct from the antiquarianism they seem to mimic, as the explication of particular works always takes a back seat to general philosophical preoccupations. In *Problems of Dostoevsky's Art* no text merits prolonged analysis, because the point is to represent Dostoevsky as the creator of a decisively new form of representation, with far more than literary significance. The very manner of Bakhtin's analysis of the 'novel' in the 1930s—an analysis which, as is well known, seizes from the genre scraps and fragments, without any interest in the exhaustive analysis of a single work—transforms it into both symptom and cure for the linguistic and cultural situation of modernity. By defining the novel as a 'stylistic' phenomenon, Bakhtin licenses the mix of philosophical generalization and brief, punctual illustration (rarely does he cite more than a few lines from any one work) through which he can constitute the novel not as a set of texts, but as the embodiment of both a historical situation and the critical principle which might address it. If the claims made for literary works in Bakhtin appear always exaggerated, this is because the texts in question do not confine themselves to artistic tasks, but reflect within themselves the social and philosophical drama of modern Europe. It would appear from recently published reminiscences of colleagues that this policy was pursued with utter self-consciousness. Bakhtin is cited as having warned the young postgraduate literary scholars who 'rediscovered' him in the 1960s that he was 'a philosopher, not a literary scholar' who had turned to ostensibly literary studies as a way of prosecuting philosophical questions in peace.[18] Yet one of those so warned, Sergei Bocharov, later pointed out to Bakhtin that this turn did not give rise to a merely sublimated philosophy, but had led to decisive and productive reformulations in his work. For later readers, it seems that the enforced turn to the literary had the effect of opening up Bakhtin's discussion of intersubjectivity to historical questions, and so helped Bakhtin, perhaps unwillingly or unconsciously, along the road to social critique.

STYLE AND DEMOCRACY

So far, however, we have spoken of modernity and history, but not politics. Does modernity pose distinctive political problems? Does it define a new kind of political terrain and require new kinds of politics? Does it alter the meaning of democracy? Bakhtin does not ask any of these questions, but he nevertheless begins to answer them. 'In this democratized language', Bakhtin observed, 'a new hierarchy (on different principles, without the sacred) is being created' (Mult., 158), and this new 'modern' hierarchy is reflected in the formal strategies of the novel itself. We find the political lineaments of modernity drawn not in Bakhtin's evocations of plebeian speech democracy, most of which are probably more indebted to Russian populism than historical scholarship, but in his analysis of the formal and linguistic features of the novel. For these descriptions are invariably 'too concrete' for their own good: the style Bakhtin describes has a greater political charge than the concepts he uses to describe it. Dialogism is supposed to be modern but beyond or above politics, yet the

---

[18] The statement was made on the occasion of Bakhtin's first meeting with S. G. Bocharov, V. Kozhinov, and G. Gachev, postgraduate students who had travelled to Saransk to meet Bakhtin. It is cited in Kozhinov's description of the meeting in 'Kak pishut trudy, ili Proiskhozhdenie nesozdannogo avantiurnogo romana', *Dialog Karnaval Khronotop*, 1 (1992), 112–13. In later interviews, Bakhtin would repeat that he was really a philosopher: in a conversation reported by Bocharov, Bakhtin evidently claimed that in his book on Dostoevsky he 'detached the form from the principal issue. I could not speak directly about the principal questions', i.e. philosophical ones, and as a consequence he was forced to turn to literary scholarship, about which he speaks in a fairly deprecating manner. See S. G. Bocharov, 'Ob odnom razgovore i vokrug nego', *Novoe literaturnoe obozrenie*, 2 (1993), 72 (an abridged English translation is 'Conversations with Bakhtin', trans. Vadim Liapunov and Stephen Blackwell, *PMLA* 109: 5 (1994), 1009–24).

'contemporaneity' it outlines is obviously and inescapably coloured by the political facts of modern Europe. Bakhtin's political case is thus lodged not in the concepts he uses but in the images of dialogism offered to us. Only by translating these descriptions of language into a critique of conceptions of language can we make plausible the otherwise bizarre claim that the style and technique of a language could be substantively relevant to a discussion of democracy.

This task will occupy the remainder of this chapter. The reconsideration of our concepts of language can be phrased as an answer to three questions: Can one attribute, in general, political meaning to the formal and stylistic structures of language? Is a concept of democracy usefully enlarged or refined by discussions of language? Does the definition of democracy itself have an inner connection to a style of language?

The Political Meaning of Style

Where is it written that politics and language don't mix? In Ferdinand de Saussure's *Course in General Linguistics*, the text which laid the foundations of modern linguistics and which was the object of unceasing critique by Bakhtin (and Voloshinov).[19] We tend to forget that linguistics had to wage a long struggle to subdue and capture its elusive, protean object, and that the domesticated creature it named 'language' bears scant resemblance to the wilder varieties which still roam beyond its territory. Beyond the sphere of linguistics language can mean many different things: a set of norms to be policed and observed, a world-view encoded in characteristic forms of speech ('they don't speak our language'), a social skill, a practice in which non-speakers are educated. In these contexts, moral, political, or aesthetic judgements on 'style' are not only natural, but often unavoidable. They seem strange and out of place, however, when they are applied to 'language' as conceived by the modern *science* of language.[20] For according

[19] Ferdinand de Saussure, *Course in General Linguistics*, ed. Charles Bally and Albert Sechehaye, trans. Roy Harris (London: Duckworth, 1983). The *Course*, which was put together from Saussure's lecture notes by his two students Charles Bally and Albert Sechehaye, was first published in Geneva in 1916. It became known in Russia, and to Roman Jakobson and the Moscow Linguistic Circle in particular, as early as 1917, when the linguist Sergei Kartsevsky returned to Moscow from a stay in Geneva. In this case linguistics and politics had an intimate connection of a different kind: Kartsevsky had been in Geneva, not for the purpose of imbibing revolutionary linguistic doctrine, but to meet with the émigré members of the Russian Social-Revolutionary Party. (As reported by Boris Uspensky in private conversation.)

[20] On Saussure's extrusion of moral and normative considerations from debate on language, see Talbot J. Taylor, *Mutual Misunderstanding: Scepticism and the Theorizing of Language and Interpretation* (London: Routledge, 1992). Deborah Cameron has brilliantly demonstrated that modern linguistics systematically ignores the constant moral and political commentary on language itself so common and inevitable amongst ordinary users: see her *Verbal Hygiene* (London and New York: Routledge, 1995).

to Saussure, while political and social history, literary life, and cultural movements and struggles all have an unquestionable influence on language, they are external to the order of meaning itself; the latter's web might be disturbed or have its strands broken by the pressures of history, but the web itself is always made of the same stuff: the grammar, lexis, and phonetic structures which together compose the system of a natural language. Rather than doubt that political, social, or geographical facts were relevant to language, Saussure chose the more modest strategy of doubting that they were relevant to linguistics, relegating them to the hinterlands of 'external linguistics'.[21] Once one has decreed that language is a closed formal system, however, whether this system is the structure of a natural language (Saussure) or the rules of a universal generative grammar (Chomsky), style, as Bakhtin shrewdly pointed out, can only consist of 'an individualization of a common language (in the sense of a system of common linguistic norms)' (DN 77/264). Talk of a democratic language, or a democratic manner of speech, is then reduced to the discussion of individual attitudes, for the common language itself can be neither more nor less democratic. The novelty of Bakhtin's position lies not in imagining 'free and democratized language' (FPND 435/71)—we can do that already—but in the suggestion that such a question can be posed technically or scientifically, in concert with the discipline of stylistics.

Nonetheless, Saussure's proposal for a new, structurally orientated linguistics unwittingly made room for this very possibility. When Saussure insisted that linguistic structure should be the sole object of linguistics, he offered two revealingly different justifications. The first was that linguistics had to find within the chaos of language an object *orderly* enough for science: 'As soon as we give linguistic structure pride of place among the facts of language, we introduce a natural order into an aggregate which lends itself to no other classification.'[22] In making this judgement Saussure naturally bore in mind requirements of science inherited from other disciplines, notably sociology and, at a different level, physics;[23] these ruled out

---

[21] See the chapter 'Internal and External Elements of a Language', in Saussure, *Course*, 21–3. Thus it seems entirely natural that Noam Chomsky, who is at once the founder of transformational grammar and one of America's leading radical political intellectuals, sees no need to integrate his critique of the language of political life in the US with the scholarly business of linguistics. See Chomsky's remarks in *Language and Responsibility*, trans. John Viertel (Sussex: Harvester Press, 1979), 3. Julia Kristeva, however, has refused to accept this admission, arguing that an ethics can be found in the deep conceptual structure of the theory of transformational grammar. See 'The Ethics of Linguistics', in *Desire in Language,* ed. Leon S. Roudiez, trans. Thomas Gora, Alice Jardine, and Leon S. Roudiez (Oxford: Basil Blackwell, 1980), 23–35.

[22] Saussure, *Course*, 10.

[23] On Saussure's relation to natural science see Sebastiano Timpanaro's excellent essay 'Structuralism and its Successors', in *On Materialism*, trans. Lawrence Garner (London: Verso, 1976), 135–219. So far as Saussure's relation to sociology goes, there is good reason to believe that he confused scientific requirements with normative ones. Was the order of the linguistic

of bounds issues of social and political history, which would lack the order-liness of grammar: 'External linguistics can accumulate detail after detail, without ever being forced to conform to the constraints of a system.'[24] The second justification, however, was entirely distinct, and itself had a whiff of democracy about it. Rejecting all claims for linguistic purism or belief in linguistic golden ages, Saussure argued that what belonged to 'the language' depended entirely on the contemporary practice of ordinary speakers, and that linguistics should therefore take an interest only in those facts which were necessary for speakers and listeners to make sense of the language they used. In asking of linguistics that it focus on structure alone, Saussure believed he would be reconstructing, in reflective form, the kind of knowledge which allowed speakers to participate in language.[25]

All that was exiled to external linguistics, or to diachronic linguistics (which examined linguistic change) was therefore put aside on the grounds that while knowledge of political and social context might be interesting for the historian of language, it was of little point for the ordinary user.[26] The test of what belonged to linguistic structure would be what entered directly into the constitution of meaningful signs; but Saussure can only keep this Pandora's box closed by positing a reduced conception of the linguistic act. If understanding entailed no more than the recognition of signs floating in space, or the reproduction of intended meanings in the mind of intended listeners (Saussure's picture of the circuit of discourse in the *Course*—two heads connected by lines representing the passage of signs between them—suggests just such a conception), then knowing what Saussure calls 'the linguistic structure' would be enough. But the act of linguistic understanding is far more complicated, and as we examine it we find elements of linguistic experience long ago exiled from the central territory of linguistic analysis clamouring to get back in. Let us follow the initial stages of this ingathering:

1. *The intersubjective or communicative nature of language.* A formalized language structure does not appear as a medium of intersubjectivity, but as a self-contained system, deployed by individualized language-users. Any

system something to be discovered, or something to be desired? It may be that, taking his cue from Durkheim, Saussure saw an orderly language as a means of social integration, and so a desideratum as much as a scientific object.

[24] Saussure, *Course*, 23.

[25] This 'democratization' has not gone unnoticed: see Roland Barthes's interesting article, 'Saussure the Sign, Democracy', in *The Semiotic Challenge*, trans. Richard Howard (Oxford: Basil Blackwell, 1988), 151–6.

[26] For this part of my argument I am much indebted to Tony Crowley's excellent article 'That Obscure Object of Desire: A Science of Language', in John E. Joseph and Talbot J. Taylor (eds.), *Ideologies of Language* (London: Routledge, 1990), 27–50. See also his 'For and Against Saussure', in *Language in History: Theories and Texts* (London: Routledge, 1996), 6–29.

explanation of linguistic structure which abstracts from the intersubjective nature of language use is forced to assume that understanding an utterance is no more than grasping mental contents encoded by the one speaking. We grasp language, however, as something *someone else* says to us: without this critical element, language loses its grounding in acts of communication. Once one splays language along the axis of intersubjectivity, changes in our sense of structure and style follow immediately, for these are orientated to the fact and expectation of communicative exchange.

2. *Linguistic authority and power.* Once one accepts the intersubjective dimension of language, a series of consequences follows. For the intersubjectivity which constitutes language is not composed of equivalent subjects engaged in random and roughly equal acts of discourse. All utterances come to us from elsewhere, but they may come endowed with varying degrees and kinds of authority. Whether it is the patriarchal and maternal authority of parents who teach you to speak, the expert or professional authority which runs through language in social and cultural institutions, or the political authority manifest in the speech of leaders, power and authority are intrinsic to the meaning grasped by subjects of language. A communicating person who could not recognize the authority of particular utterances, and gauge the changes in response these would dictate, would be an inept member of the linguistic community. Saussure imagines that speakers face a language of more or less equally authoritative or habitual forms, but in fact speakers have to recognize authority—or claims to authority—whenever they understand utterances. This fundamental feature of intersubjectivity does not remain outside language proper, but is reflected in the style of the utterances of those speaking and responding.

3. *Code-switching and multilanguagedness.* The linguistic structure itself is neither even nor homogeneous. Instead of the simple judgements Saussure imagines speakers making—where in the structure is this meaningful unit located?—speakers have to place signs in one of the alternative codes or languages available, and interpret what this choice of code or language means. Bakhtin: 'For the consciousness living in it, language is not an abstract system of normative forms, but a concrete heteroglot opinion on the world. All words taste of a profession, a genre, a movement, a party, a particular work, a particular person, a generation, an age group, a day and hour' (DN 106/293).

4. *Differences of medium in which linguistic experiences are embedded.* From the standpoint of formal linguistics, the structure of language present in oral speech, in print, and in the electronic media is identical. From an intersubjective perspective, differences in the medium of expression cannot be neutral. They determine fundamental aspects of the organization of speech, fix the roles various parties and pressures play in the composition

of an utterance (different, we assume, for the television broadcast and the chat with the grocer), and define an audience which can vary in type, disposition, and number.

5. *The process of linguistic self-reflection or 'metalinguistic discourse'*. In a now well-known letter to fellow linguist Meillet, Saussure confessed that he didn't enjoy having to reflect on language in general, preferring the work of concrete historical description.[27] The conception of language displayed in the *Course* confirms this unhappiness theoretically: the linguistic structure which is to be the unique object of linguistics appears to exist independently of the work of the linguist, as if the latter had no effect on the former. All of the above, however, testifies to the fact that language folds back on itself, in so far as it is continually modified by discourse about language itself. The *Course* is openly hostile to forms of linguistic self-reflection such as popular etymology, and since then formalist linguistics has assumed that ordinary speakers need make only the neutral judgements typical of linguistics itself. In fact, understanding utterances by others involves constant reflection of what kind of language one is hearing, on what is appropriate or proper to the situation, and registering the strengths and weaknesses of the discourse of others. Learning a language is inevitably learning about language as well; understanding language is not a simple and unreflective process, but often a highly self-conscious interpretative one.[28]

None of these issues lacks for scholarly attention. Phenomenology, religious philosophy, speech act theory, and communications-orientated critical theory have focused on the role of language in organizing and maintaining our relations with others; sociolinguistics and psychoanalysis, in different ways, examine the constitution of linguistic authority; semiotically inspired media studies and analyses of print culture have taken up the question of the specific properties of the different media of communication; multilanguagedness and code-switching is studied in scholarship on diglossia and in the theories of functional linguistics; the self-reflective properties of language are taken up in philosophy. The

[27] The relevant section of the letter is as follows: 'The utter inadequacy of current terminology, the necessity of reforming it and, in order to do that, of demonstrating what sort of object language is, continually spoils my pleasure in philology, even though I have no dearer wish than not to have to concern myself with the nature of language in general.' F. de Saussure, letter to Antoine Meillet, 4 Jan. 1894, in *Cahiers Ferdinand de Saussure* 21 (1964), 93. Cited in Françoise Gadet, *Saussure and Contemporary Culture*, trans. Gregory Elliott (London: Hutchinson Radius, 1989), 19.

[28] Deborah Cameron has criticized socio-linguistic conceptions of language for failing to account for the pervasiveness of metalinguistic conflicts, which remind us that language does not reflect society but is an object of struggle within it; see her 'Demythologizing Sociolinguistics: Why Language Does Not Reflect Society', in Taylor and Joseph (eds.), *Ideologies of Language*, 79–93, and her *Verbal Hygiene*.

problem is not that these aspects of language pass unnoticed, but that they continue to occupy the fertile ground outside the citadel of linguistics itself, supplying it with vital materials but on terms it dictates. They remain, as Saussure deemed they should, external to our definition and description of the communicative process through which meaning is made: the two heads of Saussure's imaginary circuit of speech go on passing signs between them in more or less the same way no matter who has authority, how many languages or codes are available, what medium they use, or what they think about language itself.[29] To break down this division, we would have to show not only that such historical contingencies affected the way language is used, but also that they had a presence at the heart of the linguistic structure itself. One can easily imagine a democratic situation within which language is employed, but the thesis that there is such a thing as a novelistic style means that there is a democratic way of employing it, that grammatical, syntactic, and lexical structures themselves instance or embody kinds of social relationship. 'Style' is Bakhtin's name for the place where the external 'facts' manifest themselves at the level of the sign, where meaning becomes impossible without them.

Bakhtin does not, however, synthesize these disparate factors in a comprehensive theory of communication; indeed, he shows no interest in even trying. Instead, he registers the impact of medium, intersubjectivity, self-reflection, authority, and multilanguagedness on the philosophical concept of discourse itself in an almost casual and unreflective way. The relationships embodied in the style of the novel are not so much defined as manifested in countless images of distinctively novelistic dialogue. And the invitation to decode them, to unleash the historical situation compressed in Bakhtin's images of dialogue, is contained in a dialectic of person and structure which animates all of Bakhtin's writing. For while he insists that dialogues are truly encounters between subjects and describes them as such, on closer inspection the latter dissolve into historical structures: the author turns out to be another name for the structure of the artwork, voices turn out to be 'languages', the authority of the poet turns out to be the authority of the centralized state (on the central issue of the form of the modern verbal artwork, Bakhtin oscillates gently between

[29] The problem is not that Saussure's model of language is 'abstract', and so requires additional features to make it sufficiently concrete an object, for Saussure himself insists that the linguistic structure 'is no less real than speech, and no less amenable to study' (Saussure, *Course*, 15). It is a question of which moments of language are relevant and necessary 'in reality' to acts of understanding, and which not. We may agree, for example, with Saussure, that the physiological study of sound production is not relevant. On this see Fredric Jameson, *The Prison-House of Language: A Critical Account of Structuralism and Formalism* (Princeton, NJ: Princeton University Press, 1972), 22–9.

describing this as a question of 'authorship' and as a matter of 'genre'[30]. In this way the consequences of historical development gradually burrow their way into the concept of discourse itself, and if we follow in their path we arrive at a model of intersubjective dialogue with modernity built into it, so to speak.

A characteristic example would be the concept of heteroglossia, the 'internal stratification of a unified national language' (DN 76/262) into a multiplicity of linguistic styles, jargons, and dialects, differentiated by various social pressures and contexts. Bakhtin presents this as a 'fact' with philosophical consequences for any theory of language, and with aesthetic consequences for the novel in particular. He acknowledges that there may be historical moments when there is more or less of it, or when it is more or less consciously acknowledged (when 'heteroglossia-in-itself' becomes 'heteroglossia-for-itself'; but more on that later), but from its first mention in his work it appears as a fundamental and ineluctable dimension of discourse *per se*, as part of the philosophy rather than the history of language. This has its advantage: it means Bakhtin will not treat 'heteroglossia' as an empirical happenstance without any consequences for our conception of communication and understanding. At the same time it tempts us to think of the linguistic stratifications typical of modernity as just exaggerations of tendencies within language itself, when we should be looking into the historical situation which gives rise to this 'heteroglossia'. If we did, we would find that the concept makes sense only given a distinct historical innovation: to wit, the creation of a national 'culture of print', where a new printed standard language, accessible to every literate person, could represent the still differentiated world of orality and written discourse, by portraying the multitude of dialects and styles which flourished at the oral and informal written level of the language.[31] The unity made possible by

---

[30] 'in historical perspective, the category of consummation is contextually displaced in M. M. B. from a function of an *author* in relation to a hero to a function of a *genre* in relation to the actuality represented with its help' (*SS5*, 644 n. 65).

[31] In proposing that heteroglossia is a spin-off of the culture of print, I am adapting conclusions drawn by Benedict Anderson in his book *Imagined Communities: Reflections on the Origin and Spread of Nationalism* (London: Verso, 1983). There Anderson discusses the creation of vernacular 'print-languages' in the early modern period as key elements in the establishment of the new form of national consciousness. The critical point for the present discussion is that the new national languages, with their stability of form and ability to unite regional cultures otherwise separated by dialect, were distinctively languages of print, that is, their existence as languages and their formal, structural attributes were indissociable from the historical medium which carried them. Three other works relevant to this discussion, which I rely on indirectly here, are Roger Chartier (ed.), *The Culture of Print: Power and the Uses of Print in Early Modern Europe*, trans. Lydia G. Cochrane (Cambridge: Polity Press, 1989); Lucien Febvre and Henri-Jean Martin, *The Culture of the Book: The Impact of Printing, 1450–1500*, ed. Geoffrey Nowell-Smith and David Wootton, trans. David Gerard (London: Verso, 1984); and Elizabeth L. Eisenstein, *Print as an Agent of Change*, 2 vols. (Cambridge: Cambridge University Press, 1979).

print was the precondition for the perception of a new linguistic world, that of the internally stratified national vernaculars. Bakhtin knows perfectly well that heteroglossia depended on the displacement of a controlled Latinate culture by a printed vernacular one with open lines to orality. But he would like to think that by this gesture history helped language to fulfil its immanent destiny, to become in history what it should be philosophically. One could, with justice, both admire Bakhtin for so boldly raising the stakes and admonish him for forgetting where the money to do so came from.

The novel—'artistically organized social heteroglossia' (DN 76/262)—is Bakhtin's word for those modern and democratic facts of language with which traditional stylistics cannot cope. And so as we try to grasp the distinctiveness of novelistic style we find ourselves having to reconceptualize the communicative process itself, and draw into it the historical world which had been left outside. Once we embark on this philosophical reconstruction of the idea of language, however, we may not come to rest at the point where Bakhtin did.

Thus philosophy inherits the task of keeping the conceptual structure of science up to date with historical changes in its object. This sounds odd, but it is in keeping with the situation of science in Bakhtin's own time and the very conception of the philosophical task with which he worked. Bakhtin and his friend and colleague V. N. Voloshinov write at the precise moment when the new formalist science of language is establishing its hegemony, but just after Einstein's demolition of Newtonian physics made clear just how fragile the most secure scientific hegemony could be (Bakhtin himself compares the discovery of dialogism to that of relativity in the second edition of the Dostoevsky book: *PDP* 314/272). In the 1920s linguistics is only one of the new human sciences systematically examined by the circle around Bakhtin—psychoanalysis and formalist literary criticism being two others—and in each case they are arraigned on the same charge: a lack of *philosophical* depth, a premature formalization of their objects, which dogmatically establishes the fundamental categories of science without reflecting on their meaning or appropriateness. Voloshinov, in his article 'The Latest Trends in Linguistic Thought in the West',[32] explains this dogmatism as a species of traditionalism: the twentieth-century linguist takes as given the grammatical method which, originally formed for the purpose of teaching alien languages, is handed down from generation to generation. Rejigged for service in the human sciences, grammar is made to appear as the theoretical core of language,

[32] V. N. Voloshinov, 'Noveishie techeniia lingvisticheskoi mysli na zapade', *Literatura i Marksizm* 5 (1928), 115–49. English translation by Noel Owen in *Bakhtin School Papers*, ed. Ann Shukman, Russian Poetics in Translation 10 (Somerton: RPT Publications, 1983), 31–49.

rather than its formalization for specific practical ends. Bakhtin is far less generous: he sees in the dogmatism of linguistics not the unthinking reproduction of the old but an attempt to maintain an absolutist conception of language in the face of the rising tide of popular-democratic speech embodied in the novel. The scientific theory of Saussure is not outmoded dogma, but a rearguard action within European modernity.

Philosophy's task is then to remind us that the business of every science is forever unfinished, and that no scientific fact or axiom, no matter how fundamental or apparently unshakeable (one thinks again of Newtonian physics) is immune to historical change. Matvei Kagan, one of Bakhtin's closest friends, and one from whom Bakhtin clearly learned much of his neo-Kantianism, made philosophy responsible for this unrelenting and ruthless historicization of science.[33] He pointed out that even in natural science one could not predict with absolute certainty from existing causal laws because there was no proof that the lawfulness of phenomena in the future would manifest itself as conformity with already known laws:

And if this is so, then nothing, no fact, no group of facts, no field of phenomena from the currently constituted objective development of being is in a position to be the basis and principle of being as such, of being as historical, so that one might think it permissible to explain everything historical from it and on its basis.[34]

The critique of everything 'given', the motif of neo-Kantianism most insistently present in Bakhtin, means not only that objects are dissolved into processes, but that the processes and the laws that govern them are themselves 'problematic', i.e. expressions of human activity which are constantly rewritten. Language, and the conceptual framework which makes it an object and allows us to think of its changes and modifications, is the 'given' on which Bakhtin trained his sights (although not exclusively: in his discussions of the chronotope Bakhtin, now following directly in neo-Kantian footsteps, analyses the history of that which was thought by Kant to be an unchanging and transcendental form of intuition: space and time).[35]

[33] As contained, for example, in his article 'Filosofiia kak filosofiia istorii' (unpublished), where the two are nearly equated. I am greatly indebted to Brian Poole for copies of his editions of several of Kagan's articles, which he is now preparing for publication in the forthcoming volume Matvei Kagan, Filosofiia dolzhenstvovaniia [The Philosophy of the Ought] (Moscow: Agraf).

[34] M. I. Kagan, 'Filosofiia i istoriia' ['Philosophy and History'], 188 (unpublished typescript).

[35] Marburg neo-Kantianism was committed to a historicization of science which would not undercut its truth value. They realized that Kant's identification of space and time as forms of intuition was a hostage to fortune, as they were in fact categories of science, founded in Newtonian mechanics, which would themselves be transformed together with the advance of scientific knowledge. Space and time themselves could not be treated as 'given' preconditions of experience, but would be better integrated into the historical march of science. To do this without sacrificing the objectivity of science, it was necessary to present space and time as synthetic categories, on a par with those of mathematical knowledge, which would lead to yet

In this context philosophy does not merely chart the vicissitudes of becoming but acts as its advocate. The historical sense as envisioned by Kagan and Bakhtin is not a neutral awareness of the fact of change but an 'orientation to the future' transforming the sheer flow of time into something meaningful. Brian Poole has persuasively argued that Bakhtin and Kagan take from the neo-Kantian Hermann Cohen a certain 'historical messianism', which declares that history is only possible given an ultimate redemptive end.[36] Only when reality exists as something 'set as a task' (to use Vadim Liapunov's elegant translation of the Russian *zadan*) can there be history, for true transitoriness and historical movement demand belief in the difference and otherness of that which is to come.[37] Kagan again: 'Every moment of actual history, like a mythology, objectively includes in itself both a task and its solution, the positing and justification of the being of the future in the present.'[38] History for Kagan and Bakhtin exists as a constant process of cultural creation, unpredictable yet with a logic—and a dignity—of its own. To maintain the historical character of human social life means to maintain what Bakhtin would call 'faith in miracle, in unexpected change in life and one's position in life' (HisTyp., 44).

An account of language restricted to linguistic 'science' predetermines the reach of historical change; an account restricted to philosophical insight substitutes metaphysical dogma for historical knowledge. But no matter how radically one imagines the change afflicting either linguistic science or its object, language, so long as it has the character of an objective self-propelling movement, it is still, in Bakhtin's parlance, not yet historical. A philosophical perspective on language is therefore first and foremost a 'practical', i.e. moral/ethical, perspective, which cannot account for the nature of its object in abstraction from its wish for an ultimately redeemed form of it. Every change in the substance of linguistic experience must therefore be accounted a change in the condition of moral and social life, and every new version of dialogue must be measured by its distance from a redeemed state. From this point of view the rise of novelistic style is simultaneously an ethical and a linguistic event. We should add: a demo-

---

further syntheses, no less objective than the ones they 'superseded'. See Kagan's account of Cohen's position on the significance of synthetic principles in science in 'German Kogen (4 Iulia 1842g.–4 Aprelia 1918g.)', *Nauchnye izvestiia, akademicheskii tsentr Narkomprosa*, (Moscow: Gosizdat, 1922), 114–15, and Bakhtin's summary of Cohen's argument regarding space and time, in his lectures on Kant in 1924 (Lec., 241–3).

[36] See Brian Poole, '"Nazad k Kaganu"', *Dialog Karnaval Khronotop*, 1 (1995), 38–48.

[37] See Liapunov's note explaining the term and his translation of it in Bakhtin, *Art and Answerability: Early Philosophical Essays by M. M. Bakhtin*, ed. Michael Holquist and Vadim Liapunov (Austin, Tex.: University of Texas Press, 1990), 235 n. 23.

[38] M. I. Kagan, 'Evreistvo v krizise kul'tury', *Minuvshee*, 6 (1981), 230.

cratic one as well, in ways of which Bakhtin himself seems only partially aware.

Does Democracy Need a Language?

Does democracy need help from even a reconstructed stylistics, though? Isn't it a matter of institutions and political structures first and language, if ever, afterwards? In political, as in linguistic, theory the working assumption is that political orders affect language from without, as an external condition, rather than from within. And this, so the argument goes, is as it should be: since Orwell we have been quite sure that a 'democratized' language is one which has been left alone. Nonetheless, the various strands of democratic theory and practice on which the Left has occasion to draw acknowledge, even if implicitly, that transformations in the style of speech and the available forms of communication are critical in the struggle for a just and democratic society.

In classical Marxist and Communist theory 'democracy' had the status of an interim step on the path towards the proletarian dictatorship which would establish socialism (the formula for a 'democratic dictatorship of proletarians and peasantry' which Lenin shelved is an example). In early post-revolutionary Russian debate, the reformation of language and the establishment of a properly revolutionary style were central to the project of a specifically *socialist* culture, rather than a democratic one (a project truncated by the establishment of 'socialist realism' as official doctrine in 1932–34). This meant that preferences for a particular style tended to be justified by reference to economic or social ends, clearly understood as prior to it—the ideal style expressed 'collectivism' or an already existing proletarian consciousness.[39] Such attempts to map economic forms or the consciousness of the working class directly onto language inevitably drew it away from its communicative context; by reducing questions of language to questions of content they more or less admitted that communicative forms and structures should be consigned to superstructural purgatory. This is what Bakhtin had in mind when he claimed that 'ideological' approaches to verbal art were not 'social' enough (DN 72/259).

The 'language question' has been more prominent in those situations where a ready-made identity of language, nation, and people is not available. In Irish debate, the question of a national language is not only a

---

[39] This led to some extraordinary arguments, in which, for example, grammatical invention was preferred to lexical innovation on the grounds that grammar represented the collective side of language. On just one instance of these arguments see my 'Short-Cuts to the Long Revolution: The Russian Avant-garde and the Modernization of Language', *Textual Practice*, 4: 3 (1990), 428–41.

matter of competing claims between Gaelic revival and the sheer inescapable facticity of English, but about the proper style and rhetoric of public discourse, the relation a language might draw between intellectuals and everyday life, and how an Irish English might establish itself as unique and cosmopolitan at the same time.[40] In decolonizing and post-colonial Africa and Asia, leaving language alone could not be an option, as national liberation movements often had to create, by linguistic-cultural as well as political means, the very popular mass which would constitute the 'demos' of democracy.[41] It is a nation, however, which apparently had a national language to hand which provoked the most fertile theoretical probing. Italy, home to a bona fide European vernacular, nonetheless found itself divided by dialect, by differences in literacy, and by splits between intellectual and popular linguistic taste and style. Here, too, a national-popular community had literally to be created, but the availability of a national language meant that the problems of medium, of education, and of meta-linguistic discourse were thrown into relief. In the notes on journalism preserved in Gramsci's *Prison Notebooks*, improvements in literary style are a necessary step in the process of enlightenment and, perhaps more importantly, in the establishment of enlightened forms of political leadership. 'The formation of a lively, expressive and at the same time sober and measured prose must be set as a cultural goal', Gramsci argued, because the overblown 'operatic' style adopted by the popular classes when expressing themselves in public was a serious *political* problem.[42] Although Gramsci— whose academic training had been in linguistics—did not describe this style in dialogical terms, its 'sober and measured' quality is clearly a reflection of the kind of relationships deemed appropriate for a modern national-popular movement. Journalism and education must therefore not only transmit knowledge and dispel myth and superstition, but also lay the foundations for a democratic *culture*, a style of intersubjectivity—sober and measured—which binds together the national-popular mass at the level of 'feeling and imagination'.

If we took liberal and liberal-democratic theory at its word, we would have to accept that it had little interest in language itself, and was content with the task of regulating the public sphere of discussion and debate

[40] The most interesting and sophisticated proposals have come from Tom Paulin, who makes a case for an Irish English: 'A language that lives lithely on the tongue ought to be capable of becoming the flexible written instrument of a complete cultural idea', from 'A New Look at the Language Question', in Field Day Theatre Company, *Ireland's Field Day* (London: Hutchinson, 1985), 15.

[41] For a characteristic discussion see Ngũgĩ wa Thion'go, 'The Language of African Literature', *New Left Review*, 150 (1985), 109–27.

[42] See Antonio Gramsci, *Selections from Cultural Writings*, trans. William Boelhower (London: Lawrence & Wishart, 1985), 204.

through which citizens make clear their values and choices. Liberal democracy imagines itself not so much as shaping language but as protecting the private realm which is its necessary well-spring. The familiar constitutional guarantees of freedom of speech, assembly, and press are meant to institutionalize and protect public dialogue, while processes like petition and election ensure that lines of communication are open between the private sphere of civil society and the public world of government. So vigorously, however, does liberal government pursue this regulatory task, and so frequently does it get bogged down in analysis of the minutiae of language use, that one begins to wonder whether this modesty of aim is really no more than a delusion. Even a brief glance at the US case law covering freedom of speech reveals that judges find themselves constantly having to gauge the effects of particular linguistic forms, the intent and context of speech, and the role of language in maintaining or disrupting social relationships when they are called upon merely to protect an ostensibly private process.[43] According to its self-understanding, liberalism is interested only in *procedures*, formal rules and patterns extrinsic to language itself; but to imagine that these, and the institutions they regulate (the press, the mass media, social movements, and so on), are separate from linguistic style, that they neither shape it nor are reflected in it, is to maintain precisely the individualized concept of style which is the problem to begin with. Liberal democracy would like to think that it spares no effort in its attempts to establish and maintain democratic processes. But it pulls up short before the sphere of culture, at the point where it becomes clear that democratic language is something shaped from within, not regulated from without, and that rules and their interpretation are not distinct from language but are part of it. We are thus faced with a paradoxical situation: while liberal-democratic states characteristically cannot keep their hands off language, they do so constrained by the belief that the liberal state should be no more than the efficient administrator and referee for the privately constituted interests of civil society. In that light, how one speaks, in what tone, and how loudly, is an entirely individual matter, and the state should limit itself to ensuring that private speakers play by the rules. (In practice, of course, the state's implied promise to keep its hands off

---

[43] The problem is exemplified by the US Supreme Court's famous doctrine that words can be curtailed by government action when they present 'a clear and present danger that they will bring about the substantive evils that Congress has a right to prevent' (*Schenk* v. *United States*, 249 US 52 (1919)). Oliver Wendell Holmes, who articulated this doctrine, recognized at the outset that this meant assessing not the words themselves but their possible effect in a given set of circumstances. Since that time, the Court has continually wrestled with the problem of deciding what renders a particular act of speech clearly dangerous, as well as the related problem of assessing those expressive acts (burning flags and draft cards, wearing armbands) which are obviously both expressive of ideas or ideologies and acts with definite, 'material' effects.

language is as worthless as its explicit promise to keep its hands off the economy; state intervention in education and language planning have been and continue to be the order of the day throughout liberal-democratic Europe and North America.) The end result is the characteristic liberal-democratic obsession with the rules of the game, the constitutional procedures which, because they take the form of law, are able to imagine themselves as distant and distinct from the subjects and the language they regulate. Democracy, as conceived in the liberal-democratic universe, consists of rules for discourse somehow separate from discourse itself.[44]

The consequences of this for actual democratic life are well known, and often enough rehearsed in public comment; there is no lack of ink on the fact that liberal-democratic subjects are often unenthusiastic or even hostile to the procedures which guarantee their political power.[45] Democratic procedures are not enough; they require and imply democratic dispositions and competencies as their 'subjective' support. Not merely forms and institutions, but the ability, will, and confidence necessary to work them in a sophisticated and often reflective manner is a prerequisite of democratic political life. One might say that the *experience* of democracy has never been regarded as a private affair, but that this political insight has been always used tactically, in the notionally 'private' theory and practice of political organizations.[46] In liberal-democratic theory, whether subjects take up the opportunities on offer is their own business, and those who lack the necessary motivation are in no position to complain when things go wrong. But even the ideally virtuous and active citizen—the middle-class campaigner?—is an indictment of this system. For the subject who 'fits' the procedures perfectly, who has the disposition and competence to work them effectively, by the very fact of fitting reminds us of the gap more sharply manifested when citizens relate to procedures either apathetically (choosing not to vote, nor to exercise other guaranteed political rights) or cynically (seeing them as no more than strategic moves

[44] The obvious example is the revival of Kantian political philosophy by John Rawls in *A Theory of Justice* (Oxford: Clarendon Press, 1972), in particular pp. 11–22, 118–50. Rawls's contractualist premises mean that he will only be able to characterize the ideal liberal-democratic discourse in terms of restrictions and principles of discussion. Thus: 'Understood in this way the question of justification is settled by working out a problem of deliberation: we have to ascertain which principles it would be rational to adopt given the contractual situation' (p. 17).

[45] The literature on disenchantment with liberal-democratic politics is, I assume, familiar enough not to require citation. In recent European politics, it is often expressed as support for parties of the extreme Right or those which promise some break with the status quo (e.g., the Greens in Germany). In the United States, this unhappiness receives direct statistical expression in a steady decline in voting participation; see Frances Fox Piven and Richard Cloward, *Why Americans Don't Vote* (New York: Pantheon, 1989).

[46] A rare, although sketchy, exception is found in some of the political writing of Raymond Williams. See my 'A Complex Populism: The Politics of Raymond Williams', *News from Nowhere*, 6 (1989), 12–22.

in the pursuit of political advantage). The gap between procedure and dis-position, separating the hard objectivity of the one from the contingency of the other is the core issue; in so far as liberal-democratic procedure presents itself neither as grounded in a form of life nor as embodied in styles of communication, it finds itself reduced to a means or an instrument, separated by virtue of that fact from the values which animate political subjects. In liberal democracy the use of procedures becomes a move in the game, and struggles for the mantle of democracy are played out as arguments over the relative democratic aura of different procedures. The apathetic or cynical subject merely makes explicit the fact that liberal democracy strives for a democratic state without a democratic culture, and for democratic discussion without democratic style.[47]

Jürgen Habermas has brilliantly exploited this weakness in liberal-democratic life, by pointing out that the roots of democratic constitutional practice lie in a democratic culture which lies outside it, in what Habermas calls 'the public sphere'.[48] In the public sphere, constituted first in eighteenth-century bourgeois civil society and embodied today in the so-called new social movements, private subjects meet as concerned citizens to argue over matters of public interest, with the conviction that these issues can and should be settled through the public use of reason. They may meet anywhere—in parks, workplaces, coffee houses, consciousness-raising groups—for in this case the rules that underlie democratic life take the form not of laws but of moral principles which determine whether or not we think an argument has been fairly and justly conducted.[49] Because

---

[47] Klaus Eder has made this case in terms of competing 'political cultures'. In his critique of the concept of political culture, which sought to bridge the gap between procedure and subject, Eder demonstrates that political cultures themselves are various even within the space of a single polity and that they are treated strategically by political actors. Battles for political power are accordingly battles for legitimacy between forms of political practice (between, to take the obvious example, industrial action, and the force of an elected parliamentary government). See his 'Politics and Culture: On the Sociocultural Analysis of Political Participation', in Axel Honneth, Thomas McCarthy, Claus Offe, and Albrecht Wellmer (eds.), *Cultural–Political Interventions in the Unfinished Project of Enlightenment*, trans. Barbara Fultner (Cambridge, Mass. and London: MIT Press, 1992), 95–120.

[48] Jürgen Habermas, *The Structural Transformation of the Public Sphere: An Inquiry into a Category of Bourgeois Society*, trans. Thomas Burger and Frederick Lawrence (Cambridge, Mass. and London: MIT Press, 1989).

[49] In Habermas's initial formulation, the public sphere was the creation of the English and French bourgeoisie, not substantially altered by the 'plebeian public sphere' which arose in the course of the French Revolution. Since that time, critics of Habermas and Habermas himself have been more generous in terms of where and when public spheres have been constituted. For further discussion of the public sphere's mutable locations see: Geoff Eley, 'Nations, Publics, and Political Cultures: Placing Habermas in the Nineteenth Century', in Nicholas B. Dirks *et al.* (eds.), *Culture/Power/History: A Reader* (Princeton, NJ: Princeton University Press, 1991), 297–335; Nancy Fraser, 'What's Critical about Critical Theory? The Case of Habermas and Gender', in *Unruly Practices: Power, Discourse and Gender in Contemporary Social Theory* (Cambridge: Polity Press, 1989), 113–43; the contributions by Schudson, Baker, Ryan, Eley,

the public sphere depends upon the initiative of private subjects, and relies on informal conventions often made up 'on the hoof', it reminds us that constitutional procedures are in the end only approximate institutionalizations of the principles which ground and justify them. By loosening democracy's bonds to the state, and making more explicit its connection to the communicative experience of political subjects, Habermas reconstitutes the communicative practice of democracy as a kind of culture with deep roots in the subject, as deep as those which supposedly govern it when it strikes off on its own in the guise of the just and righteous liberal 'individual'.

For if a democratic culture is to be a democratic *culture* the moral principles underlying it must be something more than convictions implanted in particularly worthy and admirable citizens. If the passion for democracy were an individual affair, we would be better off with the reassuring, if slightly alienating, coldness of procedures set in stone and backed up by law. In Habermas's account, however, the liberal individual's belief in justice does not ground democracy but encodes—in mystifying, monological form—the political experience of it. In the public sphere, universal moral principles take the form of rules for the conduct of argument, for this modern, secular, and democratic sphere holds that truths of practical life are not preserved in ancient texts or found in revelations but are argued for, and the fairness of the argument is in the end the only warrant for the moral worth of the conclusions reached. In the moral theory which gave philosophical expression to this liberal doctrine, Kant preserved the formalism of this dialogical political experience—it is how one reaches conclusions that counts—and its universalism—the process should ensure conclusions that apply to all equally—but he enclosed the process itself in the monological working of a single mind. What emerged historically as a distinction between kinds of social action, between the argument of the public sphere and the selfish activity of economic life, was therefore coded in Kantian morality as a division which sunders the subjectivity of each of us, as the moral rational self which tells us to be fair battles with the desiring, self-interested empirical one which drives us to want.

Habermas thus interprets the principles of Kant's 'practical reason', which tell us how we can rationally determine right conduct, as the principles of a new kind of intersubjectivity, which distinguishes itself from earlier forms by insisting that the conditions of intersubjectivity itself are what legitimate the end result of political discussion. Democracy dis-

Warner, and Habermas in Craig Calhoun (ed.), *Habermas and the Public Sphere* (Cambridge, Mass. and London: MIT Press, 1992); and Bruce Robbins (ed.), *The Phantom Public Sphere* (Minneapolis, Minn.: University of Minnesota Press, 1993).

tinguishes itself from the absolutism which precedes it by the assumption that open and public argument is the only test of whether a policy or value may be deemed rational and thus in the best interests of all. The convictions which make one a democrat are the assumptions one makes when engaging in this kind of argument, assumptions which have to take the form of not only good intentions but of binding rules for argument itself. Habermas calls this kind of public discussion 'discourse':

Discourse can be understood as that form of communication that is removed from contexts of experience and action and whose structure assures us: that the bracketed validity claims of assertions, recommendations or warnings are the exclusive object of discussion; that participants, themes or contributions are not restricted except with reference to the goal of testing the validity of claims in questions; that no force except that of the better argument is exercised; and that, as a result, all motives except that of the cooperative search for truth are excluded.[50]

The degree to which a social order is just and democratic is then the degree to which the formation of public opinion and the direction of political decision have been 'discursively rationalized' in this sense. Which means, of course, that institutions have to be in place which make public reason possible and its conclusions effective in government, and that the fact that a decision has been arrived at properly serves as a real motivation for citizens to abide by it. Democratic theory establishes a new *level of justification* for political argument; it tells us what kinds of reasons are acceptable when we claim allegiance to a political order or to its policies and decisions.[51] But what Rousseau or Kant have written makes no difference unless it describes the compelling force of such reasons in practice; it is only when subjects feel bound to norms and values *because* they are the result of democratic discourse that we are moving in the universe of modern democracy.

To a certain kind of political thinker, all this talk of principles and justification will sound rather fanciful, but the payoff is a concept of democracy at once more critical and more manoeuvrable (as Habermas has

---

[50] Jürgen Habermas, *Legitimation Crisis*, trans. Thomas McCarthy (London: Heinemann, 1976), 107–8.

[51] See his 'Legitimation Problems in the Modern State', in *Communication and the Evolution of Society*, trans. Thomas McCarthy (London: Heinemann, 1979), especially pp. 178–88. In this text from the 1970s Habermas describes 'modernity' as the moment at which 'the level of justification has become reflective. The procedures and presuppositions of justification are themselves now the legitimating grounds on which the validity of legitimations is based' (p. 185). As Habermas elaborated his concept of communicative action in the later 1970s and early 1980s he came to describe this evolution not as the triumph of reflection—using accepted philosophical vocabulary—but as the 'linguistification' or 'discursive rationalization' of decisions and socio-political authority. This reflects his increasing conviction that in everyday discourse itself are embedded the presuppositions of a modern and self-reflexive form of political rationality. Habermas now treats these issues under the rubric of 'discourse ethics'.

himself demonstrated, in shrewd and persuasive defences of political dissent in the North Atlantic versions of political modernity[52]). From the perspective of a discourse theory of democracy official democratic procedures appear reified when detached from the democratic intentions of public reason, and the latter, once severed from any particular institution, prove capable of the most protean transformations. The protesting citizen or striking worker, condemned as an unruly threat to democracy by the political powers-that-be, may have just as good a claim, when engaged in civil disobedience, industrial action, or a mass demonstration, to democratic principles as the state which opposes them. Contemporary arguments over democracy are thus unsurprisingly arguments over structures of expression: even the call for a national referendum or plebiscite, flagged as the purest example of the expression of popular will, is always strategic, a mobilization of a certain form of expression, with its own logic, against others (e.g. the legislative vote, industrial action, the election result), in the hope that an intersubjectivity firm enough to resist the opposition can be cemented by this political act. Those with their hands on the levers of state power manoeuvre in this way precisely because they recognize that official procedures themselves mean little without an intersubjectivity to support them, and that this is made or broken outside the sphere of the state itself. While it is decisions and regimes which are deemed legitimate, it is principles rather than procedures which make them so. Citizens of modern liberal democracies can perceive this distinction easily, and make use of it in their protests and their scepticism.

To this extent what is evidently a weakness of a theory of democratic culture—that it theorizes a democratic style in abstraction from particular political institutions and procedures—has the virtue of establishing a necessary critical distance from the forms instituted in the state. The analyst mesmerized by constitutional procedure determines democratic credentials by ticking items off his or her list (political rights of expression and organization, regular elections, an independent judiciary, and so forth), without regard for the 'private' question of how the citizenry experiences these. In the United States the procedures are ostentatiously displayed, but the intersubjectivity which leaves them for the most part unused is relegated to an individualist dustbin marked 'apathy'. In the Soviet Union (to make the obvious contrast) the procedures were singularly lacking, but the democratic elements established in languages or styles below or beyond the formal structures of the state were invisible to the formalist eye: the scientific price for this—a finely honed inability to see it coming—was heavy indeed. Intersubjective forces or communicative structures may grow or flourish in

[52] See e.g. Habermas, 'On Right and Violence: A German Trauma', *Cultural Critique*, 1 (1985), 125–39.

the absence of democratic states, and their development outside the state may furnish both the pressure for democracy and some elements of its subjective prerequisites (at the moment of writing it is not clear whether or not recent Soviet history will provide evidence for this). Formal democracy may coexist with intersubjective structures of an authoritarian type, for which the recent history of Europe has surely furnished too much in the way of illustration. For sure, one cannot underestimate the importance of legally sanctioned democratic procedures; but where these have an impact, it is because they coexist with a democratic consciousness which supports them. Without it, they remain the mere 'words on paper' that many a dictator has claimed. Like the republic, democracy is constantly fought for and defended, not instituted once and for all.

It was this evident gap between public culture and actual subjectivity that first moved Bakhtin to write. In 'Towards a Philosophy of the Act' he interprets the social crisis following the First World War as a crisis of 'responsibility', stemming from a breach between the values articulated in culture and the actual motivations of subjects. Wishing to criticize the formalism of Kantian ethics without giving up Kantian ideals, he turns to the formal features of every act, the first of which is the inevitable context of intersubjectivity. Bakhtin, too, will seek to redeem Kantian ideals of personal autonomy and moral universalism by pushing them out of the confines of the solitary 'monological' consciousness. As we know full well, however, Bakhtin eventually cashed in his doubts about formalism in a critique not of moral theory, but of language and linguistic theory. This is no accident, for there is a striking, but unsurprising, isomorphism between the conceptual weakness of modern linguistics and the practical weakness of liberal democracy. At the same moment that Saussure junked a no longer credible belief in an uncorrupted or original language in favour of a more egalitarian version of consent to the existing, the European *ancien régime* found itself forced to devise democratic means of legitimating hierarchical states and political orders, a parallel of which the linguist from Geneva was only too aware: 'For if we wish to demonstrate that the rules a community accepts are imposed upon it, and not freely agreed to, it is a language which offers the most striking proof.'[53] Actual liberal democracy, as it emerged from the ruins of the First World War, was rich in procedures which proved to be empty or uninspiring for the citizenry; indeed, they were probably designed with that in mind.[54] Interwar Europe was, in fact, an object lesson in the difference between the principles of democratic

[53] Saussure, *Course*, 71. I have substituted the translation of Wade Baskin here.

[54] The Europe which emerged in the wake of the First World War was overwhelmingly liberal–democratic; in the next two decades regime after liberal regime was to fall (almost all to the Right). For a good summary of this transformation see Eric Hobsbawm, *Age of Extremes: The*

life and the reified procedures of 'official' democracy, for liberal democracy did not 'take', but was challenged immediately by the alternative democratic structures of unions, soviets, improvised councils, and the like. To those involved, this revolution against procedure was a clear expression of the popular will, but it was mere disorder to the political classes which looked on in horror. They had hoped that the citizenry would accept the social order in much the same way that Saussure thinks the speaking subject accepts the order of a natural language—as something verified not by reason or argument but by the sheer inertia of passive popular consent (and when it became clear this was not on the cards, they made a deal with a more active form of popular consent—fascism—despite the risks involved). Saussure sees the conventions governing a language not as justified or as justifiable but as binding on all users nonetheless, regardless of what they want to say or how they feel about it. Similarly, the proponents of liberal democracy strive for a passive form of democratic consent, in which discouragement, fear, and resignation persuade the population that their best bet is to play by the rules.

Bakhtin sees in the 'concreteness' of language use a route out of the ineffective formalism of Kantian morality. For an effective critique of the abstractness of formalist conceptions of language ends up steering language in the direction of ethics. The feelings, motivations, and values of speakers, which Saussure carefully filtered out of his conception of 'the language structure' or *langue*, undergo a transformation when we interpret them as facts of language: they lose the capricious, individual quality they had when they were left to the happenstance world of *parole*. A 'concrete' language is not merely one which acknowledges its own historical mutability or social variability; it is a language which has reintegrated the act of speech into its structure, and reintegrated it precisely as an *act*, that is, as a moment of commitment or position-taking. Whereas Saussure separated the articulation of values in the language structure from the endorsement or rejection of them, Bakhtin claimed that it was nonsensical to believe one could articulate a value *without* taking a position in relation to it. For that reason, the minimal structural unit of language, the linguistic utterance, was defined by Bakhtin in notes from the 1950s as 'the minimum of that to which one can respond, ⟨with⟩ which one can agree or disagree' (D-II, 226). Language does not articulate values or principles from a neutral perspective, making their acceptance or rejection a matter for individual initiative: its meanings are positions taken or refused, its forms opportunities for ethical relationships.

Short Twentieth Century (London: Michael Joseph, 1994), ch. 4, 'The Fall of Liberalism'; on the 'progress' of liberal democracy see Göran Therborn, 'The Rule of Capital and the Rise of Democracy', *New Left Review*, 103 (1977), 3–41.

If language is an ethical substance, then its limits are the limits of our ethical life:

The genuinely good, disinterested, and loving person has not yet spoken, he has realized himself in the spheres of everyday life, he has not touched organized discourse, infected by violence and lies, he has not become a writer . . . Discourse was stronger than the person, he could not be responsible while in the power of discourse; he felt himself the herald of an alien truth, in the higher power of which he was caught. (Rhet., 66–7)

Bakhtin borrowed the concept of style to describe the mutual inter-dependence of language and ethical life. And having borrowed it, he tinkered with it to the point where it was of no use to its original owner. Style had traditionally denoted the moment at which language was infused with subjectivity, whether its source was a person, an epoch, or a move-ment; Bakhtin, to make his point, made style the truth of language itself, so that it was possible to speak of '*the style of a language as a whole*' (FPND 427/62). As intersubjectivity incarnate, a language did not leave the possibilities of ethical life to chance—it was their structure and condition. How else can one understand a passage such as the following, in which the European vernaculars, far from being the neutral tools of society, are the privileged media for the social and political relationships of modern Europe?

The specific inflection of sobriety, simplicity, democracy, and freedom inhering in all modern languages. With certain qualifications one can say that they have all (especially French) descended from the popular profaning genres, they have all to a certain degree been determined by the prolonged and complex process of the expulsion of the alien holy word and in general any holy and authoritarian discourse with its indisputability, unconditionality, and unqualifiability. Discourse with sanctified and inaccessible borders and therefore an inert discourse with limited possibilities for contact and combination. A discourse inhibiting and freezing thought. A discourse demanding reverential repetition, and not further development, correction, and supplements. A discourse removed from dialogue: it can only be cited from within rejoinders, but it cannot itself become a rejoinder amongst other rejoinders with equal rights. This discourse was dis-seminated everywhere, limiting, directing and inhibiting thought and living experience. It was in the process of struggle with this discourse and of its expul-sion (with the aid of parodic antibodies) that the modern languages were formed. The scars at the edges of alien discourse. Traces in the syntactic structure. (N70–71, 355–6/132–3)

Language is an odd home for equal rights and democracy; authoritarianism is surely more than a way of speaking. Yet it is in the strangeness of a passage such as the above, where democracy is employed as a literary-stylistic category, and where equal rights, a rogues' gallery of authoritarians, and problems of syntax appear cheek by jowl, that Bakhtin's point lies. Democracy and equal rights are not law but language, not the product of institutions above society but of the linguistic intersubjectivity which constitutes it. By insisting on it as a cultural category Bakhtin endows democracy with a depth and a reach into the lifeworld which any Kantian —Habermas included—would be wary of. And for good reason—for a deeper democracy is a more thinly stretched one.

Language and Legitimacy

Whether the stakes justify the risk can be gauged by comparing Bakhtin's concept of the ethics of intersubjectivity with a concept from political sociology which covers much the same ground: the idea of 'legitimacy'. In the classic formulation by Weber, legitimacy means that social actors treat the prescriptions of a political order as binding; they conform to these not only because to do so is habitual or expedient, but also because they believe that they *ought* to.[55] As a morally binding force, legitimacy makes it possible for subjects to act without immediate supervision or threat, that is, it creates a sphere of intersubjective norms and obligations which runs on its own steam. Is this just an option for modern, highly differentiated societies? Hans Magnus Enzensberger has argued that a twentieth-century polity cannot be satisfied with sullen obedience; it must mobilize its subjects:

When I say *mobilize* I mean *mobilize*. In a country which has had direct experience of Fascism (and Stalinism) it is perhaps still necessary to explain, or to explain again, what that means—namely, to make men more mobile than they are. As free as dancers, as aware as football players, as surprising as guerillas. Anyone who thinks of the masses only as the object of politics cannot mobilize them. He wants to push them around.[56]

Although Weber writes as if the point of legitimacy was precisely to 'push people around', his division of types of legitimate authority into legal, traditional, and charismatic types exhibits a working theory of intersubjectivity. Of these three only the legal form, which asks for obedience to a rationally organized and predictable system of rules (law), engages the kind of active consent which would allow for independent action on the part of its subjects. Although legal authority is personified in the bureaucrat with uncommon technical expertise, the fact that it is organized according to comprehensible, understandable, and impersonal legal norms means that those who accept it can become active, calculating members of

---

[55] Max Weber, 'The Types of Legitimate Domination', in *Economy and Society*, vol. i, ed. Guenther Roth and Claus Wittich (Berkeley, Ca.: University of California Press, 1978), 212–301.

[56] Enzensberger, 'Constituents of a Theory of the Media', *New Left Review*, 64 (1970), 14–15.

civil society (and for this reason it makes the possible the economic liberty of capitalist civil society). Traditional and charismatic authority, by contrast, demand obedience to a person rather than rules, and therefore restrict the independent initiative of subjects to a bare minimum. Charisma in particular is singled out by Weber as, on the one hand, an 'emotional form of communal relationship', involving devotion to a leader with aura, and, on the other hand, a form in which those who obey merely 'recognize' an authority which is itself the source of every creative social manouevre.[57] Charisma being the form of modern democracy, the point is clear: at the end of the day, democratic consent is a matter of follow the leader, not responsive but 'monological'.[58]

The language of intersubjectivity must therefore be cold, impersonal, and rational; once the personal and affective enter the scene, moral force becomes a one-way street. Habermas, always on the lookout for an opportunity to make an intersubjective turn, has argued that every kind of legitimacy—legal, mythic, or democratic—entails an ineradicable argumentative, narrative, or symbolic element; legitimacy is a process, a 'contestable validity claim'.[59] In this broadened sense, 'legitimacy' is political power seen from the perspective of intersubjectivity or 'dialogue', where obligation to a social order depends upon a working language of reciprocal (though not necessarily equal) expectation and response. Obligation and intersubjectivity are, as it were, two sides of the same social coin, and the fact that every social order depends upon legitimacy tells us that every order depends, in some fundamental sense, on dialogism or intersubjectivity as well. Despite first impressions, this does not contradict Bakhtin's distinction between sober and free vernaculars on the one hand and the alien holy word (which brooks no argument) on the other. As we shall see, even authoritarian discourse, in all its inertness and immobility, only works given a certain functioning intersubjectivity.

Habermas, however, remains true to the substance of the concept of legitimacy, even though he alters its form. Like Weber, he believes that the most advanced form of political intersubjectivity must be derived from Western European political experience, for which everything related to joy, endearment, or affect in general figures as an irrational admixture to the progress of political reason. The emergence of the modern European state and with it modern European political philosophy was predicated on

---

[57] Weber, *Economy and Society*, i. 243.

[58] This is so even though Weber realizes that the turn to a democratic form of charisma involves a reversal of the poles of legitimacy: 'But when the charismatic organization undergoes progressive rationalization, it is readily possible that, instead of recognition being treated as a consequence of legitimacy, it is treated as the basis of legitimacy: democratic legitimacy' (*Economy and Society*, i. 266–7).

[59] Habermas, 'Legitimation Problems in the Modern State', 178–83.

a separation of politics, and the issues decidable within it, from religious questions.[60] We know that this distillation meant pushing to one side the substantive issues posed in religious debate, but it also meant divorcing questions of political right from the aesthetic, affectual, and traditional elements which were constitutive of absolutist power and religious ethics (though the 'aesthetic state' would make a brief reappearance in Romanticism). In the narrative offered by Western political modernity, the ether in which political subjects respire is gradually purified until legality and its associated concepts (justice, right, consistency, transparency, impersonality) are its sole constituent. This purification of politics and its emergence as an autonomous sphere of action with its own norms meant relieving it of any contamination by ideas now ring-fenced as aesthetic, personal, or ethical. The question remains, however, whether the air in this realm is too thin to sustain political life of any complexity. From the perspective of a properly modern 'philosophy of right' Bakhtin's widening of the moral stakes in political authority appears ill advised, a reckless confusion of politics with the personal and the aesthetic. But it may be no more than a reflection of a national history which delivered as its modernity not a liberal constitutional state but the strangely different world of Stalinist authority. Can the concepts of legality and justice account for that bizarre combination of fear, awe, love, and fascination with which even some critical opponents regarded Stalin's rule? Is it enough to ascribe Stalin's authority to shrewd tactical manoeuvre, as if pure fear and terror rendered legitimacy a dispensable commodity? In the harsh glare of Stalinism, concepts of consent and legitimacy appear pallid and washed out, unable to explain or grasp the complex motives of those who consented to some of the worst twentieth-century politics has had to offer.[61]

The standard response to this problem is the word 'totalitarianism', meant to sum up the West's incomprehension of the language in which popular politics has sometimes been conducted. From the perspective of a political philosophy which identifies modernity with a purified political sphere of right, Russia's problem, and the problem of all nations where repressive regimes mobilize popular enthusiasm, is that their modernity is half-baked and incomplete. Nations which incline this way have not

[60] For this history I am relying on: Habermas, 'The Classical Doctrine of Politics in Relation to Social Philosophy', in *Theory and Practice*, trans. John Viertel (Boston, Mass.: Beacon Press, 1973), 41–81; Reinhart Koselleck, *Critique and Crisis: Enlightenment and the Pathogenesis of Modern Society*, (Cambridge, Mass. and London: MIT Press, 1988), part 1: 'The Political Structure of Absolutism as a Precondition of Enlightenment', in particular pp. 15–40.

[61] In this respect V. Turbin's controversial description of Bakhtin's interrogation by the OGPU (secret police) in 1929 as a 'dialogue' is strangely apposite. See the letter of protest by Sofia Kagan (widow of Matvei Kagan), 'Est' li pravo prostit' sistemu' [Do We Have the Right to Forgive the System?], *Literaturnaia gazeta*, 25, 25 June 1991.

quite grown up, or have missed a stage, and in adolescent fashion they carry round childhood keepsakes—Romantic notions of the people, the glamour of Absolutism, and so forth—they really should be done with. When faced with popular consent to repression, Western political philosophy characteristically looks out for archaic structures or else calls for reinforcements from psychology, psychoanalysis, or modern versions of crowd theory. If regimes survive in all their unjustified glory, perhaps this is thanks to the presence of 'the authoritarian personality' or the wiles of mass media deception; subjects who think that what is clearly wrong is right appear to disqualify themselves from the political task of justification; their psyches have not yet caught up with modern life, and suffer from the persistence of archaic structures. 'Totalitarianism' then represents the triumph of regressive or pre-modern forces in technologically or sociologically modern societies. But the inability to account for the legitimacy of so many modern political orders—we see it today when analysts throw up their hands in the face of the 'antique hatreds' of nationalism—may be the symptom of an unresolved theoretical problem: the belief that justice in pure form is enough to motivate support for a political order.

Bakhtin, too, sees authoritarianism as 'pre-modern'; his bearers of the alien holy word have supposedly been expelled from the linguistic territory of modernity. But in his account, the opposite of authoritarian fear and submissiveness is not purely 'political' reason purged of all emotion, but democratic 'sobriety' and ironic distance. The political theory which restricts dialogically maintained consent to questions of pure right panics when confronted with popular acquiescence in manifest injustice, and must call upon the psychologism it otherwise rejects. But the psychic forces in play when 'totalitarianism' is the order of the day do not disappear in democracies, and they too must be part of any intersubjectivity which supports a democratic life. In that case, democratic orders do not depend upon the mere *absence* of fear, *ressentiment*, or whatever emotion one associates with the 'totalitarian', but upon the presence of its opposite, whether this is called sobriety, confidence, civility, or respect.

In a series of essays following the formulation of his discourse theory of democracy, Habermas agreed that, on its own, public recognition that a conclusion had been justly arrived at was probably too weak a motive to be effective in practice. A morality of right and justice 'is dependent upon a form of life that *meets it halfway*',[62] because its recommendations have only 'the rationally motivating force of insights',[63] which may bind us but do

---

[62] Habermas, 'Morality and Ethical Life: Does Hegel's Critique of Kant Apply to Discourse Ethics?', in *Moral Consciousness and Communicative Action*, trans. Christian Lenhardt and Shierry Weber Nicholsen (Cambridge, Mass. and London: MIT Press, 1990), 207.

[63] Habermas, 'Discourse Ethics: Notes on a Program of Philosophical Justification', ibid.

not, so to speak, inspire us. Meeting morality half-way, however, turns out to be a matter not of altering the emotions and motives in questions, or of providing more inspiring reasons for supporting a social order, but of universalist morality creating a psyche and a lifeworld in its own image. Thus Habermas sees Kantian morality as made effective by the development of legal institutions on the one hand, and of ego-identities, superego controls, and the capacity for 'self-governance' on the other, all of which presume that subjects should internalize the essentially negative and constraining force of norms of justice, which remain as unlovable as ever.[64] Habermas remains stubborn on this point because he is convinced that while concepts of justice and right are implicit in any attempt to conduct a reasoned argument, every other moral good, however attractive, is relative to a specific, geographically and historically limited way of life: 'Negative versions of the moral principle seem to be a step in the right direction. They heed the prohibition of graven images, refrain from positive depiction, and as in the case of discourse ethics, refer negatively to the damaged life instead of pointing affirmatively to the good life.'[65] Justice may seem unduly negative as a goal, but it is the *only* value which is the presupposition of every dialogue.

As what interests Bakhtin is the very possibility of redemption which Habermas wants to exclude, he finds himself 'pointing affirmatively to the good life' every time dialogue crosses his field of vision. No doubt this reflects the fact that Bakhtin derives his concept of dialogue from religion and aesthetics, precisely the areas in which Habermas has the least interest. Religious and aesthetic dialogues do not have as their primary aim the generation of morally defensible decisions; their value lies in the relationships of love or solidarity they evoke and in their ability to keep alive an image of utter transformation or redemption. But Bakhtin is convinced that these qualities are also universal features of dialogue rather than something added onto it in the form of metaphysical beliefs. He pushes dialogue in the direction of the good life not by cutting out its universal features, but by focusing attention on aesthetic properties of language which Habermas has always put to one side and energies which Weber stored up in the idea of charisma. Are these energies and properties surplus to our political requirements? Even so sober a figure as Weber did not think so. Linking democracy to the aesthetic concept of dialogism suggests that the former may have to offer more than justice and the satisfaction of acting

[64] Thus Jay Bernstein has taken Habermas to task for overemphasizing problems of justice and right at the expense of the problem of a meaningful life, a problem he thinks may be corrected by a return to the Hegelian priority of 'ethical life' (*Sittlichkeit*). See J. M. Bernstein, *Recovering Ethical Life: Jürgen Habermas and the Future of Critical Theory* (London and New York: Routledge, 1995).

[65] Habermas, 'Morality and Ethical Life', 205.

rightly; it must also include a distinctive and rewarding form of inter-subjectivity, and the experiences of solidarity, fulfilment, and the integrity of a life story essential to a civil form of existence.[66] And one of the reasons we may want to think of democracy in these terms is that modern democratic politics, for better or worse, already occupies this terrain.

In the essays which make up the book *Signs Taken for Wonders* and in his study *The Way of the World* Franco Moretti has suggested that ideology in bourgeois society has a distinctive form, different from the kind of systematic belief which legitimized its feudal precursor.[67] Because the bourgeois world acknowledges that a multiplicity of conflicting interests and values is natural to society,

the concept of 'consent' itself has to undergo a profound transformation. It can no longer consist in the drastic and acknowledged triumph of one system of values over all others. It must assume a more ductile and precarious form: no longer that of full dialectical synthesis but the more dubious one of *compromise*.[68]

Compromise has distinctive formal features: it cannot, by definition, be incarnated in a systematic philosophy or theory of society—it must assume the form of a narrative, to wit, of the realist novel of the nineteenth century. In modernity 'culture' takes over the task of legitimation from religion, but this entails not the substitution of one system of belief for another, but the replacement of the strong and systematic belief necessary for religion by the weak, narrative kind of belief typical of the novel. Or, to put it more exactly, it entails the replacement of belief in the usual sense of the word by narrative itself, which alone can make compromise some-thing liveable and even pleasurable.

One cannot, therefore, simply confront liberal democracy with its own claim to justice and fairness, for it already has cultural mechanisms which assume the world is unfair, or cruel, occasionally arbitrary, and often violent. The culture of the capitalist democracies works not through persuasion or strong ideological argument, but by the creation of templates for a life well lived, in full knowledge of the world's dissonances and inadequacies. In which case a *critical* democratic culture must take aim at the weak, narrative kind of belief embodied in modern culture, not in order to demonstrate that it is weak, which is its premiss, but to point a

[66] Axel Honneth has argued that in the young Hegel's conception of the recognition essential to intersubjectivity we find not only relationships based on Kantian 'respect', but also those based on 'love' and 'solidarity'. See his *The Struggle for Recognition: The Moral Grammar of Social Conflicts*, trans. Joel Anderson (Cambridge: Polity Press, 1995).

[67] Franco Moretti, *Signs Taken for Wonders*, 2nd edn., trans. Susan Fischer, David Forgacs, and David Miller (London: Verso, 1988); id., *The Way of the World: The* Bildungsroman *in European Culture*, trans. Albert Sbragia (London: Verso, 1987).

[68] Franco Moretti, 'The Soul and the Harpy', in *Signs Taken for Wonders*, 34. See also in this volume 'The Spell of Indecision' and 'The Moment of Truth'.

critical gaze at the anxieties and dissatisfactions which it seeks to defuse or displace. A democratic culture therefore attacks all those features of modern culture which support what Bakhtin would call 'the usual run of life' (Rhet., 64), 'the eternal threat of the *present day*' (Rhet., 65), or 'bourgeois-philistine optimism' (an 'optimism', as Bakhtin quipped, 'not of the better but of the safe' (Flau., 131)). In short, democracy can only challenge the aesthetic satisfactions on offer if it has something to put in their place.

No doubt many will think that democracy has a hard enough time without finding itself burdened with feelings and dreams of salvation. A democracy of pure procedure and justice, however, runs the risk of giving rise to its opposite, a democracy of pure, often national, redemption. Writing in the mid-1920s, the political theorist Carl Schmitt could see that there was something not quite democratic in the legalism of the Weimar Republic, and that procedures on their own would hardly be enough to bind its citizenry.[69] To this legalism Schmitt opposed a purely aesthetic conception of democracy, in which democratic life reduced itself to the expression, even by dictatorial means, of the will of a people unified culturally and subjectively. One can reject Schmitt's own repulsive convictions (he would serve and justify Hitler's dictatorship in the 1930s) while admitting his analysis had some point. It was hardly an accident that then—and now—it was the promise of a national, collective redemption which inspired a powerful popular will, and no accident that promises of redemption so often leave constitutional procedures looking empty or like mere scheming. Weber himself more or less admitted this when he defined democracy as the absolute antithesis of legal rationality, as an irrational 'charismatic authority'. The majority who follow a charismatic leader do so spontaneously—neither procedures nor mechanisms have a role in the creation of the obligation which binds the former to the latter. They see in their leader a promise or an aura, and Weber clearly thinks that those who believe in this sort of thing are beyond the pale of rational discourse.

In Weberian theory, liberalism and populism (to give modern charisma its correct name) are the torn halves of a democracy to which they do not, as the expression goes, add up. For Bakhtin, simultaneously a neo-Kantian and a Russian populist, these two come together in novelistic style: he believes there are structures of expression imbued with a distinctively democratic sobriety and irony, which are more than feelings made democratic by virtue of their spontaneous popularity. It may be that what Habermas has dubbed 'the rationality of a form of life' is represented best

[69] See C. Schmitt, *The Crisis of Parliamentary Democracy*, trans. Ellen Kennedy (Cambridge, Mass.: MIT Press, 1985), in particular the 'Preface to the Second Edition (1926): On the Contradiction Between Parliamentarism and Democracy'.

by changes in linguistic style.[70] A democratic language can be rationalized in the sense that it is a technique to be learned, observed, and refined by constant practice and revision: its authority would lie in itself and not in its bearer, and it would be a prize won through historical effort. But changes in 'the style of a language as a whole' have consequences not just for explicitly political relationships, but for the very texture of the lifeworld itself, for the finest details of social interactions and our very sense of time, space, and the surrounding world. If language is to be the medium of a democratic intersubjectivity, then the latter must take the form of a restructuring, not a repression of the sentiments on which a successful life-world depends. That means a democratic language is simultaneously 'ethical' and 'technical', irreducible to either a set of procedures or the expression of good intentions.

Of course, social orders are more than dialogues, their structures more variegated than those of the modern vernaculars. In modern European societies, decision-making and enforcement are centralized in differen-tiated institutions of political and economic power, and one can legiti-mately ask whether attention to language obscures this central fact. For every citizen the relation to a system of decision is mediated via the insti-tutions of the state and of civil society itself. Is language, as Saussure implied, really a social institution on a par with these?[71] Yes and no. One is tempted to think of language as merely an abstract moment of a variety of institutions, with little in the way of its own logic, and correspondingly less effectiveness or force. It is, however, instituted at its own level and not a mere reflection of its contexts. The sphere of novelistic styles and techniques can be isolated precisely because it represents a set of formal possibilities or resources, the actual deployment of which takes place in situations defined by the intersection of language with other elements of the social structure. What language lacks in fullness, however, it makes up for in fluidity. The numerous and intersecting styles of a language flow through the institutions which structure ordinary social life, often by a route which includes serious diversions through the less predictable and rule-bound contexts of everyday life. Styles of language are malleable to an extent that formal procedures of state cannot be—no one ever need submit an influx of irony to scrutiny by parliamentary committee—and they may serve as conveyor belts for transferring democratic practice from one sphere to another. But at that point we have to remind ourselves that novelistic style in Bakhtin is continuous with but not identical to the modern vernaculars. In fact, it represents the style of a distinct 'public

---

[70] Habermas, 'Discourse Ethics, Law and *Sittlichkeit*', in *Autonomy and Solidarity: Interviews with Jürgen Habermas*, rev. edn., ed. Peter Dews (London: Verso, 1992), 266.

[71] Saussure, *Course*, 15.

sphere'—the world of literary prose and the printed novel—with its own specialized requirements (it is worth pointing out, for the benefit of anyone who thinks literature is rather distant from politics, that in Habermas's monograph on the public sphere it is eighteenth-century *literary* culture which first develops the principles of public debate and discussion).[72] The relationship between this particular sphere and the language around it is, as we shall see, a central problem in Bakhtin's work, and the ambiguities he navigates are ambiguities set deep in the problem of democracy itself. Let us now turn to the shape of that public sphere.

The Inner Link of Democracy to Language

The identification of democracy with a form of language is nothing new: from the moment of its modern resurrection in Rousseau, democracy has been inseparable from the discourse which makes it possible. Whether popular will is understood as preformed or arrived at after arduous debate, as homogeneous consensus or constellation of interests, it becomes manifest in expressions with a particular structure and in a public sphere with particular physical characteristics, and this fact alone puts democratic theory in debt to philosophies of language. Theories of democracy cannot construct their ideal institutions first and then figure out how language might run through them, as if poured into a mould; conceptions of language and discourse structure democratic principles from within, informing the very critical standards we use in assessing actually existing democracy.

In Rousseau's *Social Contract* one finds the paradigmatic example of this inner linkage, which has haunted democratic theory to the present day.[73] Awed by the principles announced so grandly in its opening, we tend to forget that section of *The Social Contract* which fusses obsessively over electoral procedure and how 'the people' should be arranged on the plain where popular sovereignty will be physically embodied.[74] Gallons of ink have probably been spilt debating 'the general will'—whether it exists and whether it is divine will in disguise, what its limits are and how one might bring it into being—but not too many of us have given careful thought to whether the centurions should stand over there, on the edge of the field, and the plebs in the middle, or perhaps the other way round. Neither should we; but we might bear in mind that Rousseau thinks this is worth

[72] Habermas, *The Structural Transformation of the Public Sphere*, Part II, 'Social Structures of the Public Sphere' (pp. 27–56).
[73] Jean-Jacques Rousseau, *The Social Contract and Discourses*, trans. G. D. H. Cole (London and Melbourne: J. M. Dent & Sons, 1973).
[74] Ibid., Book IV, ch. 4.

worrying about, because the general will has geographical as well as legal prerequisites, and only the right physical space and the right kind of discourse can ensure its fragile existence. Gathered together in persona 'the people' can assume their role as sovereign, for then the sensuality and immediacy of oral speech holds sway. Dispersed they no longer have authority or even the right to it, for the vagaries of print can only sow confusion and discord. Democratic speech mimics the settled conversations of village elders under the oak tree, and when a society, for whatever reason, can no longer reproduce this kind of space, these kinds of relationships, and that kind of language, popular sovereignty is no longer possible. Rousseau's insistence on 'direct democracy' reflects not only a fear of the corrupting power of state office but a philosophy of language which sees in anything other than oral speech—provincial oral speech at that—the inevitability of betrayal.

Thus in his earlier *Essay on the Origin of Languages*, Rousseau argues that 'there are some tongues favourable to liberty. They are the sonorous, prosodic, harmonious tongues in which discourse can be understood from a great distance.'[75] It is not by accident that Italian is the language of republicanism; its accent and phonic structure make it ideal for the oratory essential to the republic, and in this sense the rise of republicanism depended upon the evolution of Italian. If democracy depends upon persuasion and expression, then surely these functions are best discharged by a discourse which is face-to-face and full of sonorous Southern vowels? In Rousseauean philosophy, formal qualities of language which we consider contingent and socially meaningless acquire political significance, precisely because linguistic practice—the give-and-take of republican, we can call it democratic, argument—is a defining feature of political life. If this is so, then the limits of language itself, and of particular languages as well, will have a determining effect on our concept of a desirable political life.

We may not share Rousseau's confidence in Southern European language and we don't mind much whether the centurions sit in six ranks or seven, but Rousseau's spell still captivates much of the Left (when the Italian Communist Party changed its name to the *Democratic* Party of the Left it added—as belated thanks for Rousseau's praise of Southern Europe?—an oak tree to its emblem). When Lucio Colletti claimed that 'so far as "political theory" in the strict sense is concerned, Marx and Lenin have added nothing to Rousseau', he meant that 'direct democracy' without limit to its power still provided the standard by which all political

---

[75] Jean-Jacques Rousseau, *Essay on the Origin of Languages*, trans. John H. Moran (Chicago, Ill.: University of Chicago Press, 1986), 72–3.

society was to be judged, even though it seems inappropriate to any modestly differentiated and modern society.[76] Raymond Williams once claimed that the characteristic sin of arguments for socialist democracy was that they conceived of democratization as a simplification of social relations—getting everyone round the table, or in the field, if you wish—when it should be thought of as making these relations more complex, and in this he recognized the persistence of Rousseauean fantasies and criteria in socialist argument.[77] Two otherwise quite different philosophers, Jacques Derrida and Habermas, have tried to break the spell, by focusing on the link between the theory of politics and the theory of language. In his long critical study of Rousseau's *Essay on the Origin of Languages*, Derrida points out that Rousseau's hostility to the written word in the name of the immediacy or 'presence' of the oral provided support for a physical and spatial ideal of the body politic.[78] Meaning relies on the presence of oral language much as sovereignty depends on the presence of the people; representation in politics is thus deemed corrupting and dangerous *for the same reasons* that representation of speech by writing is deemed dangerous and unstable. In this context, 'writing' signifies a political problem, not the mere fact that no field is big enough to contain 'the people', and it is the definitive rebuke to Rousseau's concept of a homogeneous body politic which needs to learn nothing because it need only know itself. 'Writing' means not so much the physical fact of graphic language as the uncertainty, flexibility, and disputatiousness which are part of every public sphere, an openness which Rousseau hopes to shut out of modern democratic politics. Habermas sees this emergent public sphere as held back by Rousseau's distaste for the arguments of the French Enlightenment and the civility of the salons.[79] Rousseau's opposition to Parisian political life leads him to confuse two quite different questions: What principles must be satisfied for a political order to be deemed legitimate? What institutional arrangements conform to these principles?[80] Rousseau's equation of direct—today we might say 'participatory' or 'council'—democracy with democracy *per se* stems from a premature concretization of principles, a mythic embodiment of the idea of democracy

---

[76] Lucio Colletti, 'Rousseau as Critic of "Civil Society"', in *From Rousseau to Lenin: Studies in Ideology and Society*, trans. John Merrington and Judith White (New York and London: Monthly Review Press, 1974), 185.

[77] Raymond Williams, 'The Importance of Community', in *Resources of Hope*, 117, and in the same volume, 'Democracy and Parliament', 273–5, and 'Toward Many Socialisms', 301–2.

[78] Jacques Derrida, 'Genesis and Structure of the *Essay on the Origin of Languages*', in *Of Grammatology*, trans. Gayatri Chakravorty Spivak (Baltimore, Md.: Johns Hopkins University Press, 1976), 167–71.

[79] See Habermas, *The Structural Transformation of the Public Sphere*, 96–100. As Habermas elegantly puts it: 'The *volonté générale* was more a consensus of hearts than of arguments' (p. 98).

[80] Habermas, 'Legitimation Problems in the Modern State', 185–6.

which hems it in. The principle that decisions are the end result of open argument, however, has to be separated from direct or council democracy which is only one, and by no means always the most effective, means for realizing open argument itself.

When Derrida remarks on Rousseau's hostility to 'writing', and Habermas on his preference for a provincial and undisputatious public sphere, both lock onto a fundamental resistance in Rousseau's conception of popular sovereignty. The revival of ancient republican principle and practice may be itself a modern gesture, but it is combined with a distrust of developed and rationalized communicative structures, structures which make public discourse something rather more open and complicated than an act of self-expression. One might say that Rousseau places his faith in the rationality of the popular will, but only once he has deprived that will of all the modern 'rationalized' communicative means which are in fact at its disposal.

Bakhtin displays similarly ambiguous feelings about the prospects for a free and democratized language. A theory of dialogue which locates its paradigmatic expression in novelistic texts is, in a fruitful way, unsure about the role which dialogue can play in modernity. It would have us believe that unharassed and natural speech interaction will deliver up an egalitarian and cooperative intersubjectivity of its own accord, an inter-subjectivity which benefits from the political and social struggles, and the technical and social developments, of the last 300 years without itself being marked by them. But in the course of describing the novel as a dialogue, Bakhtin finds himself demonstrating the limits of the 'natural dialogue' which is supposedly its basis, and outlining the extent to which dialogue must give way to dialogism, modern in conception, different in form and aim. In saying goodbye to pure dialogue, do we admit that democracy itself has 'modern' limits—such as make, for example, representation an inevitable fact—which we cannot escape but which we should not celebrate either? My argument is almost exactly the reverse. In the concept of novelistic style one finds an intersubjectivity which depends on a historical sense, irony, a literate print culture, an eye and ear for social differentiation, and much else characteristic of modern social life. A definition of democracy which hasn't room for these facts isn't worth much, and if they imply dialogues which are uneven, asymmetrical, or distanced, this tells us not that modernity is bad but that there is more to democracy than chatting under the oak tree. If the dialogism of the novel appeals, it is not because it reduces a grand cultural form to a familiar anthropological constant, but because it shows what history can do and what it has done to linguistic interchange, what new possibilities—and new dangers as well—populate the modern discursive world. The novel tells us what has happened to dialogue, and why it is time for the Left to wish Rousseau a fond but final farewell, for the latter's direct democracy is not only impossible but, as I hope to show, undesirable and 'undemocratic' as well.

The move from dialogue to dialogism is an awkward and incomplete gesture in Bakhtin's work, full of ambiguities and evasions. But it thematizes, even if inadvertently, tensions between modernity, democracy, and dialogue. The uncertain hold of the theory of dialogism on these matters is the subject of the next chapter.

CHAPTER TWO

Dialogue with History

Bakhtin's first impulse was to solve problems in the traditional grand manner: with an ambitious and comprehensive philosophical project, a 'first philosophy' which would attack the crisis of European life at its onto-logical roots.[1] From the evidence of letters, his participation in discussion circles, and extant texts, it appears that from roughly 1918 to 1927 he worked on a systematic philosophical text in several chapters, dubbed 'The Architectonics of Answerability' by Michael Holquist and Katerina Clark.[2] But then Bakhtin thought that the early twentieth century had set him a pretty tall order, a crisis afflicting not a particular set of cultural values or norms but the very status and functioning of culture as such. The problem was not an absence of culture, for Europe was heavy with scientific accomplishment, artistic innovation, and socio-political invention. The problem was the uncoupling of this achievement from the 'contemporary act' which it was meant to guide. The web of European culture might have been finely spun and impressively patterned, but at some (unspeci-fied) turning-point of modernity it had acquired a self-propelling and objectified dynamic, a theoreticized form which rendered it useless for the 'world of life'. Separated from this rich but autonomous sphere, the con-temporary act inevitably 'descends to the level of elementary biological and economic motivation' (TPA 123/55), while Bakhtin looks on (together with a healthy chunk of the European intelligentsia) in horror. To borrow from Bakhtin's later terminology, culture had become a field rich with 'meaning' (*smysl*) but not with 'significance' (*znachenie*), a string of silent monuments, which impress us but do not obligate us.

The loss of this obligatoriness or 'oughtness' (*dolzhenstvovanie*) leaves culture in the strangely bifurcated condition I described in the previous

[1] In his notes to 'Towards a Philosophy of the Act', S. G. Bocharov traces the term 'first philosophy' to Aristotle, noting its link with the project of a general ontology. There is also, however, a more local Russian precursor—Gustav Shpet, who, in his explication of Husserlian phenomenology, *Appearance and Meaning*, describes phenomenology as a necessary fundamental philosophy, prior to all theoretical and scientific labour. Interestingly, Shpet accuses all theoreti-cal (i.e. scientific) knowledge of being 'pragmatic, even technical knowledge, a knowledge *pour agir*' (pp. 3–4). See *Iavlenie i smysl': Fenomenologiia kak osnovnaia nauka i ee problemy* (Moscow: Germes, 1914), ch. 1: 'Ideia osnovnoi nauki'.

[2] See Katerina Clark and Michael Holquist, *Mikhail Bakhtin* (Cambridge, Mass. and London: Harvard University Press, 1985), ch. 3.

chapter: on the one hand, there exist norms and values, which one might, but need not, adhere to; on the other hand, there are subjects in need of motivations. But it required no special power of analysis to see that, in the wake of the First World War, Europe's traditional sources of obligation and its corresponding subjective attribute, 'responsibility', were drying up, and Bakhtin's old-fashioned confidence that philosophy could restore some of culture's lost power was the ground-bass for scores of intellectuals suspicious of science and 'materialism'. The distinctiveness of Bakhtin's position lies in his persistent belief that philosophy should save us not by making possible uniquely philosophical or mystical experiences, but by translating actually existing culture into, or rather, back into, a primary 'ethical reality' with which it had lost contact.[3] In Bakhtin's account, 'oughtness' and 'responsibility' constitute an original dimension of all culture which disappears from view when modern science and juridical thought force it into their two-dimensional frame. Thus the mere act of restoring cultural meanings to their proper architectonic space will release an obligating significance muffled by modernity, and the essential feature of this space is the ineradicable distinction between *I* and *other*. Only when cultural meanings were put into the space between *I* and *other* would we hear the call their contents made on us, for in that context they cannot be assented to indifferently. 'The contemporary crisis is fundamentally a crisis of the contemporary act' (TPA 123/54), and the contemporary act was in crisis because it had become cut off from the fundamentally ethical nature of discourse; left to drift in a sea of interchangeable individuals, it had become rootless, contingent, and thoroughly unphilosophical.

Not every European (including Russian) intellectual took this view: some were content to leave this two-dimensional world in search of a suprasensible one, while others thought the modern age deserved its own forms of obligation, which an emerging sociology could help identify. Bakhtin is certain that science will not be able to deliver a sense of obligation, for the very good reason that obligation is something which he believes must be disclosed rather than 'proved' in the manner of science ('Oughtness is a unique category of acting and the act (and everything, even thought and feeling, is my act), it is a particular orientation of consciousness, the structure of which we will disclose phenomenologically'

---

[3] I am translating the Russian phrase *nravstvennaia deistvitelnost'* as 'ethical reality' rather than the more usual 'moral reality' because Bakhtin elsewhere uses the Russian loan term *moral'nyi* to denote the legalistic, Kantian sense of the moral to which he is opposed. By *nravstvennyi* Bakhtin means not a particular, differentiated sphere of moral questions and problems but the axiological element (mores, customs, norms) which guides action in any sphere, be it science, politics, or art. In this respect *nravstvennost'* is closer to Hegel's concept of *Sittlichkeit* (ethical life or substance) than to Kant's concept of *Moralität*.

(TPA 85/6)). At the same time, he thinks it can not be found in empty space, but has to be disclosed in existing art, science, religion and politics, that is, on actual historical material; hence Bakhtin's philosophizing must take the form of a reinterpretation of the historical record, a persistent excavation of the dynamic of *I* and *other* contained, even if unknowingly, within the art and science of the past.[4] Bakhtin promised not to scrimp in this matter: at the end of his introduction to this work, he claims that chapters devoted to the 'ethics of aesthetics', the 'ethics of politics', and the 'ethics of religion', respectively, will follow.[5] But the obligations he assumed in pursuit of obligation turned out to be too much for him, and what remains of this ambitious project are only fragments, albeit quite substantial ones: the introduction, 'Towards a Philosophy of the Act', large sections of the chapter devoted to the 'ethics of aesthetics' (which include the long essay known as 'Author and Hero in Aesthetic Activity' and possibly the article 'The Problem of Content, Material, and Form in Verbal Art'), and notes of a lecture devoted to (the ethics of) religion.[6]

This is not something for which, to borrow a phrase, history is to blame. For however tempted we are to ascribe the incompleteness of this text to the difficult circumstances following the Russian Revolution, or to fantasize about missing chapters lying on uninspected shelves or in unknown archives, the fact remains that this valiant attempt at first philosophy is incomplete in a fundamental theoretical sense, for which no remedy is possible. The evidence lies not only in Bakhtin's inability to finish this work but in the pattern of writing which followed it: he abandons his philosophical project, but then, in effect, rewrites it, and not once, but over and over again, never really moving on to a new problem, but hovering obsessively around the old one. If Bakhtin endlessly formulated what he had called an 'ethics of aesthetics' it was not because he was sticking with a winning formula; rather, it resembled a kind of philosophical neurosis, each repetition a doomed attempt to work through

---

[4] In a note entitled 'Answer to a task, posed by M. M.', clearly a reference to discussions taking place among these friends, L. V. Pumpiansky says of 'ethical being' that 'As it is (as explained above) invisible, then, if you try, you do not see it (the adequate truth which moves mountains is an exception), but must search for it by indirect paths' (Lec., 228).

[5] The introduction to this systematic work, 'Towards a Philosophy of the Act', takes as its two targets the formal-juridical ethics of neo-Kantianism, as embodied in the work of Hermann Cohen, and what Bakhtin calls 'material ethics', that is, ethical systems based on a substantive principle or principles, and includes sideswipes at the philosophy of life (Nietzsche, Bergson). A discussion of 'Towards a Philosophy of the Act' can be found in the section of Ch. 3 entitled 'Philosophy in Nevel' and Vitebsk, 1918–1924'.

[6] I am following N. I. Nikolaev's speculative, but I think persuasive, account of the chronology and role of the various pieces, as set out in his introductory comments to Pumpiansky's notes on Bakhtin's contributions to the Kantian seminar of 1924–25; see Lec., 221–32.

an original and insoluble trauma.[7] For the attempt to describe what is dialogical in the dense and differentiated culture of twentieth-century Europe, and thereby to restore a lost or hidden ethical reality, inevitably problematized the philosophical or anthropological ideal of dialogue which was its critical starting-point. As dialogism acquired flesh and historical depth, it found its substance more and more indebted to the historical developments it supposedly explained, as if the flash of heavenly lightning that illuminated modernity turned out to have an electric generator as its source. Each text which brings it forth again is thus no more than a compromise formation, an attempt to square and reconcile contradictory impulses, which has to fail, as each time the original tension between philosophical principle and cultural history is merely overlaid with new historical experience. In that respect, there really is no mythical Bakhtinian 'ur-text' which could reveal all or serve as theme for the variations embodied in the remainder of the *œuvre*.

Bakhtin's own commentary on this question is misleading:

The unity of the becoming (developing) idea. There is also a certain internal unfinishedness in many of my thoughts. But I do not wish to make a vice into a virtue: in my works there is a good deal of external unfinishedness, an unfinishedness not of thought itself, but of its expression and exposition. Sometimes it is difficult to separate one kind of unfinishedness from the other. One should not ascribe this to any definite tendency (structuralism). My love for variations and for a multiplicity of terms for a single phenomenon. A multiplicity of perspectives. A bringing close of the distant without an indication of mediating links. (N70–71, 380/155)

As is the following claim to consistency, which, discussing the relation of his texts to those of Voloshinov and Medvedev in the 1920s, is no more than a disavowal of the problem: 'To the conception of language and speech set out in the works mentioned, without sufficient detail and not always intelligibly, I have held on until the present, although over 30 years it has undergone, of course, a certain evolution.'[8] But what one finds in Bakhtin's works is not evolution in the scientific sense of the term, or the openness to development necessary for the progress of knowledge, but a constant rewriting, made necessary by historical faults too deep to be excised or pasted over. Bakhtin wants to grasp the philosophical meaning of his historical material, but the history he takes as his object leaks into the

---

[7] A neurosis which may explain Bakhtin's obsessional attachment to particular words: in an interview in 1966, Abram Vulis noted how in Bakhtin's discourse 'the fundamental words never yield their place to synonyms' as 'terminological repetition creates the unseen dynamic carcass of oral and written Bakhtinian prose'. Abram Zinovevich Vulis, *Ser'eznost' neser'eznykh situatsii: Satira, prikliucheniia, detektiv* (Tashkent: Gafur Guiama, 1984), 253.

[8] Letter of 10 Jan. 1961 to V. V. Kozhinov, cited in Bocharov, 'Ob odnom razgovore', 76.

philosophical tools themselves, and the result is an ineluctable unevenness, the constant shuttling between registers which is the hallmark of Bakhtin's prose style. Nearly every one of his significant concepts denotes both a philosophical idea and an empirical phenomenon, and this ambiguity keeps open the commerce between these two fields. One can never really say, in any particular text of Bakhtin's, whether dialogism (or for that matter, heteroglossia, responsibility, the chronotope, or the culture of laughter) designates a philosophical principle or a historical feature of specific works, and one should, as a consequence, not try to say so, for the moment one insists on a one-sided reading, the historical problem to which Bakhtin is responding appears, falsely, as solved.

Criticism, naturally enough, prefers useful insights and solutions to reminders of problems it can't quite handle, and so commentary on Bakhtin has tended to stop this dialectic of history and philosophy dead in its tracks, insisting that he is either a philosopher working on first principles or some kind of critic or social scientist making empirical discoveries. Everyone agrees that Bakhtin's concepts are ambiguous and that his works differ among themselves in their tone, theoretical idiom, and vocabulary, but the conclusion usually drawn is that some of the works are not as successful at expressing his central insights as others, not as successful because they present the insight in the wrong style or the wrong theoretical idiom. No one, of course, agrees on which works are in the wrong idiom: for some it is the 'philosophical' works of the 1920s, which are deemed too early and immature—Bakhtin knowing what he wants to say but not yet how to say it; for others it is the 'sociological' works of the 1930s, which are too late and inauthentic—Bakhtin knowing what he wants to say but being unable, for political reasons, to say it. What holds the sociological and the philosophical interpretations together is the belief that *somewhere* Bakhtin got it right—made a philosophical discovery, revealed the truth about language, pushed the social study of the literary forward a bit—and that in his other works this truth appears in dilute form.

One cannot, however, point to a single essay or book which represents Bakhtin shorn of earlier (or later) illusions, or trace a clear learning curve in the movement from text to text. There is neither a moment of original (or subsequent) insight to recover, nor a visible steady progress from one problem solved to the next. And to illustrate this point I would like to elaborate on Bakhtin's idea of a dialogism which is not quite dialogue by juxtaposing the two essays around which the different camps rally their forces. 'Author and Hero in Aesthetic Activity' (from the 1920s) and 'Discourse in the Novel' (from the 1930s), neither of which was published until the 1970s, are so ritually contrasted in commentary on Bakhtin that allegiance to one or the other often seems to determine the shape of one's take on Bakhtin as a whole.[9] 'Author and Hero' is a work of aesthetics, with heavy debts to neo-Kantianism, phenomenology, and Christian ethics; its justification of the aesthetic work in philosophical terms, as the embodiment of an 'architectonically stable and dynamically alive relation of author to hero' (AH 9/4), has made it a key text for those wishing to present Bakhtin as a philosopher later gone astray. 'Discourse in the Novel' describes a 'social dialogue of languages' somehow ideally embodied in the form of the novel, thus rendering it the unique manifestation of 'the social life of discourse' sustained by 'the people'; it depends on a critique of linguistics inflamed by a kind of populist sociology. Its clear political reference—the novel is presented as popular representative in a literary arena dominated by official 'poetry'—and sociology of language lead critics suspicious of philosophy to see in it a happy and overdue turn to sociological argument. On the surface a choice between these texts defines whether one favours a philosophical or a sociological Bakhtin, whether he is to be cast as a great moral thinker or advocate of 'the people'.

But the battle lines drawn in commentary obscure what would other-wise be obvious: however distant in idiom and vocabulary, the two essays are identical in intention and shape, and are in effect two attempts, roughly a decade apart, to describe the kind of intersubjectivity or dialogue which could heal the wounds of modernity. This common argument reveals itself in precisely parallel structures, as follows: (1) An opening declaration that the essence of the successful aesthetic work (called 'the novel' in the later essay) is its dialogical nature, the play between the form of the work and the 'everyday' expressions which it takes as its material, between the 'consciousness' of the author/novelist and that of the hero/linguistic material. (2) A description of the compromised and flawed intersubjectivity, dominant in modern life, which must be redeemed by aesthetic form; in effect, a critical picture of Bakhtin's present. (3) Lengthy technical discussion, making up the bulk of both essays, of how this ideal and redemptive form of intersubjectivity will work itself out in the details of narrative, style, and character, this in the form of a description of the

[9] Allegiance to a key work or series of essays is a pervasive feature of Bakhtin criticism, and perhaps its distinguishing characteristic. Thus Todorov argues that Bakhtin's 'philosophical anthropology', outlined in 'Author and Hero' and in the various notes from the 1970s ('From the Notes of 1970–71', 'Towards a Methodology of the Human Sciences') are the key to his work. This view is shared by many Russian commentators: by Gogotishvili and Bonetskaia (see Ch. 1 above) and by the more secularly inclined Vitaly Makhlin, who has persistently empha-sized the centrality of the works of the 1920s in his writings.

As for those who stake all on the 'sociological' and apparently more scientific texts, my own earlier work provides a perfectly adequate example. In my 'Bakhtin, Discourse and Democracy', *New Left Review*, 160 (1986), 92–113, I described Bakhtin as someone who thankfully outgrew an early predilection for the purely philosophical. I must thank Ann Jefferson and Graham Pechey for pointing out to me the loss incurred by this strategy.

ideal aesthetic work or novel. (4) To conclude, an examination of the history of this aesthetic form, in the shape of an ambitious history of European prose writing, which presents European culture from antiquity to the nineteenth century as a long struggle for this ideally balanced aesthetic work against a gaggle of monological rivals. This pattern and argument subsist underneath dramatic differences in rhetoric and conceptual vocabulary, and each work has its idiosyncratic digressions and enthusiasms (God in the first essay, 'the people' in the second). Nevertheless a juxtaposition will reveal the historical content of an essay we are accustomed to think of as strictly philosophical, and the philosophical content of a text apparently devoted to 'sociological stylistics'.

More importantly, this juxtaposition will keep our attention on the main issue—the felt need for a dialogism different from dialogue and at the same time its modern heir. Bakhtin cannot define dialogism precisely, because it always signifies both something found in every communicative exchange and something specific to the historically framed practices of verbal art. He would like these meanings to flow seamlessly into one another, so that his favoured aesthetic achievements would tell us only about timeless capabilities, but the distance between them asserts itself in each and every essay he writes. And while it may seem that the most judicious response to this confusion is to draw a line between the idea of raw dialogue and the legacy of the modern novel, Bakhtin's wish to conflate them is more than a little useful. It reminds us that the institutionalized public forms which constitute democratic life are historic achievements which at the same time need to be part of our ordinary, everyday consciousness. There are objective prerequisites to a democratic life—political institutions, legally enforceable rights, the technical means for public opinion to shape itself—but there are subjective ones, too: one needs subjects who can think and act 'novelistically' for novels themselves to function as paradigms of the dialogical. But this entails thinking hard about the historical contribution modernity makes to democracy itself, for the subjects we will then be talking about will not be the abstract creatures which sometimes dwell in political philosophy but people who bring to their speech modern expectations and resources—irony, a sense of the historical character of social life, desire for a narratively coherent existence, belief in the unalterable fact of specialization and social differentiation, a secular and scientific world-view. If the dialogism we need or want is found first and foremost in modern works of prose art, and if everyday speech is isomorphic with this artful dialogue, then these resources are not something brought into play after dialogism begins but the very precondition of dialogism itself, the features of a 'free and democratized language' which make dialogism and heteroglossia facts of both life and art.

We should therefore prepare ourselves for reading not descriptions of a dialogue which is up and running but fantasies out of proportion with the dialogue we know, fantasies which tell us why what we experience as dialogue in the twentieth century is in some sense not 'dialogical', or dialogical enough. For anyone interested in Bakhtin's relevance to late twentieth-century politics this is the nub of the issue, for in actually exist-ing democracies the question is not the presence or absence of political and social 'dialogue'—the necessity of which is a legitimating principle of the social order itself—but the relative failure of the dialogues which actually take place, the moment at which communication which fulfils the ordi-nary prerequisites for being a dialogue nonetheless falls short of the demo-cratic project. And this failure, at least in my view, is not a quantitative one, where the dialogues which take place are fine but need merely to be made more inclusive, but a qualitative one, concerning the very mode of expression constituting the public sphere and the kinds of intersubjectivity which are possible within it. Bakhtin may justify the distinctions between good and bad speech by claiming that one embodies a dialogical quality the other lacks, but the distinctions he draws in analysis are never between two-sidedness and one-sidedness, dialogue and monologue in the ordinary sense of the term, but between different forms of expression and their relation to the historical tasks of a culture. Thus in both 'Author and Hero' and 'Discourse in the Novel' we will meet a dialogue which is not quite a dialogue (the merely ethical, the poetic) and a dialogue which is clearly more than a dialogue (the aesthetic work, the novel). In the light of this, it's not surprising that things get complicated.

In the remainder of this chapter I will demonstrate the relative failure of both 'Author and Hero' and 'Discourse in the Novel' to secure a straight path from the simple 'fact' of dialogue to the higher reaches of verbal art; in each case, the redemptive intersubjectivity embodied in the latter has historical roots on which Bakhtin refuses to get a grip. Although I am interested in the transformations which lead from the earlier to the later essay, I am more interested in the fact that 'Discourse in the Novel' in no way leaves behind the project left unfinished by 'Author and Hero', and that it sharpens, but does not resolve, the ambiguities of the earlier text. I then suggest, via a brief detour to a different text of Bakhtin's, that solving this problem depends upon finding a way to maintain the idea of a redemptive intersubjectivity in a landscape which is clearly secular and modern. The model for this secular but redemptive dialogue is the style of the novel, which tries to hold together both the symmetry which any modern idea of dialogue (and any conception of democracy) implies and the transformation of ordinary speech implicit in the project of dialogism. These transformations are described by Bakhtin as the novelistic representation of speech and as the achievement of 'voice', and they suggest that a dialogical culture means not just letting everyone have their say but also a peculiar form of expression, which gives to one's utterance a historical character. I then briefly describe the relevance this has to a concept of democracy which is more than procedural. If democracy is potentially a kind of culture rather than just rules for speech, this means that its practice is not only about justice but also about the ends of human activity, that is, that it can help address the need for meaning traditionally associated with religion and art. Because dialogism is a kind of language linked to a philosophy of history, it implies that asking for speech to be fair and asking for speech to be cultured might be two sides of the same coin.

'AUTHOR AND HERO IN AESTHETIC ACTIVITY': INTERSUBJECTIVITY TAKES CENTRE STAGE

At first glance, 'Author and Hero' appears to be the old wine of German idealist aesthetics in a new intersubjective bottle. As in Kant, aesthetic form heals the rift between the lawfulness of that which we know through natural science (which Bakhtin calls cognition) and the orientation towards ends characteristic of morality: in art we experience something both sensual and apparently purposeful, in Bakhtin's words, existence as 'beautiful givenness' (AH 22/19), self-sufficient and needing no justification from beyond itself. Unlike Kant, however, Bakhtin describes the aesthetic object not as something one may chance upon or create—a beautiful sunset, a work of art—but as a transformation wrought on the given materials of ordinary experience, the 'consummation' or 'finalization' (zavershenie) of the substance of everyday existence. The life 'consummated' by the aesthetic activity of the author acquires 'the self-valuable givenness of experience' (AH 108/115); it is affirmed as valuable in itself, bounded and finite, rather than in relation to a moral value or use which transcends it, as is the case with ethically and cognitively objectified life.

One cannot—and this is the distinctive move—transform *one's own* experience in this way, because what makes an author an author is his or her distance from the experience represented in the work. To invest the given and merely existent with aesthetic value requires:

a relation of tense 'being-located-outsideness' [*vnenakhodimost'*—hereafter 'outsidedness'] of the author to all the moments of the hero, a spatial, temporal, evaluative and meaning-related outsideness, making it possible for him to draw together the *entire* hero, who from within himself is scattered and dispersed in the posited world of cognitive thought and the open event of the ethical deed, to draw together him and his life and to make of them a *whole* by means of those moments within him which are are inaccessible to him: such as the plenitude of his external image, his appearance, the background behind his back, his relation to the event of death and of the absolute future, and so on, to justify and consummate him without regard to the meaning, achievements, results and success of his own forward-directed life. (AH 18/14)

The calmness and satisfaction which accompanies the experience of the beautiful depends on removing oneself from the horizon of the subject (the hero), in which the world appears subordinate to the relentless demands of 'forward-directed life'. In order for the *integrity* of a life to become the focus of value rather than its specific and local achievements, one must apprehend that life 'not in the category of the *I*, but in the category of the *other*, as the life of another person, another *I*' (AH 79/82). Aesthetic experience is rooted in an absolute phenomenological division in our perception of human life: 'any inner experience and mental whole can be concretely experienced—can be inwardly perceived—either in the category of the *I-for-myself* or in the category of the *other-for-me*, that is, either as my experience or as the experience of this definite singular other person' (AH 26/24). One cannot aesthetically consummate one's own experience precisely because the world as 'one's own' is constituted by ethical and cognitive considerations inimical to the aesthetic as such.

The experience of the beautiful is, as in Kant, presented as a cure for the problem of subjectivity, but with the difference that in this case the cure for subjectivity is intersubjectivity. The exact nature of the alternative on offer, however, remains unclear due to a fundamental ambiguity in Bakhtin's argument, which arises first here, but nags all of his further writing. For it no doubt appears that Bakhtin is offering not a specific form of intersubjectivity, but intersubjectivity plain and simple as a cure for the trauma of solipsism, the limitations built into individual, ethical-cognitive experience. But aesthetic experience would be a strange paradigm for the mere fact of human interaction: 'Author and Hero' is not about meetings in the street or intimate conversation, but written works of art, the implication being that these are more genuinely representative of intersubjectivity than our ordinary relations with others. As in virtually every other one of his works, here Bakhtin makes the claim for a form of dialogue or relationship which can redeem us from the dangers of individualizing theories and practices—'forward-directed life', psychologism, naturalism, the 'poetic', and so on—but the danger is not that one will really exist 'as an individual', which is impossible, but the kinds of relationships to which these individualizing world-views lead. Thus the 'ethics of aesthetics' which 'Author and Hero' was to explicate turns out to be a celebration of the particular relationship Bakhtin describes (following Hermann Cohen) as 'aesthetic love' (AH 86/90), the free and unmotivated (that is, disinterested) affirmation of the value of another. The point of describing the 'loving' relationship of 'author' to 'hero' is to show what is missing from existing social relationships; the point of describing the aesthetic work itself as a relationship is to show that the intersubjectivity required is an extraordinary one, no simple matter of encounters between people.

So the 'author' and the 'hero' are subjects, but not necessarily people, in so far as they are found inside the aesthetic work, not before it or outside of it; their relationship is the irreducible tension between the ordinary cognitive and ethical intentions represented in the work and the tranquillizing power of an aesthetic context which assigns them subordinate roles. This entails a fundamental asymmetry in their roles, for while the hero appears as a creature embroiled in the world-views and knowledges of ordinary 'forward-directed life', the author is nothing other than aesthetic form itself:

the author is a uniquely active form-giving energy, present not as a consciousness psychologically conceived, but in a stably meaningful cultural product, his active reaction is present in the structure, conditioned by that reaction, of the active vision of the hero as a whole, in the structure of his image, the rhythm of his disclosure, in the intonational structure and in the selection of moments of meaning. (AH 12/8)

Although Bakhtin will insist on defining the aesthetic work as 'a meeting of two consciousnesses, in principle unmerged' (AH 85/89), the 'outsidedness' of the author refers not to the mere separateness of another empirical subject, but to the act of transcendence whereby contents of lived experience are placed on a 'new plane of existence' (AH 18/14) in the work of art.

The author therefore has to step 'outside' not the limitation of this or that horizon or world-view, but the very form of the everyday lifeworld as such. While the artist is naturally 'a participant in life (practical, social, political, moral, religious) from within', he or she becomes an 'author' precisely to the extent that he or she 'loves life from without, in the place where it is not for itself, where it is turned outside itself and *is in need* of an outside activity beyond meaning' (AH 175/191; emphasis added). A merely different consciousness of the same form would remain embroiled in life, and encounters with heroes would 'begin to degenerate into self-interested disputes, in which the centre of value lies in the problems being debated' (AH 22/19–20) rather than in the life affirmed by aesthetic form. Bakhtin makes sure that the difference between aesthetic intersubjectivity and that controlled by the play of everyday 'practical' or ethical interests is absolutely clear, and with good reason. For he is writing directly in the wake of a political and social revolution which has made uncertain both the role and aims of culture and the responsibilities of the cultural intellectual. In the early 1920s the Communist Party had not yet declared its hand so far as culture went (indeed, it probably yet did not know what was in it) and competition for favour between the modernist intelligentsia, avant-garde constructivism, and proletarian art was at its zenith. Bakhtin had suggested, in a statement published during the Russian Civil War, 'Art and Responsibility', a clean division of labour: art and life would be separate spheres, but would avoid the uncontrolled autonomous development which leads to 'unserious life' and empty art. Because aesthetics is defined as one kind of 'ethics' it is bound to the sphere of social relationships (and so also to 'life' in the broadest sense), but its meaning and value depend upon its difference from relationships governed by moral-practical or cognitive values. Bakhtin thereby navigates a kind of middle course for art, and in the context of Russian literary-critical debate Scylla and Charybdis are not hard to identify: on the one hand, the danger of 'aestheticist' Symbolism and modernism, which draws a straight line between art and the metaphysical, bypassing the 'vulgar prose of the world' in search of 'poetic' revelation; on the other hand, those proponents of a committed 'political' art who see it as little more than ethical doctrines unfolded into pseudo-aesthetic form. One must prevent 'the confusion of the author–creator, a moment of the work, with the author–person, a moment of the ethical, social event of life' (AH 14–15/10), because culture's connection to social life will be *lost* the moment one buries it in the different demands of everyday political struggle.[10]

The tendency to commit art to the expression of ethico-political values or world-views, however, is not a Bolshevik idiosyncrasy, but a Hydra-headed monster Bakhtin spends almost an entire lifetime fighting. The reduction of the aesthetic relationship either to the ethico-political (to questions of right) or to the cognitive (to a matter of abstract biological or psychological pleasure) is a constant temptation, and its particular expressions in post-revolutionary Russia are but local instances of a world-historical problem. This perception of a bad modernity provides the polemical starting-point for nearly every one of Bakhtin's and the Bakhtin circle's finished works: 'Author and Hero' protects the aesthetic not only against 'committed' art but also against a variety of modern neo-Kantian and Lebensphilosophical doctrines; the review of the critical literature which opens *Problems of Dostoevsky's Art* condemns literary critics—many

---

[10] Raymond Williams endorses the work of the Bakhtin circle precisely on account of this emphasis, which he describes as their belief in the 'specificity' of the aesthetic and the cultural. See his 'The Uses of Cultural Theory', *New Left Review*, 158 (1986), 22–3.

of them Russian Orthodox ones—for treating Dostoevsky's heroes as interlocutors in ethical debate rather than as artistic representations; the first pages of 'Discourse in the Novel' take poetics to task for interpreting statements in the novel as directly expressive, thus overriding the essential formal qualities of the genre; the lengthy critique of Russian Formalism in Pavel Medvedev's *The Formal Method in Literary Scholarship* (1928) likewise makes the mediation of all thematic and ideological material by artistic 'forms of consummation' or genres the principle of his aesthetic doctrine:

But, without losing its direct significance, the ideologeme which enters into the artistic work forms a new chemical, and not mechanical, unity with features of artistic ideology. Its ethico-philosophical pathos becomes an ingredient of poetic pathos, while ethico-philosophical responsibility is absorbed by the totality of the artistic responsibility of the author for the whole of his artistic statement. The latter is, of course, just as much a social statement as is an ethico-philosophical, political, or any other ideological statement. (*FM* 34/22)

The point being not that art must keep a distance from the ethical and political concerns which are its basic material, but that it must transpose them into a new key, where what stands out is not the rightness or wrongness of the statements themselves but the meaning they have for the life-narratives of their speakers and the relationships in which they are embedded. The aesthetic work wants to tell us something about the style and substance of existing intersubjectivity, but we have to be willing to listen to it. When Bakhtin claims at the end of the 1920s that 'every literary work is inwardly, immanently sociological' (*PDA* 3–4/276), he means that the expressiveness *in* the work tells us something about social relationships that a sociology *of* the work cannot. In that sense Bakhtin's case for the distinctiveness of the aesthetic resembles many other efforts to insist that 'culture' describes a domain of feeling and relationship which cannot be reduced to the necessarily legal and procedural categories of politics traditionally conceived. Cultural criticism often finds itself describing ways of life as works of art precisely in order to focus on satisfactions which are neither economic nor political.[11]

[11] A paradigmatic example of this would be the emergence of a left-wing cultural criticism in postwar England. Writers like Richard Hoggart and Raymond Williams saw a gap in the achievement of postwar social democracy: while its politics remained obsessed with procedures, its economic policy reduced the citizenry to individuals with natural needs and consumer wants. What fell through the gap was the 'felt' quality or style of relationships themselves, whether in community or workplace, and writers like Hoggart and Williams sensed that these had been addressed more powerfully in cultural debate and argument, even reactionary cultural argument, than in political and economic analysis. The 'culturalism' or aestheticism for which they were rebuked by other parts of the Left reflected their sense that democratic relationships had to be not only procedurally correct but also substantively satisfying: hence their evocations of an aesthetic rightness or integrity in the 'ordinary culture' of working-class English and Welsh life. See Richard Hoggart's description of working-class life in the first half of *The Uses of Literacy*

That is the very reverse of Bakhtin's procedure, which is to describe works of art as ways of life, but it renders more understandable the striking anthropomorphism of 'authors' and 'heroes'. Aesthetic experience may be the province of particular works of art, but Bakhtin also casts it as no more than an elaboration of the 'fact' that we encounter others in proto-heroic form. Brian Poole, on the basis of his study of archival materials, has argued that the ethics described in 'Author and Hero' are derived for the most part from a source Bakhtin does not even mention: the phenomenology of Max Scheler, whose text *The Essence and Forms of Sympathy* merited fifty-eight pages of synopsis in a notebook of Bakhtin's from 1926.[12] According to Poole, it is Scheler who demonstrates that the ethical relationship of sympathy is only possible because of the distance which separates *I* and *other*, a distance which sympathy, unlike mere identification, strives to maintain. Rather than merely re-experiencing suffering, the sympathetic person responds ethically, from his or her place outside the one suffering, just as Bakhtin describes it in a telling passage: 'When I empathize with the suffering of another, I experience it precisely as *his* suffering, in the category of the *other*, and my reaction to it is not a cry of pain, but a comforting word and an act of help' (AH 28/26). Even here, however, Bakhtin acknowledges that what he has described is not a peculiarly sympathetic relationship, but the very situation of all understanding, in so far as it is directed at the expressions of *others*. Our ability to encounter the content of subjective horizons in an embodied form, inaccessible to the subject itself, 'is the bud in which form slumbers, and from which it unfolds like a blossom' (AH 27/24). All of which implies that the terminology of 'author' and 'hero' has more literal meaning than might appear, and that, despite the warning shots that go off throughout the essay, the mere separateness of individuals may be enough to guarantee the 'outsidedness' that gives rise to aesthetic consummation.

One can never be sure, therefore, whether one should go to philosophical anthropology or to cultural history for an explanation of the aesthetic event: is this a relationship for which we have to step outside of history or one which is the latter's gift? 'Author and Hero in Aesthetic Activity' embodies this ambiguity in its very structure. The first half of the work is devoted to a minute phenomenology of intersubjective experience, in which the difference between the experience of our own lives

(London: Chatto & Windus, 1957) (pp. 56–7 provide a particularly evocative example) and Raymond Williams's essay, 'Culture is Ordinary', where the point is made quite explicitly, as a matter of theory, in *Resources of Hope*, 3–18.

[12] Brian Poole, 'From Phenomenology to Dialogue: Max Scheler's Phenomenological Tradition and Mikhail Bakhtin's Development from *Toward a Philosophy of the Act* to his Study of Dostoevsky', forthcoming in Ken Hirschkop and David Shepherd (eds.), *Bakhtin and Cultural Theory*, 2nd rev. edn. (Manchester: Manchester University Press).

and that of the lives of *others* becomes an unbridgeable and fundamental boundary. Space, time, desires: no category remains unified in the face of this breach within experiential space. The mere phenomenological fact that the meanings and intentions of others are, of necessity, present as expression, whether in language or gesture, becomes the foothold with which aesthetic experience will begin its climb to sublime heights. The second half of the work, by contrast—'The Whole of the Hero as a Whole of Meaning'—is a *history* of aesthetic consummation, conducted as a more or less chronological discussion of the forms of confession, tragedy, biography, lyric, and romantic and classical character. In this history, the aesthetic reworking of life requires pen, paper, and culture rather than much in the way of face-to-face intersubjectivity. As the endpoint of a historical evolution, the properly aesthetic relationship of author to hero depends on formal techniques which we would assume are not automatically available in the structures of the lifeworld.[13]

Unable to settle for one or the other, Bakhtin's intersubjective justification for the aesthetic tries to have it both ways. Aesthetic activity is, on the one hand, a properly historical affair, in need of defence in the early twentieth century and depending on the accumulated resources of a developed and expert artistic practice, and, on the other hand, no more than the setting loose of powers stored up in the ordinary experiences of intersubjectivity, the actualization of an experience of *others* which is part of the phenomenology of everyday life:

To understand this world as the world of other people . . . is the primary condition of an aesthetic approach to it . . . One must realize that all positively valued definitions of the world as a given, all valorizing bindings of worldly presence, have a justified and consummated other as their hero: it is about the other that all plots are composed, that all works are written, that all tears are shed, for the other that all monuments are erected, it is only with others that all cemeteries are filled; only others are known, remembered and recreated by productive memory, so that my memory of an object, a world, or a life might also become artistic. (AH 105/111–12)

In the end, it is the 'author' who must bear the burden of this ambiguity, for it is this figure which is called upon to be both ordinary and exceptional, a bare human being and a product of aesthetic evolution. When Bakhtin makes it a requirement that 'the author knows and sees more not

---

[13] The division between the two halves of the essay also reflects a different division, between the perceptual and narratable. The first half of 'Author and Hero' is also the half devoted to the spatial and temporal integrity of the hero, and it correspondingly accounts for the hero as something perceived. The author can be described by analogy with empirical physical outsidedness for precisely this reason, as the hero is made whole in time and space. By contrast the latter half deals with the hero as a whole of meaning, a whole constructed from plots, and this automatically draws the author away from any analogies with perception.

just in the same direction as the hero looks and sees, but also in a different direction, in principle inaccessible to the hero' (AH 17/13), the simple language makes the author's task look too easy. 'Direction' (*napravlenie*) means spatial and temporal direction—the author can see behind the back of the hero, as any of us could—but also 'direction' in a wholly different, phenomenological sense, taken more or less wholesale from Husserl. In the latter, the 'directedness' of intentions, whether cognitive, ethical, or aesthetic, is to their objects, and different forms of directedness constitute objects and worlds in dissimilar manners.[14] 'One forgets', the founder of phenomenology tells us, 'that the objects of which we are "conscious" are not simply in consciousness as in a box, so that they can be merely found in it and snatched at in it; but that they are first *constituted* as being what they are for us, and as what they count as for us, in varying forms of objective intention.'[15] On this latter definition, the objectifying intentions of the author are different not merely by virtue of the fact that the author occupies a different physical space, but as a consequence of the author's special gift, which constitutes the hero as a different kind of object, placing him or her on a 'new plane of existence'.

In this 'new plane' the pressure of ethical and cognitive activity recedes behind the question of the meaning and ultimate purpose of this activity. The author raises the question of the justification of the hero's existence and, in this essay at least, delivers the answer without the least delay. For by transforming the life of the hero into a beautiful given, Bakhtin claims the author effects the hero's 'salvation', redeeming a life hemmed in by earthly achievements which will never be enough. And if at this point we think Bakhtin has gone too far, and that asking for salvation within everyday intersubjectivity is really too much, our fears are addressed—if not allayed—once it becomes clear that Bakhtin is in effect asking only that subjects act like Christians, with all he believes that entails:

Any evaluation is an act of occupying an individual position in being; even for God it was necessary to incarnate himself in order to be merciful, to suffer and *to forgive*, to descend, as it were, from the abstract point of view of justice. Being is, as it were, once and for all, irrevocable, between myself as unique and all those who are others for me; a position in being having been occupied, every act and every evaluation will issue only from that position, they have it as their precondition. (AH 120/129)

[14] 'Experiences of meaning are classifiable as "acts", and the meaningful element in each such single act must be sought in the act-experience and not in the object, it must lie in that element which makes the act an "intentional" experience, one "directed" at objects.' Edmund Husserl, *Logical Investigations*, trans. J. N. Findlay (London and Henley: Routledge & Kegan Paul, 1970), Investigation V, p. 533.

[15] Ibid., Investigation II, §23, p. 385. For all the fuss made about Bakhtin's relationship to neo-Kantianism, it is remarkable how little his substantial and recurring debt to phenomenology is discussed in commentary; see n. 28 below.

In his lecture on religion Bakhtin locates the distinctiveness of Christian morality in the belief that 'between myself and others there is, for the Christian, a chasm' (Lec., 235) such that the demand for justice (i.e. *equal* treatment of *I* and *other*) makes no sense. The author can love the other and only the other because distance between the two is a presupposition of Christian ethics, according to which the believer demands the 'cross for himself and happiness for others' (Lec., 235). What appeared to be the result of a phenomenological investigation—the gap between *I* and *other*—turns out to be an axiom of Christian ethics.

The analogy between the work of art and the act of Christian forgiveness and salvation solves many problems for Bakhtin. In everyday life one can forgive and love, and if that is in essence what artworks do for their heroes, then perhaps the difference between the two is not as insurmountable as it seemed. But Christianity embeds the local act of forgiveness in a larger narrative, in which divine mercy and forgiveness make the unhappy history of humanity meaningful and redeemable as a whole. Ordinary subjects do not transcend the immediate exigencies of 'life' on their own, but they can borrow the means to do so, from God. If the things of the world and the world as a whole acquire a value independent of good and evil, success and failure, it is on account of the reflected power of the one who can lie outside the world as a whole and who alone can endow it with meaning. Only by faith does authorship acquire its necessary tools and 'the divinity of the artist lies in his communion with the ultimate outsidedness' (AH 175/191), because everything *in* history is caught up in the heroic rat race of cognition and practical activity. The author can manage the double act of being both ordinary subject and skilled artist if it is divinity rather than historical evolution which makes art possible.

The secular among us would give up on Bakhtin at this point, were it not for the obvious lack of fit between Bakhtin's characterization of the aesthetic and the Christian *deus ex machina* summoned up to explain it. The account of the artwork as an intersubjective fact, and the claim that there is an aesthetic moment of everyday intersubjectivity abstracted from practical interests, is convincing without the Christian justifications attached to it, and the fact of the matter is that dialogical theories of existence were springing up all over Europe in the 1920s, sometimes with, sometimes without religious world-views attached. Bakhtin is too modest when he credits his own 'scientific' discovery to the Christian ethics he inherits as a tradition. For there is no mistaking the modern cast of the experience he describes: the assumed autonomy of aesthetic experience, a 'democratic' reversibility of the roles of author and hero, utter secularity in topic and theme, an obsession with the proper relation of hero to environment, belief in the importance of subjective horizon or point of view. Instead of figuring an *I–other* relationship which lifts both author and hero out of history, Bakhtin provides a phenomenology of the inter-subjectivity of his day, or the intersubjectivity which would redeem his day, focused on its particular tensions. To call it aesthetic love is reasonable but perhaps misleading, for while the solidarity he describes is not the same as respect (which would be based on a notion of equality) or part of intimacy, it is a more reciprocal affair than he allows. Below I hope to demonstrate that Bakhtin describes a kind of solidarity which goes beyond temporary agreement on particular questions (hence its difference from mere practical ethics), but which is nonetheless reciprocal rather than sacrificial in its form. Availing himself of contemporary science and philosophy, Bakhtin may have secularized his project without quite realizing it, for the more seriously one takes the phenomenological and cultural-historical claims of the work, the less one is in need of metaphysical support from religion. To the extent that he persuades us that the other can be redeemed by some judicious combination of phenomenological inspection and aesthetic deftness, we are apt to see his call for divine aid as redundant, and the possibility of salvation as not the gift of God but a *promesse de bonheur* built into historical life.

THE GREAT TRANSFORMATION: 'DISCOURSE IN THE NOVEL'

By the time of 'Discourse in the Novel', none of this apparently matters. In the transformed theoretical universe of the 1930s, writers dream not of salvation but of 'the social life of discourse beyond the artist's study, in the open spaces of public squares, streets, cities and villages' (DN 73/259), and of dialogue which draws its virtues from below rather than from above. Hope that one might surmount the limitations of human finitude is point-less in a landscape so plainly dominated by worldly, temporal struggles, where the battle is not for the souls of all-too-human heroes but between the people and their 'novels' on the one hand, and the repressive poetics of the official, centralizing state on the other.

No one dreams of arresting the flow of history in this text, which appears to take for granted the triumph of contemporaneity and the virtues of its artistic champion, the novel. In 'Discourse in the Novel' intersub-jectivity takes the shape of a ubiquitous dialogism, standing in the way of the directly expressive *word* rather than world-view: 'No living word stands in relation to its object in isolation: between the word and its object, between the word and the speaking personality, has been deposited a resilient, often hard to penetrate environment of other, alien words about the same object, on the same theme' (DN 89/276). The struggle with the stubborn ethical and cognitive 'directedness' of utterances of others now appears as a problem constitutive of discourse as such:

A living utterance, acquiring meaning at a determinate historical moment in a socially determinate environment, cannot avoid brushing against thousands of living dialogical threads woven by socio-ideological consciousness around the given object of the utterance, it cannot avoid becoming an active participant in social dialogue. It is out of this dialogue that it arises, as its continuation, as a rejoinder, and it does not approach the object from somewhere on the sidelines. (DN 90/276–7)

This inevitable dialogism fractures language itself, giving rise to 'the internal stratification of a unified national language into social dialects, group manners, professional jargons, generic languages, the languages of generations and age groups, the languages of tendencies, the languages of authorities, the languages of intellectual circles and passing fashions, the languages of socio-political days and even hours . . .' (DN 76/262–3), a 'social heteroglossia' through which the novel 'orchestrates all its themes, and its entire represented and expressed objective and meaningful world' (DN 76/263).

The most contentious and striking difference from the earlier essay, however, is the quasi-Nietzschean populism which endows the novel with its political edge and purpose. Everyday life no longer strives to redeem itself from within, but struggles against the domination of the 'poetic genres', which aid the 'historical processes of linguistic unification and centralization' (DN 83/270). These centralizing poetic works resort to the classic strategy of the prestige 'correct' form, presenting themselves as a privileged reflection of truth, counterposed to the variety of deformed dialects and social misfits which populate the common linguistic world. In these circumstances the novel's dialogized heteroglossia naturally makes a play for linguistic diversity:

At the time when poetry, on the official socio-ideological heights, was tackling the task of the cultural, national and political centralization of the verbal-ideological world, in the depths, on fairground stages and in buffoon shows, there rang out comic heteroglossia, the mimicry of all 'languages' and dialects, there developed the literature of the *fabliaux* and *Schwänke*, of street songs, folksayings, anecdotes, where there was no linguistic centre, where a lively play with the 'languages' of poets, scholars, monks, knights and others took place, where all 'languages' were masks and there was no authentic and indisputable linguistic face. (DN 86/273)

In place of salvation, then, strife; instead of phenomenology, a theory of stylistics; no longer a struggle for consummation, but one for the relativization of every language with pretensions to truth. Nevertheless, we can isolate the distinct transformations which link 'Author and Hero' to 'Discourse in the Novel':

1. *The symmetry of language.* Although the roles of 'author' and 'hero' were in theory reversible, in any given aesthetic event there existed an active author and a passive hero. In 'Author and Hero', that is, the aesthetic event was still conceived of as the author's 'objectification' of a world and a character, in keeping with phenomenology's interest in the relationship between the individual consciousness and its objects. The heroes of 'Discourse in the Novel', however, are described as languages rather than as objects, and the intersubjectivity on which the essay focuses is not a relationship between people but a dialogue between 'voices' or 'socio-ideological languages'. Once Bakhtin begins to think of the aesthetic event as a uniquely linguistic or discursive phenomenon (a consequence of Voloshinov's work and influence in the 1920s, which I discuss in Chapter 3) it acquires a symmetry or two-sidedness it lacked in its initial formulation. An address to the *other* in language assumes transcendentally, as it were, that a response may be forthcoming: 'every discourse is directed at an answer and cannot escape the profound influence of the anticipated answering discourse' (DN 93/280). The turn to language thus appears to render impossible the principled—and, in terms of its project, necessary—asymmetry of the author–hero relationship.[16]

2. *Politics.* In 'Author and Hero' the artist struggles against 'life'; in 'Discourse in the Novel' the artist struggles against other artists, as novelists take up arms against those who work for 'poetic' verbal and ideological centralization. To aesthetic descriptions such as the following— 'In poetic genres artistic consciousness—in the sense of the unity of all the semantic and expressive intentions of an author—realizes itself entirely within its own language, it is wholly immanent to it, it expresses itself in it directly and immediately, without qualification or distance' (DN 98/285)—Bakhtin now attaches political conclusions: 'Language in a poetic work realizes itself as something beyond doubt, beyond dispute, all-

---

[16] To treat the emergence of dialogue as a 'paradigm shift', however, is possible only for those who systematically ignored the warning signs present in the earlier work which was, of course, specifically and explicitly devoted to the analysis of *verbal* art. (In a letter to M. I. Kagan of 20 Feb. 1921, Bakhtin calls it his 'aesthetics of verbal creation'; see Iu. M. Kagan, 'O starykh bumagakh iz semeinogo arkhiva (M. M. Bakhtin i M. I. Kagan)', *Dialog Karnaval Khronotop*, 1 (1992), 66.) The 'authors' and 'heroes' of Bakhtin's early philosophy are never more than language, but this isn't clear because Bakhtin is at such pains to distinguish himself from the Russian Formalist reduction of the aesthetic object to the quasi-natural properties of language. Bakhtin knows that language is the substance of verbal art, but he argues that the aesthetic object is composed of unities of meaning rather than grammatical units: 'The components of the aesthetic object of a given work are, therefore, "the city's streets", "the shadow of the night", "the scroll of memory", etc., but not visual representations, not psychic experiences in general and not words' (PCMF 52/299).

encompassing' (DN 99/286). It appears that Bakhtin is less alarmed by the rootless and shifty nature of 'life' than about the new danger of an official authoritarian culture shaping social life from on high.

But in Bakhtin's hands authoritarianism does not, as in its classical formulation, prevent speech, but gives rise to a rich, if fearsome, poetic culture. This productive, fertile official culture creates as one of its poles the very sphere of individuality. Speaking, in 'Discourse in the Novel', of philosophy of language Bakhtin comments that in its traditional form it knows 'only two poles of linguistic life . . . *the system of a unified language* and the *individuum* speaking in that language' (DN 83/269). Which applies, *mutatis mutandis*, to culture itself: the official does not merely impress itself on the contents of everyday consciousness (by enforcing some terrible alien ideology), but, perhaps more importantly, individualizes it.

In this context the 'official', while by definition requiring a state apparatus, is not equivalent to 'the state' as we know it in secular political theory, as an institution which works—however one evaluates it—in the domain of 'practical' (i.e. worldly, temporal) interests. Bakhtin has in mind something closer to the metaphysical and normative concept of the state as it appears in Hegel or the idea of 'the cultural state' associated with the neo-Kantians. The 'official' is a political form with cultural consequences, a worldly act (Bakhtin will sometimes call it a 'centripetal force') which can apparently structure the possible experience of the society as a whole. This metaphysical exaggeration of the political might account for the peculiarly undialectical shape of the struggle we witness between the official-poetic and the popular-novelistic, each of which could apparently survive on its own. For if they opposed one another in the same political space each would acquire the colouring of the worldly and temporal interestedness which is the very problem Bakhtin seeks to confront. Instead they appear as opposed, but inhabiting different spaces and even different historical epochs, the poetic representing a classical or medieval culture which has overstayed its welcome, the novelistic embodying not just a tendency in modernity but modernity itself. (Or rather, a peculiar amalgam of modernities: novelistic culture combines the humanism and scientificity of 'the era of the Renaissance and of Protestantism, which destroyed medieval verbal-ideological centralization' (DN 226/415) with the popular-democratic politics of the seventeenth, eighteenth, and nineteenth centuries.) Bakhtin thus figures politics into his theory, but only having ensured that the stakes are higher than the play of earthly interests.

3. *Populism*. Bakhtin does not, in 'Author and Hero', criticize only overly ethico-political art which is, so to speak, all hero and no aestheticizing author; he pours equal scorn on the formalist gameplaying which is all author and no hero, art which has no material or content to subdue or

work upon. In 'Discourse in the Novel' the prospective author has to travel further than his own *I-for-myself* to find these vital impulses—he must literally go out of the door, and probably downstairs, in search of 'the social life of discourse beyond the artist's study'. The distance between author and hero is now the social distance between an artistic intelligentsia and popular life, and the problem of writing cut off from 'life' apparently reflects the problem of a writer cut off from life.[17]

To this rather classical populist problematic, however, Bakhtin adds a significant individual twist, endowing 'the people' not just with life but with the ability to produce novelistic writing. Just as it became important in the earlier text to show that art could be derived from what people do every day, so in this text Bakhtin is at pains to show that the novel can be derived from what 'the people' do every day. If in 'Author and Hero', art was both a specialized practice and a simple extrapolation of everyday intersubjectivity, then in 'Discourse in the Novel' the same ambiguity reappears, with the qualification that a truly everyday intersubjectivity itself is no longer accessible to all, but is a particular historic achievement, found only in the public square. Does Bakhtin thereby historicize the very idea of art? Not in the least, for 'the people' and their novelistic consciousness are every bit as eternal as the natural aesthetic faculty Bakhtin had earlier attributed to us all. The difference is that whereas in 'Author and Hero' it was philosophy which told us that art was always possible, a decade later it is cultural history which delivers this same message. This means the people who fill the pages of 'Discourse in the Novel' must be quite extraordinary, simultaneously signifying a closeness to the historical process (described as 'becoming') and a distance from any particular element in it. They are at once more bodily and more sceptical, earthier yet more ironic, a people whose constant epistemological doubt brings them closer to, rather than more distant from, the world of things. A people who could be loved by both democrats and artists, to be sure.

4. *'Consummation' and history*. Of all the transformations one stands out as an apparent *reversal* of earlier priorities:

If on the ground of poetry there grew, as the utopian philosophy of its genres, the idea of a purely poetic extra-historical language, removed from the daily grind, a language of the gods, then artistic prose is close to the idea of the living and historically concrete being of languages. Artistic prose presupposes a purposeful feeling for the historical and social concreteness and the relativity of living discourse, for its participation in historical becoming and social struggle; and it takes

[17] For an interesting analysis of the relationship of the intellectual to the people see Dana Polan, 'Bakhtin, Benjamin, Sartre: Toward a Typology of the Intellectual Cultural Critic', in Catriona Kelly, Michael Makin, and David Shepherd (eds.), *Discontinuous Discourses in Modern Russian Literature* (Basingstoke: Macmillan, 1989), 3–18.

discourse still warm from this struggle and antagonism, still unresolved and rent by antagonistic intonations and accents, and subordinates it to the dynamic unity of its own style. (DN 144/331)

What in 'Author and Hero' was the problem is now the goal: an open-ended, forward-directed life is what we should desire and what the novel alone can deliver. Artistic prose, far from justifying life from beyond its local cognitive and ethical concerns, now focuses attention on precisely those local antagonisms and historically determinate interests which drive 'life' ever onwards and make of it something *per se* 'unresolved'. Historical 'becoming', that endlessness and 'unconsummatedness' from which the author was to rescue the hero, is now the end of every proper aesthetic act. To consummate or finalize has become the ultimate sin.

Dialogism should have been the concept which rescued Bakhtin from earlier ambiguities, yet one cannot resist the feeling that in 'Discourse in the Novel' 'art' has unconditionally surrendered to 'life'. Once dialogue and its symmetry becomes the leading principle, metaphysics and the privilege of the authorial position must go to the wall, sceptical epistemology must replace religious certainty, and the aesthetic can no longer hope to do anything more than echo—perhaps in intensified form—the imperatives of life itself. Two remarkably similar passages underscore the point. 'Author and Hero':

The author must struggle with old or not so old literary forms, must use them and combine them, overcome their resistance or find in them a support, but at the basis of this movement lies the most essential, determining *primary artistic struggle* with the cognitive-ethical directedness of life and its valid living persistence . . . (AH 181/197)

And 'Discourse in the Novel':

The discourse directed at its object enters into this dialogically agitated and tensed medium of alien discourses, evaluations and accents, and becomes interwoven with their complex interrelationships—it merges with some, recoils from others, intersects with a third group; and all this may essentially endow the discourse with form, be deposited in all its levels of meaning, complicate its expression, influence its entire stylistic profile. (DN 90/276)

In the second passage artistic form is determined by a dialogical interplay with pre-existing discourses, a process of self-definition through agreement and disagreement. But the insistence that dialogue was subordinate to a 'primary artistic struggle' simply drops out of sight in the later rewriting. Having lost its claim to be a force with a value and justification all its own, art is reduced to mimicking what exists already: the cognitive and ethical struggles of everyday popular life.

Modernity, identified as the rise of dialogue and heteroglossia, would appear to entail the end of the redemptive possibilities embodied in the ideal of aesthetic form and wholeness. In 'Discourse in the Novel' the dialogism implicit in the author–hero relationship becomes a principle of social life, but it pays a heavy price: once God has been condemned to the junkpile of outdated metaphysics, the best the novel can do is deck out life in the clothes of art. Having overwhelmed the social field, dialogue finds itself reduced to the status of a positive, and therefore unredemptive, fact of social life.

DOSTOEVSKY AND MODERNITY

'Discourse in the Novel' leaves us with an unprincipled enthusiasm for dialogism and the novel, for while the power of this self-consciously modern form is celebrated on every page, the essay itself appears to knock away every reason one might have for placing hope in it. From the perspective of 'Author and Hero', the modernity represented in 'Discourse in the Novel' is nothing other than the disintegration of every authoritative principle of culture, and while disintegration may be exciting, if it leaves nothing positive in its place it signifies chaos rather than progress. Whether modernity has indeed something of its own to offer is a question Bakhtin confronts directly when he writes about Dostoevsky, who represents for him, as for so many of his contemporaries, modernity in distilled form. Lukács had ended his *Theory of the Novel* (1920) with the future firmly in Dostoevsky's hands ('It is in the words of Dostoevsky that this new world, remote from every struggle against what actually exists, is drawn for the first time simply as a seen reality'[18]) and Bakhtin's intellectual soulmate Lev Pumpiansky had, in his lecture-turned-book *Dostoevsky and Antiquity* (1922), represented Dostoevsky's novels as the definitive announcement that classical European culture had fallen apart.[19] Bakhtin's initial estimate of Dostoevsky was along the same lines: although there is no trace of the text on Dostoevsky he supposedly finished in 1922, and though the extensive analysis of Dostoevsky promised in 'Author and Hero' never materializes, the cursory but prescient comments he hazards at the end of that fragment cast Dostoevsky as the central figure in a contemporary crisis of authorship in which 'the right of the author to be outside of life

[18] Georg Lukács, *The Theory of the Novel*, trans. Anna Bostock (Cambridge, Mass.: MIT Press, 1971), 152.
[19] L. V. Pumpiansky, *Dostoevsky i antichnost'* (Petersburg: Zamysly, 1922). The text opens with the line 'The poetry of Dostoevsky belongs to the epoch of the great disintegration (disorganization) of European poetry, the beginning of which one could see conditionally in "Hamlet"' (p. 7).

and to consummate it is disputed' (AH 186/203).[20] When 'life becomes conceivable and substantial as an event only from within' (AH 186/203), the author loses the outsidedness necessary for art, and modernity presumably resigns itself to a Godless and unaesthetic existence. But when Bakhtin next speaks of Dostoevsky—in *Problems of Dostoevsky's Art*, published in 1929—he praises him for inventing the very artistic forms which had at first been treated as symptoms of crisis. *Problems* stands midway between 'Author and Hero' and 'Discourse in the Novel' both chronologically and theoretically, combining an interest in the relation of author and hero with acclaim for a new dialogism in which they are evenly balanced. In the new symmetry the hero appears 'as if [he] were not the object of authorial discourse but the bearer, fully valued and fully endowed with rights, of his own word' (*PDA* 7–8/5), but rather than treat this independence as a sign of cultural decay, Bakhtin argues that it is the fruit of a revolution in aesthetic form.[21] Dostoevsky's dialogical renunciation of any consummating position outside the hero is not crisis but generic innovation, and the absence of a quasi-divine author strengthens rather than weakens his aesthetic hand. Registering a complete turnaround even in the lexical details, Bakhtin now congratulates Dostoevsky for having discovered an artistic method capable of representing heroes as '*unconsummated*', as if heroes could never have wanted to be anything but.

The loss of redemptive consummating form may be compensated for by a new modern equality of voice. But open-ended dialogue and equality of voice are such familiar values in twentieth-century North Atlantic culture that few critics have asked what *kind* of values they are. For although Bakhtin describes Dostoevsky's innovation as an artistic one, it's hard to avoid the suspicion that in valuing what he has previously condemned, Bakhtin has merely made an expedient substitution of politics for art.[22] If this was what Bakhtin had in mind, he could hardly have predicted the

---

[20] In his article '*Dostoevsky i antichnost'* L. V. Pumpianskogo (1922) i M. M. Bakhtina (1963)' N. I. Nikolaev proposes that Bakhtin finished a text in 1922 which was close in form and emphasis to Pumpiansky's, and that this text was the basis for a first version of *Problems of Dostoevsky's Art*, finished around 1925. The article appears in [Proceedings of] The Seventh International Bakhtin Conference, Book I (Moscow: Moscow State Pedagogical University, 1995), 1–10.

[21] Nikolaev, in '*Dostoevsky i antichnost'* L. V. Pumpianskogo (1922) i M. M. Bakhtina (1963)', argues that Bakhtin initially shared with Kagan and Pumpiansky the notion that modern culture could best be explained by recourse to the concept of a crisis, but that this soon changed. 'The mixing of tragic and comic as a fundamental artistic feature of Dostoevsky's art, about which L. V. P. [Pumpiansky] wrote in *Dostoevsky i antichnost'*, received an explanation precisely in the sphere of the genre of Menippea as a special literary field of the serio-comic, without recourse to the unwieldy theoretical construction of a "crisis"' (p. 9).

[22] In this respect also Bakhtin would be following Pumpiansky's line of argument, in so far as the latter interprets Dostoevsky as the working through of a European 'crisis of aesthetic culture' (*Dostoevsky i antichnost'*, 46).

enthusiastic support he would receive from his critical admirers. For in embracing the idea that novels may embody unfettered dialogue critics have shown themselves more than willing to trade in their aesthetic ideals for political ones. When they inspect their newly acquired wares, however, they will discover that they have been well and truly swindled, for the political goods come badly damaged. Whatever the values made flesh in the novel, the openness and spontaneity essential to dialogue in the strictly political sense are not going to be found. Novels, even Dostoevsky's, are not spontaneous acts of conversation or political meetings, and the persons or languages represented within them depend on an author even to acquire the identity and dignity of political actors. A political dialogue in which one party represented, with however much aesthetic dexterity and sincere good will, the position of the other would be regarded as a sham, and rightly so, for the political value placed on dialogue depends on a real diversity of speakers, not one supplied by the deft use of quotation marks. That much is acknowledged in the very language Bakhtin uses to describe Dostoevsky's achievement: 'everything must be sensed as *a discourse about someone present* and not a discourse about someone absent, as a discourse in the "second" and not "third" person' (*PDA* 70/64). Novelistic dialogue is described in the language of personal encounter precisely because it feeds off political and social values (equal rights, natural human dignity) dependent upon the autonomy of actually present others.

Bakhtin is more aware of this paradox than many of his followers: the entire first chapter of *Problems of Dostoevsky's Art* is a polemic with those critics who take the bait and *argue* with Dostoevsky's heroes. It is they who make the fundamental error of treating novels as political occasions, ignoring the different role that language acquires in the context of the artwork. Acknowledging that Dostoevsky's texts appear as 'chaos' to traditional criticism, Bakhtin claims this is only because it fails to perceive the 'new artistic task, which only he [Dostoevsky] was able to pose and solve in all its breadth and depth' (*PDA* 10/8). But while Bakhtin may have perceived Dostoevsky's artistic task, he was at a loss for words when it came to defining it. His description of Dostoevsky's novel as 'polyphonic' was at bottom no more than an evasion, an attempt to confer aesthetic value on Dostoevsky's work by means of an analogy from contrapuntal music in which Bakhtin himself could not have believed.

In 'Author and Hero' subjectivity took the form of soul, as opposed to spirit, when it fell under the consummating, aesthetic gaze of the *other*. When Bakhtin claims in 1929 that 'what the idealist–Romantics designated "spirit" as opposed to soul becomes in Dostoevsky's art the object of an objectively realistic, sober, prosaic representation', that what they had 'approached from within', Dostoevsky had approached 'from without'

(*PDA* 101/277–8), a distinction which had once been described as a phenomenological fact is conveniently demoted to the status of a Romantic convention. But having admitted that Dostoevsky was thus able to square the circle, he failed to make the adjustments in his phenomenology which would make sense of this achievement. If the unconsummated condition of the *I* is the initial problem, then it is not clear why it is either possible or—more importantly—desirable for it to be unconsummated by virtue of artistic representation. For Dostoevsky's work to be justified, representation must relieve, not reproduce, the problematic condition of ordinary subjectivity.

'Discourse in the Novel' radicalizes rather than solves this problem. The originality of the essay lies in the insistence that the 'social dialogue' incarnate in novels only reflects and exploits the spontaneous and 'elemental' dialogism of everyday speech: at least here Bakhtin admits that the claims of art are borrowing directly from the virtues of life. But on further inspection it becomes clear that Bakhtin has thrust dialogue into speech acts where there is no dialogue in the usual, more restrictive sense of the term, in the sense we rely on when we endorse dialogue as a feature of our social or political life. When Bakhtin asserts that 'a living utterance cannot avoid becoming a participant in social dialogue' dialogical partners are in effect buried in the recesses of language itself, guaranteeing, by a kind of theoretical sleight of hand, dialogues—and the values attached to them— even when actual speech partners are absent. While at first glance Bakhtin appears to be claiming that novels borrow their power from the dialogues of everyday life, in truth the everyday dialogical speech they depend on is no more a matter of two-sided exchange than novels are. Which leads one to suspect, naturally enough, that the open-endedness and relentless forward movement typical of dialogism is not the mere consequence of two-sidedness in speech, but the sign of a historical condition or situation which gives rise to a new kind of life and a new kind of art.

Thus the modernity which was the problem in 'Author and Hero' has become the solution in 'Discourse in the Novel', with the result that Bakhtin deprives himself of the only justification he had for the asymmetries of author and hero. Once he has renounced the semi-divinity of the author, and with it the ideal of a tranquillizing and merciful aesthetic, Bakhtin is left—or so it would seem—with only the uncertain intersubjectivity for which the aesthetic was to be the cure. Far from being unambiguously ideal or normative, dialogism teeters on the edge of the merely existing, as if it might be no more than a dignified title for the ordinary squabbling of ethical life. Yet without a redefinition of the meaning of aesthetic form, or of the role of the author, the novelistic writing on which Bakhtin stakes so much in 'Discourse in the Novel' has nothing to do: the aesthetic, strictly speaking, has no role, and finds itself reduced to the echo of the problems it was meant to solve. Having either renounced or suppressed the metaphysics of salvation, Bakhtin finds himself with an art form so in tune with the modern world that it has no project of its own.

When Bakhtin claims that 'all the categories of traditional stylistics and the very conception of a poetic artistic discourse lying at their basis are not applicable to novelistic discourse' (DN 75/261) he implies that he has solved a problem which he has in fact only posed. In so far as dialogism implies the reciprocal condition of speech, we know it is not another word for the uneven relationship of God to man; in so far as we find it in novels, where only one person speaks, we know it is not another word for political discussion, which demands a real and not virtual plurality of voices. This paradox is the real point of the matter: the specifically aesthetic intersubjectivity Bakhtin calls 'the novel' is conceivable precisely because modern dialogue demands something more than the equality and spontaneity which defines dialogue as a political form. A modern and 'democratic' intersubjectivity is not just dialogue, because it is not just politics. Or rather, politics itself may not be as self-sufficient as it wishes, for it needs a modern 'dialogical' art by its side to fulfil its own promises.

DIALOGISM AS STYLE

'Discourse in the Novel' is in essence one claim—'the novel is an artistic genre' (DN 82/269)—justified and explained for more than 150 pages. And even though this claim apparently requires a radical revision of both existing literary history and the 'existing conception of poetic discourse', by the end we still do not know *why* the novel is an artistic genre and why dialogism is artistically significant. We know that the novel is a specifically modern genre and one uniquely adapted to the aesthetic needs of con-temporaneity, but nowhere does Bakhtin tell us what these historically unprecedented needs are or how they differ from those of the past. So enthralled is he with the sharp and vivid intercourse of socio-ideological languages and the stylistic acrobatics of the novel that he hardly pauses to consider what the point of the style is or how he will justify a world so dominated by the local exigencies of 'life'. In the rush to embrace the social liveliness of discourse the idea of art seems to have been left behind.

Unless, of course, the task of art is to *provide* this very liveliness. After all, it is this sublime democracy which provokes wonder and fascination in the minds of Bakhtin critics, who rightly sense that our petty and ordinary conversation appears trivial in the shade of a dialogue embodying the drive and force of social life itself. Our natural interest in the contrast between dialogism and monologism has perhaps concealed from us the distinction which makes the essay appealing for modern readers, that between the 'living' force of 'novelistic' dialogism and the anaemic state of all dialogue founded on mere individuals. For dialogue, we should bear in mind, means not only popular debate but also private 'conversation', bounded in its topics, style, and effects by the sphere of bourgeois intimacy, and in 'Discourse in the Novel' this inherited category serves as a foil for a transformed one.[23] The novel then appears as an attempt to reinvigorate this desiccated intimacy with the power of social conflict: 'here contradictions between individuals are only the surface crests of the elemental force of social heteroglossia, an elemental force which plays through these oppositions and imperiously renders them contradictory, saturating their consciousnesses and words with its own fundamental heteroglossicity' (DN 139/326); it redeems dialogue from its enfeebled state, by drawing on the energies of a more vibrant social diversity below it. But that means that the dynamism we accept as a natural attribute of dialogism is actually evidence of its aesthetic refashioning.

If vibrant social dialogue is the hero of the artwork, then isn't the novelist logically its author? Isn't the dialogue of socio-ideological languages which inspires the novelist in fact the product of his or her own aesthetic labour? For in everyday life we do not confront socio-ideological languages, or rather, we do not confront language as a struggle of socio-ideological languages, full of sound and fury, signifying everything: this happens only in particular situations, one of which may be the reading of novels. Just as the author in 'Author and Hero' had to compose the tranquil hero out of the scattered materials of ordinary life, so the novelist in 'Discourse in the Novel' has to make socio-ideological languages—the true heroes of the novel—out of the fluid and chaotic

---

[23] Franco Moretti has persuasively argued that 'conversation' in the 19th-century European novel functions as the consciously 'softened' and consensual alternative to the hard and conflictual rationality of public discussion (*The Way of the World*, 49–52); this is obviously less true of the Russian novel of that time (where political and philosophical discussion seems, from a Western point of view, to have an inordinate role in domestic life), but nevertheless implies a background against which 'dialogism' may function. Fredric Jameson has suggested in a discussion of Nathalie Sarraute that modernism 'presupposes a situation in which the apparent surface conversation is no longer the real one; in which, beneath the routine and insignificant, contingent exchange of spoken words, there comes into view some more fundamental human contact, some deeper wordless groping struggle or interaction'. The task of the modernist writer then becomes 'the invention of a new and fresh, nonalienated *originary* language' capable of rendering that more genuine level of interaction (*Fables of Aggression: Wyndham Lewis, the Modernist as Fascist* (Berkeley, Ca.: University of California Press, 1981), 40–1). On this account dialogism is one version of the modernist distrust of ordinary language and the realist novel-writing in which it is represented. On the role of conversation in the Russian context in the 19th century see William Mills Todd III, *Fiction and Society in the Age of Pushkin: Ideology, Institutions, and Narrative* (Cambridge, Mass. and London: Harvard University Press, 1986), 31–3, 55–72.

materials of language. The conversation which embodies struggle and becoming *among* socio-ideological languages thus depends on a 'primary artistic struggle' of the author with language in its initial raw state. In which case the distinctive moment of novelistic dialogism is not, as is commonly assumed, the symmetrical dialogue between languages or points of view, but the asymmetrical 'dialogue' between the basic 'stuff' of language and the novelist/author responsible for its transformation. And in fact, the greater part of 'Discourse in the Novel' is devoted to the analysis of *this* transforming dialogue rather than the heteroglot debate which is, in a sense, its consequence.

Nevertheless, Bakhtin insists on describing this transformation as dialogism and on using this latter term to describe both the relation of the novelist to language and the relation of one socio-ideological language to another, as if he were afraid that, left to their own devices, novelists would forget that they, too, were playing an intersubjective game. We should therefore not be surprised to hear Bakhtin describe the novelist's orchestration of thematic material through 'adopted' languages as

a special *double-voiced* discourse. It serves two speakers at the same time and expresses simultaneously two distinct intentions: the direct intention of the speaking personage and the refracted intention of the author. In such discourse there are two voices, two meanings, and two expressions. In this case the two voices are dialogically related, it is as if they know about one another (as two rejoinders in a dialogue know of one another and are structured by this mutual knowledge of each other), as if they are having a discussion with each other. Double-voiced discourse is always internally dialogized. Such is humorous, ironic, parodic discourse, such is the refracting discourse of a narrator, refracting discourse in the speech of characters, such, finally, is the discourse of the inserted genre—these are all double-voiced internally dialogized discourses. In them a potential dialogue is embedded, a dialogue which has not been unfolded, a concentrated dialogue of two voices, two world-views, two languages. (DN 137–8/324–5)

The conceptual dissonance of this passage—what takes place is alternately described as an actual dialogue, a 'potential dialogue', and an 'as if' dialogue—is the sound of theoretical circles being squared and bets being hedged. For now dialogue takes place not between speakers or languages separated by time and space, but between two moments of a single utterance: *stylistic* phenomena, in fact quite diverse stylistic phenomena, are explained and justified as dialogical. Thus dialogue finds itself squeezed into progressively smaller spaces: in 'Author and Hero' the aesthetic act at least had its origins in our perception of physically distinct others, and while novels couldn't be actual political debates, their dialogues at least separated speakers with white space and punctuation marks. The concept of 'double-voiced discourse', for better or worse, eliminates even these traces of ordinary interaction by locating dialogue within the line of discourse itself.

This confirms that what is actually at stake in the stylistic phenomena Bakhtin crams into a bag labelled 'dialogism' is not a relationship between voices, but an act of 'authorial' formation or aesthetic reworking which Bakhtin seems at pains to deny. Even if one were willing to describe effects of parody, irony, or stylization—for heuristic purposes alone—as a relationship between 'heroic' linguistic materials and an 'authorially' determined place in a unified artwork, the asymmetry, never mind the incommensurability of the two sides of the equation, would be obvious. To describe aesthetic form as itself a 'voice' is a gesture necessary to establish that rough equivalence between actors—the level playing field—which is a *sine qua non* of dialogue, and in this case that playing field is the utterance itself, converted into a territory on the surface of which two intentions can coexist.

It is this radical move—the reconstitution of literary style as double-voiced discourse, as itself intersubjective—which endows the concept of dialogism with its cutting edge: from it almost every dramatic Bakhtinian insight is derived. But levelling the difference between 'author' and 'hero' in this way robs the novel of the philosophical meaning it needs to justify itself. The existence or emergence of phenomena like irony or parody appears to have no particular significance for the societies in which they arise when they are no more than further evidence of the latter's heteroglot multiplicity. Reading irony as a horizontal bifurcation in language made vertical, so to speak, renders it no more than a consequence of social differentiation and the fact of heteroglossia. No sharper contrast could be drawn than with Lukács's *Theory of the Novel*, for which 'irony is the objectivity of the novel', signifying the necessary contingency of all attempts at form-giving in a world deserted by God.[24] Bakhtin, however, does not confront irony as a unique form of objectivity, from which one might have to draw social-philosophical conclusions; instead, by reading it as only 'double-voicing', he reduces it to the side-effect of a more fundamental objectivity, the existence of many voices, buoyed up by little else than their own positivity.

In this respect, the concept of double-voiced discourse, however valuable from the point of view of a theory of intersubjectivity, sidesteps the critical issue of the novel's aesthetic form. As we shall see in Chapter 5, Bakhtin is unable to discuss the novel as dialogical and as having a distinctive form in the same essay: the more dialogical it appears, the less 'formed' it appears; the more definite its form, the less dialogical its nature. What Bakhtin hopes to avoid explaining is how language assumes the

[24] Lukács, *The Theory of the Novel*, 90.

form of 'voices' in the first place, and with it the issue of what kind of 'intentional existence' these language-heroes lead in the novel itself. If the existence of voices depends on novelistic form, then the existence of voices is a historical fact, with historical preconditions and limits, but history—at least in this text—is presented as the consequence of voices, not their cause. In 'Author and Hero' it was never decided whether the aesthetic object was the result of a happy collision between consciousnesses or a historical achievement, whether 'authors' and 'heroes' were separate individuals or moments of the artwork. The tortured vocabulary of voice reproduces this ambiguity, as we can never be sure whether double-voicedness signifies the collision of two independently given voices or whether it is simply the form in which voices exist. One suspects that the problem is that voices can only exist as 'doubled' voices and that their ostensibly natural liveliness and power depends on their being 'doubled', framed, aestheticized by the genre which embodies modernity. By imply-ing that the novel merely picks them up from the public square, Bakhtin can let himself off the hook, endow these objects with a fictitious inde-pendence, and avoid the thorny historical issue of why voices have the form they do.[25] To put him back on the hook we need to focus on how voices or 'socio-ideological languages' (to use the revealingly different term) are made.

DIALOGISM AS REPRESENTATION

To start with, we can ignore the claims, dotted throughout the text of 'Discourse in the Novel', that novelistic forms of double-voicing do no more than 'consciously organize' dialogical elements already present in the everyday use of language. For these are evasions, which throw the problem of form back into an unfathomable world of spontaneous modern speech. It is only in the middle of 'Discourse in the Novel' that one finds a discussion of novelistic dialogism which—conducted under the rubric of 'representation'—tells us something about where the voices which engage in dialogue come from. When describing the novel as a genre in which 'discourse not only represents, but is itself represented' (DN 149/336) Bakhtin is compelled to abandon, albeit temporarily, the pseudo-sociological myth of a world already populated by voices. 'The central

---

[25] In *Social Formalism: The Novel in Theory from Henry James to the Present* (Stanford, Ca.: Stanford University Press, 1998), Dorothy Hale shrewdly points out that 'Because Voloshinov/Bakhtin have made the material form of language expressive of subjectivity, it does not matter whether the subjectivity expressed is fictional or real—each is equally represented and contained by forms of language' (p. 157).

problem of the stylistics of the novel can be formulated as *the problem of the artistic representation of a language, the problem of the image of a language'* (DN 149/336). *Izobrazhenie* (representation) might also be translated as 'form-giving' (the root *obraz* means both 'image' and 'form'), and is, not co-incidentally, named the aesthetic term *par excellence* in 'Author and Hero': 'The actual aesthetic event is expressed far better by the term from impressionist aesthetics *"izobrazhenie"* [form-giving] [than by the term "expression"] both for the spatial and for the temporal arts, a word which shifts the centre of gravity from the hero to the aesthetically active subject, the author' (AH 80/83–4). In the context of the novel as well, *izobrazhenie* is the term which describes the aesthetic work of the novel and provides a clue to its philosophical significance.

That the 'representation' of language leads to 'voices' is itself telling, for it reminds us that Bakhtin had continually equated representation with giving an object bodily existence.[26] In 'Author and Hero' incarnation was the essence of the aesthetic itself, signifying the crystallization of potentially endless life in the exteriority and bodily form of the hero. This was equally true when the flesh in question was verbal rather than physical. According to the theory of language in 'Author and Hero', we confront meanings always in exterior form—as words, gestures, actions—and therefore interpret them not by stripping away the bodily shell to re-experience an ideal core, but by responding to them from our own position ('I experience it precisely as *his* suffering, in the category of the *other*'). Representation therefore means more than embodying meaning in signs, because Bakhtin's model for bodily, earthly existence is not the subject cognizing isolate objects but a subject confronting another subject. The embodiment of meaning therefore creates not sign-objects for contemplation but the distance between speaker and listener intrinsic to the speech act. Language is 'situated' once this distance is established, and it is not a terribly long step from this Christian-phenomenological belief that language is situated between *I* and *other* to the modern 'sociological' notion (represented in 'Discourse in the Novel') of a situation consisting of particular social conventions and a specific context. This nexus of sociological and Christian concerns continues into the concept of understanding which 'representa-

---

[26] Although at first glance this definition of 'representation' appears recondite, it is central to use of the term in English, where the word has both an aesthetic and a political definition. In art, representation implies the signifying or symbolizing of an object which already exists; in politics the term means asking a person or persons to speak on behalf of a group, whether defined by interest or geography. It is the latter sense which is relevant here: in medieval political theory, representation took place when a distinct person made tangible corporate or collective interests which were in themselves intangible. Political representation was the giving of concrete and earthly form to something ideal or spiritual. See Hannah Fenichel Pitkin, 'Representation', in Terence Ball, James Farr, and Russell L. Hanson (eds.), *Political Innovation and Conceptual Change* (Cambridge: Cambridge University Press, 1989), 132–54.

tion' implies. If embodiment means confronting meaning 'in the category of the *other*' then comprehension consists not of the reproduction of mental contents, but of making an appropriate response. But appropriateness can have a Christian-ethical meaning, in which the appropriate response is the one which extends love and mercy to the other, or a sociological one, which emphasizes the fact that one meets not with *others* in isolation, but with *others* in specific contexts, which determines how we ought to respond. In the latter sense, understanding, like the novel, is continually combining words 'with the image of a speaking person' (DN 149/336) not in order to trigger the sentiment of mercy, but in order to keep the social wheels rolling: 'For the everyday evaluation and the deciphering of the actual meaning of alien discourses the following can have decisive significance: who precisely is speaking and in what concrete circumstances' (DN 153/340).

With this intersubjective twist Bakhtin transcended the concept of understanding which he received from phenomenology (and which was more or less reproduced in Russian Formalist literary theorizing), and which left one with a choice between the ideality of meaning or the brute material of the signifier. In Husserl, when the perceived word—the 'word-presentation'—counts as an expression, our intention points away from it as external percept—aural or visual—to 'the thing meant'.[27] The 'materialist aesthetics' (Bakhtin's description) of Russian Formalism simply drew the consequences of this position for art, treating attention to the bodiliness of language—the aural body of the signifier—and interest in the meaning of an utterance as a zero-sum game. Verbal art would therefore sacrifice understanding to an 'orientation to expression',[28] that is, an aesthetic interest in the body of language, while practical language sacrificed the linguistic body to the meaning or content communicated.

In Bakhtin's hands representation does not create one body—an image in the mind of a subject—but two, by recasting the speech process in intersubjective terms. Once this step has been taken, the exact physiognomy of meaning and understanding will naturally depend on how one defines intersubjectivity itself. Nevertheless, any interpretation of language in intersubjective terms will define the process of understanding as a matter

[27] Husserl, *Logical Investigations*, Investigation I, §10, p. 283.

[28] According to the reported testimony of Roman Jakobson, credited with coining the phrase 'orientation to expression', this was intended as an exact borrowing from Husserl's phenomenology, the Russian *ustanovka* translating the German *Einstellung* (intention). See Jurij Striedter, *Literary Structure, Evolution and Value: Russian Formalism and Czech Structuralism Reconsidered* (Cambridge, Mass. and London: Harvard University Press, 1989), 270 n. 99. On the influence of Husserl on Formalism and Jakobson in particular see Peter Steiner, *Russian Formalism: A Metapoetics* (Ithaca, NY and London: Cornell University Press, 1984), 18, 201–4. Steiner reports that Gustav Shpet attended meetings of the Moscow Linguistic Circle, where he could have acted as a first-hand medium for the transmission of phenomenological doctrine.

of *responding* to the speech acts of another person, whether with speech or behaviour, and it will define the correct understanding of speech as an appropriate response to it. Wittgenstein would make such a case for an intersubjective concept of understanding when he coined the term 'language-games' to describe the mutual imbrication of language and context. Habermas has unfolded the consequences of this latter concept of understanding:

Within the horizon of the understanding of language there is no such thing as a 'pure' grasp of symbols. Only formalized languages, which are monadologically structured, that is, in the form of calculi, can be understood abstractly, without regard to practical learning processes . . . What is specific to the understanding of everyday language is precisely the achievement of communication. There we do not use signs as such, but adhere to reciprocal behavioural expectations. The processes through which I learn to speak imply then learning to act.[29]

In order to understand, one must therefore act: this general obligation, constitutive of language as such, then parallels the 'oughtness' Bakhtin sought to restore to modern culture. For just as ethical responsibility entails acknowledging one's position and the need to act which flows from it, so communication, understood in intersubjective terms, involves not abstractly entertaining the ideas of others but reacting to them by agreement or disagreement, doubt or conviction, with reciprocating passion or revulsion. In notes Bakhtin made for the article 'The Problem of Speech Genres' (dubbed 'Dialogue-II' by his editors), he emphasized the ethical nature of communication by insisting that dialogue was the sphere not of mere meaning, but of agreement and disagreement, assertion and negation. These acts, unlike the simple creation of well-formed sentences, imply an ethical movement: 'To evaluate, ⟨?⟩ by agreement–disagreement is to occupy some kind of position' (D-II, 230). Bakhtin therefore dismisses the idea of a theoretical understanding which postpones action till later: for him understanding itself entails action and commitment, and responsibility is something assumed in the very act of comprehension.

The ethical and verbal aspects of 'responsibility' are neatly combined in the striking defence of the concept of Revelation which Bakhtin advanced in his Leningrad philosophical circle in 1925. Responding to the charge, familiar since the Enlightenment, that Revelation was the sign of an absolute authority which undermined the Kantian ideal of autonomous humanity, Bakhtin accused this reading of endowing Revelation with 'a thing-like character, the communication of something'.[30] This 'reification

[29] Jürgen Habermas, *On the Logic of the Social Sciences*, trans. Shierry Weber Nicholsen and Jerry A. Stark (Cambridge, Mass. and London: MIT Press, 1988), 131–2.

[30] Quotations in this paragraph are from 'Objections of Bakhtin' to a lecture by M. I. Tubiansky in 1925, and a lecture by Bakhtin of 1 Nov. 1925 (Lec., 245–6).

of the Revelation', according to which the witness would grasp God as the carrier of an ideal meaning, ignores the 'most important moment of Revelation . . . personalitiness [*personal'nost'*]'. The key to Revelation is not the message passed on but 'personality as the form of God', a form of appearance which forces on the subject 'a personal orientation', embedding even the divine appearing in a context where communication means appropriate response. Those opposed to Revelation fear precisely the fact that its understanding includes by definition an obligation to respond:

Not a hostility, but a typical *fear* of Revelation. The hidden nerve of this entire position is precisely fear. Compare it to people who are afraid to receive a good turn, who are afraid that they will become obliged; here precisely there is the fear of receiving a gift and of being too greatly obliged. (Lec., 245)

The word of God, the unsolicited act which *demands* response (in either word or deed), is the paradigm of communication. It shows us, in absolute form, the obligation to act which defines understanding in everyday language.

God cannot be pure Law or Word: he or she must appear 'in person'. And languages and their world-views are subject to the same requirement: they must become the heroes of the artistic work not only metaphorically but also literally, given body by acquiring a speaker, a place in the narrative, and a social context. If in the 1920s the author's task was to 'draw together [the hero] and his life and to make of them a *whole*', the novelist's job, as defined a decade later, is to do the same thing to language, stopping up the flow of words and endowing it with form and shape by surrounding it with a worldly context. But the novel cannot choose just any old context—only a particular kind of context creates the conditions for the dialogical intersubjectivity Bakhtin believes the times demand:

What fundamentally distinguishes all these extra-artistic forms for the transmission of alien discourse from its artistic representation in the novel? All these forms, even where they most closely approach artistic representation, as, for instance, in certain rhetorical double-voiced genres (in parodic stylizations), are directed at the utterance of an individual person. These are practically interested transmissions of the isolated utterances of others, which in the best case rise to the generalization of utterances into a socially typical or characteristic alien speech manner. Concentrated on the transmission of utterances (albeit a free and creative transmission), these forms do not strive to find and attach to utterances the image of a social language realizing itself in them, but not exhausted by them; precisely an image, and not a positive empirical given of the language. Behind every utterance in a genuine novel one senses the elemental force of social languages with their inner logic and inner necessity. The image in this case reveals not just the actuality, but also the possibilities of a given language, its, so to speak, ideal limits, and its total integral meaning, its truth and its limitedness. (DN 167–8/355–6)

To endow language with the 'elemental force of social languages' is therefore the particular aesthetic task of the novel, its end result a distinctively 'historical' bodiliness. However, this move from the individual to the social should not be confused with the apparently similar one found in, for example, the criticism of Lukács, in which the social typicality of characters is what distinguishes the realist text. For the payoff in Bakhtin's case is not cognitive: when utterances become 'the surface crests of the elemental force of social heteroglossia' we are not supposed to know more about them, but encounter them on a 'new plane of existence'. When Bakhtin reworked the themes of 'Discourse in the Novel' in the 1950s he described literature as 'not simply the use of language, but its artistic cognition (corresponding to scientific cognition in linguistics), the image of a language, the artistic self-consciousness of language. The third dimension of language. A new mode of the life of language' (LArtLit., 287).

Bakhtin does not congratulate the novel for having organized a debate—remember, one should not argue with Dostoevsky's heroes—but for its stylistic achievement, which is to create a world saturated by the cut and thrust of double-voiced 'socio-ideological languages'. The value of a novel therefore does not depend upon the strictly theoretical worth of the positions enunciated within it, for the point of it is not to provide knowledge, but to throw us into a new relationship with language, to introduce us to its lost 'third dimension'. This third, intersubjective, dimension is what we might call the 'ethical' dimension of language, which does not so much add depth to the space and time of language as reorder our sense of what it means to participate in it. It is the dimension we blot out when we respond to language as 'practically interested transmission', letting our immediate and individual needs blind us to those questions which are most sharply posed by our intersubjective situation: our neediness and ultimate vulnerability, the role of the future, and the recognition of others in determining the meaning of our actions, our need and desire for narrative coherence and justification in our actions. At issue is not whether individuals are *important* in a moral sense (as some rather frightened liberal commentators have implied), but whether the individual life *as* individual life contains all the resources necessary for a fulfilled existence in the modern world. The question answers itself. In an article from the 1940s, published for the first time in the *Collected Works*, where it has been given the title 'On Flaubert', Bakhtin argues that the moral stupor of the French novelist's world stems from the fact that within it 'the event of life is played out on the most pacified inner territory, at a maximum distance from its borders, from beginnings and ends, both real and semantic' (Flau., 131). Beginnings and ends are the points at which one surrenders one's existence to others, and the subject which ignores or doubts these borders, intending to live by its own wits and values, makes a fatal declaration of its own independence. To comprehend one's life intersubjectively therefore means to see one's life both from within and from beyond it, and it is the unique virtue of language to make this possible. The novel therefore transcends the limits of individual life not by changing the content of discourse, that is, by making authoritative statements from a supra-individual perspective, but by altering its form, in a manner which dislodges its self-sufficiency: 'An acute sense (and a distinct and sharp awareness) of the possibility of a completely different life and a completely different world-view than the life and world-view of the present is a presupposition of the novelistic image of present life' (Flau., 132). This acute sense is what Bakhtin had earlier called 'double-voiced discourse'.

But why is it 'the elemental force of social languages' which catapults language into this third dimension? Individual life may have its limits (most conspicuously, individual birth and death), but there are many ways to transcend them, not all of which involve putting 'historical becoming and social struggle' in the driver's seat. In fact, poetic discourse and all the variants it spawns in the course of 'Discourse in the Novel' (different species of monologism, 'serious' discourse, authoritarian discourse, myth) are worth polemicizing with precisely because they represent a kind of false, official transcendence of the individual, a transcendence which offers power as a substitute for fulfilment and redemption. Discussing 'authoritarian discourse', Bakhtin remarks that:

It enters our verbal consciousness as a compact and indivisible mass, which one must either ratify or repudiate as a whole. It is unbreakably knit to authority—to political power, an institution, a person—and it stands and falls with it. One cannot divide it, agree with one aspect, accept another in part, refuse a third altogether. Therefore distance in relation to authoritative discourse also remains unchanged throughout its extent . . . (DN 156/343)

The problem with authority, so far as Bakhtin is concerned, is not that it shuts people up, presents the false as true, or imposes an otherwise neutral language on downtrodden subjects; the problem with authority or power is that it distorts the natural intersubjectivity of language, giving us meaning without 'voices'. Ratify or repudiate: the authority of the authoritarian can be acknowledged or recognized, but cannot be something which one responds to or develops, and to acknowledge it means to accept it as something utterly unlike oneself, at one remove, so to speak. Successful, acknowledged authority thus transcends the limits and vulnerability of life by the bizarre strategy of denying the fact of mortality and historical change altogether. For Bakhtin all power depends on a claim to immortality, embodied in literary forms like epic, which represent an always powerful past, and the material forms of monument, which preserve the memory of the powerful for future generations. Power therefore transcends the subject by denying the fact of subjectivity altogether, setting itself up as something beyond or above historical life. As a consequence, the individual who accepts power as something greater than him- or herself is not saved or redeemed as an individual, but dissolved in an order of meaning which renounces everything bodily. Rather than let language draw its meaning from its situation, power attempts to draw a situation, a world, out of 'pure' meaning.

In the context of Bakhtin's theory of language, such authoritative language does not afford subjects the opportunity to act ethically. For in the sphere of the authoritarian and monological the truth of a particular utterance is effectively disengaged from the act of taking a position. Embodying what Bakhtin in *Problems of Dostoevsky's Art* calls the 'meaning-based unity of a world-view' (*PDA* 75/79–80) the authoritarian discourse's ideality means that in either affirming it or denying it, one's act loses its intersubjective significance. In *Problems* the costs are itemized:

From the point of view of truth there are no individual consciousnesses. The only principle of cognitive individualization that idealism knows is *error*. Every true judgement is not bound to a personality, but corresponds to a certain unified systematic monological context. Only error individualizes. Everything true fits into the limits of a single consciousness and if it does not fit as a matter of fact, then it is only for reasons incidental and irrelevant to the truth itself. In the ideal a single consciousness and a single mouth is completely adequate for the full plenitude of cognition; it has no need of and no basis for a multiplicity of consciousnesses. (*PDA* 77/81)

In this slightly earlier text monologism is a philosophical and cultural fact, rather than a political one. But the dissociation of monological truth from any particular personality or individual, even that of the Leader who announces it, is an important component of Bakhtin's later account of authority. In a different context, Slavoj Žižek has argued that this disjunction between individuals and symbolic authority is constitutive of all authority relying on what he calls the *mystique of the Institution*: 'The king, the judge, the president, and so on, can be personally dishonest, rotten, but when they adopt the insignia of Authority, they experience a kind of mystic transubstantiation; the judge no longer speaks as a person, it is Law itself which speaks through him.'[31] The transcendence of the individual through the impersonality of law or tradition is therefore a dead end, so far as Bakhtin is concerned. For authority is founded on the rejection of

---

[31] Slavoj Žižek, *For they know not what they do: Enjoyment as a Political Factor* (London: Verso, 1991), 249.

historical life itself, and therefore, though it asks for nothing from the individual, it offers nothing in return.

In the novel, by contrast, all authority becomes a matter of *figures* of authority, all authoritative language a matter of style: 'The speech subjects of the high, pontificating genres—the priests, prophets, preachers, judges, leaders, patriarchal fathers, and the like—have passed from life. The writer has replaced them all, simply the writer who has become the heir to their styles. He either stylizes them (that is, assumes the pose of a prophet, a preacher, and so on) or parodies them (to a greater or lesser degree)' (N70–71, 355/132). The Law still speaks, one could say, but with a human face which no longer has an accidental, contingent relation to it. And this very fact alters the nature or 'mood' (in the linguistic sense) of the Law, turning it into a historical project which can no longer comport itself with the self-assurance of absolute dogma. But Bakhtin does not dissolve symbolic authority in the acid bath of actual, particular individuals: the human face the Law acquires is not that of William Rehnquist or Lord Denning, but that of 'the judge'. Because when individuals participate in this language, they do so not as a whole, with their entire being, but precisely as judges, lawyers, defendants, jurors, and so on. To reduce the Law, religion, political discourse, the language of a particular art, to the expression of a particular individual would be to destroy their relative integrity and thus the actual multiplicity of language and discourse. And this in turn would reduce historical life itself to something rootless and contingent, and thus convert it once again into something to be redeemed, almost arbitrarily (in the spirit of predestination), by a power beyond or above it. The priority of 'ethical reality' can be established, or re-established (if this is what Bakhtin thinks is happening), only if the world itself remains the arena in which human fulfilment is sought. Therefore the individual life is transcended not by a stroke of metaphysical salvation, but through its integration (but not absorption) into the historical projects embodied in the developing languages of modern life, for which redemption is not, to take the neo-Kantian phrase, 'given, but set as a task'.

The novel is Bakhtin's word for this integration or transformation—it can evoke what Adorno called 'the possibility of relations without purposes',[32] that is, the idea of an intersubjectivity devoted solely to its own elaboration, only by making language worldly in this particular sense. Its genius is to make the starting-point of this transformation not individuals as such, but individuals at the point of their own self-transcendence, at the point where they become 'more than themselves', at the point where they participate in the historically transformative process of culture: in short, at

---

[32] Theodor Adorno, *Minima Moralia*, trans. E. F. N. Jephcott (London: Verso, 1974), 41.

the point of language, as Bakhtin conceives of it—'The search for my own discourse is in fact a search precisely not for my own, but for a discourse which is greater than myself; it is a striving to exceed my own words, with which nothing essential can be said' (N70–71, 374/149). Grasped as biological creatures bordered by birth and death, individual lives are inert, finished, closed up; grasped as moments of the 'elemental force of social languages' they are as open and meaningful as the historical process to which they contribute. To take a disinterested, aesthetic view of human life is therefore to intensify its historical forcefulness, not to reduce or ignore it; otherwise, the bodies one redeems are no more than biological entities, elements of the natural, but not historical, world.

Paradoxically, the more effectively the novel embodies an aesthetic relation to languages, the more utterly riven by strife language itself appears. For aesthetic disinterest and social conflict are complementary once we acknowledge that the novel is meant to represent not the overcoming of earthly feeling and social passion, but the transformation of its form and its meaning. There is, of course, no actual novelist embodying the disinterest of the aesthetic itself, just as the author of a decade before was not an empirical individual but a 'moment' of the artwork. The style of the novel represents the form in which social 'voices' ought to emerge, not the product of individual creative effort; it is a form of expression, not something externally imposed on recalcitrant material. If it requires, as Bakhtin writes, not just 'the discovery of the multilanguagedness of a cultural world and the heteroglot nature of one's own national language', but, more importantly, 'the discovery of the *essentialness of this fact*' (DN 179/367; Bakhtin's emphasis, occluded in the English translation), that is, the recognition that this multiplicity represents not tragic Babel, but the only shape human history can take, while remaining human, then novelistic representation cannot reject 'social struggle', which by nature always has an ideological component, but must extract from it that moment which addresses what Bakhtin will sometimes call the 'ultimate questions'. No particular struggle can, in the Marxist sense, represent the interests of humanity as a whole, but viewed as a totality social struggle embodies the process of cultural creation itself. The task of the novel is to intervene in that struggle aesthetically: to push aside from it those moments of 'practical interestedness' (*zainteresovannost'*) which link social struggle to the limited horizons of 'life', while drawing out of it those moments which address the 'undecidable' question of the meaning and shape of modern life itself.

Authority can be brought down to earth only if we think of earthly life as a socio-historical process, that is, in a modern European manner; the truth of our intersubjective condition only emerges when we think of other people as social beings. *Pace* those for whom sociology is a vulgar excrescence on the Bakhtinian corpus, the theory of the novel claims that we can only populate the world with voices if we are willing to indulge sociologists and historicists. On what grounds? First, because it is the essence of modern social identities that they are self-consciously human artefacts, relying on no external principle—'great chains of being', analogies with nature, and so on—for their legitimation. Socio-ideological languages—the true heroes of the novel—float on the surface of social life, and can therefore move with the tide of history and participate in its making in a way that older, traditional identities cannot. Secondly, for the reason given above: according to Bakhtin, the unity and integrity of the individual depends on the ultimate unity of the historical culture in which he or she lives; if the continuous intersubjectivity which constitutes human culture does not, in the end, add up, or does not aim to add up, then individual lives are left stranded by their own earthly limits. 'Contradictions between individual wills and minds' cannot serve as the basis for dialogism; they must be 'immersed in social heteroglossia, reinterpreted through it' (DN 139/326) if the immediate ethico-political concerns of 'life' are to acquire historical form.

What is striking is that Bakhtin will not represent the modern social world as a struggle amongst individuals *à la* Adam Smith (or Social Darwinism), the simple reason being, that individuals, in the very strictest sense, can only be represented as culturally 'contingent', as inessential to the language they speak. To act 'as an individual' is therefore to disembody language, to approach it 'only *from inside*' (DN 99/286), to be trapped by the calculating experience of the *I-for-myself* and unable to take part in the give-and-take of actual intersubjectivity. And if language cannot provide the values which motivate action, then these motivations will take the form of what modern social theory has chosen to call 'interests', those stable passions which are not concerned with their own transformation. In 'Towards a Philosophy of the Act' Bakhtin declared that to be motivated by money or biological need was to be literally uncultured, and in the context of his later theory of the novel this means such motivations are beyond aesthetic representation, irredeemable because uninterested in the 'ultimate questions'.[33] Dialogism is first and foremost a commitment to those questions and to the knowledge that taking them seriously would drive you beyond the boundaries of individual selfhood and well-being. Not taking this step amounts to confessing a lack of interest in one's true historical situation. The Dostoevskian characters who disappoint Bakhtin

---

[33] See TPA 123/55: 'All the forces of responsible accomplishment pass into an autonomous sphere of culture, and the act torn from them descends to the level of an elementary biological and economic motivation, it loses all its ideal moments: this is the condition of civilization.'

are not, therefore, the nihilists with convictions, but those content to ride on the surface: 'Those for whom no truth is necessary (Luzhin, the Miusovs, the Karmazinovs, and others) do not participate in dialogue. But atheists and nihilists participate in this dialogue . . . Only such a *truth* shatters the monological plane. Lebeziatnikovs cannot shatter it' (Dos61, 374). The forward-driving interest of *homo œconomicus*, or other liberal models of the individual, remains monological, that is, aesthetically unrepresentable, because the desire to make money or to get ahead cannot express itself in the 'inner form' of a particular language: it expresses itself in whatever language suits it at the time. None of its acts have any particular meaning, because all of them have, if you like, the same meaning.

The movement from individual will to socio-ideological language is thus qualitative: a voice cannot emerge at the level of the individual not because the latter is too small, but because the points of view or cultural values which voices express depend upon a distinct linguistic expression. Interests, even very big ones (national or class, to take the obvious examples) are human passion in 'given' unhistorical form, orientated to 'life' rather than 'truth'. Of course, social life being what it is, groups often have other things on their mind besides their aesthetic representation, and act according to their interests rather than their values, despite the regrettable consequences for art. Therefore, for the plebeian who wants never to be fooled 'what is important is the actual, always interested use of this meaning and its expression by the speaker' (DN 212/401): while in theory interests and values may be distinct, in practice socio-ideological languages may involve some of each. To the ambiguity between the critical and utopian dimensions of heteroglossia one should add this tension between interests and values: when dialogism is critical, it unmasks interests, when it is prefigurative, it represents values. An ambiguity which according to Bakhtin's theory ought to find aesthetic expression in novels themselves: the language of social interests should appear object- or thing-like in the text; while only the language which embodies ideology can take the form of a social voice, moving in the stream of historical culture.

One decisive consequence of the above: Bakhtin's position has nothing to do with the liberalism with which it has so often and so sloppily been confused. At the centre of any liberal social philosophy lies belief in a realm of the private, protected from social intervention; at the centre of most liberal doctrine lies belief in the irreducibility, even the dignity, of 'interests' as motivating forces for action. But to be private within Bakhtin's world is to give up the only chance of dignity one has. For a language driven by something private could only be presented as an inert object, to which one could not respond, even given the most tolerant of dispositions. Desires which remain too close to life, too far from culture, renounce their historical aspirations, and while their bearers can man-oeuvre for position, they cannot engage in dialogical interaction, for the latter entails giving up one's claim to self-sufficiency. By endowing human desire with dialogical form, the novel refuses desire's claim to independence and rescues it for intersubjectivity.

DIALOGISM AS A VOCATION

Like many gifts, this gift of form comes with strings attached: in demonstrating the historical truth of a language the novel demonstrates its 'objective specificity and boundedness' as well. Socio-ideological languages express world-views which have historical meaning, but historical limits as well. Such voices sound very modern, and we are apt to think that what is modern about them is that there are lots of them, reflecting both fundamental social differentiation and an accompanying scepticism about the authority of any one world-view. But the double-voicedness which brings these languages to our attention is not a matter of accumulation or collection, but of the fundamental condition in which *any* modern voice must exist. A voice can appear, and ideology acquire stylistic flesh, only as stylization, parody, irony, or character; it can exist only on condition that there is an author present—a 'second voice'—to distance it. What appears in Bakhtin to be a sociological claim about modernity is also a philosophical one, about the nature of voices and the world-views they represent, not how many there are. One could say that, contrary to appearances, dialogism is about the distinction not between double-voiced discourse and single-voiced discourse, but between discourse in which there are voices and discourse where there is no voice at all.

The struggle Bakhtin describes with such passion is therefore not to listen to voices which are already out there, pieces of the world which the novel will attend to and nurture, but a distinctively modern struggle for voice itself. The second voice of dialogism is never heard and cannot be, for it is in actuality nothing but the form in which the first voice exists, when and if it reaches some kind of expression. Bakhtin is closer to Lukács than at first appears—double-voicedness is the objectivity of voice itself—with the difference that what Lukács regards as regrettable and accomplished fact Bakhtin treats as the prize yet to be won. This should make it clear to us, however, that the authorial second voice is not something which undermines the authority of already existing socio-ideological languages, as if it were a perspective from afar, but the very condition of their possibility and their value.

It is, in fact, only through such voices that there can be 'value' as such in a post-metaphysical world. Helmut Kuhn has noted that, with the death of metaphysics: 'The loss of status which the good suffers ultimately leads to an attempt by a substitute word to occupy its place. The notion of "value", imported from political economy, is the *caput mortuum* of this once living concept.'[34] Bakhtin does not, as I have argued above, regard modernity as mere disintegration, or as the death of value, but as a moment in which values themselves come down to earth and a more independent ethical experience becomes possible. In this respect he can be usefully compared to another neo-Kantian who believed in the possibility of distinctively modern values: Max Weber, whose essay 'Science as a Vocation' makes a parallel claim for the possibilities of a life both modern and cultured.[35] Weber, from whom much of the modern discourse on values is derived, sees in the possibility of a vocation a chance to live like a modern without surrendering oneself to the vulgar play of interests. In the case of scholarly life, vocation demands first of all submission to the specialized values of one's discipline.[36] Scholarly genius and 'personality' are available only to those with a sober sense of limits and a willingness to plough one's chosen intellectual field. The scholar unwilling to renounce global ambitions will end up, in Weber's view, not a hero but a dilettante, an unserious and frivolous intellectual. Instead of great synthesis, the modern world demands a level-headed heroism, which respects the specialized methods of the particular sciences and steers clear of all metaphysical speculation.

A substantial payoff, however, awaits the one who can live within these bounds. To the specialized scholar, science will represent a vocation, or to use an alternative translation of the German *Beruf*, a calling. It will exist not merely as a means of making a living, but as something of value in its own right, with an ethos rising above the mere calculation of benefits. Weber thinks one can live by common ideals and norms, rather than by individualizing self-interest, so long as the ideals are of the right size and shape. In short, vocation represents a modern style of culture in societies dominated by the market, a place where one can be responsible and where work can have moral value and justification, even if these values come from secular disciplines rather than cosmology. Like Bakhtin, Weber wards off the possibility of a society reduced to pure 'practical interestedness'

---

[34] Cited in Herbert Schnädelbach, *Philosophy in Germany, 1831–1933*, trans. Eric Matthews (Cambridge: Cambridge University Press, 1984), 163.

[35] On Weber's neo-Kantianism see Guy Oakes, *Weber and Rickert: Concept Formation in the Cultural Sciences* (Cambridge, Mass. and London: MIT Press, 1988).

[36] Max Weber, 'Science as a Vocation', in *From Max Weber*, ed. H. H. Gerth and C. Wright Mills (London: Routledge & Kegan Paul, 1991). On Weber's concept of a vocation see Perry Anderson, 'Max Weber and Ernest Gellner: Science, Politics, Enchantment', in *Zones of Engagement* (London: Verso, 1992).

or endless egoistic calculation by acknowledging the differentiated and historical character of modern ethical life. The very existence of value in this sense indicates the breach made by modernity in moral experience, for it presupposes the possibility of *choosing* among values and of a subject capable of making that choice.[37] The normative spheres represented by the sciences make possible an enlightened, *gesellschaftlich* form of moral experience and commitment, which doesn't need metaphysical presumptions to prop it up.

When Weber said science, however, he meant it. Although differentiated, Weberian culture only works in so far as the subject can lose itself in the larger 'objective' tasks of the discipline it has chosen. Weber's vocational culture is a historical culture: his ideal scholar participates in an openly structured sphere, where a continuing process of discovery and learning is built into the self-understanding of all participants and the form of the activity itself.[38] This tells us something else about modern values— that they are not revealed once and for all but elaborated and tested in human experience, and that the possibility of their radical transformation is built into our sense of what it means to adhere to them. That is the reason why it so important that the Bakhtinian 'voice' maintains contact with 'the language-stratifying forces of historical becoming' (DN 138/325) which orientate all dialogue to the future. 'The inner dialogicity of authentically prosaic discourse . . . cannot be essentially dramatized and dramatically consummated (authentically finished)' (DN 139/326) because the need for historical development is not an accidental, but a constitutive feature of modern culture. The double-voicedness of language, its three-dimensionality, is therefore not the cue for some generalized scepticism about all ideology, but the mark of 'the future, lodged in the negated present' (Sat., 15). This means, however, that the world-views of social groups, embodied in such languages, are expected to acquire a structure quite unlike the one they may wish for themselves, one not grounded on an exemplary past or a mythical and closed-off image of identity, but on an orientation towards the future. In a text from 1943 Bakhtin remarks that in the novel 'everything good is precisely beyond the world which is represented, in the future; in the world which is represented there is only the need for and expectation of this future' (Rhet., 63). The idea of a novelistic voice is inseparable from this expectation.

This returns us to our initial problem: the fact that the aesthetic of the 'unconsummated' novel appears as the exact antithesis of the aesthetic

[37] I am indebted to Patrizia Nanz for pointing this out to me.

[38] Pierce had put forward a similar theory of science when he associated the dynamic character of scientific knowledge with the very form of scientific research and scientific communities. See his 'The Scientific Attitude and Fallibilism', in *Philosophical Writings of Pierce* (New York: Dover, 1955), 42–59.

formulated in 'Author and Hero'. The 'open, inconclusive present' so fundamental to our sense of modernity was, in Bakhtin's earlier writing, precisely the problem which the aesthetic was called upon to solve. In the 1920s, the condition of modernity appeared to Bakhtin as simply the phenomenological form of experience in the register of the *I-for-myself*:

From within myself, in the value-meaning context of my life an object *stands over against* me as an object of my living (cognitive-ethical and practical) directedness; in this case the object is a moment of the unified and singular open event of being in which I, necessarily interested in its outcome, am a participant. From within my active participation in being the world is the horizon of my acting, deed-performing consciousness. I can orient myself in this world as an event, I can order its objective composition, only (remaining within myself) in cognitive, ethical and practico-technical categories (the good, the true and practically purposeful) and this conditions the visage of every object for me, its emotional-volitional tonality, its value, its meaning. From within my consciousness as it participates in being the world is an object of the deed, of the deed as thought, the deed as feeling, the deed as word, the deed as activity; its centre of gravity lies in the future, as that which is desired and that which ought to be, and not in the self-sufficient givenness of the object, its presence, its being-on-hand, its integrity, its already-actualizedness. My relation to every object of the horizon is never consummated, but set as a task, for the event of being as a whole is open; my position must change with every moment, I cannot linger or remain calm. (AH 92–3/97–8)

From within 'the unified and singular open event of being' the meaning of objects and actions is always cast ahead into the future, giving rise to an 'infinite discontentedness'. We are now in a position to unearth the historical presuppositions of an experience which Bakhtin had at first assumed could be explained by phenomenology and philosophical anthropology alone. In 'Discourse in the Novel' and the later lecture-turned-essay 'Epic and Novel' (1941), openness to the future separates the modern novel from all that precedes it. The epic and the authoritarian are defined by their reliance on an exemplary and thus distanced past, but with the novel 'time and the world become, for the first time, historical for artistic-ideological consciousness: they are revealed, albeit at first in a still unclear and confused way, as becoming, as an uninterrupted movement into a real future, as a unified all-embracing and unconsummated process' (EN 473/30). As in 'Author and Hero', 'every object of artistic representation loses its consummatedness', but in the later work this loss is a consequence of a wholly positive 'revolution in the hierarchy of times' (EN 472/30) which places the 'unfinished present' on the throne formerly reserved for the idealized past.

The pressure of the future on the present, the orientation of consciousness to a future which rules on the justice of acts and judgements, the emergence of 'history' as an all-embracing world process: these are the defining features of the 'time-consciousness of modernity' whose histori-cal roots in eighteenth-century Europe have been unearthed by Reinhart Koselleck amongst others.[39] In this context, the problematic experiences which Bakhtin summarily named the *I-for-myself* become a more recogniz-able starting-point for theoretical and historical research. For while we can dismiss as implausible Bakhtin's claim that the *I*'s crises were an inevitable consequence of human intersubjectivity, if we imagine the *I-for-myself* as the name for the late nineteenth- and twentieth-century European subject its difficulties sound rather familiar. The *I-for-myself* is perhaps as good a description as one could find for the modern and enlightened subject which, in the absence of the authority of kings, bishops, and sages, must generate and justify every new norm from its own resources. The excess of this subject above each and every given situation is the principle of its sovereignty: 'the *I-for-myself* will remain . . . in the act of seeing, feeling, thinking, and not in the object that is seen or felt. I cannot put all of myself into the object, for I exceed any object as the active subject of it' (AH 40/38). Trapped within 'life', having to justify its actions by reference to an endlessly receding future (the 'yet-to-be meaning', as Bakhtin calls it), unable to be satisfied with any particular historically given object or event, the *I-for-myself* experiences its own sovereignty as a cause for anxiety. It is the weakness of this particular historical form of lived experience which gives rise to the need for art and, as Habermas has argued, for philosophy: 'such a need is forced on philosophy as soon as modernity conceives itself historically, in other words, as soon as it becomes conscious of the dis-solution of the exemplary past, and of the necessity of creating all that is normative out of itself, as a historical problem'.[40]

When the subject itself becomes the source of justification, every value it establishes will eventually appear as no more than a temporary resting-place, a historical given liable to pass away into the mists of time. Bakhtin believed the problem lay in our refusal to see that the subject is always both an *I-for-myself* and an *other-for-me* and a consequent exaggeration of the first half of the equation at the expense of the second. But when he comes to describe how this confusion issues in the current crisis, he tellingly switches from the genre of philosophical anthropology to that of literary history. In the section of 'Author and Hero' entitled 'The Whole of the Hero as a Whole of Meaning' (AH 128–72/138–87), Bakhtin does not derive the *I-for-myself* from phenomenological reflection, but locates its emergence in a series of discrete cultural forms. And although Bakhtin *lists* these genres

---

[39] See the essays in Koselleck's *Futures Past*.
[40] Habermas, 'Modernity's Consciousness of Time and its Need for Self-Reassurance', 19–20.

rather than putting them in chronological order, it is not difficult to reconstruct a history of the *I-for-myself* and the *other-for-me* from the patchwork account he leaves us with. Thus the initial distinction between *other* and *I* can be glimpsed in the confrontation between classical (i.e. Greek) tragedy and monotheistic religion, the first standing for the power of objective authority beyond the self—the authority of the *other*—and the second for the *I*'s emerging powers of self-reflection. Classical tragedy's reliance on the authority of 'kin' is, in this historical account, challenged by the new Christian belief, which makes ethics both subject-centred and abstract: 'The ethical *I-for-myself* is kinless (the Christian felt himself to be kinless— the immediacy of heavenly fatherhood destroys the authoritativeness of earthly fatherhood)' (AH 165/179). The guilt at stake in classical tragedy is therefore a 'guilt of being', guilt as betrayal of existing positive authority, as opposed to the moral guilt, the 'guilt of meaning', which depends on standards generated through the subject's reflection on the divine. This fundamental historical opposition establishes the ground for the two genres which define, as it were, the limit cases of *otherness* and subjectivity— biography and so-called 'confessional self-accounting'. Biography follows in classical tragedy's wake, grounding itself in earthly historical values, that is, values maintained by the opinion of peers or descendants, but lacking any absolute or final justification. In 'confessional self-accounting', on the other hand, the attempt to find an absolute justification for any value from within the resources of subjectivity alone leads to a parallel endlessness, as the attempt to reflect on one's actions from the perspective of some absolute notion of the 'ought-to-be' climaxes in a spiral of self-objectification and 'pure valuational going-beyond oneself alien to any justified ending from within itself' (AH 133/143). Neither objective nor subjective values prove stable, which allows Bakhtin to wheel on the modern aesthetic work as the antidote to the complementary, but equally unhappy, destinies on offer to the modern individual.

But if the dialogized voice of the novel also lacks a 'justified ending', this implies that Bakhtin could not, in the end, solve the historical problem posed by modernity, and chose instead simply to endorse its relentless forward motion. A closer scrutiny of Bakhtin's work, however, reveals that he consistently distinguished between the 'historical becoming' which structured the world as we know it and the sheer endlessness of individualized 'life'. Throughout the mid-1920s Bakhtin was a member of a philosophical circle meeting regularly in Leningrad; notes from one of the participants have left us with a detailed account of a series of lectures on philosophy,[41] and the status of Kantian philosophy in particular, which

---

[41] These are the 'Lectures and Interventions by M. M. Bakhtin': for full details see the Bibliography, under 'Notes from the Philosophical Seminar, 1924–1925'.

Bakhtin delivered in 1924–25. The most striking feature of these lectures is the contrast drawn between the 'logic of the horizon' in which the modern subject is trapped, and the 'historical being' which only becomes accessible to a systematic philosophy orientated to science. In this context, the difference between sheer endlessness and historical being is the difference between history as experienced by an individual subject and history as the form of intersubjectivity itself, for which 'science' stands as the exemplar. What threatens the objectivity and security of this 'historical becoming' are those philosophies or pseudo-philosophies (the philosophy of life, as enunciated by Nietzsche and Bergson, for example) which are essentially no more than elaborations of the subjective experience of the horizon: 'Bodily-spiritual man everywhere wishes to subordinate philosophy to his own ends, to distort the axiomatic unconsummatedness of thought' (Lec., 238). Here—in a text which is either earlier than, or roughly simultaneous with, 'Author and Hero'—unconsummatedness is a value, but one which demands the displacement of the centrality of the subject, for 'the unity of consciousness is only the image of a unity of culture which, in principle, cannot be realized in a single consciousness' (Lec., 237).

Some readers may be surprised to hear that a writer so often hailed as the unswerving opponent of systematicity placed so much store by science and critical philosophy, but that aspect of Bakhtin's reputation owes more to the enthusiasms of his interpreters than to the sources.[42] According to the

---

[42] There are a few versions of the myth of Bakhtin's unsystematicity, but the most rigorous is surely Morson and Emerson's. In their *Mikhail Bakhtin: Creation of a Prosaics* they assign pride of place to a concept of 'prosaics' which they claim as an extrapolation from Bakhtin's usage. While they are right that Bakhtin distinguishes prosaic art and prosaic form from other kinds of art, they are wrong to imagine that prosaic art puts philosophy in its place rather than vice versa. They are able to contrast 'prosaics' to systematic thought in Bakhtin's work only by systematically ignoring the philosophical roots of his vocabulary and argument, and the intellectual-historical context of his work. This is, of course, a scholarly weakness, but it is intimately entangled with a political one: the utterly absurd belief that systematic philosophy is somehow of a piece with Stalinism. While I am not sure whether we would feel better or worse if we thought Stalin, Beria, Voroshilov, *et al.* were systematic thinkers, I am certain that notions like 'semiotic totalitarianism', which equate formal scientific thought with political repression, are little more than academic mud-slinging.

Of course, Morson and Emerson might have argued that they had not read Pumpiansky's notes of Bakhtin's lectures. But Emerson no longer has this excuse: in her recent *The First Hundred Years of Mikhail Bakhtin* (Princeton, NJ: Princeton University Press, 1997) she misreads Bakhtin's discussion of systematic philosophy completely, presumably because the evidence conflicts so radically with her earlier belief in Bakhtin's 'prosaic' mentality (p. 234 n. 35). Having announced the necessity of systematic philosophy, Bakhtin explains why unsystematic philosophy emerges as a historical fact (Lec., 238–9), and in the course of his argument provides three grounds for its 'persuasiveness' or 'convincingness' (*ubeditel'nost'*). Emerson, ignoring the initial demand for systematic philosophy, interprets this discussion as an attempt to *justify* unsystematic philosophy. Accordingly, she presents the three grounds as reasons why this philosophy is both 'plausible'

records we have of Bakhtin's participation in the philosophical seminar, while he was critical of both Kant and neo-Kantianism, he nevertheless thought they could only be criticized systematically: any other approach would be no more than an authoritarian extrapolation of one's immediate horizon—'The logic of the horizon is the source of unsystematic philosophy' (Lec., 238); 'philosophical discussion of systematic philosophy is possible only from within systematic philosophy itself' (Lec., 238).[43] Bakhtin was to retain his sense of identity as a philosopher, and his sense of philosophy as a 'strict science' rather than mere 'free intellectualism', until the end of his life, as recently published interviews have shown.[44] And this traditional neo-Kantian definition of the task and nature of philosophy involved more than a mere methodological preference, as can be gauged from an earlier programmatic statement made not by Bakhtin, but by the editors of the first issue of *Logos*, the joint Russian–German organ of neo-Kantianism published from 1910 to 1914 (from which Voloshinov and Medvedev would cite directly and Bakhtin without attribution).[45]

(which Bakhtin thinks it is, in the sense of being believable) and 'valid' (which Bakhtin thinks it is not—the word occurs nowhere in the passage in question).

At any rate, Bakhtin's enthusiasm for systematic philosophy was not something he left behind: even in the text of *Rabelais*, submitted for publication in the 1960s, Bakhtin refers to the 'strict scientific seriousness' of modern times as one of those forms of non-dogmatic seriousness which, like carnival, stands for freedom and opposes everything official. His description of this seriousness as 'problematic' and self-critical by its very nature makes clear that he is thinking of a line of philosophical and scientific thought which climaxes in neo-Kantianism (Rab., 133–4/122).

[43] Belief in the centrality of Kant hardly distinguishes Bakhtin, even among ostensible modernists. Walter Benjamin was also trained as a neo-Kantian philosopher and acted like one for a little while. His 'On the Programme for a Coming Philosophy', written in 1917–18, bears a striking resemblance to Bakhtin's first programmatic efforts, but is most striking for its opening affirmation: 'The central task of the coming philosophy will be to turn the deepest intimations it draws from our times and our expectation of a great future into knowledge by relating them to the Kantian system' (trans. Mark Ritter, in Gary Smith (ed.), *Benjamin: Philosophy, Aesthetics, History* (Chicago: University of Chicago Press, 1989), 1).

[44] See Bocharov, 'Ob odnom razgovore', 81. See also Ch. 1 n. 18 above. In the interview with Duvakin, which took place in 1973, Bakhtin insists at length on his identity as a philosopher. Speaking of his youth in Odessa:

Duvakin: You were more a philosopher than a philologist?
Bakhtin: More a philosopher than a philologist. And I have remained so until the present day. I am a philosopher. I am a thinker. (*Con.*, 42)

[45] The Russian edition of *Logos* (it was published simultaneously in Russian and German editions in Tübingen and Moscow) was edited by Sergei Hessen, Fedor Stepun, and E. K. Metner and had on its joint editorial board figures such as Husserl, Weber, F. F. Zelinsky (Bakhtin's ostensible classics tutor), Peter Struve, Nikolai Lossky, and Heinrich Rickert. In *Marxism and the Philosophy of Language* Voloshinov mentions articles from *Logos* by Georg Simmel and by the linguist Karl Vossler, as well as Husserl's 'Philosophy as a Strict Science' (*Marksizm i filosofiia iazyka: Osnovnye problemy sotsiologicheskogo metoda v nauke o iazyke* (Leningrad: Priboi, 1929). Recently a new version of *Logos* has begun publication in Moscow, although it is strongly orientated to phenomenology (Husserl and Heidegger) rather than neo-Kantianism.

Recognizing the dangers of the 'contemporary cultural disintegration' caused by the differentiation of spheres of life, the editors were nonetheless all too aware of the dangers posed by an irrational, subjective synthesis, such as they found in one of their main philosophical opponents, religious Slavophilism. In Slavophile thought the synthesis of spheres is drawn from life immediately, as an intuitive fact of inner life. 'But unity as the givenness of inner life is something completely different from unity as the projected task of theoretical thought.'[46] 'Held captive by life', Slavophilism provides a 'rational sanction for the rule of the irrational'; thus the act of synthesis becomes an act of despotism. Lest the political stakes be in doubt, the editors spelled it out: 'It is necessary to remember that just as the cultural state cannot exist without the inner freedom of its citizens, so authentic philosophical synthesis must unavoidably demand the full freedom of development of all these separate motifs, which only in totality constitute the face of authentic culture.'[47] Bakhtin is critical of the logic of the horizon because it identifies culture with the intuitive unity of an individual consciousness rather than the multiform cultural unity which only science and philosophy can deliver.

Bearing this in mind, it is entirely consistent that those who take the brunt of Bakhtin's criticism in the opening chapter of the Dostoevsky book are religious philosophers (Merezhkovsky, Shestov, Rozanov), who similarly want to reduce Dostoevsky's work to the elaboration of a truth grasped by a single consciousness: they wish to surrender the paradigmatic artist of modernity to the logic of the horizon. By contrast, Bakhtin will stand up, from the very beginning, for a conception of truth which acknowledges modernity in a manner strikingly close to Weber: 'As a subject I never know anything; the scholar ceases to be a scholar as soon as he becomes a sage, i.e. someone who wishes to create a *subjective* unity of consciousness' (Lec., 237). The sage thus stands at the head of that long line of authoritarian, pre-modern figures who will make the fatal mistake of identifying truth with their earthly person or their institution, imagining it as something grasped by the subject rather than unfolded in intersubjectivity. What will change in Bakhtin's account is not the problem, but the genre charged with guarding against this confusion. For at this early date it is up to philosophy and philosophers to defend the differentiated and historical character of modern culture against authoritarian illusion. Soon this task will be passed on to the literary form which is modern in its very essence and structure, a kinship Bakhtin acknowledged in the 1940s: 'All the [classical] genres are orientated to myth (the ultimate whole), the novel to philosophy (and science)' (StyN 138).

[46] 'From the editors', *Logos*, 1 (1910), 2.   [47] Ibid. 6.

The novel protects culture by keeping its eye fixed on heteroglossia; philosophy does so by continually interpreting science 'as a vocation', that is, as the exemplary instance of a culture orientated to the future rather than the past. But while we might assent to Bakhtin's claim that 'the orientation to science is an orientation to a system of judgements, a system in principle open and limitless' (Lec., 240), we tend to see in this open-endedness of judgement proof that science never reaches the objective and universal knowledge it claims as its goal (if we are good Popperians this permanent self-correction does not question the objectivity of science, but if we believe in the 'social construction of science' it is a riposte to the self-understanding of science itself). Bakhtin, however, takes from Marburg neo-Kantianism a wholly different interpretation of the fact of scientific progress. According to the neo-Kantian rereading of Kant, science elaborates all of its categories and all of its objects out of itself, leaving no room for a contribution from something external to experience (in Kant, the notorious thing-in-itself).[48] If all science is, as Hermann Cohen argued, of a piece with the a priori science of mathematics, then there is no question of comparing it with an external world, for it creates the objects and consistency of that world to begin with. The incompleteness of science therefore represents not a deficit in knowledge (for what, the neo-Kantian would ask, could possibly lie behind the screen of knowledge, but metaphysical things-in-themselves?), but the incompleteness, the 'problematic' character of reality itself. From the fact of scientific progress one should draw not epistemological conclusions, but ontological ones: reality is not something complete, it is something 'set as a task'.[49]

But not, one should stress, a task for the subject. The neo-Kantians had to identify objectivity with an a priori science precisely so that no one could trace the substance of scientific knowledge back to any kind of subjective (and therefore uncertain) experience. 'Objectivity (and reality) are given not in nature, not in consciousness, but in history and culture; objectivity and unbroken objectification in cultural labour' (Lec., 237) and this objectivity is—Bakhtin will use this exact word—*transgredient* to subjective consciousness, just as the author must be to do his aesthetic work. As soon as one identified science with the contents of a consciousness, it descended to the status of a reflection—whether adequate or not—of

---

[48] I am relying here principally on Klaus Christian Köhnke's account of Hermann Cohen's systematic philosophy in his *The Rise of Neo-Kantianism: German Academic Philosophy between Idealism and Positivism*, trans. R. J. Hollingdale (Cambridge: Cambridge University Press, 1991), ch. 3.

[49] Matvei Kagan describes history—conceived of as cultural labour—as 'the task of *overcoming the curse of the Fall*'. See his 'Kak vozmozhna istoriia?' [How is History Possible?], *Zapiski Orlovskogo gosudarstvennogo universiteta, seriia obshchestvennykh nauk*, 1 (Orel: Gosizdat Orlovskoe gubernevskoe otdelenie, 1921), 137.

something outside and beyond it ('nature'). Historical becoming only retains its objective character when it is conceived of as a process of cultural creation and labour which makes subjective experience possible.

But if scientific progress thereby retains a kind of permanent objectivity, the meaning of its development has radically altered. Once understood as one more form of 'unbroken objectification in cultural labour', science becomes less a matter of technical knowledge than of historical creation, and its own logic is subordinated to the general task of a culture aimed at the future. As argued in the Introduction, according to Bakhtin and Matvei Kagan, progress in science must lose its 'meaningless', objectivistic character and be reinscribed—by philosophy, of course—into a larger cultural narrative. Kagan, who had moved to Moscow by the time of Bakhtin's Kant lectures, but who had by then already left his philosophical mark on Bakhtin, argued that the European crisis of culture derived precisely from the dichotomy which a 'paganized' Christianity had established between the 'canonically sacred' on one hand, and the historical 'technically organized' sides of life—state, economy, science—on the other.[50] The consequence was science as an independent *force*, in the literal sense, which established historical change as movement without meaning or moral point. Re-establishing the 'sacredness of culture', to use Kagan's phrase, would entail, on the one hand, making science one more form of cultural creation, and, on the other, endowing the inert sphere of the sacred with a historical character.[51]

'Man lives not in nature, but in history': when Boris Pasternak placed this in the mouth of one of *Doctor Zhivago*'s many intellectuals, he paid implicit homage to his own days in Marburg.[52] Bakhtin regards living in history, however, not as the fate of humanity but as a challenge to it, a

[50] Kagan, 'Evreistvo v krizise kul'tury', 234.

[51] Ibid. 235. Some of Bakhtin's comments on Cohen and neo-Kantianism in the 1920s imply that to his mind they, too, were guilty of endowing culture and science with an objectivistic character. The charge of 'transcendental logicism' was levelled at the Marburgians from several different quarters in Russia; see S. Askol'dov, 'Vnutrennyi krizis transendental'nogo idealizma', *Voprosy filosofii i psikhologii*, 125 (1914), 781–98, and N. Lossky, *Vvedenie v filosofiiu*, vol. i (St Petersburg: Stasiulevich, 1911), 214–31.

[52] Boris Pasternak, *Doctor Zhivago*, trans. Max Hayward and Manya Harari (New York: Pantheon, 1958), 10. Pasternak has described the Marburg experience in his autobiographical *Safe Conduct: An Autobiography and Other Writings* (New York: New Directions, 1958), 31–78.

The belief that this was Kant's principal lesson was a central tenet of neo-Kantianism. Whether Kant had grasped the nature of his own achievement was less clear, at least to his Russian followers. In the inaugural issue of *Logos*, a lengthy exposition of neo-Kantian principles by B. Iakovenko credits Hegel with uncovering the truly historical nature of philosophy, but in a form distorted by Hegel's belief in the dialectical nature of philosophical progress. The neo-Kantians take over the idea of historically progressive knowledge but recast that progress in the form of a straight line. See B. Iakovenko, 'O teoreticheskoi filosofii Germana Kogena', *Logos*, 1 (1910), 199–249.

challenge which those who indulge themselves in 'poetic' and monological culture have refused to take up. To allow history to persist as the inevitability of change, without reason or justification, is to theoreticize or objectify it; to try to master it through the acquisition of earthly power or by acting as a member of an organization with world-historical ambitions is to treat it as the mere arena or tool of subjective ambitions. Living historically is therefore not a technical problem—a matter of power or effectiveness—but a willingness to stick tight to the 'ultimate questions', to the quest for a justified and, in that sense, redeemed life. It is the primacy of ethical reality which makes the world historical, and the subject who just lets things happen wants to deny this fact.

Ethical reality as the primary 'actual' reality, embodied for us moderns in social struggle and historical becoming, opposed to a theoretical and contemplative view of the real—this ought to sound rather familiar ('The chief defect of all hitherto existing materialism . . . is that the thing, reality, sensuousness is conceived only in the form of the *object or of contemplation*, but not as *sensuous human activity, practice*, not subjectively'[53]). And though Bakhtin blends his philosophical method with the historical facts rather less deftly than others, it is this combination which explains why the novel appears at once closer to the world than everyday discourse and yet an aestheticization of it. For the novel is supposed to escape the confusions of 'life' via a paradoxical double movement: on the one hand, it plunges us into the densely knit intersubjectivity of a functioning social world, where obligations, goals, conscience, and norms of response provide the texture of ethical life; on the other hand, it ascends to a disinterested apprehension of and engagement with the task of historical redemption. But does it take a philosopher or novelist to attain this level of apprehension? Bakhtin depends upon a 'struggle among socio-linguistic points of view' to make his vision of history persuasive, but he does his level best to disguise its modern sources. For the consciousness that one is acting historically, in a manner which transcends immediate interests and results, has been the historic birthright of modern social and political actors themselves (even Hegel acknowledged that the historical spirit coursed through Napoleon's veins, not his). Europe did not become a continent of self-interested individuals once divine right went to ground; it became a land of social and political movements, now aware that history was not only the element in which they worked but the fact which made their work possible. Bakhtin is afraid that these movements will remain mired in interest and earthly concerns, but they are the birthplace of the very socio-ideological languages he uses as evidence that ethical reality is alive and well. Which

[53] Karl Marx, 'Theses on Feuerbach', in *Early Writings*, trans. Rodney Livingstone and Gregor Benton (Harmondsworth: Penguin Books, 1975), 421.

is to say that the battle between local interest and historical disinterest is one which must be fought out within social and political causes themselves, not between these causes as a whole and the novelist/philosopher who sees them from on high.

The novel's struggle for 'voice' is thus a struggle for this kind of 'historical being'. It is the struggle for a language which gives the subject an entrance into history, an opportunity to transcend itself by means of language, and it is this ethical self-transcendence which endows all dialogism with its distanced and indirect style of expression. Voices which merely express the world-view of a single consciousness, without, as Bakhtin put it, quotation marks, are literally uncultured—mere cries, at several removes from the always incomplete task of making a social world. Only the voice which has been 'submerged in social heteroglossia and reinterpreted through it' participates in historical becoming, because only that voice is bound to the intersubjective interaction which 'makes history'. What Habermas calls 'strategic action'—dialogue where actors aim not at knowledge but at manipulation of the other—and Bakhtin calls 'rhetorical dialogue' can never, in this account, be truly historical, for it assumes an unchangeable solidity of subject positions (in actual language, of course, this is a matter of degree rather than ideal type):

Rhetoric, to the extent that it is something false, strives to call forth precisely fear or hope. This belongs to the essence of rhetorical discourse (these passions were emphasized particularly by ancient rhetoric). Art (authentic art) and knowledge, by contrast, strive to free us from these feelings. (Rhet., 63)

To the extent that it frees itself from the local calculations of success and failure (fear and hope), the voice can take part in the ethical reality which is always an element of language, but not always the dominant one.

THE AESTHETIC OF DEMOCRATIC LIFE

Of course, the novel cannot really escape the vicissitudes of 'life' and its partial interests altogether, for however worthy it may be, it is not the only genre on the block. Bakhtin, rather infamously, cannot explain why novelistic consciousness must put up with competition from a poetic-monologic culture at all, or what it is that impedes the formation of a modern and democratic intersubjectivity. Nevertheless, incarnations of an official culture which blocks access to history are a continual presence in his writing (in particularly explicit form from the 1930s onwards), working as a kind of empirical check on what otherwise would be a stirring but unworldly evocation of the promise of modernity. Though Bakhtin claims that 'we live, write and speak in a world of free and democratized language' (FPND 435/71), the very energy and necessity of his own project testifies that this is not so, not yet. But even if this ambiguity itself remains untheorized in Bakhtin's work, it is strikingly accurate. For while the early twentieth century may not have brought democracy to European politics and culture, it certainly brought a decisive change in the rules of the political game. After the First World War and the end of the *ancien régime* across Europe, however history was made, it was made in the name of the people. Democracy, no, but some kind of 'popular' mass politics, yes, and across the continent: this fact draws together the otherwise dissimilar phenomena of historical Communism, fascism, and bourgeois-liberal democracy. The struggle for a novelistic voice over rival language forms, in a modern world where heteroglossia reigns, describes at the level of culture a struggle between different kinds of popular politics.

Why describe this struggle at the level of culture, when it also involved explicit and violent political repression, battles over the organization of the state and its relation to civil society, and even civil war? Because these struggles were interwoven, and had to be, with a struggle over the meaning of democracy itself which, despite the pleading made for the pedigree of this or that variant, has remained ambiguous throughout the modern period. That is to say, democracy is not just a system or mechanism suited to agreed ends but involves philosophical and cultural questions as well: the claim that it involves only the functioning and legal requirements of limited political institutions reflects not the facts of the matter, but a specifically liberal-democratic world-view. Is the subject of democracy rights-bearing individuals or a people united culturally? How do these subjects relate to the history of their polity? What they should expect from political life itself? Not only shouldn't we rule these questions beyond the bounds of politics, but we can't, for strictly pragmatic reasons. For even when we don't ask them, the actual subjects of democracy do.

The concept of a dialogized, novelistic voice bears on these issues in four important respects. First, because it suggests that democracy entails not only symmetrical dialogues but asymmetrical ones as well. Where democracy is conceived of as liberal-democratic procedure, balance and equality amongst voices is the pre-eminent value. The intersubjectivity instanced by the novel is not, however, a symmetrical one, entailing in its very definition a functional distinction between author/novelist and hero. In this intersubjectivity the stake is representation rather than consensus or decision, and representation is an ineluctable, and not in the least regrettable, feature of modern democratic life. The concept of the novel suggests that representation is also a form of intersubjectivity and one for which the egalitarian norms of symmetrical intersubjectivities are not adequate.

In the second place, the concept of a novelized voice bears on the relationship between historical institutions and everyday consciousness in democracy. Even though dialogism describes a form of representation, Bakhtin insists that it is found both in a particular kind of printed literary work (the novel) and in the practice of ordinary language (the public square). One does not have to accede to Bakhtin's unconvincing populism to see that something important is at stake here. His mistake is not to confuse the everyday with the literary, but to assume that popular discourse produces a novelistic style *automatically*. Yet everyday language can surely develop just as literary language does, and perhaps it, too, must 'modernize' itself to acquire the style and voice appropriate to its democratic task. That is, while novelistic style is obviously a model for the public sphere, it must also embed itself in the structures of ordinary communication if the former is to have much point. Whereas Habermas has spoken of the need to rationalize, i.e. make rational, the life-world, we might speak of the need to 'novelize' it. Democracy has not only objective institutional prerequisites, but subjective ones as well.

Thirdly: in the world of the novel, democracy is a matter of knowledge and self-exposure rather than expression and conviction. The logic of democratic intersubjectivity includes an element of *risk* for all: there is no telling where things will go. This willingness to risk (Bakhtin describes it as openness to the future, faith in the possibility of the miraculous, the psychology of the threshold, and so on) is an ineluctable feature of the dialogized consciousness, which surrenders the security of simple self-expression as the price of historical engagement (Richard Sennett has described this experience as an 'engagement in worldly experience beyond one's control'[54]). Even in the most procedurally democratic conditions, public discourse can assume the character of an expression of already shared convictions, appearing to give vent to feelings and positions bound up with an existing cultural identity. Of course, in actual fact, the sense that public discourse only externalizes already existing sentiment may be an illusion, but part of the work of *populist* discourse has been to persuade, by means of a cathartic public expression, a group that this indeed is who they are and what they want. Bakhtin himself had first-hand experience of expressive popular politics, and the key to his critique is his identification of this expressive pathos with the ideal of a single consciousness. A democracy which is no more than a shared or agreed consciousness, or a commonly held, but 'consummated' culture, has already surrendered its intersubjective and experimental character, and with it, the future.

Finally, Bakhtin presents not just democratic life, but a democratic

---

[54] Richard Sennett, *The Fall of Public Man: On the Social Psychology of Capitalism* (New York: Vintage, 1976), 534.

world, as if democracy had not only political features, but phenomenological ones as well. Whereas an epic and monological form of culture is premissed on the distance between a valued past and the experienceable world of the present, 'experience, knowledge and practice (the future) define the novel' (EN 459/15). Just as science implies not only a certain understanding of the world but also a certain kind of relationship between the subjects who cooperatively elaborate it, so democracy implies not only a relationship between subjects but also a certain kind of world: historical, open-ended, contemporaneous, 'set as a task'. It matters to Bakhtin that 'a new, sober, artistically-prosaic novelistic image and a new critical scientific understanding, grounded in experience, were formed alongside one another, simultaneously' (EN 481/39) because a democracy which empowered individuals as subjects but did not render the world scientifically knowable—'open to the future'—would be pointless; indeed, to act morally or politically in such a world would be impossible. Conversely, the project of the official power is not merely to shut everyone else up, but to alter the phenomenological texture of the world itself, by giving time a non-historical, epic form. A scientific experience of the world and a democratic experience of the world are two aspects of a single phenomenon and, as well, of a single struggle.

These features of the novelistic voice derive from the fact that even when Bakhtin is discussing the sociology of dialogue and the novel, the redemptive intentions first evidenced in 'Author and Hero' are at work. Although the novel seems bound to political tasks—to dialogue, the unmasking of interests, and so on—it remains at bottom an aesthetic form. But by the 1930s it has become clear that the aesthetic is not the moment when history stops and one gazes with awe or satisfaction at the sublime or the beautiful, but the moment when history begins and one feels swept up in its forward movement. In linking intersubjectivity to this aesthetic of history, Bakhtin provides grist for a theory which links democracy with science rather than expression, with knowledge rather than interests, and with a collective future rather than the veneration of the past. But only grist: Bakhtin may have sought to restore ethical reality, but he never looked to politics to do it. In the 1920s it was a philosophy of intersubjectivity which was to do all the necessary work, and the implied symmetry between author and hero remained in the background. But a decade later the idea of dialogism effectively secularized all the older distinctions, and with this secularity philosophy ceded its privileged role to the novel. As the novel, rather than philosophy, becomes the privileged form of culture, intersubjectivity itself came, so to speak, down to earth. Bakhtin did not intend this; indeed, he seems to have resisted it. The logic of this unwilling transformation is the subject of our next chapter.

PART II

The Matter of History

CHAPTER THREE

Bakhtin Myths and Bakhtin History

For a long time we knew very little about Bakhtin's life. Thanks to the efforts of post-*glasnost* Bakhtin scholarship, we now know even less. For example:

1. *A simple matter of biographical fact.* For many years it was assumed that Bakhtin's father was from an old gentry family which had lost most of its land and wealth the generation before, and that the bank he worked at was one which Mikhail Bakhtin's grandfather had actually founded. Bakhtin personally related the story of how the land was lost and the bank was founded to Viktor Dmitrievich Duvakin, in the course of one of their discussions in 1973 (later published), informing Duvakin along the way that his great-great-grandfather had founded a cadet corps at the time of Catherine the Great (*Con.*, 17–20). Unfortunately, it appears that none of this can be true: S. S. Konkin's research in the Orel regional archive has revealed that there were no familial connections between the Bakhtins who interest us and the noble Bakhtins who founded a cadet corps and the like (in fact, the noble Bakhtin who founded the corps, far from being Bakhtin's great-great-grandfather, died childless), and that Mikhail's grandfather was a merchant hardly in a position to found a bank.[1] Where did the myth of noble origins come from? Its first public appearance was in a biographical note devoted to Bakhtin and published in 1973.[2] But the source for this part of the note turned out to be another biographical note, which had appeared in England many years before and had been devoted to the life of Mikhail's brother Nikolai, who had died there. It is, of course, odd that Nikolai Bakhtin should be so mistaken about his family origins

---

[1] Konkin first suggested this in his biography, but has gone into more detail in the following papers: 'Pora zakryt' vopros o rodoslovnoi M. M. Bakhtina', *Dialog Karnaval Khronotop*, 2 (1994), 119–23; 'Posleslovie k stat'e "Pora zakryt' vopros o rodoslovnoi M. M. Bakhtina"', *Dialog Karnaval Khronotop*, 3 (1994), 135–7; 'Esli obratit'sia k pervoistochnikam . . . (k rodoslovnoi M. M. Bakhtina)', [Proceedings of] The Seventh International Bakhtin Conference, Book II, 244–50.

[2] See, for the first mention of the story, V. Kozhinov and S. Konkin, 'Mikhail Mikhailovich Bakhtin: Kratkii ocherk zhizni i deiatel'nosti', in S. Konkin (ed.), *Problemy poetiki i istorii literatury* (Saransk: Mordovskii gosudarstvennyi universitet, 1973), 5. Kozhinov discusses his source for the story, with admirable openness, in Kozhinov, 'Kak pishut trudy', 110–11. Clark and Holquist, presumably also relying on Nikolai's biography as a source, present the same account (*Mikhail Bakhtin*, 16).

(assuming that it was Nikolai who initially provided the information and that he was, in fact, mistaken), but it is surely odder that Mikhail Bakhtin should repeat the mistake, for it can only mean that he used the biographical note devoted to him as a source for the creation of his own biography. When in a later interview Duvakin presses him on the information he has on his family's history, Bakhtin hints at the source of the myth—'I myself have nothing [no information], because I was not interested in this, but my brother was interested in it. He knew the genealogy . . .' (*Con.*, 219)—but seems happy enough to collude in it. It may have been indifference, or a desire not to rock the biographical boat, or may it have been Bakhtin willingly seizing an opportunity to trade in his petty-bourgeois origins for noble cultured ones (while the Russian people benefit from the fact that their name, *narod*, is also the word for 'nation', its petty-bourgeoisie suffer from the fact that their name—*meshchantsvo*—is also the word for philistinism)?[3] Either way, we have learned that Bakhtin's biography depends upon a network of sources, and that Bakhtin depended upon this network as much as his followers.

2. *A weightier issue—the fate of one of Bakhtin's texts.* One of the reasons we know, or knew, so little about Bakhtin is that so few of his texts were published near the time they were written. The casualty list, a striking compendium of what you might call spectacularly poor political luck, is worth enumerating. Having published a one-page philosophical piece in 1919, Bakhtin's next effort to make his philosophical project public is a long critique of Formalism, commissioned by the Soviet journal *Russkii sovremennik* (*The Russian Contemporary*) for publication in its fourth number in 1924. Before publication of that issue, the journal is shut down by the Party, and the text benefits from the gnawing criticism of mice until extracts are published in 1974. Leaving aside the so-called disputed texts for the moment, we can pass to *Problems of Dostoevsky's Art*, published shortly after its composition as history's minimal concession to normality. When it comes out in 1929, Bakhtin has already been arrested, along with part of the intelligentsia which might have formed a sympathetic audience, all in the first round-up of so-called rightist intellectuals in 1928–29. (The arrest makes possible two further publications—prefaces to works by Tolstoy, written at the invitation of his interrogators—but these are not so much

---

[3] Pan'kov, in a typically shrewd response to Konkin, has suggested that one can find in the interview itself indications that Bakhtin knew he was playing a game, and that Duvakin mischievously pushed it along. Pan'kov also mentions the conviction of friends that Bakhtin had a naturally aristocratic bearing and, discussing his motivations, suggests: 'it is possible that at certain periods in his life a substantial concept of the distance between a certain "elite" and the mass "mob" may have meant a great deal to him'; see his 'Predislovie k zapozdavshemu "Poslesloviiu . . ." S. S. Konkina', *Dialog Karnaval Khronotop*, 3 (1994), 133. At which point I should probably consider retitling this book.

independent compositions as extended pleas for mercy.) In the early 1930s Bakhtin publishes not his long essays on the novel, but a short piece on practices of collective farm accounting, reflecting his hardly chosen employment at the time. His article 'Satire', written on commission for the tenth volume of the Literary Encyclopedia just before the war, finds itself condemned to the filing cabinet of history when the project is abandoned later; it is published only in 1996.

This brings us to the most notorious absence in the Bakhtin archive—the great book on the *Bildungsroman* from the late 1930s, which would have capped Bakhtin's work on the novel and even provided us with his evaluation of socialist realism. The story is almost too tragic: the text is accepted for publication by the publishing house Sovetskii pisatel', but the copy lodged with the publisher is destroyed in a German bombing raid, while Bakhtin's own copy endures a slower inflammatory death: deprived of cigarette papers in the course of the war, Bakhtin himself smokes the manuscript of his great work, page by page.[4]

Correction: the story *is* too tragic. The legend regarding the fate of Bakhtin's second copy, which assured us that this most ascetic of scholars was nevertheless in equal measure casual as regards his texts and passionate about one of life's more suspect pleasures, always suffered from the excessive meaningfulness of myth. But according to the most recent editorial information, the myth of the smoking copy only distracts us from a more fundamental illusion: the belief that this text existed in the first place. There is plenty of material in note form, there is a plan, there are letters to the publisher—but no evidence that a book on the *Bildungsroman* was ever completed or sent to press.[5]

3. *Bakhtin's legendary erudition.* Every reader of translated Bakhtin is familiar with the gasps of editorial awe and the extensive notes to obscure literary figures which accompany his works. Bakhtin was not merely well read: he had mastered the literature of modern Europe in several languages and had a knowledge of classical and medieval sources so deep, we require the help of experts merely to identify them. Some have ascribed his profound knowledge of classical sources to his work at university, where, as the story goes, he studied with the Polish classicist and, perhaps more interestingly, Nietzschean F. F. Zelinsky (except that we do not know whether

---

[4] This by now legendary story is recounted in detail by V. Kozhinov in 'Kak pishut trudy', 113.

[5] E-mail to the author from Brian Poole, 13 Aug. 1997. According to Poole, who is the editor responsible for the volume of the Russian *Collected Works* devoted to the *Bildungsroman* text, the relevant materials consist of 716 manuscript pages (half of which became 'Forms of Time and of the Chronotope in the Novel'), a sixty-page plan of the work sent to the publisher in 1937, a draft of a letter to the publisher from 1937, and several notebooks 'which suggest that work continued from 1937 onward'.

Bakhtin did go to university—see below). But careful examination of Bakhtin's writings in the 1930s has revealed a dependence on secondary literature in German which explains how he could apparently be familiar with so much while having direct access to so little.[6] The German literature on classical, medieval, and Renaissance writing on which Bakhtin took extensive notes accounts for much of his field of reference—which is to say that Bakhtin may have not read many of the texts he confidently slots into his philosophy. Brian Poole's shrewd detective work has revealed, for example, that several pages of *Rabelais and His World* are lifted word-for-word from Ernst Cassirer's *The Individual and the Cosmos in Renaissance Philosophy*.[7] Bakhtin may well have read the works of Pompanazzi, Ficino, and Pico della Mirandola discussed in *Rabelais*, but he did not have to, for everything he has to say about them there comes directly from this secondary source.

These myths are not myths generated by Soviet censorship, but myths generated in the course of its demise. Indirectly, therefore, they reveal to us the founding myth of Bakhtin scholarship itself—that all that stands between us and Bakhtin is the heavy hand of official politics and Stalinist repression. Those reclaiming Bakhtin's work rightly believed they were undoing the distortions of the past. But scholarship can never afford to forget that history is not only the storm that blows it off course, but also the wind that fills its sails. And the winds of change which propelled Bakhtin into the public world were not all blowing in the same direction. When Bakhtin was initially 'rehabilitated' in the early 1960s, a complete record of his life and work did not emerge—no such thing existed. The texts and their relevant context had literally to be reconstructed, and this process was no more immune to the pressures of social and historical life than the texts themselves. When Bakhtin claimed that 'every word tastes of the context and contexts in which it has lived its socially tensed life' (DN 106/293) he forgot to add that the definition of a context, a biography, an intellectual source, is a historical act, too, rent by social tensions and struggles. Because he was not part of the public culture until the end of his life, the works and life of Bakhtin have come to us not in the form of an inheritance, carefully preserved and lovingly handed on to the next

[6] The editors of the *Collected Works* note that Bakhtin's transliteration of Greek names reflects not ordinary practice for Greek–Russian transliteration, but the system used by Erasmus for putting Greek into Latin. There follows a guarded comment: 'It is possible that this reflects the influence of German sources—for which there is a clear preference—and similarly the wish to regulate in the proper manner the transliteration of Greek words into scholarly language . . .' (*SS5*, 407 n. 1).

[7] Brian Poole, 'Bakhtin and Cassirer: The Philosophical Origins of Bakhtin's Carnival Messianism', *South Atlantic Quarterly*, 97: 3/4 (1998), 542–4.

generation, but as something forcefully disinterred in the midst of an argument amongst competing heirs.

We are thus denied the usual advantages of a relative scholarly consensus: the complete and reliable editions of relevant texts, the authoritative commentary and discussion of sources, and the associated material such as letters, notes, and drafts, which guide the critic in his or her journey through past conflict. The belated and contorted history of Bakhtin publication has bequeathed to us not a full record of work but an *œuvre* full of sidelong glances. No piece of biographical information, no letter, no edition or reminiscence appears which does not play a part in a campaign for Bakhtin's reputation, however purely intentioned the provider or scholar. So all-encompassing are the splits in the interpreting community that even a relatively neutral assembling of biographical fact has proved impossible; the documentary materials, reproduced correspondence, new editions, and apocrypha which appear only seemingly at random in Russian bookshops or Russian conversation are evidence that for Bakhtin at least, the historical weather is still pretty rough.[8] Caryl Emerson has charted the weather in detail in her recent *The First Hundred Years of Mikhail Bakhtin*; in what follows I want to focus on the link between the myths which displace Bakhtin's own history and the attempt to eradicate any sense of history itself from his work.

When in 1961 three young literary scholars boarded a train to Saransk to visit the author of a book on Dostoevsky from 1929, they could not have known that forty years of texts were awaiting their first publication.[9] *Problems of Dostoevsky's Art* had effectively served as a message in a bottle, revealing to those who followed it to its source an entire body of work which had, in effect, been buried. Political circumstances, more precisely the attempt at cultural and political liberalization which had taken place under Khrushchev's leadership, made the publication of previously

---

[8] A characteristic example: in 1973 Kozhinov and Konkin's 'Mikhail Mikhailovich Bakhtin: Kratkii ocherk' appeared in one of the first of many Russian collections devoted to Bakhtin. This first effort at biography, which was self-consciously brief and bare-boned, was nevertheless attacked vociferously in the émigré journal *Sintaksis* (Maiia Kaganskaia, 'Shutovskoi khorovod', *Sintaksis*, 12 (1984), 145–8) for skating over Bakhtin's arrest and enforced exile and the reasons for his move to Nevel' in 1918 (there was little food to be had in Petrograd). However, even the union of Kozhinov and Konkin was apparently under strain. When Konkin together with L. S. Konkina published their book-length biography (*Mikhail Bakhtin: Stranitsy zhizni i tvorchestva* (Saransk: Mordovskoe knizhnoe izdatel'stvo, 1993)), in which Bakhtin's Muscovite admirers were accused of leading him astray, Kozhinov went into print to attack Konkin and his account of Bakhtin's time in Saransk (where Konkin had taught). In the course of his attack Kozhinov let it be known that even in 1973 he had fallen out with Konkin and had only left his name on the biographical sketch to keep the peace. See V. V. Kozhinov, 'Ob odnom "obstoiatel'stve" zhizni M. M. Bakhtina', *Dialog Karnaval Khronotop*, 1 (1995), 151–60.

[9] Kozhinov has described his discovery that Bakhtin was living and the first trip to meet him in '"Tak eto bylo . . ."', *Don*, 10 (1988), 156, and in 'Kak pishut trudy', 112–13.

condemned or suppressed work possible, but the rehabilitation would take initiative, and that was to come not from Bakhtin himself or his academic peers, but from Vadim Kozhinov and Sergei Bocharov, two of the three who had made the first pilgrimage. Clearly moved by their meeting, Kozhinov and Bocharov fought a by now thoroughly documented campaign for a new edition of the book which first brought them to Bakhtin.[10] Their protracted struggle with the apparatus of Soviet publishing was successful, but it could not, of course, erase the history which lay between them and 1929. And as a result, what emerged from their heroic efforts in 1963 was, on the one hand, a substantially *revised* and enlarged text, *Problems of Dostoesky's Poetics*, and, on the other, the first of many mythologies.

This mythology concerned the rediscovery of Bakhtin himself. For while no one could deny the central role played by Bocharov and Kozhinov, they were not the Robinson Crusoes they were made out to be in later accounts. This is not only because Bakhtin was well known and much respected in Saransk itself, where he had a substantial academic position, but also because a revised edition of the Dostoevsky book had been set in motion before the legendary pilgrimage took place and without the struggles necessary for the Russian one. Did any reader notice the careful editorial claim that the revisions embodied in the notes called 'Towards a Reworking of the Dostoevsky Book' were written '*immediately preceding*' (my emphasis) Bakhtin's work on a new Russian edition?[11] Who doubted Kozhinov's strategic wisdom when he recalled that, during his campaign for the book's republication, he asked the now eminent Italian Slavist Vittorio Strada if he would, as a favour, approach Bakhtin with an offer to republish *Problems of Dostoevsky's Art* in Italy, in order to put pressure on the Soviet establishment (who would be afraid of a repeat of the *Zhivago* debacle, when Pasternak's masterpiece was first published abroad, by Feltrinelli, and went on to win the Nobel Prize)?[12] No one doubted that Bakhtin had been rediscovered by a younger, post-Stalin generation of Russian intellectuals, but they should have. For Strada has

[10] Kozhinov has described his role in the republication of *Dostoevsky* and the first publication of *Rabelais* in some detail. See his '"Tak eto bylo . . ."', 156–9; 'Kak pishut trudy', 118–20; and '"Ia prosto blagodariu svoiu sud'bu . . ."', *Dialog Karnaval Khronotop*, 1 (1994), 104–10.

[11] Preliminary notes to the text 'K pererabotke knigi o Dostoevskom', *Estetika slovesnogo tvorchestva*, 2nd edn. ed. S. G. Bocharov (Moscow: Isskustvo, 1986), 424.

[12] The most complete account of this strategic manoeuvre is found in Kozhinov, '"Tak eto bylo . . ."', 157–8, where he describes the conversation in which he apparently first told Strada about Bakhtin's book and persuaded him to help; it is briefly referred to in 'Bakhtin i ego chitateli: Razmyshleniia i otchasti vospominaniia', *Dialog Karnaval Khronotop*, 2–3 (1993), 121, and, perhaps most interestingly, in footnotes to some Bakhtin letters from 1961–65, where Kozhinov explains that Bakhtin's references to an Italian edition of the Dostoevsky all relate to this strategic manoeuvring ('Pis'ma M. M. Bakhtina', *Literaturnaia ucheba*, 5–6 (1992), 145 n.).

come forward with documents that show that he had written to Bakhtin
in early 1961, before he had ever met Kozhinov, with an entirely sincere
and independent offer to republish the Dostoevsky book as an introduction
to an Italian edition of Dostoevsky's works, and his version of events has
been confirmed by the editors of the new Russian Academy of Sciences
Collected Works.[13] The offer was accepted, a revised text was written, permission from the relevant authorities was granted, and a finished manuscript delivered to the Italian publisher Einaudi through Strada by the
summer of 1962, without any public campaign. Work on a Russian edition began only in March 1962, and the revision notes for this text have
only just been published in Russian.[14] It was an Italian Communist (as
Strada was at the time) who provided Bakhtin with the first possibility of
re-entry into public life, a fact which no doubt embarrasses the present
generation of Bakhtin's Russian devotees on two counts.

To publish Bakhtin in Russian, however, required a struggle, and
Kozhinov and Bocharov therefore had to mount a sustained public campaign for *Problems of Dostoevsky's Poetics* in 1963 and for a reworked version
of Bakhtin's dissertation on Rabelais, which came out as *The Art of François
Rabelais and the Popular Culture of the Middle Ages and the Renaissance* in
1965.[15] In retrospect these struggles, however thorny and protracted, appear
relatively lucid: the opposing sides were well defined, the stakes the
apparently simple act of publication. Public and private resistance to the
books came from entrenched elements of the literary apparatus, and in the
name of the traditional emphases of Soviet Marxism;[16] the revisions
required by the censors were thoroughly predictable (religious and 'idealist' philosophical references were to be deleted: for example, the Husserlian
term 'intention' was deleted from the republication of *Dostoevsky*[17]).

[13] Vittorio Strada, Letter to the Editors (with supporting documents appended), in *Bakhtinskii
sbornik*, vol. iii (Moscow: Labirint, 1997), 373–9; S. G. Bocharov and L. A. Gogotishvili, editorial commentary to '1961 god. Zametki', *SS5*, 650–1.

[14] The editors of the *Collected Works* point out that this explains why Bakhtin refers to his
Dostoevsky book as an 'introductory article' in 'Notes from 1961' (*SS5*, 354/295). There are thus
two extant sets of revision notes relating to the Italian edition ('Notes from 1961' and
'Dostoevsky 1961') and one relating to the Russian edition ('Notes from 1962–63'), although this
will doubtless change when the volume of the *Collected Works* containing *Problems of Dostoevsky's
Poetics* and its preparatory materials is published.

[15] The editor of the Rabelais book, S. L. Leibovich, has described the manoeuvres leading
to its publication in 'Tridtsat' let spustia: Redaktor "Rabelais" S. L. Leibovich vspominaet o
podgotovke knigi k izdaniiu', *Dialog Karnaval Khronotop*, 1 (1997), 140–86.

[16] See, e.g. the hostile review of the Dostoevsky text upon its republication in 1963 by A.
Dymshits, 'Monologi i dialogi', *Literaturnaia gazeta*, 82, 11 July 1964, which accuses it of formalist
tendencies.

[17] The editors of Bakhtin's revision notes claim that the publisher required the deletion of this
term in order to make the text more 'popular' (*SS5*, 666 n. 89). Kozhinov has claimed that
Bakhtin's willingness to delete a term so 'characteristic of neo-Kantianism' from the revised text
indicates how distant from that tradition he had become ('Bakhtin v zhivom dialoge', in *Besedy*

Younger scholars, spurred by the liberalizing 1960s, were enlisting the support of elder figures, in fact a very unlikely group ranging from the Formalist survivor Viktor Shklovsky to Marxists such as Fridlender and Ermilov, for the publication of texts which, whatever their relation to Soviet Marxism, were of undeniably great scholarly significance.

But it was the simplicity of the stakes which made the sides seem clear-cut. Once the texts were out in the open, their own historical manoeuvres and evasions made themselves felt in dramatically contrasting interpretations. The unified front supporting publication began to fall apart, as it immediately became clear that Bakhtin had not married Formalism, Marxism, and idealist philosophy, but had merely housed them in the same quarters, so that old arguments could be conducted once again in an arena where relations were more intimate and more ambiguous. The heirs to Formalism struck the first solid blow. In 1970, Viacheslav Ivanov delivered the paper 'The Significance of M. M. Bakhtin's Ideas on Sign, Utterance and Dialogue for Modern Semiotics'[18] at a conference at Moscow State University in honour of Bakhtin's seventy-fifth birthday, in which he claimed him as a brilliant forerunner of the undeniably modern and technically impressive semiotics of the Moscow–Tartu school. For the latter, Bakhtin's literary-theoretical achievements represented nothing less than a refinement of sign theory, which could easily be accommodated in the narrative of progress which characterized a scientific discipline like semiotic analysis. It was this paper, rather than any written by anti-Formalist opponents, which was soon translated into English, a sign of the semioticians' great advantage—international prestige and clout. Ivanov would continue to translate Bakhtin's concepts into a purely scientific idiom—a project which attained an apogee of sorts in a recent attempt at melding the theory of carnival with neuropsychology—while other members of the semiotic school interpreted Bakhtin as a particularly gifted interpreter of the semiotics of culture, and assimilated his stylistic insights accordingly.[19]

By that time, however, it had become clear that the struggle over Bakhtin would continue as a division of *positive* opinion. At issue was no

V. D. Duvakina s M. M. Bakhtinym, ed. V. B. Kuznetsova, M. B. Radzishevkaia, and V. F. Teider (Moscow: Progress, 1996), 280). Given the term's actual, phenomenological provenance, this is a strange claim.

[18] V. V. Ivanov, 'Znachenie idei M. M. Bakhtina o znake, vyskazyvanii i dialoge dlia sovremennoi semiotiki', *Trudy po znakovym sistemam*, 6 (Tartu: Tartu gosudarstvennyi universitet, 1973), 5–45; trans. into English in Henryk Baran (ed.), *Structuralism and Semiotics* (White Plains, NY: International Arts and Sciences Press, 1976), 186–243.

[19] Boris Uspensky, for example, would integrate Bakhtin's idea of polyphony into a sophisticated theory of point of view, without paying particular attention to the philosophical stakes; see his *A Poetics of Composition: The Structure of the Artistic Text and Typology of a Compositional Form*, trans. Valentina Zavarin and Susan Wittig (Berkeley, Ca.: University of California Press, 1973), 10–11.

longer the significance of Bakhtin's work, but its essential shape and emphasis. As Bakhtin's work remained for the most part unpublished, in privately held archives (Kozhinov and Bocharov would eventually become the executors of Bakhtin's literary estate), one could endow the *œuvre* with shape in the most direct and literal way—by determining what was published, in what forum, and with what gloss. Although interpretation is traditionally a second-order process—a discourse on a corpus of texts already in public view—in Bakhtin's case it became part of the first-order business of editing the texts themselves, that is, *writing them*, for publication. After *Rabelais* virtually every remaining text existed in archival form alone, and from these the first selected (but by whom? and after what negotiations or struggles?—we do not know) to go into print was a series of essays and lectures on the novel drawn from the period 1934–41 (published in English in the collection *The Dialogic Imagination*) and, the odd man out, the critique of Formalism destined for, but failing, publication in 1924.[20] The former essays appeared in the Gorky Institute's house journal *Voprosy literatury*, the latter in the yearbook *Kontekst*, and they were published together as a collection, *Voprosy literatury i estetiki* (*Questions of Literature and Aesthetics*), with virtually no editorial apparatus and only notional dates of composition, in 1975, the year of Bakhtin's death. The publication of texts on the novel may have been the logical next step after books on Rabelais and Dostoevsky, but they happily confirmed Bakhtin's status as a literary critic with an axe to grind about Formalist theories of language. The anti-Formalist leitmotif draws 'The Problem of Content, Material and Form' into the body of the collection, for as the only text from the 1920s, and the only philosophical text in the collection, it otherwise stands out. It was hardly surprising that this was the text which first appeared in *Kontekst*, a periodical regarded by many as a continuous riposte to the all too successful semiotics practised by Ivanov, Boris Uspensky, and Iuri Lotman.[21] By selective publication, the one-time critic of Formalism could serve as a prestigious 'humanist' opponent of Formalism's semiotic progeny.[22]

---

[20] The publication details were as follows: an extract from 'From the Prehistory of Novelistic Discourse' entitled 'Slovo v romane', *Voprosy literatury*, 8 (1965), 84–90; 'Epic and Novel', *Voprosy literatury*, 1 (1970), 95–122; an extract from 'Discourse in the Novel', entitled 'Slovo v poezii i v proze', *Voprosy literatury*, 6 (1972), 54–86; an extract from 'Forms of Time and of the Chronotope' entitled 'Vremia i prostranstvo v romane', *Voprosy literatury*, 3 (1974), 133–79; an extract from 'The Problem of Content. . .' entitled 'K estetike slova', *Kontekst 1973* (Moscow, 1974), 258–80.

[21] For an account of the battles over Tartu–Moscow semiotics see Peter Seyffert, *Soviet Literary Structuralism: Background—Debate—Issues* (Columbus, Oh.: Slavica, 1985), 193–357.

[22] That the unity of this collection lay in its polemical force was borne out by its fate in English translation, where the stakes were not as high. In his introduction to *The Dialogic Imagination* Michael Holquist points out that 'The Problem of Content, Material and Form' doesn't fit the

For those deaf to the leitmotif, a chorus was added. In his review of the volume, the eminent Soviet critic Georgy Fridlender articulated the polemical theme: 'And now, following the appearance of the book *Questions of Literature and Aesthetics*, we can see that this struggle [with Formalism] was not something contingent for Bakhtin: it was inseparably bound up with the fundamental task and pathos of this scholar's life . . . '.[23] The neo-Kantian angle of this struggle, and the ambiguous relationship it supposed between science and philosophy, did not come into the picture: the book's virtues would 'guarantee it the greatest significance for the struggle with the formalism and antihistoricism of bourgeois literary scholarship'.[24] One need only add that for many in the West its translation, *The Dialogic Imagination*, continues to play this role.[25]

Across the page from Fridlender's review is a second one, which, though apparently presenting one more perspective, claims to offer us the truth of them all. In 'The Personality and Talent of a Scholar' Sergei Averinstev opposes not Fridlender's arguments but the fact that Fridlender argues: 'The essence of Bakhtin's position always consisted not of "against" but of "for", not of contention or of rejection but of affirmation, of defence of the rights of the whole in the face of the unjustified pretensions of the part.'[26] To 'drag Bakhtin into the dualism of arguments between circles' is to miss the humanistic task which Bakhtin set himself, and which can only be accomplished as philosophy. That task is the defence of the object of humanistic thought itself—'expressive and speaking being'—and it requires not ordinary scholarship but 'thinkers' whose philosophical wisdom puts them in touch with the free and dialogical being over which scientific circles ride roughshod. Bakhtin as philosopher of the humanities: is this not one more position, and quite a defensible one? It might be, but it encapsulates the logic which lies at the bottom of the Bakhtin phenomenon as a whole—the identification of his insight with his person. 'He is perceived not only as one who solves particular scientific tasks, who reaches such

essays on the novel, and has accordingly been omitted from the translated collection. It was finally to appear in 1991 in more appropriate company, with the other 1920s philosophical text on aesthetics, 'Author and Hero in Aesthetic Activity'.

[23] G. Fridlender, 'Real'noe soderzhanie poiska', *Literaturnoe obozrenie*, 10 (1976), 62.

[24] Ibid. 64.

[25] The appearance of Bakhtin in the 'English-speaking West' (for want of a better term) has its own logic. Although *Rabelais* had been translated into English in 1968, and *Problems of Dostoevsky's Poetics* in 1973, it was only in 1981—when *The Dialogic Imagination* appeared—that conditions were ripe for the 'Bakhtin industry' to take off. If intellectual quality were the only issue, would I have been able to buy *Rabelais* at an MIT Press remainder sale for a single dollar? Probably not. What had happened in the interval between 1968 and 1981 was 'literary theory', a movement masquerading in the neutral colours of an intellectual discipline, which at that time meant structuralism and so-called 'post-structuralism'. In 1981 Bakhtin appeared as the literary critic who had made the linguistic turn without losing his humanist baggage on the way.

[26] Sergei Averintsev, 'Lichnost' i talant uchenogo', *Literaturnoe obozrenie*, 10 (1976), 59.

and such conclusions, but above all as a personality.'[27] As a philosophical personality, Bakhtin cannot participate in the anonymity of science, which demands a strict separation between the value of the person and the value of discovery or scientific knowledge. A philosophy which preaches the value of the person cannot maintain this distance without contradiction. This, of course, explains why Bakhtin is, whatever the various positions, a cult figure for all of them, in a quite literal sense of the term, his value transcending the rightness or wrongness of any particular argument. If Bakhtin has gradually appeared more and more in the person of the philosopher and less and less in that of the literary critic it is in part because his fame depends upon this identity.[28]

Averinstev does not promote Bakhtin as a religious philosopher, as a number of Russian commentators—with varying degrees of Russian Orthodox chauvinism—were to do later. But he does not need to; for in drawing a line in the sand between philosophy and science, he more or less admits that Bakhtin must be a pre-scientific philosopher, which does not leave much room for doubt. Whatever the substance of his ethical arguments, Bakhtin's identity as a metaphysician who preaches and lives an ethical doctrine endows even his secular arguments with a prophetic and occasionally saintly air.[29] But once Bakhtin is transformed into an otherworldy man preaching an otherworldy doctrine, it is no longer possible to see him as interesting and thoughtful in a more sober, scientific spirit—he is already weighed down with the burden of being exemplary.

In 1979 the posthumous publication of the philosophically inclined texts of the early 1920s and the postwar period, with a markedly more thorough editorial apparatus (the extensive notes were prepared by Averintsev and Bocharov), in the collection *Estetika slovesnogo tvorchestva* (*The Aesthetics of Verbal Creation*—Bakhtin's own description of one of his projects in 1921), provided this philosophical school with more in the way of essential ammunition. Flanked by philosophical work before and after, the essays on

---

[27] Ibid. 58.

[28] For example, Vadim Kozhinov, centrally responsible for Bakhtin's rehabilitation, has nearly always limited himself to an interest in Bakhtin's literary-critical and cultural ideas. Nonetheless, he will describe Bakhtin in the following tones: 'I think that Mikhail Mikhailovich is a very great figure. Above all because this person was a representative of that essentially heroic type in Russian culture, to which there is none comparable in the world, especially in the twentieth century . . . And it seems to me that this heroism enters into the concept of culture as a constituent part of it, that is, it raises it still higher, because culture, if you like, is intrinsically valuable . . . In what sense? It is intrinsically valuable within humanity and in the end it is a kind of exit in a higher sense out of the narrow limits of the temporal, the spatial, the everyday, even the historical boundedness of the individual.' Kozhinov, 'Kak pishut trudy', 111–12.

[29] For a contrasting view of philosophy, see Jürgen Habermas, 'Themes in Postmetaphysical Thinking', in *Postmetaphysical Thinking*, trans. William Mark Hohengarten (Cambridge: Polity Press, 1992), 28–53, and 'Philosophy as Stand-In and Interpreter', in *Moral Consciousness and Communicative Action*, 1–20.

the novel took on the appearance of a mid-course diversion, and Bakhtin of a writer who strays—either by intention or force of circumstance—from the high road of philosophy in his middle years, only to return to its reassuring monumentality at the end of his life.[30] In the 1980s, therefore, the scene was dominated by the publication of yet more fragments of the earliest philosophical writing. Earlier sections of Bakhtin's grand project for a 'first philosophy' came out in a piecemeal manner which could seem ordinary only in pre-perestroika Russia. A collection of largely already published work in 1986 included a new twenty-five-page fragment of 'Author and Hero'; in 1986 'The Architectonics of the Act', a heavily abridged extract from what appeared to be the first philosophy's introductory section, was published; in 1988 a version of the same text twice as long (although still abridged by the requirements of the censor) was published as 'Towards a Philosophy of the Act'.[31] As Soviet power waned, the trickle of material being published grew, so that by the early 1990s new texts, usually in the form of lecture notes or notebook materials, were coming out steadily in journals or in the collections of articles which were now cropping up at the rate of two or three a year. A steady stream, and then the dam finally broke: when the Soviet Union collapsed as a state, it became possible for the Gorky Institute to embark upon a proper scholarly edition of Bakhtin's Collected Works, a project which promised to put

[30] The Anglo-American assimilation of Bakhtin has mirrored the Soviet/Russian one. Initially, Bakhtin's reputation, and the reputation of the circle, was as a literary theorist and a semiotician. The translation of Voloshinov's *Marxism and the Philosophy of Language* in 1973 by Ladislav Matejka and I. R. Titunik was accompanied by an afterword quite reasonably entitled 'On the First Russian Prolegomena to Semiotics'; extracts from Bakhtin and Voloshinov appeared in Ladislav Matejka and Krystyna Pomorska (eds.), *Readings in Russian Poetics* (Cambridge, Mass.: MIT Press, 1971). The translation of the essays on the novel in 1981 (in *The Dialogic Imagination*) brought Bakhtin out of the orbit of semiotically inspired poetics and into circulation within Anglo-American literary theory. The biography by Katerina Clark and Michael Holquist published in 1985, however, suggested something quite different. Clark and Holquist, with access to the materials which Bocharov could publish only after perestroika, made a case which seemed bizarre to some at the time, but was wholly congruent with the flow of commentary in the then Soviet Union: Bakhtin was really a philosopher, his essential ideas were contained in an early philosophical work and were then varied and elaborated. At the time of publication, this claim was met with no small degree of suspicion, fuelled, no doubt, by the fact that Clark and Holquist relied on written sources which they could not publicly document. As time has passed, however, Westerners have fallen into line. Thus while Gary Saul Morson, when reviewing the biography, claimed that it 'is sometimes hard to see from the biographers' account why he [Bakhtin] was not just another second-rate philosopher' ('Two Voices in Every Head', *New York Times Book Review*, 10 Feb. 1985), five years later, in his and Emerson's *Mikhail Bakhtin: Creation of a Prosaics*, he adopted the same 'philosophy first' (or 'first philosophy' if you like) strategy; not because he claims that all of Bakhtin's work was an elaboration of his earlier writings, but in so far as Bakhtin is celebrated for essentially philosophical (and particularly ethical) rather than literary-critical insights.

[31] Thus a section of the text critical of Marxism was only published as a fragment in a brochure edited by V. L. Makhlin, *Mikhail Bakhtin: Filosofiia postupka*, Znanie 6 (1990), 40–1.

into print nearly every significant text, in uncensored form, with an editorial apparatus at last worthy of its subject. And in 1996 one of its seven projected volumes, Volume 5, devoted to works from the early 1940s to the early 1960s, appeared, with more than a dozen new texts, existing texts in startling new form, and 300 pages—virtually half the book—of notes and commentary.

It is tempting to let the last feature—the sheer weight and precision of the editorial commentary, which describes in detail the physical facts of the texts presented: colour of pencil or pen, number and disposition of sheets, idiosyncrasies of handwriting, titles of notebooks—stand for the opening up of Bakhtin's written legacy, and in many ways it can. The texts are presented scrupulously, evidence for dating is discussed openly, sources are noted and earlier errors are corrected. From this edition we learn, for example, that references to religious discourse were deleted from an early version of the important text 'Towards Philosophical Bases of the Human Sciences', that an extra line of white space in the 1979 publication of 'The Problem of the Text' concealed three pages of text excised from the published version, and, most worryingly, that the Russian text of Bakhtin's most famous essay, 'Discourse in the Novel', was published with excisions (none of which are indicated in the text itself) of which one is a reference to Lev Iakubinsky, author of the 1923 article 'On Dialogic Speech', the absence of whose name in that essay had seemed until then a puzzle (it has since emerged that other names deleted from the published version were those of Georg Misch, Ernst Cassirer, Leo Spitzer, and Oskar Walzel).[32] But we also learn things we might rather not have known. The editors make no reference to the fact that they have restored references to 'bourgeois linguistics' (PSG 168) and 'idealist linguistics' (PSG 167) in the essay 'The Problem of Speech Genres' which were absent, again without indication of a deletion, in the version published in *Estetika slovesnogo tvorchestva* (in which Bocharov himself played a significant role). They openly admit that they have taken the liberty of excising from this authoritative version of 'The Problem of Speech Genres' 'references . . . explained by the official character of the text' (*SS5*, 536) as if it were part of the editorial task to decide which elements of a text were merely external incrustations and which part of its argumentative essence. And while they never fail to point out the earlier excision of a philosophical or religious reference, the following passage, previously excised from the notes known as 'Towards a

---

[32] That deletions were made from the published text of 'Discourse in the Novel' was revealed in an editorial note to 'Dialogue-II' (*SS5*, 573 n. 20), a set of rough notes which includes a conspectus of 'Discourse in the Novel' in which passages not present in the published text are referred to. Brian Poole has uncovered the missing references to the writers mentioned above, as well as references to Marr and Dilthey (e-mail to the author, 6 Apr. 1998).

Reworking of the Dostoevsky Book' (in this edition redubbed 'Notes from 1961'), now appears without comment, apparently because it cannot be explained away as something related to the 'official character' of a text:

Marx on the restoration of man to himself in pure relationships, on the exchange of love. Dostoevsky didn't know the *real* paths to this, on which the Russian people embarked (Marx noted them). He saw the final goal, but he did not see the earthly paths and means. (N61, 345)[33]

In short, the *Collected Works* alerts us, intentionally, to the fact that virtually every Bakhtin text in print is corrupt and, unintentionally, to the fact that despite its descriptive detail, it, too, is an edition with an axe to grind. For both the editorial procedures at work and the massive notes and commentary are dedicated to demonstrating that even the most ostensibly scientific text of Bakhtin's is beyond science, containing at its heart a religious-philosophical argument.

Despite the efforts of editors, however, the texts themselves remain too strained, the tensions too deeply embedded, for the mere act of publication to clinch any particular reading. Publication of the texts has therefore always been shadowed by the slow but deliberate seepage of material—letters, reminiscences, recollections of casual discussions—aimed at establishing a decisive context of interpretation. Given how few extant works there are and given the fact that Bakhtin was a relatively unknown figure for most of his consequently undocumented life, these play an even greater role than usual in endowing a life and *œuvre* with shape. The very thinness of the biographical atmosphere surrounding Bakhtin endows each known relationship with remarkable importance, and arguments about context turn out to be arguments over the relative significance of personal influences and relationships. Claims to intimacy are made through the publication of personal correspondence and the recollection of conversations, and, ironically, the more trivial the topic, the more persuasive the claim; in this way, discussions of automobile accidents and cigars from Havana add weight to arguments over issues in poetics and philosophy.[34] If Bakhtin was so close as to discuss freely smoking and cars, imagine with what intimacy he discussed the history of the novel! The publication, in 1993–94, of a transcript of Bakhtin's lengthy (eighteen hours in total) inter-

---

[33] Bakhtin is referring to two passages from the third of Marx's 'Economic and Philosophical Manuscripts' of 1844; see Karl Marx, *Early Writings*, 345, 379.

[34] Without doubt, the master of this genre was the recently deceased scholar V. N. Turbin, whose game of epistolary cat-and-mouse entailed apparently random publication of brief personal correspondence in as many different public arenas as possible. Turbin himself justified this procedure in a three-and-a-half-page introduction to an apparently short and uninteresting letter, itself embroidered with two pages of footnotes explaining, among other weighty matters, the provenance and purpose of cigars alluded to in the letter. See V. N. Turbin, 'Po povodu odnogo pis'ma M. M. Bakhtina', *Dialog Karnaval Khronotop*, 1 (1992), 53–9.

views with Duvakin in 1973, a great part of which are devoted to discussion of Bakhtin's various friendships and acquaintances, might have decisively settled these issues. But once again length and detail indicate not freedom from historical pressures but a more elaborate engagement with them—the transcript was first published in severely edited form, and by the time the more accurate and unexpurgated book version came out in 1996 it was clear both that Bakhtin was happy to collude in the myths about his past created by a later generation and that Duvakin could not know where and on what issues he should have pressed his interviewee.[35] The way was still clear, therefore, for the practice whereby the establishment of links by one party would imply the disparagement of links claimed elsewhere. An ineluctable feature of Bakhtin debate has become the recollection of comments which throw doubt on claims made for the intimacy of rivals.[36]

Once again the form of the argument is itself revealing. That the credentials of friendship will somehow ensure a particular reading of texts makes sense only for an intelligentsia which has never shaken off the moral elements of its self-conception. For the Russian *intelligent* the act of intellectual creation remains indissolubly bound to the quality of moral courage and example, a morality which must take the form of an ethics of conviction rather than one tempered by political or social calculation. It is, of course, ironic that having trained his critical sights on the Russian concept of the *mudrets*, the sage imbued with or personifying wisdom, Bakhtin should then be described even by a scientific intellectual such as Ivanov as 'above all else, a person to whom in the authentic sense of the word, the concept *mudrets* applies'.[37] But in a public sphere where intellectual effort depends more than usual upon fluid, uninstitutionalized contexts, and where productive relationships were therefore often sustained on the moral

---

[35] The interviews were initially published as 'Razgovory s Bakhtinym' ('Conversations with Bakhtin'), in the journal *Chelovek*, 4–6 (1993), 1–6 (1994), and 1 (1995), but in this version passages were deleted, material was rearranged so that the discussion proceeded in strict chronological order, and the halting, oral pattern of the proceedings was smoothed over. The book version, by all accounts a strictly accurate record, is *Besedy V. D. Duvakina s M. M. Bakhtinym*.

[36] A pair of examples will suffice to illustrate. In an interview Vadim Kozhinov has described in detail Bakhtin's efforts to avoid meeting Roman Jakobson, participant in the Moscow Linguistic Circle and structuralist linguist and critic. Kozhinov explains this in terms of Bakhtin's disinterest in 'foreigners', perhaps structuralist foreigners in particular (although one senses this might be a redundant description for Kozhinov). The conclusions to be drawn need no elaboration. On the other hand, the lengthy and polemical reminiscence of Bakhtin in the émigré journal *Sintaksis*, edited by the exiled writer Andrei Siniavsky, includes reported comments by Bakhtin to the effect that Kozhinov was himself anti-Semitic, and therefore distant from the great Master's sympathies. For Kozhinov's glee over Bakhtin's rejection of Westernized intellectuals see 'Kak pishut trudy', 116–17; for the report on Bakhtin's distance see Kaganskaia, 'Shutovskoi khorovod', 142, 144. Bakhtin himself defended Kozhinov from the charge of antisemitism during one of his interviews with Duvakin (*Con.*, 217–18).

[37] Viacheslav Ivanov, 'O Bakhtine i semiotike', *Rossiia/Russia*, vol. ii (Torino: Einaudi, 1975), 284.

basis of friendship or the intellectual 'circle', it is inevitable that closeness to the person and closeness to the intellectual commitment are considered of a piece. In the absence of an institutionalized collaborative form of work—such as one expects of the natural sciences or finds in the patterned working relationships of Western university life—insight and intellectual vision appear to be embedded in the truthfulness of personal relationships.

Of those personal relationships, it is the ones from 1918 to 1929 that matter most. Although it is intellectuals of a later generation who are the providers of anecdote and correspondence, their own claims for intimacy matter less for us, as nearly all of them adopt the role of admirers or students of Bakhtin's work. When the topic is Bakhtin's earlier life, the time of his various circles, the stakes are much higher, for in this case we are dealing with intellectual influences which are deemed formative and project-shaping. Apparently—so goes the logic of this kind of argument— Bakhtin cannot be everybody's friend, and the relationships upon which light is shone are meant to displace others in the pecking order of collegial influence. P. N. Medvedev and V. N. Voloshinov, both of whom participated in circles with Bakhtin as early as 1920 and 1918 respectively, and continued as his close friends into the late 1920s, have recently been put in the line of fire, and the question of their relationship to Bakhtin is inextricably bound to the resolution of the question of the so-called disputed texts.

ON THE 'ACCURSED QUESTION'

Voloshinov had died of tuberculosis in 1936, and in the relative liberalization of the Khrushchev period his monograph *Marxism and the Philosophy of Language* (1929) had been revived as a subject of discussion, as was his critique of psychoanalysis. Medvedev had been arrested and shot in 1938, and had been well known not only as a Blok scholar and a literary theorist, but also as the author of *The Formal Method in Literary Scholarship: An Introduction to Sociological Poetics* (1928), which represented the most intellectually serious attack on Formalism on record. At the meeting at Moscow State University in 1970, Ivanov not only claimed Bakhtin for semiotics, but claimed these books and other articles published under the names of Voloshinov and Medvedev for Bakhtin. Ivanov was making public a claim which had circulated as oral folklore amongst the intelligentsia since at least 1960. Having been pronounced at the meeting, Ivanov's claim was then obliquely referred to in a published report of the meeting, and recorded as a footnote in the paper published in 1973.[38] The local reasons for this

[38] See O. G. Revzin's account of the meeting in *Voprosy iazykoznaniia*, 2 (1971), 160–2.

bibliographical assault probably relate to the content of the paper itself, which, presenting Bakhtin as a semiotician, needed to credit Voloshinov's theory of the sign to Bakhtin in order to make credible the description of Bakhtin as a figure in the development of a regional 'science'. (Voloshinov's text, while by no means unperturbed by philosophical questions, nonetheless casts its conclusions in the form of scientific rather than philosophical ideas, despite its title.)

In 1970, both of the authors in question were dead, leaving Bakhtin and the surviving widows of the two as the only direct sources of evidence. In the five years before Bakhtin's death a number of curiously indirect attempts to verify the claim were made, with, it appears, mixed results. Bakhtin refused to sign an official document for the Soviet copyright agency claiming authorship, but Russian sources insisted that in private he had confirmed his authorship, and a number of provocations (for example, placing a copy of *Marxism* before Bakhtin to gauge his reaction) were adduced as supporting evidence. Even at this time, however, the claims made were of an oddly hedged kind: Ivanov had claimed not authorship but that the 'basic text belonged to Bakhtin' and that Voloshinov and Medvedev had 'made only small insertions and changes of individual parts'; in 1973 the biographical sketch provided by Konkin and Kozhinov made a slightly different argument: 'On the basis of discussions with Mikhail Mikhailovich [held in Vitebsk in 1920–24] devoted to problems of philosophy and psychology, philosophy and aesthetics, a series of books and articles was later composed.'[39] The exact method by which the texts were written and the consequent degree of contribution from each party appeared to be either a matter of doubt or consciously muddled.

Ivanov had declared that eyewitness testimony was available, but the inability of Russian scholars to produce the promised smoking pen cast doubt, especially amongst some Western writers, on their claims (the endorsement Russian claims received in the biography of Clark and Holquist seemed to stoke opposition as much as solidify support). Indeed, the reticence and indirectness with which the entire affair has been conducted has made scholarly determination of the issue virtually impossible. In an article published seven years ago, Iuri Medvedev, son of Pavel, pointed out that the circuit of unofficial assertion has created a climate of opinion within Russia in which the claim for Bakhtin's authorship is supported less by evidence than by the international velocity of the discourse surrounding it:

One of the chief devices of the 'campaign' is precisely the creation of 'scholarly' opinion from abroad, in order to compensate for the tendentiousness of domestic

[39] Kozhinov and Konkin, 'Mikhail Mikhailovich Bakhtin: Kratkii ocherk', 6.

arguments. Passed onto the West as rumour, as the opinion of an authoritative person which it would be awkward for a courteous foreigner to dispute, it then returns to us as something having currency in the competent circles of judgement, to which those who 'launched' it can refer and on which they can rely.[40]

There is something in this: one cannot help feeling uncomfortable with the fact that nearly every assertion is the second-hand report of a conversation, especially given the fact that Bakhtin refused the opportunity to make his putative authorship a matter of official record. In an article published in 1994, Sergei Bocharov has made the case for Bakhtin in terms as clear as is possible. He reports a conversation with Bakhtin from 9 June 1970 (supplementing it with snippets from a later one on 21 September 1974), in which, faced with a copy of Voloshinov's *Marxism* and queried directly about it, Bakhtin claims:

You see, I thought this was something I could do for my friends, and it wasn't a difficult thing to do, since I really thought that I would write my own books, and without these unfortunate additions (here he nodded at the title with a grimace). I really did not know that everything would turn out the way it has. And then, what significance does all this have—authorship, a name? Everything that has been created in this half-century, on this barren ground, under this unfree sky, all of it is to a greater or lesser degree flawed.[41]

To this comment Bocharov adds the testimony of others (including Voloshinov's widow) but is yet forced to admit that 'even the personal testimony of Bakhtin himself is not enough to decide the question'.[42]

Scholars from societies with relatively liberal academic spheres are, in one sense, poorly placed to complain about the necessarily informal nature of the information they are forced to rely on. Nonetheless, even the impeccable fairness of Bocharov coexists with an appeal to intuitive truth which inspires in us an unexpected passion for the sobriety of positivist scholarship. While Bocharov concedes that 'there are no proofs and most probably there will never be any . . . There is already more than a little *testimony*, but it cannot be *proof*',[43] he follows this admission with quotations from Bulgakov (heroic figure for the intelligentsia) and Dostoevsky, in which the desire for proof of the existence of God is mocked for its narrow scientist pretensions. Furthermore, too much of the evidence depends upon a kind of literary hermeneutic deftness. The following

[40] Iu. P. Medvedev, '"Nas bylo mnogo na chelne . . ."', *Dialog Karnaval Khronotop*, 1 (1992), 98.

[41] Bocharov, 'Ob odnom razgovore', 71.

[42] Ibid. 73. Bocharov reports that Nina Arkadievna Voloshinova told him in April 1975 that 'Mikhail Mikhailovich wrote these books' and that she repeated the claim in a letter of 14 March 1978 to Radovan Matijašević, the Yugoslav translator.

[43] Ibid.

letter from Bakhtin to Kozhinov, only recently published (although dated 10 January 1961), is read against the grain by Bocharov, as support for Bakhtin's authorship:

The books *The Formal Method* and *Marxism and the Philosophy of Language* are very well known to me. V. N. Voloshinov and P. N. Medvedev were my friends; in the period when these books were being written we worked in the closest creative contact. Furthermore, these books and my book on Dostoevsky are based on a *shared* conception of language and speech. In this respect V. V. Vinogradov [the source of the information for Kozhinov] is completely right. I should point out that the presence of a shared conception and contact in work does not diminish the self-sufficiency and originality of any of these books. As for the other works of P. N. Medvedev and V. N. Voloshinov, they lie on a different plane and do not reflect our shared conception, and I did not play any part in their creation.[44]

Bocharov interprets 'shared' conception and 'different plane' as signals of differing authorship: a possible reading, but one which depends on an already made *symbolic* interpretation of the situation, in which Bakhtin is cast as the leader of the pack. The issue of authorship is inextricably bound to a concept of truth attached to the person of Bakhtin himself, whose polemics with positivism are applied reflexively to the authorship question. The deficiencies of merely scientific 'theoretical' truth mean that the question of authorship is construed as first and foremost a moral and symbolic one.

Bocharov appeals to the inwardness of conviction against the surface meanings of text and proof, a contrast which neatly corresponds to the inwardness or separation which Bakhtin apparently maintained in relation to the 'official' social and political world beyond him. From the very beginning of this curious dispute it has been clear to all that the stakes are ideological and that the issue is not the attribution of works which would merely add lustre to a reputation, but the ideological repercussions of Bakhtin's possible authorship. But the crux of the question is not, as might be supposed, Bakhtin's relationship to Marxism, for barely a word of the commentary addresses in any substantive sense the Marxist or non-Marxist content of these works, or indeed, of any of the later works written by Bakhtin (although Bocharov is an honourable exception here). Marxism itself in this debate signifies not a body of social theory, but an external and secular world of political power and social relationship, necessarily degraded in comparison with the purity of quasi-religious inwardness. The real issue is not whether Bakhtin was or was not a Marxist, but the extent to which his theory was informed by 'external' social and political realities. Would Bakhtin be condemned for believing the theory of surplus value?

---

[44] Ibid. 76. The letter was also published by Kozhinov, as one of several, in 'Pis'ma M. M. Bakhtina', 145.

No, he would be condemned for believing that such a local 'merely cognitive' question was of much importance at all. The question of whether Bakhtin was or was not a Marxist has been transformed into a moral one, in which the intellectual merits of a theoretical choice are displaced by the issue of affiliation to or distance from the values of a secular and social existence.

A similar displacement works to opposite effect in the United States. The scholars in America who contest Bakhtin's authorship—Gary Saul Morson and Caryl Emerson, I. R. Titunik—are also in no doubt as to the stakes.[45] They are certain that the authors of the disputed texts, whoever they are, are Marxists, and therefore insist that the barrier between these Marxist works and writings appearing under Bakhtin's name must on no account be breached. As in Russia (though here there are fewer excuses), intellectual questions are cast in moralized form. Neither Morson and Emerson nor Titunik have much time for arguments when the time comes to decide whether or not a text is Marxist; instead, they treat the presence of emblematic words and phrases as the decisive test of a general intellectual position. The mere existence of significant terms—'class struggle', 'dialectics', 'sociological', and so forth—is taken as evidence against, irrespective of their significance in analytical terms.[46] But words and phrases can serve as independent counters, in abstraction from arguments, only when interpreted as indices of moral commitments and decisions made elsewhere, as the sediment of existential choices between good and evil. Only if being a Marxist is a movement of the soul rather than the mind, which one makes all at once or not at all, is saying 'class struggle' evidence enough that one has gone over the edge.

The critic on the lookout for signs of that all-or-nothing decision is therefore liable to overlook the argument itself. Few recent commentators have been as perceptive as Boris Pasternak was when he wrote to Medvedev, having read *The Formal Method*, that 'It is with difficulty that I imagine that, given such a methodological substance, you have been recognized as an orthodox Marxist.'[47] Having made his own pilgrimage to Marburg, Pasternak was well placed to recognize the influence of neo-Kantian beliefs (of course, by no means flatly contradictory to Marxism) in

[45] See the special Bakhtin section in *Slavic and East European Review*, 30: 1 (1986), and Morson and Emerson, *Mikhail Bakhtin*, 101–19 (ch. 3: 'The Disputed Texts'). For a fuller list of texts on this question, see the Bibliography.

[46] Titunik has analysed the revision of *Problems of Dostoevsky's Art* in precisely such terms, tracing the replacement of the term 'sociological' by the term 'metalinguistic'. See his 'Bakhtin &/or Vološinov &/or Medvedev: Dialogue &/or Doubletalk', in Benjamin A. Stolz, Lubomir Doložel, and I. R. Titunik (eds.), *Language and Literary Theory* (Ann Arbor, Mich.: University of Michigan, 1984), 535–64.

[47] Letter from Pasternak to Medvedev, *Literaturnoe nasledstvo*, vol. xciii (Moscow: Nauka, 1983), 709.

the work of the Bakhtin circle in the 1920s. He could see what few after have: in the disputed texts, claims for the priority of 'the social' amount to something more complicated than an endorsement of positivist sociological verities. Voloshinov and Medvedev defend the 'objectivity' of culture in order to protect it from reduction to an aggregate of individual dispositions, and thus, in effect, a creature of psychology or biology. When the former makes his case for the social character of language in *Marxism and the Philosophy of Language*, the point is not to displace the rights of consciousness by sociological laws (in fact, sociology's main representative in linguistics, Saussure, gets a critical chapter all to himself), but to defend consciousness from the idealism which buries it under logic and the psychologism which reduces it to the natural laws of physiology or the spontaneity of 'life'.[48] Whatever fantasies certain writers may have about philosophy defending the individual against the predations of the collective, sociology, Marxism, and the rest, in this case philosophy found itself defending culture against the reckless individualism which would reduce everything to nerve endings or neuroses. (Of course, in Soviet cultural thought there was plenty of 'collectivist' Marxism, but then there was Marxism aligned with 'philosophy of life', Marxism inflected by religion, and so forth; all of which might suggest to the open-minded that there is no single Marxist dragon to slay). Those hoping to place these works beyond the pale of a mythical 'sociological turn' might remind themselves that continental sociology itself was the creation, for good reason, of professors of philosophy, and not statisticians.[49] Even discussion of the specific character of capitalism, which one might legitimately expect as a minimal guarantee of Marxist credentials, is not to be found in any disputed text; neither is any particular analysis of it relevant to the various claims made about literary theory, language, or the psyche. Nothing in these works flatly contradicts Marxist arguments, but nothing absolutely requires them, either. To demand that they declare themselves is to enact precisely the test of orthodoxy of which they fell foul in the Soviet Union.[50]

Attempts to separate Bakhtin once and for all from the moral contagion

---

[48] See Voloshinov's discussion of the contest between psychologism and anti-psychologism (*MPL* 41–2/31–2), where Husserl, for all his idealism, is enlisted in the struggle against the main enemy, philosophy of life and naturalizing psychology.

[49] On the emergence of sociology as a discipline, see Wolf Lepenies, *Between Literature and Science: The Rise of Sociology*, trans. R. J. Hollingdale (Cambridge: Cambridge University Press, 1988), and Harry Liebersohn, *Fate and Utopia in German Sociology, 1870–1923* (Cambridge, Mass. and London: MIT Press, 1988). The intellectual ancestry of sociology was, naturally, different in England, where the statistical societies endowed it with a more empiricist bent.

[50] *The Formal Method* was condemned for its neo-Kantianism (naturally). See Albert Wehrle, 'Introduction M. M. Bakhtin/P. N. Medvedev', in Bakhtin/Medvedev [sic], *The Formal Method in Literary Scholarship* (Cambridge, Mass. and London: Harvard University Press, 1985), pp. xxi–xxii.

of Marxism are at any rate doomed, not because he caught the disease—on his own evidence, he didn't—but because his work shows no particular interest in dividing up its constituent elements into Marxist and non-Marxist ones.[51] Even if the quarantine imposed on the disputed texts was successful, there would be fresh outbreaks in Bakhtin's later works to deal with. The populist enthusiasm of the essays on the novel owes more to Russian Populism and Nietzsche than to Marx, but then Russian Marxism itself had a heavy debt to Populism and, in strictly political terms, these essays are rather more militant than anything found in Voloshinov and Medvedev. Furthermore, there are passages such as the following:

The *reification* of man in the conditions of class society, taken to its extreme in the conditions of capitalism. This reification is accomplished (realized) by means of external forces, acting from within and without on the personality; it is violence in all the possible forms of its realization (economic, political, and ideological), and struggle with these forces is possible only from without and with equally external forces (justified revolutionary violence); but the goal is personality. (N61, 356–7)

The critic who separates the sociological shell from the philosophical kernel in this note from 1961–62 will not be left with much of a text. That capitalism is put in the dock for the crime of reification rather than exploitation at once distinguishes this critical position from more orthodox ones; that personality rather than a proletarian dictatorship is the endpoint of a revolutionary process demonstrates a careful distance from the politics of the Third International. But this paragraph would not look much out of place in Lukács's *History and Class Consciousness*, in which reification is also the crucial feature of the objective social forms engendered by capitalism. This similarity is hardly surprising, and should serve to remind us that Bakhtin and Lukács, like an entire generation of European intellectuals, drew heavily on neo-Kantian social philosophy for the terms of their social critique, whatever their local political allegiances. This no more makes Bakhtin a Marxist than it makes Lukács a non-Marxist; it tells us that Marxism, neo-Kantianism, philosophy of life, and religious argument constituted not moral options but an intellectual force-field within which different writers made their way.

[51] An unequivocal statement of identity, for those who feel comforted by that sort of thing, has been recorded twice. Kozhinov recounts that at his first meeting with Bakhtin, he and his colleagues were warned 'Bear in mind, I am not a Marxist' ('Kak pishut trudy', 113); Bocharov has confirmed the first claim and added his report of another conversation from 1974:

> *Bocharov.* Mikhail Mikhailovich, maybe at some time you were enthused by Marxism?
> *Bakhtin.* No, never. I was interested, as in many other things, in Freudianism, even spiritualism. But I was never a Marxist to any degree. ('Ob odnom razgovore', 76–7)

See as well the critical comments on historical materialism contained in 'Towards a Philosophy of the Act', excised from the original Russian publication of the text and revealed later (in Makhlin, *Mikhail Bakhtin: Filosofiia postupka*, 40–1).

In the United States, the question of Marxism is inevitably a question of national loyalty. The choice between a non-Marxist Bakhtin and his Marxist comrades appears as a choice *between* social systems, allowing a critic such as Morson to enlist Bakhtin in the fight for 'American progressive ideals'.[52] In Russia, however, the moral choices are structured differently, and this is reflected in the fact that ostensibly similar anti-Marxist strategies have led to opposite conclusions on the authorship question. In asserting Bakhtin's authorship of the disputed texts, Russian commentators hope to flush out the philosophy hidden cleverly beneath the Marxist underbrush. Bocharov, in the same article in which he recounts his crucial conversations with Bakhtin, has made a case for the 'shared conception' uniting Bakhtin's texts with the disputed ones, and has quite correctly asked us to look to the conceptual structure rather than the lexical surface. For Bocharov, as for a number of other Russian critics— N. I. Nikolaev, Natalia Bonetskaia, L. A. Gogotishvili—the language of the disputed texts is a 'sociological shell', masking philosophical contents capable in principle of standing on their own: the doctrine of *I* and *other* is the template from which even Bakhtin's most militant discourse is made. Yet it appears that for these writers all sociology is a shell and cannot be otherwise, and that the price of a truly moral intellectual position is a philosophical inwardness capable of resisting the historically finite and ceaselessly changing world both mapped and supported by sociology. They retain a belief in a metaphysical conception of the philosophical task, in which insight into the true nature of things (hidden, of course, from the social sciences) is the only source of reliable moral truth. And a metaphysical conception of the philosophical task demands a metaphysical conception of the philosopher, who must steer clear of the secular and strife-ridden world if he is to maintain his moral bearings.

If this is a shared conception, it is not one shared by Bakhtin, Medvedev, and Voloshinov. Nonetheless, the authorship question remains a question of affiliations and common work. If Voloshinov and Medvedev are pushed aside as intellectual influences, it is not so that Bakhtin may stand apart from the culture surrounding him, but so that a different intellectual formation, from an earlier time, can take their place. The recently published notes taken by Lev Pumpiansky from 1919 to 1925 have been marshalled by their editor N. I. Nikolaev as evidence for a 'Nevel'' school of philosophy, named after the town in which the first philosophical circle met in 1918–19. Voloshinov was a member of this circle, and Medvedev joined the group when it continued in Vitebsk from 1920 to 1924, but the

---

[52] 'Introduction' to the Russian Cluster, *PMLA* 107: 2 (1992), 227. David Shepherd and I responded to this vulgar conscription in 'Bakhtin and the Politics of Criticism', *PMLA* 109: 1 (1994), 116–18.

members of the circle whom Nikolaev wants us to attend to are Lev Pumpiansky and Matvei Kagan, who have the virtue of being interested in philosophy and defined as philosophers (there is some irony here, as Kagan was not only a philosopher, but also a former member of the Bolshevik party, who, having been appalled by the events of 1917, took a more supportive, on occasion enthusiastic, view of the revolution in the mid-1920s).[53] In asserting the rights and achievements of an earlier Bakhtin circle against those of a later one, in effect 1918–24 against 1924–28, Nikolaev establishes Bakhtin as a different kind of intellectual, akin to the 'philosophical' Kagan and Pumpiansky rather than Voloshinov and Medvedev (Natalia Bonetskaia has pushed sources even further back, locating Bakhtin in a St Petersburg school of Russian philosophy centred on his teachers at the university there; in her account, Kagan hardly exists at all).[54] If Bakhtin has written the later 'disputed' texts, then imagining a formation—call it, if you will, a 'Leningrad' school of philosophy—consisting of Bakhtin, Medvedev, and Voloshinov becomes pointless or implausible. That this is a genuine risk can be gauged from the very different constellation established by the critic Raymond Williams, who in an article of 1986 described a 'school of Vitebsk' consisting of Bakhtin, Voloshinov, and Medvedev, with intellectual affiliations quite different from those Nikolaev and Bonetskaia have in mind.[55]

Of course, this biographical thesis depends on a philological one—the by no means certain assumption that Bakhtin wrote his 'early works' while in Nevel' and Vitebsk, during a period of pure philosophical reflection which he was forced to surrender after returning to Leningrad. According to the model of the kernel and the shell, the core of Bakhtin's position would have been worked out first, in appropriate philosophical prose and with appropriate philosophical interlocutors. The later 'disputed' works could then be at once Bakhtin's and yet not Bakhtin's; they could be interpreted as translations of another position because there already existed

[53] In Kagan's autobiographical notes he says that he joined the Russian Social Democratic Workers' Party in 1904, was arrested in 1905, and continued to work for the party until at least 1908 (Iu. M. Kagan. 'O starykh bumagakh', 64); he does not tell us when he left the party. In an interview with Nikolai Pan'kov, Kagan's daughter Iudif and wife Sophia (who died shortly afterwards, described his enthusiasm for the ideals of the Revolution; see 'O pamiatnom, o vazhnom, o bylom . . . (ustnye vospominaniia S. I. Kagan i Iu. M. Kagan)', Dialog Karnaval Khronotop, 2 (1995), 178–9.

[54] According to Brian Poole, the connections drawn with philosophers at the University of Petrograd are largely mythical and serve to disguise the fact that Bakhtin's real philosophical education depended on his contact with Kagan (letter from Poole to David Shepherd, 21 Jan. 1994). In the Duvakin interview, Bakhtin claimed that his philosophical education was more or less do-it-yourself, and that his acquaintance with neo-Kantianism and with the existentialism of Kierkegaard came from reading outside of his university education; see Con., 35–42.

[55] Williams, 'The Uses of Cultural Theory', 22–3.

something they could be translations *from*. But the dates of composition for
'Author and Hero' and 'Towards a Philosophy of the Act' are purely con-
jectural (the manuscripts themselves are apparently undated) and those
offered by the editors are appropriately vague—'in the first half or the mid-
1920s' for 'Author and Hero', 'apparently during the author's time in
Vitebsk' (1920–24).[56] But what if, as Brian Poole has suggested, 'Author
and Hero' was written in 1927, or at least no earlier than 1925, that is, at
more or less the same time as the disputed texts?[57] Could the kernel and
the shell be taking shape at the same time? Hardly likely. For the hypothesis to work, Bakhtin's formative work has to take place early on, in a
strictly philosophical context, so that the work which comes later can be
classified as neither original nor influential.

The pathos of this belief in the priority of earlier affiliations rests on
more than an intellectual commitment to Christian religion rather than
Marxism; it draws its energy from the conviction that the distinction
between these different, perhaps artificially constructed, groups has a moral
dimension. The influence which is denied to Voloshinov and Medvedev
when disputed texts are attributed to Bakhtin is not only a matter of
sociology or even Marxism itself, but of a possible form of intellectual life,
which takes seriously secular power and relations, and sets, in a principled
fashion, its intellectual and cultural goals accordingly. Medvedev and
Voloshinov, in particular the former, were distinguished by their involve-
ment with the institutions of Soviet cultural life; they appear as intellectuals
who do not keep a philosophically sanctioned distance from the actually
existing. When Bocharov remarks that 'all the principal actors in Bakhtin's
biography . . . were unofficial people' he is forced by the logic of his argument to exclude Volshinov and Medvedev from Bakhtin's inner circle,
despite Bakhtin's own testimony to the contrary.[58] When Kozhinov's first
words to describe Medvedev are 'a social activist' the intention is clearly to
taint this intellectual with the accusation of worldly and unphilosophical
compromise.[59] This worldliness reflects a conviction of the seriousness of

[56] Commentary to 'Author and Hero in Aesthetic Activity' (S. S. Averintsev and S. G.
Bocharov), *Estetika slovesnogo tvorchestva*, 404; Commentary to 'Towards a Philosophy of the Act'
(Sergei Bocharov) *Filosofiia i sotsiologiia nauki i tekhniki* (Moscow: Nauka, 1986), 81.

[57] Poole, 'From Phenomenology to Dialogue', typescript, 2–4, 20.

[58] S. G. Bocharov, 'Sobytie bytiia' [introduction to the first instalment of the transcription of
Duvakin's interviews with Bakhtin], *Chelovek*, 4 (1993), 137; Bocharov's list of Bakhtin's close
circle includes M. V. Iudina, L. V. Pumpiansky, M. I. Kagan, A. A. Meier, and K. K. Vaginov.
See the letter from Bakhtin to Kozhinov quoted on p. 129 above, where Bakhtin describes
Medvedev and Voloshinov as 'friends' with whom he worked 'in the closest creative contact'.
In the interviews with Duvakin, Bakhtin describes Voloshinov as his 'close friend' (*Con.*, 77) and
Medvedev as 'My friend, also very close' (*Con.*, 171).

[59] Vadim Kozhinov, 'Kniga, vokrug kotoroi ne umolkaiut spory', *Dialog Karnaval Khronotop*,
4 (1995), 140.

social and political values in all their historical and local limitedness, which does not sit comfortably with the vocation of religious philosopher assigned by some of posterity to Bakhtin.

No other explanation accounts for the curious imbalance one finds in the assessment of relative tragedy in the lives of these three intellectuals. Those inclined to represent Bakhtin as the tragic figure among them either forget or ignore the fact that Bakhtin died in bed, while it was Medvedev who was shot shortly after having been arrested. On any ordinary estimation, one would expect the hero's laurels to fall on the head of the latter rather than the former, but they have not. This reflects not ill will or personal enmity, but, as it were, the conviction that Bakhtin's path was somehow both more proper and more difficult. As an intellectual whose freedom depends on a self-conscious distance from 'results', he refuses—or so we assume—to be guided by the expectation of earthly reward or social and political success (hence the legends about Bakhtin's indifference towards the prospect of publication). By contrast Medvedev and Voloshinov's participation in public life and interest in Marxism, in however original or unorthodox a fashion, reflect a belief in the value of the secular, itself embodied in the 'social-scientific' flavour of the disputed texts. For while the shared conception tying these works to Bakhtin's is clear, the stylistic difference which sets them apart—systematicity of exposition, sobriety of expression, and absence of philosophical pathos— and endows them with a more scientific rather than philosophical character has an undoubted secularizing effect. The mention of 'class struggle' in *Marxism and the Philosophy of Language* does not clinch Voloshinov's commitment to the secular—some of the theologically inclined (including A. A. Meier, whose circle Bakhtin participated in) interpreted revolutionary class struggle itself in religious terms—but his style does. Not Marxism, but a secular concept of the intellectual is the alien force which might be embodied in an intellectual circle comprising Medvedev, Voloshinov, and Bakhtin.

Just as Marxism is not the real issue, so the disputed texts themselves are not the real prize. Bakhtin's essays on the novel represent a far deeper plunge into profane social life and its all too partial values than any of the disputed texts, and their militant tone and easy talk of popular subversion leave little room for transcendental manoeuvre. Accounts which subsume all of Bakhtin's work under metaphysical 'fundamental categories' therefore find themselves forced to make long and unconvincing detours around the very works which remain the cornerstone of Bakhtin's reputation in the West. The leap which carries them from *Problems of Dostoevsky's Art* (1929) to the book on Rabelais (1946) is all too conspicuous, and it is no accident that it is the very texts in which philosophy is brought down to earth that cause the trouble.[60] Such a detour is a temporary expedient at best, and it has become increasingly clear that the real aim of the authorship dispute is not to establish Bakhtin's rights to works by others, but to establish a mode of reading which will make it possible to assimilate the most awkward of Bakhtin's *own works* to a philosophical model of his career. Once it becomes acceptable to read texts by Voloshinov and Medvedev for their hidden philosophical content, there is no reason why this same method cannot be used to displace and discredit sociological or scientific language whenever and wherever it appears in Bakhtin's texts. In this vein Bocharov has allowed himself to extend the metaphor of the shell or surface to the concepts of realism and popularness (*narodnost'*) which structure the essays of the 1930s, and Nikolaev has suggested that the 1929 text of *Problems of Dostoevsky's Art*—a text which is entirely Bakhtin's— must be understood as a sociologized rewriting of an earlier, utterly unsociological, Dostoevsky text.[61] But for the ultimate exposition of this strategy we have to turn to the recently published Volume 5 of the *Collected Works*, which is guided by the conviction that every time scientific language appears on the horizon we should prepare to separate the wheat from the chaff. In her commentary to the preparatory materials for the text 'The Problem of Speech Genres', Gogotishvili reveals that labelling Voloshinov's work 'deuterocanonical', that is, Bakhtinian with reservations, was merely a dry run for a more wholesale revaluation of the entire canon:

However, on their [the preparatory materials'] basis one can at a minimum come to the conclusion that the text of 'The Problem of Speech Genres', usually perceived as the direct discourse of Bakhtin is, conventionally speaking, as 'deuterocanonical' as the text of *Marxism and the Philosophy of Language*. They are constructed on identical principles and from analogous authorial positions, from which it follows in particular that the language of positive and normative linguistics, and likewise the logical presuppositions of structuralism, were as distant from M. M. Bakhtin as the language of Marxism. All these languages are to an equal degree conventional and *equally alien* to him. (SS5, 558–9)

Every engagement with modern social science is therefore not a true engagement, but a feint or ruse. Even to talk about language in a scientific spirit, to think of it as something with historical shape and rules which must be empirically ascertained, compromises the removed and inward character of philosophy. These interpretative moves make clear that the ultimate stakes in the disputed texts debate are not works by Medvedev and Voloshinov, but Bakhtin's most historically acute and secular texts,

---

[60] See Ch. 1, p. 7 n. 7.
[61] See Bocharov, 'Ob odnom razgovore', 78–9; Nikolaev, '*Dostoevsky i antichnost'* L. V. Pumpianskogo (1922) i M. M. Bakhtina (1963)', 5–6.

which might add up to something uncomfortable if placed in a constellation where their historical energies could be set loose. The ideological
struggle is only apparently between works by Bakhtin and the disputed
texts; it is actually being waged on behalf of certain Bakhtin texts against
others, in effect the Bakhtin of *Estetika slovesnogo tvorchestva* (1979) against
the author of *Voprosy literatury i estetiki* (1975).

Whether Medvedev and Voloshinov composed the disputed texts is not
itself a trivial issue, but it is now so weighed down with moral baggage that
it is impossible to separate the dry facts from the ideological stakes. The
endlessly changing stories and justifications (Bakhtin did it as a favour,
because he could not get published, as a carnivalesque joke, and so on) tell
us that no one really has conclusive evidence of the truth, but they also tell
us something about the symbolic weight of the issue itself. One cannot
separate the question of attribution from questions of interpretation or—
more difficult, this—from the symbolic identity Bakhtin himself acquired
in the intellectual world of metropolitan Russia. What kind of philosophy
he practised, and what accommodation it made with the emerging world
of social science, is at the same time the question of what kind of intellectual he was to be. As might be clear already, this issue seems to me easier
to decide than the empirical one of who wrote what. Interpretations which
lock Bakhtin into philosophical solitary confinement are not only damag-
ing in themselves, but crude in relation to the texts. The neo-Kantians
from whom Bakhtin took his philosophical bearings knew that philosophy
could no longer run the show on its own, but had to be orientated to the
facts of science and to social and political actuality.[62] The literary historians
from whom he took ideas of genre and their historical development
showed him that once history had been let out of the bottle, it was impossible to put it back in again. The tensions between philosophical aspiration
and the sciences of actuality make Bakhtin's work difficult, but they also
save it from being either mere chronicle or empty philosophy.

Remaining true to this principle, we must realize that the historical fact
of authorship is separate from the symbolic debate conducted through it.
Even if Bakhtin did write the disputed texts, one should defend their
integrity (as indeed Bocharov, having made his case, does). The evidence,
however, is not very convincing. Although Bakhtin is reported by several
reliable sources to have claimed authorship of the disputed texts, he also
evidently refused to sign the document which would seal his claim to
copyright, told Kozhinov in the letter to him quoted earlier that a 'shared
conception' did not compromise the 'self-sufficiency and originality' of the

---

[62] On neo-Kantian social philosophy and its link to social and political affairs, see Thomas E.
Willey, *Back to Kant: The Revival of Kantianism in German Social and Historical Thought, 1860–1914*
(Detroit, Mich.: Wayne State University Press, 1978).

texts in question, and described Voloshinov to Duvakin in his 1973 inter-view as 'the author of the book *Marxism and the Philosophy of Language*, a book which has, so to speak, been attributed to me' (*Con.*, 77–8). Only a strong counter-intuitive reading of inconvenient evidence can conjure something consistent out of these self-evidently contradictory materials. The fact of collaboration is agreed by all, though its exact form—rewrit-ing, composition based on discussion, dual authorship—is in dispute. And finally, archival materials from other members of the Leningrad circle imply that independent work on both psychoanalysis and the philosophy of language was being pursued in the mid- and late 1920s. Notes from the archive of I. I. Sollertinsky reveal the circle's plans for collectively pro-duced works on psychoanalysis, and include the beginning of an article strikingly similar to the opening of the disputed text on Freudianism.[63] Even more persuasive is the batch of academic files drawn from Voloshinov's time as a postgraduate student in linguistics, which have been uncovered by Nikolai Pan'kov. These include not only numerous reports on work in progress, but also a detailed plan of the book *Marxism and the Philosophy of Language* made at the end of the academic year 1927–28.[64] The plan implies a shorter book than the one we know, covering only the first two sections of the final published text (but including material on the status of the word in contemporary Russian writing which never made the final cut). Voloshinov's discussion of the syntax of indirect and quasi-direct speech—the third section, and the one which would preview Bakhtin's conception of double-directed or double-voiced discourse—takes the form not of a part within *Marxism and the Philosophy of Language*, but of an entirely separate article entitled 'The Problem of the Transmission of Alien Speech', apparently destined for publication in a collection in 1928. This evidence, also, is not decisive, but it supports what would have been the obvious conclusion to begin with—that Voloshinov wrote his 'disputed texts' while he was immersed in the study of linguistics, and had expertise which Bakhtin did not. This might remind us that for close on fifteen years

---

[63] L. Mikheeva, *I. I. Sollertinsky: Zhizn' i nasledie* (Leningrad: Sovetskii pisatel', 1988), 52–3.

[64] A transcription of the files was published as 'Lichnoe delo V. N. Voloshinova', *Dialog Karnaval Khronotop*, 2 (1995), 70–99, while the plan of the book alone was published as part of 'K istorii knigi V. N. Voloshinova *Marksizm i filosofiia iazyka*', *Izvestiia Akademii Nauk, seriia literatury i iazyka*, 54: 3 (1995), 67–76. In Pan'kov's introductory article to the first transcription, he notes enigmatically that the plan of the book is made out in a hand different from the one which appears in the documents filled out by Voloshinov himself, but also says that the hand-writing in question is not Bakhtin's; see N. A. Pan'kov, 'Mifologema Voloshinova (neskol'ko zamechanii kak by na poliakh arkhivnykh materialov)', *Dialog Karnaval Khronotop*, 2 (1995), 66–9. In the introductory article accompanying the second publication of the plan, V. M. Alpatov suggests that Voloshinov may have completed the book and the article by the beginning of 1928 and then, while staying with the Bakhtins over the summer of that year, revised it on the basis of conversations with Bakhtin ('K istorii', 63–6).

no one was able to elicit written proof from Bakhtin to substantiate what was an utterly counter-intuitive and hearsay case. Proof is required for claims like these, and none is forthcoming.

A review of Bakhtin's life therefore works from materials inseparable from their polemical origins. Even the publication of the basic texts remains strewn with controversy: one can purchase Russian editions of *Freudianism* which list Bakhtin as the author, Voloshinov as the author, or both as joint authors (and each edition has a preface justifying the decision made).[65] Every year texts we thought we knew turn out to be corrupted and biographical facts turn out to be fictions, while the monumental project of the *Collected Works* threatens to unsettle everything already agreed. The following account of the relevant biography is therefore organized around the works of which we are aware, and may turn out to sustain as many myths as it debunks.[66]

CHILDHOOD AND EDUCATION, 1895–1917

Texts

None extant.

Mikhail Bakhtin was born on 17 November (new style) 1895, in the city of Orel. He was one of six children, flanked by an elder brother Nikolai, and four younger sisters (one of whom had been adopted); their father, whatever his origins, worked for an Orel commercial bank. In 1905 the family moved to Vilnius (Lithuania), where Bakhtin entered one of the city's gymnasiums, after which they moved to Odessa, apparently in the middle of 1911.[67] In the Duvakin interview Bakhtin has trouble remembering the exact details of his higher education, but eventually he recalls that having

---

[65] 'Bakhtin pod maskoi, maska pervaia: V. N. Voloshinov' ['Bakhtin Under a Mask, First Mask: V. N. Voloshinov'], *Freidizm* [*sic*] (Moscow: Labirint, 1993); Valentin Voloshinov, *Filosofiia i sotsiologiia gumanitarnykh nauk* [includes *Freudianism* and *Marxism and the Philosophy of Language*] (St Petersburg: Asta Press, 1995); M. M. Bakhtin–V. N. Voloshinov, *Freidizm: Kritischeskii ocherk* (New York: Chalidze Publications, 1983).

[66] Some of what follows is at variance with the account offered in Clark and Holquist's impressive reconstruction of Bakhtin's life. This reflects the numerous new sources which have become public and entered print since the publication of their biography, and, more particularly, since glasnost; only occasionally (as with the question of the 'disputed texts') does it stem from a different judgement about the available facts.

[67] The exact dates of the family's movements and Bakhtin's secondary education are now the object of rather intense scrutiny. Pan'kov, on the basis of school records, has provided a hypothetical sketch of Mikhail's and his brother Nikolai's schooling. See his 'Zagadki rannego perioda (Eshche neskol'ko shtrikhov k "Biografii M. M. Bakhtina")', *Dialog Karnaval Khronotop*, (1993), 74–89.

studied at Novorossiskii University in Odessa for a year, he transferred to Petrograd University, graduating in classics and philology in 1917, which mirrors his account on several official forms. 'I do not remember the dates exactly. There are reminiscences of my brother, they are . . . in this . . . English . . . memorial volume' (*Con.*, 35). That Bakhtin should refer to the biographical note on his brother sounds curious, but is in fact perfectly natural, for the educational background he has just described belongs to Nikolai and not to him. For Bakhtin 'may perfectly well have "borrowed" certain biographical episodes from his older brother' (as it has been delicately put) in order to provide what was in effect self-education with an official veneer—recent work on university records shows there is no record of Mikhail having been registered at either university.[68] In actual fact, it would appear he moved to Petrograd a year after his brother, in 1914, together with the rest of his family; he may have attended the university without actually registering. (This explains why a moment later he tells Duvakin how little formal education matters, anyhow: 'But I have to say that nevertheless, despite the fact that I cannot complain about either the gymnasium or the university, all the same I acquired the fundamentals through independent study . . . Because such educational establishments, official educational establishments, cannot, at bottom, cannot provide the kind of education which can satisfy a person' (*Con.*, 35).)

Even if Bakhtin did not attend university, he has been clear on his retrospective sympathies, which lay closer to the philosophical culture of the professors than the political interests of the radical intelligentsia. Confessedly 'completely apolitical' (*Con.*, 69), Bakhtin condemns the 'democratic students who made trouble' (*Con.*, 66) and showers praise on three professors who, perhaps rather too neatly, point to three distinct influences on his philosophical world-view. According to Bakhtin, his most significant teachers—but perhaps these, too, were 'borrowed'?— were F. F. Zelinsky, the Nietzschean classicist,[69] A. I. Vvedensky, at that time the leading figure in Russian neo-Kantianism, and the religious philosopher N. O. Lossky (*Con.*, 56). If, as is so often the case at universities, the most important play was off the ball, then what mattered most was not lectures and tutorials but neo-Kantianism, the ins and outs of which dominated student discussion in the humanities as well as the salons of

---

[68] Ibid. 85.

[69] On Zelinsky's Nietzscheanism and its possible influence on Bakhtin, see James M. Curtis, 'Michael [*sic*] Bakhtin, Nietzsche, and Russian Pre-Revolutionary Thought', in Bernice Glatzer Rosenthal (ed.), *Nietzsche in Russia* (Princeton, NJ: Princeton University Press, 1986), 331–54. Hans Günther has pointed out that Russian Nietzscheanism was filtered through the populist ideas of Viacheslav Ivanov; see his 'M. Bakhtin i "Rozhdenie tragedii" F. Nitsshe [F. Nietzsche]', *Dialog Karnaval Khronotop*, 1 (1992), 27–34.

Petrograd intellectuals[70] (Bely, among others, has written of conflicts between neo-Kantian tendencies maturing—if that is the right word—into social squabbles[71]). While Bakhtin was in Petrograd attending university (or not, as the case may be), his future close friend and intellectual colleague Matvei Kagan was involved in the classic Russian pilgrimage to the philosophical fount, Germany, where he studied at Leipzig, then with Hermann Cohen and Ernst Cassirer at Berlin, and finally with Paul Natorp at Marburg, thus completing a superb neo-Kantian education.[72] In Heidelberg, neo-Kantianism's other wing, comprising Wilhelm Windelband and Heinrich Rickert, worked on an epistemological justification and definition of the *Geisteswissenschaften* (sciences of culture or spirit). In the words of a friend and contemporary, Nikolai Bakhtin had 'entered the dead-end of neo-Kantianism', and his younger brother apparently followed him: 'I was', he confessed late in his life, 'captivated by the Marburg school—that's all there is to say.'[73] So captivated, it seems, that in 1920 one more official form persuaded him to borrow an educational pedigree even more neo-Kantian than his brother's—that of his friend Kagan ('From 1910 until 1912', Bakhtin wrote, 'I lived in Germany, where I studied for four semesters at Marburg University and one semester in Berlin').[74] While Bakhtin was busy being captivated, *Logos*, the neo-Kantian journal published in simultaneous Russian and German editions

---

[70] The reminiscences of Iu. G. Oksman have emphasized the pervasiveness of neo-Kantian debate amongst students of philology. Thus:

> The lectures and books of A. I. Vvedensky preached neo-Kantianism, and thus almost all of the student-philologists were fierce opponents of vulgar materialism . . . We knew the history of modern philosophy according to Windelband, and looked askance at those who preferred Paulsen, Mach and Avenarius. Following W. Dilthey and Rickert (both of whom we knew only by hearsay) we contrasted the 'sciences of spirit' to the natural sciences. In the sciences of spirit there could not be conformity to law, because there the unique and unrepeatable was studied, while in the natural sciences, the 'mass' was studied. (M. O. Chudakova and E. A. Toddes, 'Tynianov v vospominaniiakh sovremennika', *Tynianovskii sbornik: Pervye Tynianovskie chteniia* (Riga: Zinatne, 1984), 93)

The above pertains directly to the Russian Formalist Tynianov, but is equally relevant to Formalists such as Shklovsky and Eikhenbaum—the latter confessed that the Heidelberg neo-Kantian Rickert was his favourite philosopher. Much Anglo-American discussion of Russian Formalism misinterprets central elements of the doctrine because it does not acknowledge the heavy theoretical debt owed to neo-Kantian and phenomenological philosophy. A sophisticated account is Steiner's *Russian Formalism*.

[71] See Andrei Bely, *Mezhdu dvukh revoliutsii* (Moscow: Khudozhestvennaia literatura, 1990), ch. 14.

[72] See Brian Poole's account of Kagan's philosophical career and his influence on Bakhtin in '"Nazad k Kaganu"'.

[73] Reported in Bocharov, 'Ob odnom razgovore', 81. Bakhtin claimed an interest in Hermann Cohen's work dating from his time in Odessa (*Con.*, 35–6).

[74] A. G. Lisov and E. G. Trusova, 'Repliki po povodu avtobiograficheskogo mifotvorchestva M. M. Bakhtina', *Dialog Karnaval Khronotop*, 3 (1996), 165.

from 1910 to 1914, was providing a ready conduit for the reception of German philosophical work in Russia.[75]

Neo-Kantianism was central to Bakhtin's project, but in embracing it Bakhtin was not—as in his own self-presentation—tracking into unknown territory, but riding the crest of a cultural wave. It could flow into his work from a variety of sources—the university at which he didn't register, the pages of *Logos*, the philosophically accomplished Kagan (whom he met in Nevel'), independent reading—and the evidence shows it flowed continuously and influentially, well into the late 1930s, rather than just providing a soon to be surpassed starting-point.[76] It provided, first of all, a conception of philosophy as, on the one hand, something necessarily strict and systematic, and, on the other, something historical and critical, justifying and explaining the achievement of the human and natural sciences rather than offering itself as their substitute.[77] Secondly, as a consequence of this definition, it focused attention on the distinctiveness of knowledge in the human sciences (as opposed to natural-scientific forms), a problem on which Bakhtin would later superimpose the distinction between dialogical and monological relationships. Thirdly, in the hands of the Russian neo-Kantian Vvedensky, it demonstrated that the question of distinctively cultural knowledge was first and foremost a question of how, and with what limitations, we could know the meanings, intentions, sensations, and so forth of *others*. The *Geist* of the *Geisteswissenschaften* was neither Hegel's World-Spirit nor those feelings and ideas of our own to which we had, as it were, direct access; it was the spirit or mind of others, available to us only in the form of human expression. In *Psychology Without Any Metaphysics* Vvedensky would ask how the gestures, expressions, and language of others could be interpreted by us as indications of psychic phenomena without resorting to metaphysical speculation.[78] Finally, neo-Kantianism in

---

[75] On *Logos* see Ch. 2, p.. 100 n. 45.

[76] The conventional judgement that Bakhtin had outgrown neo-Kantianism by the time he returned to Leningrad in 1924 is belied not only by textual evidence, but also by Bakhtin's own testimony (which is perhaps more reliable when it comes to intellectual matters than biographical ones) and evidence from the archive. In the Duvakin interviews Bakhtin says that he participated in Leningrad discussion circles in the mid-1920s 'as a Kantian' (*Con.*, 144). But, more importantly, the neo-Kantian work on which he showers the greatest praise is not one of Hermann Cohen's texts from the early part of the century, but Cassirer's *Philosophy of Symbolic Forms* (*Con.*, 42 and 230), published in German between 1923 and 1929 and probably read by Bakhtin in the 1930s (see n. 128 below). On Cassirer's extensive influence see Poole, 'Bakhtin and Cassirer'.

[77] Bakhtin is reported to have compared Russian 'free intellectualism' unfavourably with the strictness of German philosophy on at least a couple of occasions. See Bocharov, 'Ob odnom razgovore', 81, and Kaganskaia, 'Shutovskoi khorovod', 141, where Bakhtin claims philosophy is a 'particular field of human knowledge. Knowledge, yes. As mathematics is.'

[78] A. I. Vvedensky, *Psikhologiia bez vsiakoi metafiziki*, 2nd edn. (Petrograd: Stoeiulevich, 1915). Vvedensky understood that the transformation of psychology from a discipline 'about the spirit'

the person of Kagan presented Bakhtin with the demand that all human culture be made historical, orientated to the future and justified by its own achievements, and in the person of Cassirer with the claim that the Renaissance was the moment when this historical consciousness blossomed in Europe.

In all these respects, Bakhtin was following the lead of not just German, but German Jewish philosophers, a fact which visibly unnerves some of his less open-minded Russian followers. But while the intellectual substance of Bakhtin's philosophical culture was taken from German academic philosophy, its form and style remained unacademic and Russian. On his own account, in Petrograd the new, independent, and unofficial culture was a creature of informal societies, cafés, and salons rather than universities. Of these, Bakhtin apparently preferred the philosophically orientated milieu of the Symbolists to the self-consciously avant-gardiste and more 'scientific' culture developing in Futurist haunts. At the same time, his own independent activity, at least in the beginning, took its distance both from high philosophy and new science. In 1911–12, during an earlier, apparently extended, visit to St Petersburg (as Petrograd had been called until 1914), he was part of a group which has more reason than any other to be called the 'Bakhtin circle', for this one included two Bakhtins, Mikhail and Nikolai. 'Omphalos' consisted of the two brothers, Lev Pumpiansky, whom they knew from Vilnius, and three other friends.[79] Its distinctiveness in literary terms derived from its unrelenting devotion to parody and parodization, including the composition of long poems which Bakhtin could recite sixty years later. 'We were scholar-jokers. Jokers of science . . . or, if you prefer, clowns of science' (*Con.*, 52) is how Bakhtin described the group, and this devotion to life (which evidently also took in feasting and the smoking of hashish on at least some occasions) was evidently its strong point in comparison to other rival circles: 'OPOIaZ [the Russian Formalist group] lacked the most important thing, which the circle had, specifically a profoundly critical, but happily, not gloomily critical relation to all the phenomena of life and of contemporary culture' (*Con.*, 54). Perhaps happy critique, in all its Nietzschean glory, appears only in the retrospect of one who has written a book on carnival culture

to one 'without the spirit', created problems. But could he solve them? In his own *Filosofskie ocherki* (Prague, 1924), he would argue, following Kant, that only in moral feeling are we given sure signs of the existence of other subjects like ourselves.

[79] Bakhtin himself discusses 'Omphalos' in *Con.*, 40–1 and 50–5. Further information can be found in William Edgerton, 'Iu. G. Oksman, M. I. Lopatto, N. M. Bakhtin i vopros o knigoizdatel'stve "Omphalos"', in *Piatye Tynianovskie chteniia* (Riga, 1990), 211–37, and O. E. Osovsky, '"Neslyshnyi dialog": Biograficheskie i nauchnye sozvuchiia v sud'bakh Nikolaia i Mikhaila Bakhtinykh', in K. G. Isupov (ed.), *M. M. Bakhtin i filosofskaia kul'tura XX veka*, vol. ii (St Petersburg: Obrazovanie, 1991), 43–51.

and Rabelais. But it may also be that the relentlessly redemptive intention not of even hard-headed criticism is a mark of Bakhtin's debt to Christianity, but to formative cultural experiences of a different kind.

No work survives from this period: in Mikhail's biography, a richly embroidered background has nothing to front it. Of his reaction to February and October 1917 we have no evidence from the time, but the usual conflicts of retrospective accounts. Bakhtin is reported to have confided to his friend V. N. Turbin that he, like others, had assumed that power would pass over to the Constituent Assembly once it met.[80] In his interview with Duvakin he paints a much gloomier picture:

VDD. So in February subjectively you felt that it was to be either the monarchy or the extremist parties?

MMB. Yes, yes. And that the monarchy, in a word . . . that the victory of the extreme elements was inevitable. In addition, I would say we were inclined to be very pessimistic: we thought that the business was finished. Of course, the monarchy could not be restored, there was no one to restore it, no one to rely on, inevitably victory would belong to these great masses of soldiers, soldiers and peasants in soldiers' overcoats, to whom nothing mattered, the proletariat, which is not an historic class, it has no values of its own, it has nothing at all. They had spent their whole lives fighting only for very limited material goods. And that they were the ones who would seize power. And there would be no one to overthrow them, because all these intellectuals were incapable of doing that.

VDD. So, you didn't go to meetings?

MMB. No, I didn't go to meetings, no, no. I sat at home and read, and went to the library when the heating was turned on. (*Con.*, 118–19)

The political revolution will not solve anything because its very terms are part of the problem: a revolution by an economically defined class is limited to the necessarily degraded interests of the economic—goods (*blaga*) rather than values (*tsennosti*). But can one find culture in any other place besides the library? Bakhtin's reaction to the events of his day does not inspire confidence in his political judgement.

His brother Nikolai, who apparently shared and probably pioneered Mikhail's neo-Kantian and Nietzschean concerns, took a rather different path: he joined the White Army, and left Russia after some years of fighting, eventually arriving in England, where he completed a doctorate at Cambridge, taught briefly at the University of Southampton (by the sheerest coincidence—I hope—a former employer of the present writer), and went on to found the Linguistics Department at the University of

---

[80] From Osovsky, '"Neslyshnyi dialog"', 51 n. 14: 'V. N. Turbin once remarked in conversation that M. M. Bakhtin spoke of himself as a "fortnighter", i.e. in the early days of the October Revolution he assumed that in the next few days power would pass to the Constituent Assembly.'

Birmingham. When he later became a member of the Communist Party of Great Britain, he understandably questioned his earlier political judgements.

PHILOSOPHY IN NEVEL' AND VITEBSK, 1918–24

Texts

'Art and Responsibility' (1919).
'Towards a Philosophy of the Act' (1920–7: exact date in dispute).
'Author and Hero in Aesthetic Activity' (see under 1924–1929 below).

Selected Texts by Other Members of the Circle

Matvei Kagan: 'Hermann Cohen' (1918); the triptych 'On the Personality in Sociology' (1918–19), 'How is History Possible?' (1919), 'On the Course of History' (1920); 'Paul Natorp and the Crisis of Culture' (1922); 'Judaism in the Crisis of Culture' (1923).

Pavel Medvedev: 'The Theory of Artistic Creation'; 'Methodological Presuppositions of the History of Literature'; 'Russian Literature of the Twentieth Century' (none extant, reportedly confiscated by KGB: see below).

Lev Pumpiansky: *Dostoevsky and Antiquity* (1922); Gogol book (unpublished).

By the spring of 1918 food had become extremely scarce in Petrograd; at the suggestion of Pumpiansky, who lived there already, Bakhtin moved to the provincial city of Nevel', where the means to live were more plentiful. For two years Bakhtin taught at a local school. The decisive and unlikely importance of this provincial town, however, stems from the establishment there of a philosophical circle, dubbed the 'Kantian seminar' by its participants, which met regularly in the living quarters of its members for discussions on what were perceived as the critical intellectual questions of the time. This was the initial institution of a circle which, with some changes of membership, would be the principal focus of Bakhtin's intellectual life until 1928. The notion of a 'Bakhtin circle' arose with Voloshinov and Medvedev in mind, and was for a long time moored to the problem of the disputed texts, but it makes more sense to apply the term to the members of this remarkably stable group as a whole, whose systematic examination of the crisis of European culture provided a focus and inspiration for individual research. After his arrest, Bakhtin described the activity of this circle in the period in Leningrad (1924–27) in a manner surely relevant to its earlier incarnations:

The lecturing activity of myself and my friends was an expression of certain intellectual strivings and of an intellectual restlessness, born of the necessity to work out a new [. . .] materialistic world-view, adequate to social reality. This process of elaboration for us, for people already intellectually matured and possessing great and many-sided theoretical knowledge, could not be a process of the passive and easy assimilation of elements of a set world-view; it inevitably had to take on the character of the difficult and laborious work of the revaluation and testing of all our previous knowledge and convictions.[81]

In Nevel' the circle included Voloshinov, then a poet and musicologist, Kagan, who had just returned from Marburg, Lev Pumpiansky, a philosopher and literary scholar, Maria Veniaminovna Iudina, who would later become one of the Soviet Union's most important pianists, and the poet Boris Mikhailovich Zubakin. Of the group's work we have some short publications, some notes taken by Pumpiansky, and some strikingly enthusiastic reminiscences. One of Pumpiansky's notes from the summer of 1919 points to the central task of recovering a lost practical life: 'He [Bakhtin] has established unerringly the logical conditions of ethical reality and reduced them to a word: responsibility.'[82] Apparently, Bakhtin announced the principles of his ethical philosophy to Pumpiansky and Iudina in the course of a walk around a lake which, as a consequence, acquired the rather burdensome title of the Lake of Ethical Reality (*Con.*, 237).[83] The experience of 'responsibility' thus became the defining quality of ethical life, and the fact which even so dramatic an event as the revolution had sidestepped. When Bakhtin published the one-page 'Art and Responsibility' in the local journal *Den' iskusstva* in summer 1919, the emphasis was on an art which remained a part of that ethical reality, and an ethical reality which had a place for the lessons of art.

Bocharov has written of the 'pathos of participation' evident in this article, a pathos manifested in the energetic *public* cultural activity of the members of this circle. During his residence in Nevel' Bakhtin and his colleagues participated in numerous public debates and lectures, the very

[81] KGB Archive, Leningrad region, d. 14284, t. 3, l. 7; cited in Iu. P. Medvedev, 'Na puti k sozdaniiu sotsiologicheskoi poetiki', *Dialog Karnaval Khronotop*, 2 (1998), 47 n. 85. The ellipsis in this quotation marks a point where the transcription of the interrogation is confused: the Russian is 'novoe dlia nas, adekvatnoe sotsialnoi deistvitel'nosti trevog i materialisticheskogo mirovozzreniia'. Having consulted expert opinion, I have decided to assume that the typist recording the interview made an error, particularly with the word 'trevog' and with the ending of 'mirovozzreniia'; Medvedev himself offered a corrected and therefore comprehensible version of the passage in an earlier quotation of it; see his '"Nas bylo mnogo . . ."', 95.

[82] From Pumpiansky's archive, cited in Nikolaev's introduction to the the 'Lektsii i vystupleniia' (Lec., 227).

[83] On the basis of comments by Pumpiansky, Bakhtin, and Iudina, and the examination of Pumpiansky's writings from that summer, N. I. Nikolaev claims that the precise walk in question must have taken place in June 1919. See Nikolaev, 'M. M. Bakhtin v Nevele letom 1919g.', in *Nevel'skii sbornik*, vol. i (St Petersburg: Akropol', 1996), 96–101.

titles of which disclose an atmosphere in which open, public argument feels free to address both the most transcendental and the most private experiences—'God and Socialism', 'Art and Socialism', 'On the Meaning of Life', 'On the Meaning of Love', 'Christianity and Criticism', 'Nietzsche and Christianity', 'The Russian National Character in Literature and Philosophy'.[84]

The circle could continue to articulate its concerns in public when Bakhtin, Pumpiansky, and Voloshinov moved to Vitebsk (Bakhtin in early autumn 1920), which had, as a consequence of the internal emigration described earlier, become a major centre of intellectual and cultural life (one of Bakhtin's closer acquaintances being, for example, Kasimir Malevich, the instigator of Suprematism and the Vitebsk School of Art).[85] Pumpiansky left in 1920 and Kagan had gone to Moscow, but there was also a fresh infusion of talent into the circle: Pavel Nikolaevich Medvedev, a literary scholar, and the future director of the Leningrad Philharmonic, Ivan Ivanovich Sollertinsky. The latter has recorded the titles of lectures given in Vitebsk from September 1920 to April 1921, which display no less scope than those in Nevel'—from Bakhtin 'The Moral Moment in Culture', 'On the Word', 'New Russian Poetry', the history of modern philosophy, and Russian, French, and medieval literature; from Pumpiansky lectures on the philosophy of music, the philosophy of antiquity, 'On Heroism', and 'The Work of Constructing a System of Morality'; from Medvedev a series on Russian literature of the twentieth century and on the Moscow Art Theatre.[86]

Bakhtin's correspondence with Kagan reveals a restlessness of focus as well as of spirit. 'Lately I have been working almost exclusively on the aesthetics of verbal creation'[87] (February 1921); 'I am working a great deal, especially on aesthetics and psychology'[88] (March 1921); '[while I was ill] I began a work which I now intend to continue—"The Subject of Morality [nravstvennosti] and the Subject of Law". I hope in the near future to put this work in its final and finished form; it will serve as an introduction to my ethical philosophy'[89] (October–November 1921); 'Now I am writing a work on Dostoevsky which I hope to finish very soon; for the time being, I have put aside the work "The Subject of Morality and the Subject of Law"'[90] (January 1922): in the course of one year, three apparently different

---

[84] See Bocharov, 'Ob odnom razgovore', 84; and 'Gazeta *Molot* (1918–1920)', in *Nevel'skii sbornik*, vol. i (St Petersburg: Akropol', 1996), 147–57, for the list of topics.

[85] Bakhtin describes their friendship in *Con.*, 137–40.

[86] Listed in Mikheeva, *Sollertinsky*, 28–9.

[87] Letter of 20 Feb. 1921, Iu. M. Kagan, 'O starykh bumagakh', 66.

[88] Iu. M. Kagan, 'O starykh bumagakh', 68.

[89] Ibid. 71.

[90] Ibid. 72.

projects, on aesthetics, ethical philosophy, and Dostoevsky.[91] Were these three different projects or the different faces of a single one? The text 'Towards a Philosophy of the Act' presents itself as the introduction to an ambitious project of ethical philosophy, within which a critique of aesthetics would figure as but one element:

The first part of our investigation will be devoted to an examination of precisely the fundamental moments of the architectonics of the actual world, not as it is thought, but as it is experienced. The following part will be devoted to aesthetic activity as an act, not from within its product, but from the point of view of the author as a responsible participant and ⟨?⟩ to the ethics of the artistic work. The third part is on the ethics of politics and the final one, of religion. (TPA 122/54)

There follow fifteen pages on aesthetics, culminating in an interesting analysis of Pushkin's poem 'Parting', and then . . . nothing: the project was not, as I pointed out earlier, to be completed. Instead we have a number of fragments: 'Author and Hero in Aesthetic Activity', which clearly follows the discussion on aesthetics, but may have followed from a distance of several years; 'The Problem of Content, Material and Form', a critique of Formalism, apparently composed around 1924; notes by Pumpiansky, dated summer 1924 by Nikolaev, on the first of a series of five lectures called 'The Hero and the Author in Artistic Creation' (Lec., 233–4); notes on a lecture devoted to the philosophy of religion entitled 'The Problem of Grounded Peace' (Lec., 234–6); and symptomatically, no trace of anything on the ethics of politics. You can put these together so that they look like the haphazard fulfilment of Bakhtin's project, and if you add the Dostoevsky book to the end, then Bakhtin seems to have made good on all his plans. But in truth what has been left to us is not a complete work but a trail of fragments, each marking a slight change of tack in Bakhtin's voyage through the 1920s.

The breadth of the project for an 'ethical philosophy' confirms what we might have gathered from Bakhtin's discussion of February and October: that politics itself cannot provide the normative basis for a society. But neither, on Bakhtin's account, can moral or ethical discourse itself. For once one defines the ethical as a particular field of problems, with its own methods, concepts, and arguments, it is reduced to a kind of science, which advances in a theoretical manner akin to natural science itself. The subject of Bakhtin's ethical philosophy is therefore not a distinct sphere of ethical or moral action or a domain of distinctly ethical considerations (which one would then apply to otherwise independent fields like politics,

[91] Announcements in the press at the time slightly complicate this picture. In March 1921 the Vitebsk journal *Isskustvo* announced that Bakhtin was continuing work on a book devoted to moral philosophy. The expected publication of the Dostoevsky book was announced in August 1922, but no manuscript of it is known (see above, Ch. 1, p. 12 n. 16).

science, art, and so on), but the absolute pre-eminence of the ethical reality which endows all spheres of action with meaning and purpose. Ethics would be not a science or a domain of reason, but a 'recognition' (*uznanie*) of the ontological facts, from which everything else would follow.

Bakhtin's philosophical task is thus not the derivation of a new set of norms, more convincing than existing options, but a persuasive disclosure of the intersubjectivity which endowed every distinct norm with the 'oughtness' (*dolzhenstvovanie*) described in the previous chapter. '[T]here are no specifically ethical norms, every substantive norm must have its validity specifically grounded by the appropriate discipline: by logic, aesthetics, biology, medicine, one of the social sciences' (TPA 98/22); but unless this norm was experienced as part of ethical reality, its theoretical truth would have no effect on our behaviour. A cultural world dominated by the separation of spheres and a belief in their individual, self-propelled progress leaves the decision to act responsibly to chance and accident:

I can agree with this or that position as a psychologist, a sociologist, a jurist *ex cathedra*, but to assert that by this alone it becomes a norm for my act means to leap over the fundamental problem. Even for the very fact of my actual assent to the validity of a given position *ex cathedra*—as *my act*—the validity of the position in itself and my psychological faculty of understanding is not enough, there must be something which comes from me, namely the morally obligating orientation of my consciousness in relation to a position which is in itself theoretically valid . . . (TPA 99/23–4)

Mere theoretical validity is like 'a document without a signature, not obligating anyone to anything' (TPA 115/44), for it separates off *the fact* that something is valid from those *for whom* it is valid.

Yet the world Bakhtin confronted, or thought he confronted, was in effect no more than an accumulation of the theoretically valid. Bakhtin calls this sense of the world 'theoreticism' and most of 'Towards a Philosophy of the Act' is organized as its critique. 'Theoreticism' constructs a world which is historical but which has no point, irremediably divided into 'two value contexts, as it were, two lives: the life of the entire infinite world as a whole, which can be known only objectively, and my little personal life. The subject of the first is the world as a whole, the subject of the second is a contingent, solitary subject' (TPA 119/50). This vision of a theoretical-scientific reason cut loose from life, creating powers for which it can provide no meaningful guidance, wreaking havoc with its cold instrumentality, is a familiar one, of course, virtually the theme song of the Central European intelligentsia. And at first glance, Bakhtin appears to be placing the blame on familiar shoulders—the overweening ambition of scientific, instrumental reason, which culminates in the creation of the weapons so dramatically effective in the First World War:

It is like the world of technology, which knows only its own immanent law, to which it subordinates its uncontrolled development, despite the fact that long ago it deviated from an understanding of its own cultural purpose, and may serve evil rather than good; these instruments are perfected in accordance with their own inner law, as what were originally a means of reasonable defence become a terrible, ruinous and destructive force. (TPA 86–7/7)

However, 'theoreticism' is *like* the world of technique, not the consequence of its dominance; its real roots lie elsewhere. Neither does Bakhtin criticize theory and science in the name of 'life' in the manner of Bergson and Nietzsche, for 'philosophy of life' rejects culture in the name of an equally blind and irresponsible devotion to biological impulse and intuition.

Theoreticism's paradigmatic expression, to which the bulk of the essay-fragment is devoted, is not natural science, but formalism in ethics, as it is formulated in Kant and his neo-Kantian followers. Bakhtin reiterates the well-known objection that Kantianism transforms morality into law-like, juridical form, to which 'the will' adheres only given a certain leap of faith. For while Hegel may have philosophically dealt with this weakness in Kant, in sociological and political terms, Kant continued to hold sway. The liberal constitutionalism which 'progressives' hoped for throughout Europe, and which failed so spectacularly in Russia, consecrated the split between the obligation demanded by law and the free play of private interests which would sustain civil society; it surrendered the dream of an ethical life to the rationality of a bureaucratic-legal order. Bakhtin's point is not that this bourgeois legality is evil, but that purely legal norms cannot and will not obligate, and from the perspective of his historical moment he appears to have a point. Classical liberalism had played its part in destroying the legitimate authority of the Church and Crown, but it had not quite figured out what to put in its place, and even if it could have delivered an endless rise in living standards (it had already become clear it couldn't, though its most spectacular demonstration was yet to come) it was not clear that it could translate this material change into something meaningful enough for its subjects.[92] As even Weber, one of liberal constitutionalism's most eloquent defenders, recognized, bourgeois legality and an efficient bureaucracy would not be enough to preserve the social order; its existence had to be morally compelling, not just temporarily advantageous.

---

[92] For an analysis of this shared concern with establishing the means of moral consensus in societies abandoned to the unreliable social cement of the market see Lepenies, *Between Literature and Science*, 47–90.

The inevitable need for meaning was proved by the fact that the most formally rational norms only acquired legitimacy by virtue of where they came from and how they were passed on. As Bakhtin points out, good form is never enough:

The norm is a special form of the free-willing of one person in relation to others, and as such, is essentially characteristic only of right (laws) and religion (commandments); and here its actual obligating quality—as a norm—is evaluated not from the perspective of its semantic content but from the perspective either of the actual authority of its source (free-willing) or of the authenticity and precision of its transmission (references to a law, to scripture, recognized texts, interpretations, verifications of authenticity, or—in more principled fashion—to the grounding of life, the grounding of a legislative authority, the proven divine inspiration of scripture). (TPA 99/24)

In effect, Bakhtin radicalizes the crisis of legitimacy, in so far as he claims that 'law'—precisely the thing which a liberal, limited state would count on—cannot be a reliable source of moral feeling. For law treats all equally, whereas the basis of the ethical sphere is what Bakhtin would later describe as the 'absolute inequality of I and all others' (QuSelf, 73), the acknowledgement of which is the only possible of source of a feeling of 'ought-ness'.

At the same time, Bakhtin wants to push forward to ethical action via heightened philosophical reflection, not beat a strategic retreat to it from the exposed positions of modern reason and science. His appeal is not to the fatally wounded authority of tradition and metaphysics, but to what he sees as the actual, but ineffectual, content of modern culture. Although he rejects the formalism of neo-Kantianism and its devotion to the ideal of law, he continues to believe in a philosophy orientated to 'the fact of science', in so far as he seeks to disclose 'oughtness' within the differentiated reality which modern natural science, social science, and art have bequeathed to us.[93] He will not, therefore, renounce the differentiation of moral life from science, and both from art, which is emblematic of modernity itself. But the strength of this position depends upon the neo-Kantian revision of Kant himself, according to which the distinction between moral *philosophy* concerned with the suprasensible and natural *science* anchored in experience is old hat.

[93] Neither is 'Towards a Philosophy of the Act' a regression from strict philosophical reflection to loose and casual observation about the ambiguity of the everyday. In the commentary of some critics this text appears as a bizarre mixture of empiricist belief in the immediacy of experience and intuitivist ethics: with eyes unclouded by theory, one grasps the concrete situation and just knows what the right thing to do is. 'Concrete', however, marks not an exit from theory, but a moment of it; Bakhtin reaches the concrete by phenomenological analysis, which reveals the inner structure of the consciousness within which every 'thing' achieves some kind of objectivity.

Kant had had to clear a separate space, which he called the suprasensible or noumenal, for subjects to be free and so responsible for their actions. But in so far as the neo-Kantians treat both law and natural science as equivalent parts of culture, both of which create their own sphere in a manner analogous to that of mathematics, they render this distinction nonsensical. Law, no less than biology, becomes a science, and both take their place in the objectivity of a historically developing culture. Thus the primacy of practical reason, which Kant had postulated so that morality was guaranteed some sort of foothold, is refigured in Bakhtin as the primacy of the ethical–practical in all spheres of existence, with responsibility replacing the categorical imperative as the last word in moral discourse. The ethical subject comes to life not by escaping from experience into the realm of the suprasensible, but by going deeper into it, finding in the ordinary practice of art, politics, and religious ritual a consciousness always structured as 'responsible' and 'responsive'. Bakhtin need not establish morality as a higher calling, for he will maintain ethical reality as the unique and unconditioned reality which indisputably is, in relation to which every theoretical act and reality has only a secondary and technical status.

Bakhtin is willing to accept the substance of modern science, modern law, and modern art—throughout his work this Kantian trio is his point of reference—and the fact of historical movement in each field, but he insists that this substance can be made meaningful only when framed by the essential inequality of *I* and *others*. Without that, science of any kind is empty theory, and its progress pointless movement. But the mere fact of intersubjectivity does not, *pace* Bakhtin, lead to ethical conclusions, nor does its acknowledgement automatically catapult the subject into ethical space. One could recognize intersubjectivity and remain unmoved, unless one believes, as Bakhtin does, that the meaning of this intersubjectivity has been revealed by the example of Christ himself. Responsibility in Bakhtin's sense does not flow from intersubjectivity plain and simple, but from a certain kind of intersubjectivity, framed by a particular philosophy of history. Only if one believes in the need for salvation does the fact of intersubjectivity serve as a reminder of one's weakness and dependence on the mercy of others. Bakhtin counts on strict phenomenology to lead us to these conclusions precisely because he believes that the presence of the Divine is manifest in the very structure of the world. Replying to the objection that Revelation interrupts the laws of nature, which make the world determinate, Bakhtin claims: 'Why would the world not lose its determinateness without the presence of Revelation? This characterizes the world to the same degree as a law of nature' (Lec., 245). The obligation sedimented in the structure of reality itself is therefore proof that the world was touched by God, but even Bakhtin cannot resist pointing out that it is Christ's example which makes the meaning of intersubjectivity crystal clear: 'The world from which Christ departed will no longer be the same world as the one in which he had never been, it is in principle different' (TPA 94/16). This kind of religiosity permits Bakhtin to have his philosophical cake and eat it, too: he can avoid a return to the authority of the metaphysical, while at the same time ensuring that religious belief will regain the empire it lost in the modern division of spheres. Faith will display itself not only within the confines of ecclesiastical institutions or as the strictly demarcated act of Christian charity, but in the responsibility which the believing subject will demonstrate in all its activities: political, ethical, artistic, and scientific–technical.

The phenomenological investigations initiated in this text, and continued in Bakhtin's other work, however, have persuaded many without faith; so many, that one begins to wonder whether the ethical reality Bakhtin discloses really does depend on learning the lesson of Christ's example. In the lecture on philosophy of religion which followed this introductory fragment, Bakhtin pointed to the existence of God as the only possible stopping-point for an otherwise endless cycle of self-justification. The subject who 'would make immanent his own justification' (Lec., 235) at once becomes unjust, for it is intrinsic to justification as such that it is justification to an *other*, and the only *other* ultimately good enough is the divine one. For this reason Bakhtin will turn to confession and the affliction of the religious conscience as a higher sphere of the ethical than law: confession which is 'completely inexplicable in terms of morality, i.e., in effect, on juridical grounds' (Lec., 235) embodies the need for an *other* central to Christian ethics; '*conscience*, i.e. not ethical but unique obligation' (Lec., 235) attacks the subject in its individuality rather than as an instance of something general.[94] One hardly needs God, however, to accept the critique of formal ethics, or the fact that justification is necessarily an intersubjective process. While Bakhtin was melding neo-Kantianism and

[94] As one utters these words, it is impossible not to hear the armies of psychoanalysis coming over the hill, and for good reason. The self as constantly guilty in the presence of the Other, as striving to maintain its identity in the face of endless self-negation: all this is the stock-in-trade of psychoanalytic theory, particularly its Lacanian variant. In this scheme of things Bakhtinian 'faith' would occupy the place of fantasy: it is what settles the subject, and allows it to get on with things. In Slavoj Žižek's account of Pascal's wager, religious belief is not what motivates the practice of the subject, it *is* the practice of the subject, its mute compliance with ordinary ritual; see Žižek, *The Sublime Object of Ideology* (London: Verso, 1989), 36–40. The moment of faith then appears as a formal recognition of what the subject 'knew' all along. Thus it is with Bakhtin's concept of responsibility and its phenomenological discovery: the subject with faith simply understands the responsible practice in which subjects without faith might also engage. Bakhtin's text is, of course, composed during the high point of Freudian theorizing (the early 1920s), which he and others would later confront head on.

Christian ethics, Cohen was taking the same materials in the direction of reform Judaism, while Weber and Durkheim, neo-Kantians to begin with, searched for secular equivalents for the morally binding force of religion. The moment of faith which Bakhtin thinks will put the subject at ease will appear in Durkheim as the authority of collective consciousness (or perhaps, more relevantly, in Saussure as the mute but inevitable authority of the speaking community itself, which alone puts an end to the potentially endless anxiety set in motion by the arbitrariness of the sign). As for conscience: Freud had something to say about that.

In short, the ethical intersubjectivity Bakhtin discovered may have been itself a historic fact, and the shape of the redemption to which it pointed may have owed as much to Kant, Marx, and Russian Populism as to Christian revelation. Bakhtin comes close to admitting this himself, in so far as he knows this intersubjectivity has different forms in art, science, ethics, and religion. But he tries to evade the implications of this insight by establishing a hierarchy of these forms with, as we shall see, religion and art somewhere near the top, science and politics closer to the bottom. But while Bakhtin may be right to see in law and legal respect too weak a bond for social life, too indirect an address to the subject, his belief that the norms he needs—boundless love and charity—are encoded in our phenomenological condition is unlikely to inspire any kind of faith, Christian or otherwise. In his scheme faith and intersubjectivity make history go, but they have no history themselves, and this confers on them an unworldliness which will not dissipate until Bakhtin buries himself in the contemplation of particular cultural forms.[95] Bakhtin may have believed that it was his own faith which ultimately revealed to him the ethical reality concealed in modern intersubjectivity, but belief in the priority of the ethical and hope in the immediacy of redemption was widespread in crisis-ridden Europe. The fluid concept of the Divine which appears and disappears in his writing may be no more than the device which allows him, in Adorno's words, to 'contemplate all things as they would present themselves from the standpoint of redemption'. As Adorno himself notes, 'beside the demand thus placed on thought, the question of the reality or unreality of redemption itself hardly matters'.[96]

To the ambiguity over the relative weight of secular knowledge and

---

[95] Russian religious philosophers like A. A. Meier, in whose circle Bakhtin participated, had no compunctions about amalgamating the worldly and the redemptive, combining belief in Russian Orthodoxy with advocacy of social revolution. Bakhtin describes Meier's politics in *Con.*, 89–90. Alexander Mihailovic has described how Meier translated theological terms into an image of a classless society in 'With Influence and Without Separation: Bakhtin and the Chalcedonian Ideal', [Proceedings of] The Seventh International Bakhtin Conference, Book II, 351–5.

[96] Adorno, *Minima Moralia*, 247.

Christian belief in Bakhtin, we should add another, with possibly greater repercussions for his future work. 'Towards a Philosophy of the Act' assigns to aesthetic activity an apparently subordinate role, which can only appear ironic in light of the fact that after this introduction Bakhtin would not write a single text on ethics, but endless texts on aesthetics. As 'a justified vision, if it does not pass beyond its boundaries' (TPA 94/17) the aesthetic has a decisive part to play, providing a necessary stepping stone to that love for the *other* which will become the cornerstone of inter-human relations in this Christianized moral world. But it is also a deceptively immediate form of vision, allied to what Bakhtin will call in his lectures on Kant 'the logic of the horizon', which must be transcended through philosophy. Its tendency to consummate the world leads to 'the peace of self-satisfaction, i.e. of the aesthetic mythologeme', from which 'I must be freed precisely by the unease which, through confession, will become faith' (Lec., 236). Aesthetic experience is necessary, but illusory, and it needs a distinctly 'ethical' philosophy to remind us that it is only a subjective moment of the intersubjective whole.

This conviction of the leading role of philosophy unites the variously composed 'Bakhtin' circles and seminars. The collective form of this philosophizing is, however, itself significant: the role assigned to philosophy by Russian neo-Kantianism makes possible a simultaneous assault on the human sciences on separate fronts. Bakhtin and Pumpiansky focused on Dostoevsky and aesthetics—Pumpiansky's efforts leading to the lecture-turned-book *Dostoevsky and Antiquity* in 1922, as well as articles on Gogol which, according to notes left in his archive, were intended as part of a dialogue on the concept of responsibility.[97] Kagan's extant texts turn to philosophy to protect labour and history itself from mythification: in 'How is History Possible?' and 'Judaism in the Crisis of Culture'[98] the rights of historical being are asserted in contraposition to myth and paganism, which threaten to displace the world as a context of action with a settled, quiescent reality: 'History must not be objectified, it must also be justified being, having meaning.'[99] Medvedev's work from this period is clearly orientated to a philosophically informed poetics: by 1924, according to his personal notes, three texts existed in manuscript—'The Theory of Artistic Creation', 'Methodological Presuppositions of the History of Literature', and 'Russian Literature of the 20th Century', as well as the article 'Towards a Philosophy of Russian Literature' and the critique of Formalism, 'The Morphological (Formal) Method, or Scholarly Salierism'.[100] As

---

[97] See N. I. Nikolaev, introduction to 'Lektsii i vystupleniia' (Lec., 223–7).

[98] M. I. Kagan, 'Kak vozmozhna istoriia?'; 'Evreistvo v krizise kul'tury'.

[99] M. I. Kagan, 'Evreistvo v krizise kul'tury', 233.

[100] Based on the archival materials held by his son; see, by Iu. P. Medvedev: '"Nas bylo

the titles and topics make clear, the form of philosophical labour chosen by the Bakhtin circles of the early 1920s render nonsensical the distinction between the sociological and the philosophical. A philosophy which no longer seeks to provide metaphysical insight, but orientates itself to the 'fact of science' cannot function without commerce with the knowledge— faulty or not—of the human and social sciences themselves.

LENINGRAD AND THE TURN TO SCIENCE, 1924–1929

Texts

Lectures and other contributions to the philosophical circle, from notes taken by Pumpiansky (1924–25).

'The Problem of Content, Material and Form in Verbal Art' (1924).

'Author and Hero in Aesthetic Activity' (1924–27?).

Lecture on Mayakovsky (1926–27).

Lectures on Russian literature, from notes taken by R. M. Mirkina: on Viacheslav Ivanov, Esenin, Tolstoy, Leonov, Ehrenburg, Fedin, Zoshchenko, Tynianov, Bely and Sologub (1920s).

Problems of Dostoevsky's Art (1929).

'Prefaces' for the Collected Works of Tolstoy edited by Boris Eikhenbaum, on the dramatic works, and on *Resurrection* (1929).

Selected Texts by Other Members of the Circle

Valentin Voloshinov: 'Beyond the Social: On Freudianism' (1925); 'Discourse in Life and Discourse in Poetry' (1926); *Freudianism: A Critical Sketch* (1927); 'The Latest Trends in Linguistic Thought in the West' (1928); *Marxism and the Philosophy of Language* (1929).

Pavel Medvedev: 'Scholarly Salierism: On the Formal (Morphological) Method' (1925); 'Sociologism without Sociology: On the Methodological Works of P. N. Sakulin' (1926); *The Formal Method in Literary Scholarship: A Critical Introduction to Sociological Poetics* (1928).

In the early 1920s the members of Bakhtin's circle moved away from Vitebsk—the majority to Leningrad (Kagan was already in Moscow)— where they began the search for a role within the rapidly emerging institutions which were to play a leading part in the drive towards a long overdue cultural revolution. Strained material circumstances, genuine uncertainty as to what cultural revolution might mean, struggles within the

mnogo"', 92; Letter to the Editors, *Dialog Karnaval Khronotop*, 4 (1995), 149–50; 'Vitebskii period zhizni P. N. Medvedeva', in *Bakhtinskie chteniia*, vol. i (Vitebsk: N. A. Pan'kov, 1996), 74.

Communist Party, and the local acts of thrust and compromise which attend all such institutional upheaval led inevitably to a confused and changeable cultural life, in which intellectuals, whether well or ill disposed towards the Communist political leadership, could never be secure in their positions. The principal sources of employment were the various state-sponsored research institutes and publishing houses, the leadership of which had, for the most part, passed to a younger generation of scholars in the humanities, of a notably different formation than their elders. After Bakhtin's return to Leningrad in 1924, he found occasional work in the Institute for the History of the Arts (where, for example, Medvedev also worked) and the State Publishing House, and gave lectures at his own lodgings for modest, sometimes optional, remuneration.

The principal arena for his intellectual work, however, remained the philosophical circle, duly reconstituted in Leningrad after his return in the spring of 1924. In the printed debates so important to Russian cultural life in the 1920s and the public lectures and arguments sponsored by the new or reformed institutes, Bakhtin appears to have played no part. The reasons for this are not clear. During the 1920s other members of the circle—Pumpiansky, Medvedev, Sollertinsky, for example—sharing Bakhtin's intellectual commitments, were active as public speakers and polemicists; Bakhtin restricted his activities to private meetings and circle discussions, where he delivered lectures on philosophical and literary topics. Suggestions that Bakhtin was uniquely out of step with the terms of public debate, even as early as 1925 or 1926, are not very convincing, for Pumpiansky shared Bakhtin's religious sympathies, and in 1928 Bakhtin had his manuscript on Dostoevsky accepted for publication (granted, with help from Medvedev). For whatever reasons, Bakhtin, except for his failed attempt to publish 'The Problem of Content, Material and Form', stayed out of sight and out of print until the end of the decade.

This raises the unavoidable question of the meaning of the institutional form of the 'circle', which played so historically significant a role in Russian intellectual and political life. Jürgen Habermas and Reinhart Koselleck have drawn attention to the new forms of intellectual association and discussion—the public sphere—which institutionalized the Enlightenment in eighteenth-century England and France.[101] Coffee houses, the new private press, the Masonic lodges: all these institutionalized a space where a new form of secular reason with political aspirations could take shape, a form which would ground the power of liberal parliamentarianism and liberal public opinion in the capitalist democracies of the nineteenth century. Russia, of course, witnessed neither the rise of parliamentary

[101] See Habermas, *The Structural Transformation of the Public Sphere*, and Koselleck, *Critique and Crisis*.

power nor the formation of the active public sphere which might have been its precondition. Not the enlightened bourgeois but the educated 'superfluous man' dominated its socio-intellectual landscape: individuals dependent on state privilege, from whom modernizing powers of reason were demanded, without their political correlate.[102] In the 1830s the institution of the private discussion 'circle' arose to fill the vacuum created by the lack of an Enlightenment worthy of the name. Conducted not only in private but in secret, the meetings of these circles witnessed debate on political, social, and philosophical questions by intellectuals from a variety of social origins (landowning, officer class, clerical, and petty bourgeois, for the most part). However, only in contradictory fashion could they emulate the public sphere of the West. The presupposition grounding debate that the better argument could and should win through, no matter by whom delivered, might still hold; likewise the secular intention to settle issues of public moment through the exercise of reason—defined as open debate and argument—alone. (In this respect the circle could distinguish itself from the salon life of a slightly earlier period, which would elaborate a Russian version of 'polite conversation', often conducted in French and without the conflictual atmosphere which distinguishes argument.[103]) But the act of criticism could not be addressed to the state itself, or openly to a bourgeois public with autonomous means (public opinion) capable of exercising influence, nor could it enter into detailed or informed debate on issues of government which had no public airing. In this respect the implied address of Russian critical debate to, as it were, third parties, removed from government—the people, God, the West—seems at one with its predilection for philosophical abstraction and the construction of world-historical narratives. Lacking a clear connection between the exercise of reason and political power, the commitment to reason takes on a moral coloration: it represents a commitment to unworldly ends. Unable to embody the openness that structures a public sphere, circles construed themselves as arguing on behalf of an extra-governmental power.

In the wake of a revolution itself set in motion by descendants of the 'circle' intelligentsia, circles find themselves forced into a new role. Unable to oppose the revolution but unwilling to support it, circles of intellectuals

[102] The classic account of this intellectual formation is Marc Raeff's *Origins of the Russian Intelligentsia: The Eighteenth-Century Nobility* (New York and London: Harcourt Brace, 1966). The fullest historical account of the various 19th-century groupings is Franco Venturi's *Roots of Revolution: Populist and Socialist Movements in Nineteenth-century Russia*, trans. Francis Haskell (Chicago, Ill.: University of Chicago Press, 1960). On the rapid rise of educational institutions in the period of self-consciously pursued tsarist modernization see Nicholas V. Riasanovsky, *A Parting of Ways: Government and the Educated Public in Russia, 1801–1855* (Oxford: Clarendon Press, 1976).

[103] On the conversation of Russian salon life see Todd, *Fiction and Society in the Age of Pushkin*, 31–3, 55–72.

could always take the line that the political revolution was not revolutionary enough, and that the 'science' which guided it should give way to the deeper, more fundamental genres of philosophy or poetry. What remains striking about the discussions conducted by the Leningrad circle of 1924–28 is the expectation that philosophical debate would beget something 'adequate to the social actuality of crisis' and that an appeal to 'ultimate questions' was the proper level at which to confront the all too apparent social crisis (but not for all: Matvei Kagan in later years would remark that his sudden decision to take a job at an energy institute in 1924 was a measure of the guilt he felt over the 'failure of my exclusively extra-economic relation to actuality'[104]). Rather than address scientific questions about their historic present, Bakhtin's circle carried on a predominantly philosophical struggle against the myths and psychologisms which threatened their vision of a historical culture.

In the Leningrad period the circle—now made up of Bakhtin, Medvedev, Voloshinov, Pumpiansky, Zubakin, I. I. Kanaev, Iudina, M. I. Tubiansky, A. S. Rugevich (a religious philosopher), and Konstantin Vaginov (a writer)—therefore embarked on a critical assimilation of the new human sciences.[105] In 1924 Bakhtin read his series of lectures on 'The Hero and the Author in Artistic Creation' (sic) and his lecture on the philosophy of religion to his friends, and then delivered a series of nine lectures on Kant and the neo-Kantian reading of Kant. In brief, he argued

[104] In Iu. M. Kagan, 'O starykh bumagakh', 82 n. 9. The entire passage, excerpted from a letter from Kagan to his wife in 1936, reads as follows:

The failure of my exclusively extra-economic relation to actuality, which I interpreted as my own despairing flaw and guilt, compelled (or allowed) me then to throw myself with childish rashness into the first business to come my way, which seemed to me at that time (and for a long time afterwards) useful. It really is a scandal, that when I went to VSNKh [the energy institute where Kagan began work] in 1924, I did not even know what it was and where it was located! And yet between 1918 and 1924 such enormous economic and social events took place! It is clear that at that time I felt guilt over this as well. And I threw myself with gratitude, headlong, into the first work that came my way, which brought me in a socially and economically everyday manner into the common ranks of life . . .

[105] On the basis of Bakhtin's testimony to his interrogators in 1929 and his discussion of his 'circle' activities with Duvakin, we can roughly characterize the meetings in which he participated. Many involved the fairly intimate circle whose members are named in the text, and who typically met at Bakhtin's, Rugevich's, or at the home of one P. M. Osokin. But Bakhtin also attended larger meetings, with a more varied membership, focused on the reading and discussion of poetry (and some philosophy), and at these he rubbed shoulders with intellectuals like Meier and other members of the religious-philosophically inclined intelligentsia. In the light of what we know, it seems fair to assume that the smaller group represented the philosophical circle bound by a common project and programme, and the larger meetings were more occasional events. The most detailed account of Bakhtin's activity is found in his response to interrogation by the OGPU after his arrest; see Iu. P. Medvedev, 'Na puti sozdaniiu sotsiologicheskoi poetiki', 46–8 n. 85; I. A. Savkin, 'Delo o Voskresenii', in Isupov (ed.), M. M. Bakhtin i filosofskaia kul'tura XX veka, ii. 110–11, 113; his reminiscences about circle and salon life, and the arrest of several of the participants, are found in Con., 144–51 and 172–87.

first, that 'the issue in Kant is the substitution of historical consciousness for natural consciousness (and its loopholes)' (Lec., 237), second, that philosophy—genuine, systematic philosophy—had to be the guardian of this historical consciousness, and finally, that one had to draw a firm and sharp distinction between the 'unity of culture' which was the true bearer of history and the 'unity of consciousness', inevitably relative to a personal position, to which this culture was so often reduced (this final argument would be repeated in Bakhtin's book on Dostoevsky, when he argued against the monological reduction of truth to the contents of a single consciousness). In 1924–25 the circle devoted time to study of the principal works of psychoanalysis, including not only works by Freud but also texts by Otto Ranke and Ernest Jones; according to Bakhtin's own testimony, the member of the circle principally responsible for reviewing Freudian work was neither himself, nor Voloshinov, but Pumpiansky.[106] An oft-cited letter from Pumpiansky to Kagan tells us that around 1925–26 theological texts constituted the focus of the circle's efforts.[107] Other topics covered at one time or another appear to be art scholarship (perhaps the material which would find its way into the early chapters of Medvedev's *The Formal Method*), Pushkin, Dostoevsky, and, of course, the philosophical tradition itself, with Bakhtin lecturing on Kant, Hegel, Schelling, Rickert, Cohen, Husserl, and Scheler.[108]

To Bakhtin also fell the task of rescuing art from the art critics and scholars. Philosophy could disclose the ethical substance of art, but it had to contend with the various naturalisms and psychologisms which reduced art to the natural, the economic, and the biological, laying waste the very heartland of ethical reality. Bakhtin's first long text on aesthetics would be a lengthy critique of Formalism, 'The Problem of Content, Material and Form', reportedly composed in 1924, in which he establishes a pattern of polemic he would maintain throughout his career. His hostility to the Formalist project for a 'science of literature', which he calls polemically 'materialist aesthetics', is not merely a matter of method or theory. For in setting out a science of literature without first locating the aesthetic in philosophical terms, the Formalists commit more than an epistemological sin: without philosophy, they reduce the ethical, value-laden content of the aesthetic process to the meaningless 'natural' processes of excitation and habituation. With the disappearance of the aesthetic as such, the ontology

---

[106] Pumpiansky, Sollertinsky, and Voloshinov were all involved in lecturing or writing on psychoanalysis at this time; see the reference to Sollertinsky above in n. 63 and N. L. Vasil'ev, 'V. N. Voloshinov—biograficheskii ocherk', in V. N. Voloshinov, *Filosofiia i sotsiologiia gumanitarnykh nauk* (St Petersburg: Asta Press, 1995), 10–11.

[107] Printed in Iu. M. Kagan, 'O starykh bumagakh', 73–4.

[108] Record of Bakhtin's interrogations, cited in Iu. P. Medvedev, 'Na puti k sozdaniiu sotsiologicheskoi poetiki', 46–8 n. 85.

of human existence finds itself flattened, and there seems little choice left but to treat others as objects of nature. Constant excitation and defamiliarization, the recognizably urban pleasures of Formalism, not only displace meanings *in* the aesthetic, they displace the meaning *of* the aesthetic, as if the occasional jangling of nerve endings were adequate compensation for the loss of ethical life.

Nikolaev believes that this article is the 'lost' first section of 'Author and Hero'. But in fact the article appears *within* 'Author and Hero' itself, in the shape of the section with the *déjà vu* title 'Content, Material and Form' (and part of the following section as well), which takes up a few pages in the third part of this long fragment, clearly offers a summary of the longer article, and introduces material (in particular, the idea of 'material' itself) which has only a weak connection with what precedes it. An astute reader would notice the remarkable similarity between the important passage discussing the 'primary artistic struggle' in 'Author and Hero' (AH 181/197) and a passage in the 1924 article (PCMF 35–6/284); an astute Russian reader would realize that one of these passages is a nearly verbatim transcription of the other, an identity obscured by the fact that the passages have been differently rendered in English. All of which supports the argument that 'Author and Hero' was written not in Nevel', but in Leningrad, after 1924, and not before Bakhtin decided to write books on linguistics, Freud, and Formalism, but while Voloshinov and Medvedev were writing their own, related but 'original' and 'self-sufficient' works.

This may explain why 'Author and Hero in Aesthetic Activity', which was supposed to be the 'aesthetics' chapter of a larger work devoted to a grand ethical philosophy, has a tendency to strike off into alien territory. It provides not one, but two justifications for the act of aesthetic consummation, one phenomenological, the other religious. On the one hand, artistic consummation flows from the very act of human perception, from the surplus of vision which defines our relation to the *other*; on the other hand, it is described as a quasi-divine act ultimately dependent on religious faith: the author has a special responsibility 'but this specialization of responsibility can be founded only in a profound faith in the highest instance which blesses a culture, faith in the fact that the highest other answers for my own special responsibility, that I do not act in a value void' (AH 189–90/206). Slowly and surreptitiously, art seems to absorb religious experience into itself, while on the other hand it does its level best to demonstrate that morality and politics are never serious sources of value in the first place. In 'Author and Hero' Bakhtin speaks not of the *nravstvennyi* (as in his phrase *nravstvennaia filosofiia*—'ethical philosophy') but of the *etichnyi*, the merely ethical or immediate relation to good and evil. His belief in the precariousness of this narrow field of morality and social norm, in its dependence on the forward-driven and ungrounded values of 'life', leads to the conclusion that the aesthetic is not so much a sphere different from ethics as a superior Christianized form of it, in which the certainty of love replaces the local calculations of moral judgement. The 'ethics of aesthetics' thus appears not as the complement to a planned 'ethics of politics', but as a substitute for it, and the polemics Bakhtin conducts with juridical and legal conceptions of the moral in this text and 'Towards a Philosophy of the Act' cast state–person relationships as a problem to be overcome rather than a necessary ingredient in a larger ethical system. Having soaked up the divine power of religion on one hand, and undermined the claims of the juridically moral on the other, the aesthetic establishes the entire range of human relationships as its privileged sphere of influence. The aesthetic focus which holds sway for the following fifty years thus represents not a narrowing, but a new constellation of the impulses which in the early 1920s are arranged in a more classically Kantian taxonomy.

While Bakhtin probed the science of literature, Voloshinov took on the science of the mind. The opening lines of his book on Freudianism describe its rapid evolution from a 'modest *psychiatric method*' to a 'philosophy of culture' deserving of critique as such. Far from interesting Voloshinov as a therapeutic method or as a set of empirical hypotheses, in principle disprovable, psychoanalysis is set in his sights for quite different reasons: 'Therefore, *anyone wishing to comprehend the spiritual face of contemporary Europe more profoundly cannot ignore psychoanalysis: it has become too characteristic, too indelible a mark of contemporaneity*' (Fr., 13/8). Psychoanalysis will be examined as one more example of the biologism promoted by the philosophy of life, and Freud finds himself at once placed in the company of Nietzsche, Simmel, Bergson, and Spengler, the philosophical opponents of the Bakhtin group. And even though this is the first text of the group to draw a contrast between 'official' and 'unofficial' modes of consciousness, nonetheless its main project is to prevent the reduction of a forward-directed culture to the meaningless movements and pulses of the drives. As philosophy, psychoanalysis is arraigned for trying to dissolve the fact of ethical reality, manifest in the dialogues of the therapeutic encounter, into the state of nature, with all that implies for the degradation of action.

Indeed, each of the human sciences encountered by Bakhtin, Voloshinov, and Medvedev in the 1920s turns out to suffer from the same incipient psychologism and biologism, and so the planned critical assimilation turns into an unyielding defence of historical culture against assaults from the new sciences of the spirit. Not only psychoanalysis, but Russian Formalism and contemporary linguistics, the three objects of systematic critique in the texts *Freudianism*, *The Formal Method in Literary Scholarship*, and *Marxism and the Philosophy of Language* respectively, split the field they analyse into an objectivistic system of culture on one hand, and, on the other hand, individuals whose actions relate to the system in a voluntaristic and contingent manner. In each of these human sciences:

The act of our activity, of our experience, like a two-faced Janus, looks in different directions: towards the objective unity of a cultural field and towards the un-repeatable uniqueness of experienced life, but there is no unique and singular plane where both faces might determine one another in relation to one unique unity. (TPA 83/2)

The theoretical reason which objectifies psychic life as a realm of physical drives, language as a system of signs, and literature as a system of material devices, must as a consequence expel the subject from the inner workings of culture itself, leaving us stranded between 'the world of culture and the world of life, the unique world in which we create, know and con-template, have lived and are dying; the world in which the act of our activity is objectified, and the world in which this act actually flows, is accomplished once' (TPA 82–3/2). In *The Formal Method*, Medvedev's sharp critique of Formalist literary history and of the concepts of motiva-tion and device demonstrates how the subject facing the text is reduced to the status of a quasi-behaviourist creature, reacting to meaningful contents as if they were merely signals. In *Marxism and the Philosophy of Language* Voloshinov discovers that the individual speaker/listener of Saussure's linguistics has no interpretative, and therefore no creative, power what-ever: its role reduced to the act of recognizing elements of an objectivized system.

The critiques of Voloshinov and Medvedev are thus demands to reinte-grate the psyche, language, and literature respectively back into the ethical reality which will make their forward movement mean something. We are accustomed, however, to think of these works as Marxist critiques, demanding not so much the priority of the ethical as the primacy of the social. But the description Bakhtin had himself offered of historical exist-ence in his lectures of 1924–25 implies that these may not be as different as we suppose:

Objectivity (and reality) are given not in nature, not in consciousness, but in history and culture; objectivity and unbroken objectification in cultural labour. Not in the image, not in the act of fixing, but in labour . . . Subjective unity is only a technical apparatus for the realization of the reality of culture. Unity of thought must be understood as the unity of science; the unity of Will is *Einheit*; the unity of consciousness is only the image of a unity of culture which, in principle, cannot be realized in a single consciousness. (Lec., 237)

This formula radicalizes the early Marxist dictum that 'men make history', for whereas Marx had assumed that nature was a given on which humanity laboured, the neo-Kantians argue that nature itself is an object which humanity creates through the ceaseless activity of science. The 'whole' is therefore not the world as it is reflected and unified in the necessarily individual consciousness, but the whole of human activity, which Bakhtin calls 'culture' in the passage above. If culture is all there is, then humanity has nothing to fall back on—it is 'responsible' for the world, in the sense that it has no other choice than to continue to create it, moving, as Bakhtin once put it, 'ceaselessly into the future'. But the crucial point, shared by Marx and Bakhtin here, is that the world can only become 'active' if activity is made worldly, if it transcends the individual, who in isolation can only contemplate it or experience it as something hardened against his or her intentions. Voloshinov and Medvedev make this point, but the usual prejudices have led people to assume that when they mention responsibility (such as in Voloshinov's *cri de cœur* at the end of *Marxism and the Philosophy of Language*) they are demanding that people step into line. In fact, they do no more than show that a sociological turn can have an ethical-philosophical point. To make reality ethical, one makes the activity of its creation social: Durkheim and Weber will confirm this axiom by drawing sociological theory (a 'science of ethics'—Durkheim) out of the neo-Kantian philosophy in which they were schooled. The common ground shared between Bakhtin's earlier essay and the critical texts of his colleagues—the 'shared conception' to which he referred in his letter thirty-five years later—is evidence not of single authorship, but of a shared philosophical tradition, which did not dismiss social life but saw in it the very possibility of a meaningful, ethical existence.

Of course, it is always possible that the achieved synthesis will break down, and that the ethical and the social will appear once again as alternatives. In much Soviet Marxism of the 1920s the identification of the social with the advance of culture was transformed into an identification of the collective with the coolly rational (and by contrast, the individual with the soppily romantic), with a technical reason bereft of any moral purpose or end. The aesthetics of Russian Constructivism and much of the argument circulating through the Left Front in Arts were the product of just such an abstraction, where the progress of culture became uncoupled from the meaning of culture itself.[109] Bakhtin turned to religion for the ultimate guarantee against such an objectivized sense of culture; by focusing on the ideal of a community of believers he could ensure that the fact of collective

---

[109] The identity of the collective and the rational became the leading aesthetic principle of the journal *LEF* and of groups like the Constructivists. In the pages of the former, poets were 'producers' and 'engineers of language', engaged in a constructive process rather than having an ear for the muse. On the ethical belief in the priority of the collective in avant-garde art see John Willett, *The New Sobriety: Art and Politics in the Weimar Period, 1917–33* (London: Thames & Hudson, 1978), 105–17.

existence never lost its ethical bearings. In a lecture on Max Scheler from this period he described confession in revealing terms: 'The essence of Scheler's views comes down to the argument that confession, according to its phenomenological meaning structure, is a disclosure of the self before the other, making social ("discourse") that which had been striving toward its own asocial, extraverbal limit ("sin") and was an isolated, persistent foreign body in the inner life of the person.'[110] The social is rendered here in the form of the Christian community, and confession as affirmation of one's membership in it (compare this to the Protestant relation to God, for which inner speech is adequate). Only when memory or intention have been externalized can they become an object of ethical action, in particular an object of mercy and forgiveness. Compare this to a similar passage from *Freudianism*:

The broader and deeper the split between official and unofficial consciousness, the more difficult it is for motifs of inner speech to pass into external speech (oral, written, printed; in a narrow, in a broad social circle), so as to become formed, clarified and strengthened in it. Such motifs begin to decay, to lose their verbal form and little by little are actually transformed into a 'foreign body' in the psyche. Entire groups of organic phenomena can in this way be thrust beyond the limits of verbal behaviour, can become asocial. Thus is the sphere of the 'animal' in a person, of the asocial in him, broadened. (*Fr.*, 134/90)

For both writers the key to an ethical existence is the disclosure of the self, the entrance into community through speech. But Voloshinov has stolen a march on Bakhtin: he has attributed to language itself some of the healing force Bakhtin reserves to religious discourse alone.[111] This is an absolutely central insight, and there is no reason to doubt that it was Voloshinov who grasped it first.

Since 1925 Voloshinov had been working and studying at the Institute for the Comparative History of Eastern and Western Literatures and Languages (its Russian acronym—ILIaZV), where he worked with, among others, Lev Iakubinsky (the scholar of 'dialogical speech'). Although formally he was considered a specialist on the methodology of literature and 'sociological poetics', his written works deal almost entirely with linguistic matters. According to the Institute's records, in the period up until 1929 Voloshinov produced not only the articles and books we are familiar with, but also four chapters of a book entitled *An Introduction to*

---

[110] From the record of Bakhtin's interrogation, in Iu. P. Medvedev, 'Na puti k sozdaniiu sotsiologicheskoi poetiki', 46 n. 85.

[111] Voloshinov thereby comes close to the account of psychoanalysis offered by Habermas in *Knowledge and Human Interests*, trans. Jeremy J. Shapiro (Cambridge: Polity Press, 1986), in which the open discourse which is the mark of a democratic community presupposes the absence of psychic repression of particular contents. On this similarity see Gerald Pirog, 'The Bakhtin Circle's Freud: From Positivism to Hermeneutics', *Poetics Today*, 8: 3–4 (1987), 591–610.

Sociological Poetics, the article 'The Problem of the Transmission of Alien Speech' (mentioned above), and translations of an article by Karl Bühler and the first two parts of Ernst Cassirer's *Philosophy of Symbolic Forms*.[112] But Cassirer was not just the subject of a translation: Brian Poole has shown that Voloshinov simply spliced some of Cassirer's text directly into 'Discourse in Life and Discourse in Poetry' (1926), and, in the abstract of *Marxism and the Philosophy of Language* taken from the Institute's files, Cassirer rates a far more prominent role than in the published text. According to Voloshinov, Cassirer had demonstrated in *The Philosophy of Symbolic Forms* that the 'word' could become a '*mediating point* between transcendental validity and concrete actuality', thereby overcoming the scientism and logicism which had deformed the work of the Marburg School.[113] This, of course, is precisely the role which language would serve for Bakhtin, but not quite yet, for he was still, as far as we can tell, placing his faith in the phenomenology of the author and the hero. Only after Voloshinov had discovered a neo-Kantian turn to language would Bakhtin realize that the key to a new type of modern art was a new relationship to discourse.

The lateness of Bakhtin's linguistic turn is manifest in the very structure of *Problems of Dostoevsky's Art*. Divided into two long sections, the book begins with a novel interpretation of the ethics of author–hero relations in Dostoevsky. In the 'polyphonic' novel which Dostoevsky initiates, heroes are drawn out of the theoreticized universe in which they were embedded in the 'monological' social-psychological realism of the nineteenth century, so that they can appear as moral beings who can answer us and to whom we must ourselves answer. They are part of the work and yet independent, thereby embodying the resistance to enclosure which Bakhtin made the mark of the aesthetic even in 'Author and Hero'. In Dostoevsky's works, the writer, just as required, 'collides and struggles immediately with the raw cognitive-ethical elementality of life, with chaos (elementality and chaos from the aesthetic point of view)' and so 'strikes the purely artistic spark' (AH 181/197). In the first half of the book this elementality takes the form of a person endowed with a world-view, an ideologue, and the ethical point stands out. But in the second half of the text, 'Discourse in Dostoevsky', Bakhtin takes a different tack, extending the line of argument opened by Voloshinov in *Marxism and the Philosophy of Language*, in which language itself (rather than the person) is the hero to be treated as *other*. The typology of forms of dialogism and monologism laid out in the latter half of *Problems of Dostoevsky's Art* marks the point at which philosophical anthropology drifts into what Bakhtin will later call 'sociological stylistics'.

---

[112] 'Lichnoe delo V. N. Voloshinova', 75, 77–8.

[113] Ibid. 87.

True, the classification of different kinds of literary writing according to the degree of dissonance between constituent voices represents an attempt to present languages as if they were persons, but this only masks the transformation of the paradigm itself. The dissonance in the book's structure is clear, and has led Nikolaev to a striking hypothesis: he has suggested that the first half of the book represents what is left from the text finished in 1925 (or possibly an even earlier variant) and that the second half of the text, including the very idea of dialogism, is the result of reworking and rewriting carried out after Bakhtin had composed the 'disputed texts' themselves.[114] On this reading 'Discourse in Dostoevsky' is Bakhtin 'under a mask', 'deuterocanonical', just as much as the Medvedev and Voloshinov texts are supposed to be. That is to say, this reading resolves the book's ambiguity decisively in the direction of the Christian-philosophical Bakhtin.

I would prefer to stick with the ambiguities and accordingly to interpret dialogism, which first appears in Bakhtin's work in *Problems of Dostoevsky's Art*, as an attempt to synthesize the ethical project and the new emphasis on language and verbal art. Voloshinov had used the term as early as 1926 and had interpreted it as a stylistic phenomenon, but he did not burden dialogism with redemptive intentions as Bakhtin did. It was only in the writing of the latter that transcendence and actuality were truly kept in balance. Dialogism was the ethical relationship between *I* and *other* rejigged as a form of language, but once the move was made, the historical actuality it opened up began to exert its own force on the course of Bakhtin's writing.

To publish in 1929 was a cruel stroke of fate. On 24 December 1928 Bakhtin was arrested on suspicion of having participated in an organization described as anti-Soviet, the religious-philosophical discussion group Voskresenie (Resurrection), formed after the revolution by religious intellectuals (many of whom, it should be said, were not opposed to the revolution itself). In the course of interrogations held in December 1928 and March 1929 Bakhtin described the meetings in which he had participated since 1924; the transcripts of these interrogations are the source for much of the above. Although he appears not to have had any formal connection with Voskresenie, members of the circle had, not surprisingly, attended meetings at which he was present (about a hundred people were arrested in the 'Voskresenie affair'). Bakhtin was found guilty on 22 July 1929 and sentenced to five years in Solovki concentration camp.[115]

Since 1923 Bakhtin had suffered from chronic osteomyelitis, of a severity

[114] Nikolaev, '*Dostoevsky i antichnost'* L. V. Pumpianskogo (1922) i M. M. Bakhtina (1963)'.
[115] On the arrest and interrogation see S. Konkin, 'Arest i prigovor', *Sovetskaia Mordoviia*, 26 Mar. 1991, 3; Savkin, 'Delo o Voskresenii'; *Con.*, 144, 148–9, 295–6 n. 42.

which laid him up in hospital, frequently for long periods (in 1938 he would have to have his left leg amputated at the knee). After his sentencing, a campaign was waged by his wife and friends to have the sentence changed to exile, on the grounds that his invalidity meant that a stay in Solovki would in all likelihood prove fatal. To this campaign both Maxim Gorky and the author A. N. Tolstoy lent their names, evidence that Bakhtin was hardly an unknown figure. Its most important element, though, was an evidently unsolicited review of the Dostoevsky book by A. V. Lunacharsky, head of the Commissariat of the Enlightenment and noted old Bolshevik.[116] Extremely complimentary and entirely directed to the text as a literary intervention, Lunacharsky only quibbled with Bakhtin's limitation of dialogism to Dostoevsky. Bakhtin remained in hospital for most of the campaign; on 23 February 1930 the sentence was changed to exile in the town of Kustanai, on the border of Siberia and Kazakhstan. One month later, the Bakhtins left to serve the sentence.

This episode had one other consequence for Bakhtin's writing. In keeping with the combination of suspicion and calculation which marked Stalinism's relationship to the literary intelligentsia, Bakhtin was encouraged to use what was perceived by the authorities as his 'Marxist methodology' to produce works of an acceptable character. In the spring of 1929 he did just that, writing two prefaces to a collected edition of Tolstoy then under preparation. Not only in tone but in substance, these texts appear as works of a completely different person; they show no interest in either linguistic or phenomenological ethics, but are marked by a tragic adherence to the windless language of the day.[117]

WORK ON THE NOVEL, 1930–1946

Texts

'Discourse in the Novel' (1934–35).
Materials from the *Bildungsroman* project (1936–38).
  Extant Fragments
  'Forms of Time and of the Chronotope in the Novel' (1937–38).
  'Towards a Historical Typology of the Novel' (1936–38).

[116] A. V. Lunacharsky, 'O "mnogogolosti" Dostoevskogo', *Novyi mir*, 10 (1929), 195–209. Gorky's and Tolstoy's help, which took the form of telegrams to the OGPU asking for Bakhtin's sentence to be commuted to exile, is described in S. Konkin, 'Arest i prigovor'; it has been reprinted, with some alterations, in Konkin and Konkina, *Mikhail Bakhtin*, 194.

[117] Nevertheless, the prefaces are not without their ambiguities; for a detailed and shrewd reading of them see Ann Shukman, 'Bakhtin's Tolstoy Prefaces', in Gary Saul Morson and Caryl Emerson (eds.), *Rethinking Bakhtin: Extensions and Challenges* (Evanston, Ill.: Northwestern University Press, 1989).

'Posing the Problem of the *Bildungsroman*' (1936–38).
'Time and Space in the Works of Goethe' (1936–38).
Book plan (*c.*60 pp, unpublished, 1937).
'Towards Questions of the Theory of the Novel' (1940, unpublished).
'Satire' (an article for the *Literary Encyclopedia*, 1940).
'From the Prehistory of Novelistic Discourse' (1940).
'Multilanguagedness as a Precondition of the Development of Novelistic Discourse' (*c.*1940).
'"The Lay of Prince Igor" in the History of Epic' (*c.*1940–41).
'On the History of the Type (Generic Variety) of the Novel of Dostoevsky' (1940–41).
'Towards Philosophical Bases of the Human Sciences' (*c.*1940–43).
'On Questions of the Historical Tradition and the Popular Sources of Gogolian Laughter' (1940–45).
'On Questions of the Theory of the Novel. On Questions of the Theory of Laughter. On Mayakovsky' (*c.*1940–45).
'Epic and Novel' (1941).
'Rhetoric, to the extent that it is something false . . .' (1943).
'The Man in the Mirror' (1943).
'On Questions of Self-Consciousness and Self-Evaluation' (*c.*1943–46).
'On Flaubert' (*c.*1944–45).
'On the Stylistics of the Novel' (*c.*1944–45).
'Questions of Stylistics For Russian-language Classes in Secondary School' (*c.*1944–45).
Book/dissertation: 'Rabelais in the History of Realism' (1940–46).
'Additions and Amendments to "Rabelais"' (1944).

The theory of the novel, on which Bakhtin's reputation in the West is founded, actually occupied him for little more than a decade. From 'Discourse in the Novel', written in 1934–35, to the defence of his dissertation on Rabelais in 1946, novels, invested by theory with the democratic and historicizing energies of the plebeian, play the leading role in his dramatization of the struggle for a modern ethical culture, after which they drop permanently into the background. When Bakhtin returned to the themes of 'Discourse in the Novel' in 1952–55, he attributed what had at first been properties of the novel to the broader, and now less plebeian, phenomenon of 'artistic literature'. Likewise for the concepts with supporting parts in this 'novelistic' complex—heteroglossia, the public square, the popular—all of which recede after their brief moment onstage. The idea of dialogism remains long after this burst of conceptual invention, to be further explored and refined in later works, but the novelistic fervour inextricably linked to it drops out, mere pacemaker for the concept which in the end will go the distance.

But the 1930s and early 1940s are not only distinguished by their conceptual apparatus; they are also suffused with a distinctively *political* pathos which marks them off from everything preceding and following. Philosophical passion in defence of the human and moral here yields to quasi-Nietzschean celebrations of the power and plebeian feeling of 'the people', incarnate in a popular-novelistic consciousness which sweeps all before it. In Bakhtin's earlier work theoretical reason appeared as a constitutive and general defect of modernity; in the decade of the novel it is the strategic tool of an 'official' political project of cultural-ideological centralization and domination. And the antidote is no longer to exhume by means of philosophy a hidden layer of historical reality, but to unearth an actual but forgotten tradition, the popular-festive culture which thematizes the future orientation and historical consciousness Bakhtin deems necessary to the present. Dividing-lines which were once vertical, separating off ethical reality from its denuded 'theoretical transcription' or the objectivity of culture from the subjective trap of mere consciousness, now swing round to bisect the socio-cultural world, setting in opposition the 'poetic' and the 'novelistic', 'epic' and 'novel', the 'carnivalesque' and the 'serious', the official and the unofficial. The change of perspective which was to be accomplished by philosophical disclosure now depends on the writing of partisan cultural history.

One therefore wants to grab at the easy historical explanation—Stalinism—which will excuse this exceptional decade as an understandable, if theoretically regrettable, loss of philosophical composure. Take the completion of Bakhtin's work on Rabelais in the early 1940s as the endpoint and one has more or less circumscribed the severest period of Stalinist repression, both as it affected Bakhtin personally and as it redrew the cultural landscape he inhabited. In 1930 Bakhtin and his wife moved to Kustanai to serve his sentence of exile; in 1934 the assassination of Kirov signalled the end of any liberal possibilities opened up by the creation of the non-Party Union of Soviet Writers;[118] in 1937 the purges and trials came to a climax, with Bakhtin himself apparently surviving 'a big scrape'.[119] In the presence of such neat correspondences, the intrusion of the political and the militant expression of loyalties in Bakhtin's theory appear as no more than choices made in the heat of historical crisis, to be set apart from the smoother meditative surface of his earlier and later works.

[118] See A. Kemp-Welch, *Stalin and the Literary Intelligentsia, 1928–39* (Basingstoke: Macmillan, 1991), 190–239.

[119] So described by Matvei Kagan after a meeting with Bakhtin in Moscow: 'A great many of the party members among the teaching staff of the pedagogical institute were dismissed. M. M. was also involved in a big scrape, but the matter turned out rather well for him: it was those who had persecuted him without any foundation who ended up in trouble.' Letter from M. I. Kagan to S. I. Kagan, 15 July 1937, in Iu. M. Kagan, 'O starykh bumagakh', 77.

But while the crisis experience of Stalinism may have provoked this sudden change in register and conceptual structure, the irruption of the bare facts of political history into cultural argument needs to be handled with care. Crises do not necessarily distort intellectual work—they may also trigger its forward movement, and the experience of Stalinism may have yielded something more durable than a local polemic. The 1930s may have been a moment of truth for Bakhtin, not only in the colloquial, but also in a literal sense. As we shall see, the theory of the novel incorporates the experience of Stalinism not by a violent displacement of its basic categories, but by modifying what was always, in large part, a historical argument about a peculiarly modern crisis. Stalinism does not merely invade or affront European culture; sadly enough, it has something to tell us about it, and a theory unwilling to learn from the experience is hardly worth much. And learning from it in this case meant altering the theory in the light of a historically unprecedented (not in its savagery, but in the shape it took) phenomenon. Stalinism was not just an example of repression, to be slotted into the existing category, but a precise form of it, the uniqueness of which demanded an adequate theoretical response.

In particular, the expressive aspects of Stalinism had to be accounted for, and these were not reducible to the mere dictates of theoretical reason. Stalinism might have made its practical demands in the name of an abstraction (the Party, the nation, the Leader), but these were accompanied by a national-popular moralism which distinguished this regime from the legal-constitutional states to which Bakhtin's earlier critiques applied. 'Socialism in one country' depended upon the strength of a party and state bureaucracy, and to this extent it was a creature of the theoretical reason Bakhtin already feared. But it was a new kind of bureaucracy both in terms of its personnel and its self-appointed tasks—it sought not to regulate or free up the obstructed forces of private society, but to inspire and mobilize social action itself. The 1930s were therefore not just about breakneck industrialization, forced collectivization, and Five-Year Plans; they were suffused with new kinds of images and new kinds of writing, from the grotesquely staged show trials and the exhortations of Stakhanovite propaganda to the varied cultural forms sailing under the colours of 'socialist realism'. In short, Stalinist terror had to be cultural as well as political, taking aim not only at explicit enemies, but also at the conscience and consciousness of the mass of the population. And in the wake of a popular revolution, it had to assume a necessarily demotic (if not democratic) and modernized form, depending on constant mass mobilization, secularized ideals, and lip-service to the concept of popular sovereignty. In this respect, any serious coming to grips with Stalinism would have to treat it neither as an atavism or mark of Russian backwardness, nor as an exceptional hiccough on the road to civilization generated by a power-crazed elite, but as a somehow symptomatic or typical experience of European modernity, from which one might have to draw general, even philosophical, conclusions.

Bakhtin's shift from ethical philosophy to a 'philosophy of discourse' made this possible. The attempt to design an architectonics of ethical reality was always held in check by its phenomenological method and presuppositions; although the separate fields of human activity were themselves historical, the relationships they instanced (ethical, religious, natural-scientific and so on) could only be variations on the dyad of *I* and *other*. When Bakhtin—following Voloshinov—began to interpret these relationships in terms of linguistic style, the deadlock was broken. Having been elevated to the status of a social institution—by Saussure amongst others—language could serve as both barometer and model of modern social relationships.[120] It was sensitive, in a way the *I–other* axis was not, to empirical changes in the form and nature of social life, and, given an adequately historicized linguistics, it was possible to read changes in its structure and style as indices of social transformations and struggles beyond it. The identification of language and world-view, inaugurated by Humboldt, argued for by Russian philosophers like Gustav Shpet, and accepted by Bakhtin, meant that in language ethical life found the incarnate form where it was accessible to historical study and analysis.[121] Bakhtin's decision to describe the novel as a distinctive form of language use was therefore not, as Tzvetan Todorov has claimed, the expression of a theoretically incomprehensible and so merely 'affective' attachment, but a calculated attempt to tie the project of a modern ethical culture to a substantive historical phenomenon.[122] But modern repression and exploitation were also ethical facts of which Bakhtin had to take account, and they therefore informed the theory of the novel from the very beginning.

[120] Saussure, *Course*, 15.

[121] In *On the Logic of the Social Sciences*, Habermas identified linguistic analysis, in a broad, reconstructed sense, as the place where social science could combine the empirical bent of scientific research with the transcendental achievements of philosophical reflection. Phenomenology would always be bound to the philosophy of consciousness and to the individual lifeworld; the analysis of language allowed us to make the break with the egocentricity of this procedure. As we now know, it also allowed Habermas to make the break which led to his theory of communicative action. Although Bakhtin never made this break self-consciously, I think Habermas's description of the advantages of the move apply to his Russian forerunner as well. See *On the Logic of the Social Sciences*, 111–19.

[122] Todorov, *Mikhail Bakhtin: The Dialogical Principle*, 86. As examples of this we could adduce criticism which has contrasted the weakness of Bakhtin's historical claims with the appropriateness or efficacy of his 'conjunctural' or 'strategic' intervention. See Richard M. Berrong, *Rabelais and Bakhtin: Popular Culture in Gargantua and Pantagruel* (Lincoln, Nebr. and London: University of Nebraska Press, 1986); and Robert Young, 'Back to Bakhtin', *Cultural Critique*, 2 (1985), 71–92.

'Discourse in the Novel', the first turn towards a theory of the novel, was written at the end of Bakhtin's exile in Kustanai, during which time he apparently supported himself by working on the accounts of a local consumer cooperative (the essay—a pleasant irony, this—was typed up by the wife of the political exile, N. N. Sukhanov, author of *Notes on the Revolution* and a noted Menshevik; *Con.*, 314 n. 24). Its date of composition suggests that the decision to focus on the novel was prompted by continual public discussion of the lineage and future prospects of this genre, which was expected to play a leading role in the new ethical culture which would be called 'socialist realism'. In 1934 this discussion was coming to its climax: Gorky was battling for a conservative and exemplary realism, from which colloquial language would be expunged, a government commission was busy formulating a compromise which would allow authors to put socialist wine into Russian realist bottles, and, as Michael Holquist and Katerina Clark have shrewdly pointed out, the Communist Academy, still a central organ of cultural hegemony, was staging a debate on the past and future of the genre. The debate was published, in 1934–35, in the pages of the new state-sponsored journal, *The Literary Critic*, where Lukács and others sought to define a realist aesthetic which would not succumb to Stalinist dogmatism; it began with the presentation of Lukács's entry on 'The Novel' for the Soviet *Literary Encyclopedia* and contained an extensive discussion involving leading figures of the Soviet literary establishment.[123] Perhaps the turn to this genre, which Bakhtin, in accord with Soviet practice, continually defined as the privileged carrier of realism, represented a conscious attempt to contest the definitions of ethical reality then circulating in the Soviet public sphere.

Whatever its motivation, 'Discourse in the Novel' laid aside phenomenology and religion in favour of new strategies for demonstrating that dialogism was the inner truth of every fact of culture. In the first two-thirds of the essay, Bakhtin offered a grand reprise of the last half of his Dostoevsky book (which had been entitled, naturally, 'Discourse in Dostoevsky'), laying out a typology of dialogical styles which culminated

---

[123] Clark and Holquist, *Mikhail Bakhtin*, 99. The debate appears as 'Problema teorii romana', *Literaturnyi kritik*, 2 (1935), 214–49, and 3 (1935), 231–54. Bakhtin's career seems to be uncannily linked to the rise and fall of Lukács himself. According to Clark and Holquist, in the 1920s Bakhtin embarked on a translation of *The Theory of the Novel*, which was abandoned; Galen Tihanov has discovered from archival materials that Pumpiansky had read it by 1924, and assumes that the circle had read and discussed it as well. In 1940, when *Literaturnyi kritik* was attacked, and Lukács fell from grace, Bakhtin was invited to speak at the Gorky Institute. See Clark and Holquist, *Mikhail Bakhtin*, 275; Michel Aucouturier, 'The Theory of the Novel in Russia in the 1930s: Lukács and Bakhtin', in John Garrard (ed.), *The Russian Novel from Pushkin to Pasternak* (New Haven and London: Yale University Press, 1983), 227–40; and Galen Tihanov, 'Bakhtin, Lukács and German Romanticism: The Case of Epic and Irony', in Carol Adlam *et al.* (eds.), *Face to Face: Bakhtin in Russia and the West* (Sheffield: Sheffield Academic Press, 1997), 273–98.

in the ideal of double-voiced discourse. What was new, leaving aside the populism for a moment, was the direct link drawn between the aesthetic dialogism of the novel and the dialogism intrinsic to language as such, which, it appeared, tended spontaneously to the double-voicedness which Dostoevsky had had to work so hard at. Here language itself embodied ethical reality as the secret of its operation. It was in the last third of the essay, however, that Bakhtin unveiled the case which would dominate his writing for the next ten years and which he probably settled on soon after going into exile in 1930.[124] In his first attempt at a 'prehistory of novelistic discourse' (as he would later call it), Bakhtin told the story of how forms of classical and medieval realism, nourished in plebeian culture, burst into the mainstream of European literature in the form of the novel, much as the people themselves had burst into the centre of European political life in the eighteenth and nineteenth centuries. Rather than outlining a matrix of possible forms, Bakhtin described a succession of historical genres, tracing in their rise and fall the gradual emergence of a historical consciousness both contemporaneous and ancient, orientated towards the future yet the legacy of a long past. However modern the ideal moral or political culture would be, it would redeem promises made and renewed for millennia. If the fate of Soviet Russia was to be embodied in the 'popularness' (the Russian *narodnost'*) and the historical awareness of the novel, Bakhtin would need a new sense of the past to make his argument.

He would, however, have to make it alone: in the years immediately following his exile, Bakhtin gradually gained access to Soviet academic institutions, but lost his circle. In 1936 Medvedev helped Bakhtin secure teaching work at the Mordovian Pedagogical Institute in Saransk, to which he and his wife moved in the autumn.[125] Although Bakhtin was destined to spend most of his remaining career in this institute, the path to semi-normalcy would not be easy. As the purges acquired a head of steam in early 1937, the local Party Committee began working its way through the

[124] I make this assumption because Bakhtin claimed in his dissertation defence (1946) that he had been working on the Rabelais text for ten years before its submission in 1940. See 'Stenogramma zasedaniia Uchenogo soveta Instituta mirovoi literatury im. A. M. Gorkogo: Zashchita dissertatsii tov. Bakhtinym na temu "Rable v istorii realizma" 15 noiabria 1946 g.', *Dialog Karnaval Khronotop*, 2–3 (1993), 55; N. A. Pan'kov, '"Ot khoda etogo dela zavisit vse dal'neishee . . ." (zashchita dissertatsii M. M. Bakhtina kak real'noe sobytie, vysokaia drama i nauchnaia komediia)', *Dialog Karnaval Khronotop*, 2–3 (1993), 30.

[125] V. I. Laptun supplies a fairly detailed account of how Bakhtin was invited to teach at the Institute and of the manoeuvres and machinations leading to his sudden dismissal in 'Pervyi priezd M. M. Bakhtina v Saransk (1936–1937gg.)', in *Nevel'skii sbornik*, vol. i (St Petersburg: Akropol, 1996), 61–74. The director of the Institute, A. F. Antonov, who dismissed Bakhtin after considerable pressure had been put upon him, was himself arrested. The parts of his interrogation which concern Bakhtin have been published in V. I. Laptun and V. N. Kuklin, 'K biografii M. M. Bakhtina', in *Bakhtinskii sbornik*, vol iii (Moscow: Labirint, 1997), 368–72. Antonov was shot in 1938.

Institute, and Bakhtin's position swiftly became precarious. Bakhtin, in his own words, 'ran away', resigning his appointment and leaving for Moscow and Leningrad, where he stayed illegally with various friends and family until settling in the town of Savelevo, a few hours north of Moscow, in the autumn of 1937 (*Con.*, 208–9). By every account these few years were, even by his standards, very difficult: in the spring of 1938 his left leg was amputated, and by 1939 he had no money and no source of income. He was, however, lucky in comparison with his friends: Voloshinov died of tuberculosis in 1936; Kagan died of a heart attack at the end of 1937, convinced that he would soon be arrested; Medvedev was arrested and shot in 1938; Pumpiansky would die of cancer in 1940; Zubakin, Rugevich, and Tubiansky all died in the camps.[126]

In these desperately isolated circumstances, Bakhtin became extraordinarily productive (the amputation may have led to an improvement in his health) and began, for the first time, to make a concerted effort to secure a place for himself in the now more settled world of Soviet cultural institutions. In 1940 he agreed to write an entry on 'Satire' for the *Literary Encyclopedia*; in 1940 and 1941 he delivered lectures at the Gorky Institute of World Literature, a section of the Soviet Academy of Sciences, and attended lectures at the Institute's theoretical department; in the early 1940s articles on Flaubert and Mayakovsky (of which drafts are extant) were prepared; in 1945, having been urged to do so by friends and colleagues, he decided to submit the book he had written on Rabelais to the Gorky Institute as a dissertation. But his first attempt to enter into public discourse concerned his projected book on the *Bildungsroman*, for which he entered into negotiations with the publishing house Sovetskii pisatel' in 1937.

In résumés of his published work written in the 1940s Bakhtin referred to completed texts called 'The *Bildungsroman* in Germany' and 'The Artistic Prose of Goethe', but in 1936 these appeared to be parts of one projected text, for which there existed a detailed plan and over 700 pages of draft work. No final copy of the text exists—what remains of it are drafts and myths about its disappearance. In 1975, Bocharov put about half of the draft pages together as 'Forms of Time and of the Chronotope in the Novel'; in 1979, a few fragments were published with the book's projected title, *The* Bildungsroman *and its Significance in the History of Realism*. Most of the draft material will be published as Volume II, Part One, of the *Collected Works*, but the story of the text will probably remain forever incomplete.

At first glance, the material justifies the rather placid description given it by S. S. Konkin, who claimed these texts represented a turn to 'problems

---

[126] These tragic fates are recorded in Vasil'ev, 'V. N. Voloshinov—biograficheskii ocherk', 15; Iu. M. Kagan, 'O starykh bumagakh', 62; Clark and Holquist, *Mikhail Bakhtin*, 264–5.

of the *historical* development of literature and culture'.[127] As a series of attempts at a typology of the organization of time and space in different narrative forms, they have the comprehensive ambition and the sobriety of the methodologically precise survey. Nonetheless, the moral torch which Bakhtin has passed to narrative form remains lit, even if its flame illuminates a new landscape. The various 'chronotopes', or patterns of time and space, Bakhtin traces are not simply lined up end-to-end, each equally close to God; they fall into their own narrative, in which 'the assimilation of real historical time and space and of the real historical person revealed within them' (FTC 234/84) by the realistic 'novel of becoming' is the redemptive endpoint, the true or concrete chronotope in comparison with which everything earlier is but a pre-modern approximation. Like dialogism, 'chronotopicity' is both fact and value, a transcendent reality which only reaches visible expression in modern novelistic prose. More precisely, in the prose of Goethe, who becomes, alongside Dostoevsky and Rabelais, the third great realist, standing out from the crowd both for doing the right thing, as a novelist of 'becoming', and for knowing what he is doing, as a philosopher of the same.

Of course, narrative was there all along. In 'Author and Hero' bounding the hero in time and space, being able to visualize the hero's life as a consummated whole, meant enclosing it in a narrative, and *Problems of Dostoevsky's Art* included a brief chapter on the author's use of the adventure plot. But in the earlier works the secular time and space of the modern plot was only a technique, used, whether by Dostoevsky or the generic 'author', to set up the absolute confrontation or dialogue which was the real substance of the aesthetic. The redemption at which they aimed takes place in a flash—the moment of aesthetic love or faith—by its nature beyond the representational grasp of a secular, 'historical' narrative. Dostoevsky is both the artist of dialogue and the artist of crisis, because dialogue becomes purer as it becomes simultaneous. Even in 'Discourse in the Novel' the concept of double-voiced discourse participates in the sleight of hand whereby a narrative event, the dialogue, is collapsed into a single temporal point.

In the *Bildungsroman* project, by contrast, being is stretched out on the horizontal rack of history, and the function of the ultimate question is assumed by the narrative concept of *transformation* or 'becoming'. The abyss which had opened up between the 'world of culture' and the 'world of life' now takes shape in various storylines, where either the world or the hero stands still while its complement moves in arbitrary, meaningless directions. In the first case, the hero is a 'fixed and hard point' (*Bil.*, 211/21) reacting in a set pattern to random events around it; in the second, 'the person

[127] Konkin and Kozhinov, 'Mikhail Mikhailovich Bakhtin: Kratkii ocherk', 9.

becomes, but not the world itself' (*Bil.*, 214/23)—the latter exists as the school in which young heroes learn to adapt to the way of the world. Only when the abyss is closed up narratively, and the hero 'becomes *together with the world*' (*Bil.*, 214/23; emphasis Bakhtin's) can we begin to speak of real historical time, for then the hero's quest for meaning flows outward into the world itself, and the latter's meaning becomes as much an open question as the fate of the hero him- or herself. This amounts to something more than a variation on the idea of a text orientated to the future, because the change of focus effects a minute but crucial transformation in the substance of that future itself. Once the emphasis shifts from the possible salvation of the individual to the uncertain future of a self-consciously historical world the moment Adorno wished for, when 'the question of the reality or unreality of redemption itself hardly matters', has arrived. In the *Bildungsroman* religious faith is no longer necessary to weave chronological events into a meaningful history, for the 'organizing power of the future' has learned to survive in the absence of faith in the possibility of salvation. For the hero of the modern chronotope life becomes meaningful in the only manner possible, as a continually revised estimation of the future and its possibilities. Once narrative acquires this level of self-reflexiveness, aesthetics can finally assume the burden of a meaningful history without any help from religion. Accordingly, the text on the *Bildungsroman* is the one least inflected by religious terminology.

With this change in emphasis comes a change in the characterization of the problem prose narrative must avoid. The enemy of responsible meaning is no longer the abstraction of formal, legalistic ethics or authoritarian monologue but 'mythological' thought, a pseudo-history which provides the wherewithal for ethical obligation, but at the cost of removing the 'ought' from cultural creation itself:[128]

This trait is manifested above all in so-called '*historical inversion*'. The essence of such an inversion consists of mythological and artistic thought locating in the past categories such as the goal, the ideal, justice, perfection, the harmonious condition of man and society, and so on. Myths about paradise, a Golden Age, a heroic age, ancient verities, and later representations of a state of nature, of naturally given rights, and so on, are expressions of this historical inversion. Defining it somewhat simplistically, one could say that here we find represented as already part of the past that which in fact can be or should be realized only in the future, that which in its essence is a goal, an obligation, but by no means a past reality. (FTC 297/147)

---

[128] In his choice of enemy Bakhtin was no doubt influenced by his reading of the volume of Cassirer's *The Philosophy of Symbolic Forms* devoted to 'Mythical Thinking'. Brian Poole, editor of the *Bildungsroman* volume of the *Collected Works*, has informed me that a lengthy conspectus of this work, probably written between 1936 and 1938, exists in the Bakhtin archive and will be published with the *Bildungsroman* materials (e-mails from Brian Poole to the author, 26 Mar. 1998 and 6 Apr. 1998).

Myth contains moral contents in a distorted relation to the practical 'reality of the act', reducing the becoming of culture to the dull echo of tradition. Mythic contents obligate, but in an authoritarian, traditional manner which makes responsibility in its modern sense impossible. When the normative or ideal becomes something given and substantial it disappears from the field of the present, and the only way it can be made part of a history is by being put in a past absolutely distant from contemporaneity, 'lacking all relativity, that is, lacking those gradual, purely temporal transitions which would link it to the present' (EN 459/15).

Bakhtin's own narrative, the narrative of the development of the chronotope, is therefore not merely descriptive, but normative, tracing the achievement of a historical existence deemed valuable in itself. Of course this preference itself has to be justified—'real historical time' without any justification would be nothing but surrendering oneself to the enforced fact of mutability. But this time Bakhtin does not appeal to the architectonics of an ethical reality. Whether from tactics or principles, philosophical insight is laid to one side, and three different arguments for the superiority of modern historical time are offered in its stead. *Christian* motifs are deployed in so far as the novel of becoming, the happy terminus of literary history, is opposed to the narrative embodiments of the juridical-ethical standpoint. In the novel of becoming the hero is the centre of value while remaining an admixture of good and bad, virtue and vice, intelligence and foolishness; this is, as it were, a narrative of compassion and mercy, which endows a life with aesthetic value irrespective of its ethical rights and wrongs. *Anthropological* arguments make an appearance in 'Forms of Time', where the unity of life and culture in the lost world of undifferentiated agricultural society provides a primitive communist norm to which modern society should aspire; there the reintegration of the hero with the surrounding world restores—on a higher plane?—the unity which was lost with the death of cyclical and ritualized agricultural life. *Enlightenment* and *populardemocratic* motifs appear in the foreground when Bakhtin takes Goethe and Rabelais as the exemplars of the novelistic narrative. There the *visibility* of modern history is what sets it apart from every mystical or allegorical reduction. The identification of the real with the historical establishes experience and secular knowledge as the ultimate arbiters of truth, and it rejects every justification of values or norms which depends on privileged access to the invisible and otherworldly. A world wholly visible is a world accessible to reason rather than insight, 'prediction not prophecy', as Bakhtin will put it.[129]

To whom is this historical world visible? Who can see the movement of

---

[129] Koselleck has described the transformation of a prophesied future into a predicted future in his 'Modernity and the Planes of Historicity', in *Futures Past*, 3–20.

history without getting caught up in any of its local tangles? Appreciating history 'in itself' demands a certain philosophical disinterestedness, which in the *Bildungsroman* fragments appears to be reserved to Goethe. But in the numerous writings from his recently published wartime notebooks, it is clear Bakhtin thought he had discovered a disinterestedness built into the historical process itself, in the form of the millennial knowledge of popular culture. In the anonymity of the collective products of popular culture lies a guarantee that its vision will not be subordinate to the merely pragmatic and technical needs of the human horizon:

> The system of folklore symbols formed over the course of the millennia, which represented a model of the ultimate whole. In them is the great experience of humankind. In the symbols of official culture there is only the petty experience of a specific part of humankind (at a given moment, and with an interest in that moment's stability). Characteristic of these petty models, created on the basis of petty and partial experience, is a specific pragmatism and utilitarianism. They serve as a scheme for the practically interested action of a person, in them, indeed, practice determines thought. (QuSelf, 77)

While official culture is bound to the exigencies of practical need, the system of folklore symbols manages to take the larger view: from this unlikely position Bakhtin developed his last great historical work on the novel, the book 'Rabelais in the History of Realism'. If realism was the order of the day—very well then, Bakhtin would describe realism, but one absolutely distant from the 'scientific' and lawlike naturalism then taken for granted. Bakhtin's gesture recalls that of phenomenology, which claimed that to go 'back to the things themselves', it was necessary to adopt an absolutely disinterested attitude, which would have no truck with the distorting practical orientations of ordinary life. These formed the basis for merely scientific knowledge, which, whatever its pretensions, ultimately aimed to make of everything 'a practically convenient object of use' (AddAmR, 122). Bakhtin therefore equates the scientific spirit with the 'mortification' of the object, its separation from the historical process and the ever-present possibility of transformation.[130] But if our grasping of objects is what distorts them, then we are most likely to see things as they are when we are not grasping, but relaxing, celebrating, in a receptive attitude.[131] Therefore true realism will be found not in science or the labour process, but in the historic culture of popular festivity ('carnival'), where a sudden distancing from the needs of action makes possible a

---

[130] See the passages on the characteristic tendencies of knowledge in AddAmR, 122–3 and Rhet., 65.

[131] Brian Poole claims that a direct source and precedent for Bakhtin's attempt to make laughter philosophically respectable is found in Paul Natorp's comments on the significance of the moment of relaxation. See Poole, '"Nazad k Kaganu"', 42–5.

radical restructuring of experience. Popular-festive culture gets back to the things themselves—and the most natural things at that, like eating, drinking, sex, and defecation—by insisting that they have a philosophical, rather than naturalistic-scientific, meaning. And just as Bakhtin had claimed to find the essence of the aesthetic in the ordinary routines of perception, so he now draws out the complex of medieval and Renaissance popular-festive culture from the anthropological constant of 'laughter'.

Rabelais's novel *Gargantua and Pantagruel* 'could serve as the key to this world of grotesque forms', in so far as 'the language of Rabelais is simultaneously our language and the language of the medieval public square'.[132] Only the language of the medieval public square will do, for the modern market allows workers not festivity, but rest, and rest is a concept of leisure with a merely scientific, rather than philosophical, meaning:

Festivity (of any kind) is a very important *primary form* of human culture. One cannot deduce it from or explain it by the practical conditions and goals of social labour or—an even more vulgar explanation—by the biological (physiological) need for periodic rest. Festivity has always had an essential and profound interpretative, world-contemplative content. No 'exercise' in the organization and perfection of the social labour process, no 'play in work', and no rest or breathing-space in labour can *in themselves* ever become *festive*. For them to become festive, something from a different sphere of being, from the spiritual-ideological sphere, must be added. They must be sanctioned not by the world of *means* and necessary conditions, but by the world of the *highest ends* of human existence, that is, by the world of ideals. Without this there is not and cannot be any kind of festivity. (*Rab.*, 13–14/8–9)

With modernity comes disenchantment, and disenchantment first and foremost of the body and of its labour and leisure activities. Bakhtin must return to a medieval concept of everyday life precisely because this predates the moment at which everyday life becomes a 'private affair' and the human body becomes the mere physical substrate of *homo œconomicus*. Once the body becomes the property of the individual (one's original item of property, according to Lockean theory) its pleasures and pains, suffering and achievement are subjectivized: 'Everything that happens to it concerns it alone, that is, only this individual and enclosed body. Therefore all the events that occur to it acquire a *single meaning*: death here is only death' (*Rab.*, 356–7/321). Far from having philosophical meaning, it exists for the individual only as 'a meaningless and deathly obstacle to all ideal aspirations' (*Rab.*, 30/23).

Bakhtin therefore again links the possibility of a philosophical perspective to deliverance from the individualized 'point of view'. The Rabelais

---

[132] From Bakhtin's presentation at the defence of his dissertation; see 'Stenogramma', 56.

book has disturbed many commentators, Morson and Emerson most strik-ingly, who see in it an irresponsible and uncharacteristic celebration of the utopian, the open-ended, and the collectivistic, at odds with the sobriety of Bakhtin's earlier, more philosophical works.[133] But Bakhtin has done no more than maintain his initial philosophical conviction that truth demands some kind of distance from the pragmatism of the individual horizon. In his various writings on popular-festive culture, it is the perspective of the historic 'people as a whole' which provides the distance, and grotesque imagery—in which death (negation) is always also birth (the future)—which keeps alive the promise of possible transformation, that is, of redemption. And if this were not clear enough from Bakhtin's repeated insistence on the positive, philosophical substance of carnival throughout the text of *Rabelais*, it has been established beyond reasonable doubt by the publication of his wartime notebooks in the *Collected Works*, where Bakhtin's older philosophical arguments are presented cheek by jowl, separated by a few lines rather than a few decades, with discussion of the nature and forms of popular-festive culture. In the 'Additions and Amendments to "Rabelais"' (1944), the notes titled 'Rhetoric, to the extent it is something false . . .' (1943) and in 'On Questions of Self-Consciousness and Self-Evaluation' (undated, *c*.1943–46) the familiar motifs of *I* and *other*, of the loving nature of the artistic image, and of a planned 'ethics of literature' reappear, with carnival truth as their natural counterpart. The revision notes to *Rabelais* in particular (composed for a new edition, when Bakhtin thought book publication a genuine possi-bility) present in the starkest terms precisely what it is that carnival rescues you from: 'the profound tragedy of the *individual* life itself, condemned to birth and death' (AddAmR, 86); exactly the same fate from which the author rescued the hero some fifteen or twenty years earlier.

The 'tragedy of the individual life': it turns out Bakhtin means this quite literally. For the genre of literary tragedy, Bakhtin argues, provides us with the ultimate truth about individuality—its tragic plot is set in motion by a transgression which ultimately expresses nothing less than the 'profound crime (the potential criminality) of all self-asserting individuality' (AddAmR, 86). Bakhtin does not forget about the individual in the 1940s: he merely reminds us of the weakness of individualism, which, confronted by the fact of historical change, can produce great art, but only by showing us its own limits. In this respect, tragedy turns out to be, perhaps surprisingly, laughter's more serious twin. From the still unpublished text, 'On Questions of the Theory of the Novel' (*c*.1940–41):

---

[133] Morson and Emerson, *Mikhail Bakhtin*, 90–6.

Tragedy and laughter are equally nourished by the most ancient human experience of world changes and catastrophes (historical and cosmic), by the memory
and premonitions of humankind, stored up in the fundamental human fund of
myth, language, image, and gesture. Both tragedy and particularly laughter strive
to expel *fear* from these, but they do this differently. The *serious* courage of tragedy,
remaining in the zone of closed-up individuality. Laughter responds to change
with joy and abuse . . . Tragedy and laughter equally fearlessly look being in the
eye, they do not construct any sort of illusions, they are sober and exacting. (*SS5*,
463 n. 1)

Bakhtin will also introduce, but not pursue, the idea of the 'unofficial
seriousness of suffering, fear, fright, weakness' (AddAmR, 81), that is, what
he would later call the problem of sentimentalism, in which the individual
exists primarily as an object of pity and sympathy. The laughing images of
carnival are hyperbolic, larger than life, exaggerated and expansive, visual
representations of a sublime history; the individual is weak, ultimately
defenceless, and elicits our sympathy by confronting his or her fate either
meekly (the sentimental hero) or defiantly (the tragic hero). History is
therefore elided only in the median case, in writing where 'the representation of the real is knit together with the representation of something
average and small (normal) and with mistrust of everything great, huge, as
something unreal, fantastic, invented, false, exaggerated, illusory' (Mayak.,
57–8). In his drafts of articles on Flaubert and Mayakovsky, Bakhtin singles
out these writers precisely for contesting this realism of the 'average', the
realism of the small group in an 'indoor little world' (*komnatnyi mirok*)
(Mayak., 55). If individualism means depending on the 'category of everyday security and stability' (Flau., 131), if it means confusing the real world
with 'the indirect struggle for life (condensed in money), which avoids
death and real struggle, which takes place in the most comfortable and
secure locations of banks, exchanges, offices, rooms, and so on' (Flau., 131)
then commentators nervous about carnival are right—Bakhtin wants to
have nothing to do with it. Only this was Bakhtin's position from the very
beginning, expressed in his philosophical texts as the problem of a life
demanding justification from beyond its own confines.

But Bakhtin's work on Rabelais is famous for describing two cultures,
not one. 'Official culture' is just as modern and significant as carnival, and
a useful reminder that the period Bakhtin describes bequeathed to us not
only modern individuals, but modern states and social structures as well. In
Bakhtin's analysis, however, the absolutist state represents not an alternative collective principle but the apotheosis of individualism itself. Modern
political power is defined as individual seriousness writ large, that is, individualism which, rather than face the prospect of death and transforma-
tion/rebirth, seeks to preserve and prolong itself by means of monuments,

glorifying prose, and links to an eternal sphere set somewhere above the mutable historical world. In effect, official seriousness is the attempt to *force* one's way into the future, rather than acknowledge one's historical condition. But if Bakhtin borrows the design of official culture from that of the individual consciousness, one has to wonder to what extent his conception of the individual horizon might have been modelled on the pretences of modern political power.

This is true of liberal states, or states in so far as they are liberal in conception and design, almost by definition: liberalism asks the state to regulate the activities of individuals, who are the only ones deemed fit to determine ends. Yet surely the Stalinist state had a historic and collective project (the making of 'Socialism in One Country' and the defence of the motherland) and surely there are few states which are only liberal? The implicit argument is that, appearances notwithstanding, the Stalinist project is not historic, but mythic in conception, and that in so far as it projects the task of the community forward into history, it glorifies action in the criminal guise of 'self-assertion' rather than as a striving towards a redeemed future. Even the most 'material' achievements of socialism—for example the massive and largely successful campaign for industrialization—were to be meaningful not only as material achievements, but also as examples of successful self-assertion by a nation and people. But if the self-assertion of a nation is modelled on the individual horizon, then it is condemned to a similar endlessness: no victory will be enough, no success ever satisfying, and the people will be condemned to an endless and necessary diet of mass mobilization.[134] The iron will of Stalin—symbol of the nation and exemplar for the people—is therefore the epitome of the 'serious' individual will, which in the end will sacrifice all for a future which has no real substance. We will return to Stalinism in the final chapter; suffice it to say here that while Bakhtin appears to have shrewdly connected the viciousness of Stalinist politics with its high humanist seriousness, he can do so only by forgetting that this was just one state in the midst of others, and that mass mobilization answered some practical necessities, too.

It was the attack on 'humanist' seriousness that was to be the book's undoing. Having researched and completed the text by 1940, Bakhtin made several unsuccessful attempts to have it published (one of which nearly led to the text's being published by Louis Aragon in Paris) before resigning himself to defending it for a degree at the Gorky Institute in 1946.[135] Submitted for the degree of Candidate of Science (the Russian

---

[134] Charles Taylor, from a rather different but not altogether distant perspective, has pointed to the need for endless mobilization as endemic to this kind of state. See his *Hegel* (Cambridge: Cambridge University Press, 1975), 455–6.

[135] The text of 'Rabelais in the History of Realism' was sent by Goslitizdat (a state publishing

equivalent of a Ph.D.), the thesis was the occasion for a discussion of seven hours' length in the Academic Council of the Institute. The three official opponents proposed that the thesis be awarded not the degree of Candidate but the higher degree of Doctor of Science (in effect, an English D.Litt. or German *Habilitation*). Others, however, were unhappy with the fact that in Bakhtin's study 'Rabelais ceases to be a great humanist', the 'ideologue of a new, growing society'.[136] The very strategy of using Rabelais to re-establish contact with a forgotten medieval realism (called 'gothic realism' in the original dissertation) was the fundamental source of conflict; even if unconsciously, Bakhtin's opponents realized that he had in his sights the ideology of 'progressive humanism' which was central to Stalin's mix of nationalism and Marxism. Bakhtin was unanimously awarded the Candidate's degree, and although the vote was just in favour (7–6) of the award of the Doctorate, the latter decision was passed on to the Higher Attestation commission. The Zhdanovite ideological offensive of the late 1940s put paid to any lingering prospect of the higher award; in 1947 an unsigned (and therefore editorially endorsed) article in the cultural press attacked the Gorky Institute in general and Bakhtin's thesis in particular for its 'anti-scientific' and 'Freudian' orientation. When in 1951 the commission refused the higher degree, it cited, amongst other objections, the lack of effort made to link Rabelais to European humanism.

The genius rebuffed by mediocre, ideologically zealous officialdom: the thesis defence easily lends itself to more myth-making, even though it has been pointed out that most of those present were prominent scholars without Stalinist connections, and opinion on the thesis did not break down on Marxist/non-Marxist lines.[137] Nevertheless, with this saga Bakhtin's prospect of reintegration into metropolitan intellectual life came to an end. In 1945 he moved from Savelevo back to Saransk, where he would remain a teacher at the Mordovian Pedagogical Institute (University, from 1957) until his retirement on grounds of ill health in 1961.

house) to Aragon at the end of 1945, by whom it was apparently going to be published. For reasons we do not know, this did not come to pass. See Pan'kov, '"Ot khoda etogo dela"', 36.

[136] From the speech of E. Ia. Dombrovskaia, cited in 'Stenogramma', 83.

[137] See V. M. Alpatov, 'Zametki na poliakh stenogrammy zashchity dissertatsii M. M. Bakhtina', *Dialog Karnaval Khronotop*, 1 (1997), 70–97. Alpatov points out, for example, that one of the examiners Bakhtin selected precisely on the basis of his nonconformist and independent convictions, N. M. Nusinov, was probably the most dedicated Marxist present at the defence.

PHILOSOPHY OF LANGUAGE AND SARANSK, 1945–1961

Texts

'Mariia Tiudor' (1954; review of Victor Hugo's 'Mary Tudor').

'The Problem of the Text' (1959–60; previously known as 'The Problem of the Text in Linguistics, Philology and the other Human Sciences: An Essay in Philosophical Analysis').

'The Problem of Speech Genres' (1953).
Preparatory Materials for 'The Problem of Speech Genres'
Dialogue (1952)
Dialogue-I (1952)
Dialogue-II (1952)
Preparatory Materials (1952–3)

'Language in Artistic Literature' (1954)

'The Problem of Sentimentalism' (1958–9)

Bakhtin's single-minded attention to novelistic culture was relatively brief and intense, although it permanently altered the shape of his project. And although his shift of focus to cultural history gave his writing a historical and social edge it lacked earlier, it did not entail any loss of philosophical perspective. Nevertheless, a subtle change of emphasis differentiates the philosophy of the 1940s and 1950s from that of the so-called early works. 'Towards Philosophical Bases of the Human Sciences', probably written between 1940 and 1943, announces the change of tack in its very title. No longer would Bakhtin place on philosophy the entire burden of defending the priority of ethical reality, in the hope that it might single-handedly restore a lost dimension of responsibility. In the postwar period ethical reality, in its new linguistic guise of dialogism, becomes something manifest above all in the distinctive disciplinary practice of the human sciences. All that philosophy has to do, to keep ethical reality in view, is to ensure that the distinctiveness of this practice is acknowledged and safeguarded. The orientation to the other and the historical consciousness which was first disclosed by philosophy, then made the exclusive province of verbal art, now passes to the act of interpreting linguistic expressions as such. Not a 'first philosophy' but a 'philosophy of expression' (TPBHum., 9) has become the order of the day.

This, however, requires a cessation of hostilities between the ethical and what had been condemned as the merely theoretical or scientific. The writing of the postwar period may appear like a return to the placid domain of philosophy, but this placidity is in fact something new for Bakhtin. In the philosophical efforts of the 1920s *and* in the theory of the novel Bakhtin seeks total victory over theoretical reason and the official ideology of the poetic; in the 1940s and 1950s only an equitable division of labour, as the 'practical interestedness' embodied in theoretical cognition is allowed its jurisdiction. In the essay 'The Problem of the Text', formalist linguistics, representing theoretical reason in the sphere of language study, is deemed not only acceptable, but even necessary:

Therefore, behind every text stands a system of language. To this corresponds everything in the text which is repeated and reproduced, repeatable and reproducible, everything that can be given outside a given text (its givenness). But simultaneously every text (as an utterance) is something individual, unique and unrepeatable . . . (PTxt, 308/105)

Such peaceful coexistence was inconceivable in the theory of the novel, when the least trace of formalism called forth the sweeping power of historical becoming. But now, while Bakhtin may reduce the strictly linguistic to a technical and subordinate moment in the scheme of things— 'from the point of view of the extralinguistic ends of an utterance everything linguistic is only a means' (PTxt, 313/109)—he nonetheless admits such a technical moment is inevitable, and therefore willingly divides the study of language into 'linguistics' and an apparently parallel field of 'metalinguistics'.[138]

In her commentary on 'The Problem of Speech Genres' and 'Language in Artistic Literature', Gogotishvili claims that the placid, even scientific tone of these pieces in particular reflects Bakhtin's tactical decision to translate his insights into the language of linguistics.[139] 'The Problem of Speech Genres' followed closely on Stalin's speech on 'Marxism and Questions of Linguistics' (which was quoted in the body of the essay, but editorially deleted) and was apparently intended as a publishable intervention in a then live linguistic dispute. But the *scientific* turn evident in these essays and in 'The Problem of the Text' is more than a superficial response to circumstances. In the 1950s the distance which once separated the public square from the world of official power has been reduced to that separating the faculty of the humanities from the natural sciences. Bakhtin had not forgotten his earlier positions: in the notebook containing plans for 'The Problem of Speech Genres' named 'Dialogue-II' by the editors, Bakhtin made a lengthy précis of 'Discourse in the Novel' (which still lay unpub-

[138] The term 'metalinguistics' first appears in 'The Problem of the Text', 321/114. See Gogotishvili's note on the origins of the term, SS5, 641–2 n. 59.

[139] In her commentary to 'The Problem of Speech Genres', Gogotishvili notes 'The present work and the working notes of 1954 entitled "Language in Artistic Literature" . . . were, probably, M. M. Bakhtin's final attempts to graft the speech phenomena which interested him directly onto the tree of linguistics' (SS5, 541). For a fuller account of how Bakhtin tried to address the linguistic polemics of his time see her commentaries on 'The Problem of Speech Genres' (SS5, 535–42), the 'Archival materials' for that article (SS5, 555–60) and 'Language in Artistic Literature' (SS5, 591–8).

lished), and the sketch 'Language in Artistic Literature' is a clear reworking of the themes of that militant essay from the 1930s. But in the postwar
context the social conditions which made a certain kind of novelistic
dialogism possible are recast as either the methodological features of a
certain kind of scholarship or the attributes of 'artistic literature' in general.
The exemplary sphere of dialogical language turns out to be the human
sciences themselves; interpretative sensitivity and tact become the very
embodiments of ethical behaviour. As 'the sciences of the person in his or
her specificity' (PTxt, 311/107) the humanistic disciplines are presented
as the most refined and elaborate occasions for that 'free revelation of
personality' which is the prize asset of dialogue. Bakhtin therefore seems
reconciled to the idea that the dimension of ethical reality will be something which comes to the fore only on certain humanistic occasions, and
then by virtue of an old-fashioned belief in the special task of the sciences
of the spirit.

This had to have consequences for Bakhtin's theory of language.
Throughout his work, it had been the elaborated 'generic' form of the
dialogical, whether it was a novel or a prayer, which effectively determined
the contours of his theory of language. Although the essays presented
genres or works of verbal art as the blossoming of inner tendencies of
language, it was always clear in the actual argument that matters were
vice versa, and that Bakhtin had crammed the properties of the grander
historical forms into language itself. Trading the novel for the act of
humanistic interpretation therefore has the effect of transforming the condition of language itself in his theory. No longer does everyday language
contain the social and historical energy of the novel *in micro*, 'punching its
way to its meaning and its expression through an alien-verbal multi-
accented environment' (DN 91/277); now it is enough for it to behave
like a text awaiting interpretation: 'A human being in his or her human
specificity always expresses him- or herself (speaks), that is, creates a text
(even if only as potential)' (PTxt, 311/107). Similarly the 'metalinguistics'
Bakhtin now calls on to describe these 'textual' relations, has no need, like
the earlier stylistics of genre it has replaced, to make generic distinctions
between the dialogism of different historical moments. As a consequence,
the old line in the sand between novelistic and rhetorical dialogue is
washed away; in the world of texts, whether an utterance is treated as the
expression of an individual or of a culture, 'from the everyday reply to the
multivolume novel or scientific tract' (N61, 329/118) makes no qualitative
difference. Dialogism seems more like a permanent but occasional condition than something set in motion by the historical energies released in
modern Europe.

In 'The Problem of Speech Genres', the once historical condition of forward-moving heteroglossia is now reduced to the simple coexistence of speech types: 'All the various fields of human activity are connected with the use of language. It is completely understandable that the character and forms of this usage should be as various as the fields of human activity, which, of course, in no sense contradicts the national unity of language' (PSG 159/60). 'In no sense contradicts the national unity of language': Bakhtin's direct concession to Stalin's claim regarding the national unity of a language leaves him stranded somewhere between functionalism—the presupposition of a coordinated fit between language games—and mere empiricism, in which the unity of language is simply the sum of more or less arbitrary 'speech genres'. Of course, the very identification of a genre entails judgements about its purpose, value, and direction. But Bakhtin here gives way to empirical sociology, in terms of the philosophy of his *method*, far more whole-heartedly than at any earlier time. Hence the distinction between the novelistic and the everyday is presented as no more than the difference between 'secondary' and 'primary' genres, as if mere chronology or spatial purview was at stake. In the ghostly form of a secondary genre, lacking a distinctive ethical or social task, the novel is condemned to roam a somewhat barren and unchangeable discursive universe.

Without detailed information or personal testimony, one cannot conclusively link this change in the stance of Bakhtin's work with any particular alteration in his living conditions. Even the circumspect observer, however, cannot resist the hypothesis that this placidity depended upon the relative ease and security of Bakhtin's institutional existence in this period. After returning to the job he had briefly held in Saransk, Bakhtin led what was by all accounts a successful, if modest, academic existence until his retirement in 1961. As first a lecturer, then a head of department, he taught literature and aesthetics for fifteen years not only at the university but in a number of public contexts. His status as a former exile was apparently no bar to this provincial success; at the same time, he effectively dropped out of the metropolitan cultural scene with which he had once been so closely associated. Although his book on Dostoevsky was mentioned in the late 1950s by Dostoevsky scholars and in an important new book by the old Formalist Shklovsky, and although Roman Jakobson took the trouble to revive Voloshinov as an object of interest, Vadim Kozhinov at the Gorky Institute could still be unaware of the fact that Bakhtin was alive in 1960. With nearly all of his friends from the Leningrad circle dead, and himself apparently frozen out of Moscow and Leningrad, Bakhtin was destined to live out his days without notoriety. Until, that is, a casual remark revealed to Kozhinov that he was alive and well.

REDISCOVERY AND LATE PHILOSOPHY, 1961–1975

Texts

'Notes from 1961' (1961–62; the second half of these notes was previously known as 'Towards a Reworking of the Dostoevsky Book').
'Dostoevsky 1961'.
'Towards Dostoevsky' (1962).
'Notes 1962–1963'.
Problems of Dostoevsky's Poetics (1963).
The Art of François Rabelais and the Popular Culture of the Middle Ages and the Renaissance (1965).
'Answer to a Question posed the Editors of *Novyi mir* (1970).
'Rabelais and Gogol' (part of 1940 dissertation; revised for separate publication, 1970).
'From the Notes of 1970–71'.
'Towards a Methodology of the Human Sciences' (1974).
'Concluding Remarks' to 'Forms of Time and of the Chronotope in the Novel' (1973).

The route by which Bakhtin was finally made part of the public world in the Soviet Union has already been described. The initial stages of the campaign on Bakhtin's behalf focused on the republication of the text on Dostoevsky and the first publication of his text on Rabelais. The various notes made while revising *Problems of Dostoevsky's Art* for the Italian and Russian editions include themes which never made it into the new text (such as the connection between the loss of personality and the condition of Russian capitalism), but their focus is the role of Dostoevsky's artistic technique in saving the represented personality from reification and the legacy of the carnivalesque in Dostoevsky. The latter topic had concerned Bakhtin since the 1940s, when he first began to work on a revision of the Dostoevsky book, focusing on the 'specifically Saturnalian conception of "truth" in Dostoevsky' (HisType, 44).[140] These interests eventually became the basis for the greatly enlarged chapter on plot, which effectively made Dostoevsky the modern endpoint of the tradition of carnivalesque Bakhtin had earlier set out in the study of Rabelais. The ease with which this reframing of Dostoevsky's 'polyphonic' achievement could be accomplished reveals how closely linked were these apparently quite different

---

[140] A letter of 1946, from Bakhtin's friend and colleague E. A. Tarle, refers to Bakhtin's intention to take 'Fedor Mikhailovich in hand again' (SS5, 418). Extensive discussion of carnival motifs in Dostoevsky is found not only in the text cited, 'Towards a History of the Type (Generic Variety) of Dostoevsky's Novel' (1940–41), but also in 'On Questions of Self-Consciousnsess and Self-Evaluation' (c.1943–46) and 'Rhetoric, to the extent that it is something false . . .' (1943).

texts. *Rabelais* suggested that popular-festive culture could dissolve ordinary identities in the flow of an ever-moving history; Dostoevsky would strip characters of their social identities by arranging a meeting 'outside' of history, on the terrain of Christian ultimate questions. What both aimed at was a sudden rupture with the everyday, which places all on a temporarily equal footing, but this rupture is not conceived of as a utopian exit from history, but as the redemptive possibility which makes history, as a meaningful sequence of events, possible. 'Not the usual run of life, but faith in miracle, in the possibility of that usual run's radical violation' (Rhet., 64): it is this faith which made history meaningful and prevented its degradation into a mere struggle for power or biological survival. As Walter Benjamin once gloomily remarked, the problem is 'that things just go on'—Bakhtin and he shared the belief that only faith in the Messianic task could break the grip of this form of the everyday.

In the 1960s Bakhtin remained in Saransk while his postgraduate admirers and figures from the Soviet literary establishment battled to have his work published and discussed. In 1969 worsening health meant that hospitalization was required. A quirk of fate (Iuri Andropov's daughter—he was then head of the KGB—was in a seminar led by Bakhtin's follower and friend, Vladimir Turbin) provided Bakhtin's champions with the connections necessary to get him into the Kremlin hospital.[141] There he and his wife Elena stayed until May 1970 when they had to be moved to a home in a town close to Moscow, where they lived until Elena's death in December 1971.

In this period, Bakhtin made a number of jottings, which were collected together by his editors as 'From the Notes of 1970–71'. There are thirty separate entries, on a variety of topics, and one cannot say what principles guided editorial selection (they were published posthumously). The temptation to regard these as the marshalling of accumulated resources for a final assault on a world racked by the narrow arguments of the rhetorical and the serious is nearly irresistible; and, indeed, through the melange of topics one can glimpse the outline of a central preoccupation, slowly worked into shape. On the one hand, Bakhtin wants to affirm the absolute difference which separates the higher 'dialogical sphere of the life of the word' and its concomitants—'creative' understanding, the alien word, the disclosure of personality—from the world of practical rhetoric and scientific thought. On the other hand, he will mark out the fate of this difference in the history of language and writing, as it is embedded in carnival laughter, the literature of sentimentalism, the gradual triumph of the European vernaculars, and the works of Dostoevsky and Gogol. The metalinguistics which might bring these two together would trace the

[141] See Joseph Kraft, 'Letter from Moscow', *The New Yorker*, 31 Jan. 1983, 105.

historical events which constituted and which could maintain the 'fragile and easily destroyed' (N70–71, 375/150) sphere of the dialogical and the personality: 'Stylistics should be orientated to the metalinguistic study of the great events (events taking several centuries) of the speech life of peoples' (N70–71, 356/133). Great events, perhaps because they defined great and all-encompassing divisions, as well as great possibilities, which persist to the present day.

However, the task assigned to metalinguistics is also embodied in a question Bakhtin poses to modernity rather than to the centuries past: how would the writer replace 'the speech subjects of the high pontificating genres—the priests, prophets, preachers, judges, leaders, patriarchal fathers, and the like'? What substance would define the role of the writer, who is the only 'authoritative' subject in modernity? The writer inherits not only the styles of the pontificating genres but their transcendental pretensions as well; it is to the writer that the problem of a sphere above or beyond the practical and resolvable worries of the everyday falls. This means the search, initiated in 'Author and Hero', for the redemptive discourse of the author continues:

An author's search for his own discourse is fundamentally a search for a genre and a style, a search for an authorial position. Right now this is the most acute problem in contemporary literature, leading many to renounce the genre of the novel, to substitute for it a montage of documents, a description of things, to bellelettrism, to a certain degree to literature of the absurd. (N70–71, 374/149)

With only an apparently secular language to hand, and lacking the institutions which underpinned the authority of the older transcendence, the writer must nevertheless find a genre and style which will take us beyond our own words. Is this merely a stand-in for metaphysical certainties no longer possible, or does the 'sobriety, simplicity, and democracy' of the modern languages furnish the basis for a modern 'kingdom of ends'?

That last phrase recurs twice in these notes, trace of a never surrendered Kantian aspiration. 'Laughter and the kingdom of ends (means themselves are always serious)' (N70–71, 358/135); 'The word as means (as language) and the word as that which gives meaning. The meaning-giving word belongs to the kingdom of ends. The word as the ultimate (highest) end' (N70–71, 357/134). In Kant the kingdom of ends depended upon the postulates of practical reason, a metaphysical supposition necessary to preserve the freedom of decision which made morality possible. Bakhtin would apparently like to find historical sources—in popular-festive culture, in the novel, in modern language itself—for that kingdom, without giving up its metaphysical heart. But Kant was giving voice not so much to metaphysics as to the dreams of an emerging liberal constitutionalism and republicanism, and some more history may have seeped into this prospective kingdom in the two centuries between him and Bakhtin, perhaps to the point where it has a more democratic flavour than would be to God's liking. Whether Bakhtin constructed a socio-cultural edifice for which religion was then mere scaffolding is a question which only interpretation can settle: his work tries to maintain ground in both camps.

The death of his wife was naturally a crushing event for Bakhtin. After a short stay in Peredelkino, a suburb which was a retreat for writers, he moved to a cooperative apartment in Moscow, where he lived until his death in March 1975. In the course of his last years he was often visited, and participated in the preparation of a volume of his essays on the novel. His last two compositions were apparently the 'Conclusion' to the essay (really a collocation of various materials) 'Forms of Time and of the Chronotope in the Novel' and the short piece 'Towards a Methodology of the Human Sciences'. The latter is a series of jottings similar in form to the earlier notes, but also a reworking and expansion of the text 'Towards Philosophical Bases of the Human Sciences'. Here, as before, the redemptive power of language is vested in the discursive forms of the 'interpretative' human sciences, which, in their search for knowledge, disclose the sphere of the personality. In formal terms, the substance of this redemption is the same, the establishment of an ethical reality in the face of excessive theoretical reason: 'Our *thought* and our *practice*, not technical but *moral* . . .' (TMHum., 391/168); but in the intervening life, the means have changed a great deal. Does the transformation of means dictate changed ends? This is the question to which we should now turn.

PART III

Refinements

CHAPTER FOUR

Language

Bakhtin did not regard his turn to language as a secularizing move, for he believed that the structure of language reflected the precepts of Christian ethics. Careful analysis of our linguistic experience would lead us to the axioms of religious existence, as surely as curved space and black holes lead to the Big Bang. When he spoke of 'metalinguistics' he did not therefore have in mind a better or even more reflective linguistics, but an altogether different discipline, with an entirely dissimilar interest in its object. The linguist looks on language as a neutral reality, which can be described but not judged, and which should function as humanity's pliant instrument; Bakhtin saw in language the substance of ethical life, in which was sedimented the very possibility of a 'kingdom of ends'. The history of language was the history of social life, and the modern European vernaculars, with their flexible structures and their capacity for irony and indirection, were ethical achievements in their own right. One did not have to make an abstract argument for the Christian point of view; one merely had to point out how language worked, and what kind of intersubjectivity it held in place. Bakhtin may have written a great deal about language and very little about religion, but he may also have thought analysis of the first rendered discussion of the second superfluous.

For reasons discussed in the Introduction, I think the claim that language is something more than a tool is convincing. But there is something suspicious in the perfect fit Bakhtin describes between our experience of linguistic intersubjectivity and the architectonics of Christian life. Does recognition of the intersubjective gap that structures all language lead so inexorably to 'absolute sacrifice for myself, mercy for the other' (AH 56/56), as Bakhtin eloquently put it? Or is there enough slippage between the two to allow secular writers (like myself) to draw different conclusions from the dialogism Bakhtin revealed? 'Our *thought* and our *practice* are not technical, but *moral* . . .': sure, but no one is saying what *kind* of morality is reflected in the varieties of dialogism. After Voloshinov, with the article 'Discourse in Life and Discourse in Poetry' (1926), had made the linguistic turn—identifying ethical reality with the sphere of language—Bakhtin was free to entrust his theory of discourse with the tasks he had originally assigned to his ethical philosophy. But once language was open to investigation as an ethical substance, there was always a danger that discourse would reveal a moral universe different from the one demanded by Christ's presence. There is every reason to believe that Bakhtin shifted his perspective convinced that the intersubjectivity he would uncover would retain its religious bearings, and that matters simply got out of hand.

'The task consists of forcing an environment *of things*, acting mechanically on the personality, to speak, that is, to disclose in it a potential discourse and tone, to transform it into a context of meaning for a speaking, thinking and acting (including creating) personality' (TMHum., 387/164). Environments don't usually speak, except in novels, of course, where the linguistic constitution of things is complete and without residue. In the linguistified reality of verbal art, the world is not a neutral field for the subject's actions, but a place which will foreground the question of the meaning of those actions, which, so to speak, is willing to understand and evaluate them. And the more intently it tries to understand and evaluate, the more plausible will it be for the personality to seize the opportunity to define itself ethically, accept its uniqueness, and lay itself open to the judgement of others. Therefore the most ethical and realistic of writers is Dostoevsky, in whose works environments not only talk, but talk back: 'Not one element of such an atmosphere can be neutral: everything must touch the raw nerve of the hero, must provoke him, interrogate him, even polemicize with and mock him; everything must be addressed to the hero himself' (*PDA* 70/64). The dream-like narrative which critics had claimed set Dostoevsky off from realism, to Bakhtin's mind brings him closer to it. It is the nineteenth-century naturalist writer intent on depicting a precise environment of things who destroys the world, because he or she subordinates language to the inertness of quasi-natural existence.

This identification of the ethical and the linguistic marks a break with Kantian moral philosophy in three significant respects. First, it implies that ethical choice takes the form not of a decision 'to be moral' but of a choice *among* different values. Bakhtin was familiar with Max Scheler's critique of Kantian formalism, which focused on the latter's assumption of humanity's 'radical evil'.[1] Scheler demonstrated that this assumption, which he regards as an unnecessary concession to Hume and Hobbes ('*Kant's* error, for he borrowed it from the English on blind faith'—an interesting sentiment, even if the nationalities aren't quite right), determined the form of Kantian

---

[1] Bakhtin indirectly refers to Scheler's *Der Formalismus in der Ethik und die materiale Wertethik* (Halle: Verlag Max Niemeyer, 1921) in 'Towards a Philosophy of the Act', 98–100/22–4; in *Problems of Dostoevsky's Art* a footnote on p. 78 describes this work and Scheler's *Wesen und Formen der Sympathie* (Bonn: Verlag Friedrich Cohen, 1927) as the beginnings of a 'principled critique of monologism'. On the very substantial influence of Scheler on Bakhtin in the 1920s see Poole, 'From Phenomenology to Dialogue'.

ethics.[2] If humanity's nature was evil, then to act morally would be to repress it, following the dictates of the law-based will rather than one's own natural inclinations:

This 'attitude' I can only describe as a basic 'hostility' toward or 'distrust' of the given as such, a fear of the given as 'chaos', an anxiety . . . Hence this attitude is the opposite of *love* of the world, of trust in and loving *devotion* to the world. Strictly speaking, this attitude belongs only to modern times, which are permeated by a *hatred of the world*, a hostility toward the world, and a distrust of it, and by the *consequence* of this hatred: namely, the limitless need for activity to 'organize' and 'control' the world . . .[3]

Scheler's preference was to understand all human willing as orientated by value preference, not by quasi-natural drives, a point of view Bakhtin takes over and recasts in linguistic terms. If needs and desires are mediated by language, they are caught within the web of culture and difficult to disentangle from the values embodied in any cultural system. Secondly, the assumption that the reality confronted by the subject is already moralized or endowed with values renders unnecessary the leap into the suprasensible or 'noumenal' which Kant equated with the passage from the natural to the moral. With the doctrine of a unique ethical reality the distinction between a noumenal realm of free moral choice and a phenomenal realm of scientific necessity falls away, and with it all excuses for the preservation of a non-scientific, purely philosophical approach to moral issues. Finally, as a consequence of the first two points, the representation of the world as ethical reality and of other subjects as moral beings is absolutely realistic; in fact, only such a description deserves to be called realist.

The last point is the critical one. It is not Dostoevsky's moral beliefs, but his *representational* achievements that impress Bakhtin: 'This . . . narrow ideologism, searching above all for purely philosophical understandings and insights, does not grasp the very thing in Dostoevsky's art that has outlasted his philosophical and social-political ideology: his revolutionary innovatoriness in the field of the novel as an artistic form' (*PDA* 4/276). For the most part, Bakhtin finds the ideology banal; Dostoevsky's value lies in his development of means for the representation of the human as an ethical being and of the idea as such, in his devotion to 'realism in a higher sense' (*PDA* 101/277). The dialogical attitude does not stem from an ethical decision—to be considerate, to protect the other's room for manoeuvre, and so on—but from an interest in an absolutely objective approach to the intentions, desires, and needs of the *other* whom one confronts.

[2] Max Scheler, *Formalism in Ethics and Non-Formal Ethics of Values*, trans. Manfred S. Frings and Roger L. Funk (Evanston, Ill.: Northwestern University Press, 1973), 66.
[3] Ibid. 67.

LANGUAGE AND PERSONALITY

It is in the philosophical text composed at the end of his 'novel' period, 'Towards Philosophical Bases of the Human Sciences', that this utter realism is most sharply elucidated:

Knowledge of things and knowledge of personality. These must be characterized as limits: the pure dead thing, having only externality, existing only for the other and capable of being completely and finally revealed by the one-sided act of this (knowing) other. Such a thing, lacking its own inalienable and unconsumable core, can only be an object of practical interestedness. The second limit is thought about God in the presence of God, dialogue, questioning, prayer. The necessity of free self-disclosure of personality. Here there is an inner kernel, which cannot be swallowed up or consumed, where a distance is always preserved, in relation to which only pure disinterestedness is possible; disclosing itself to the other, it always remains at the same time for itself also. A question is in this case posed by the one knowing not to himself nor to a third in the presence of a dead thing, but to the one known. The significance of sympathy and love. In this case the criterion is not precision of knowledge, but depth of penetration. Here knowledge is directed at that which is individual. This is the sphere of openings, of revelations, of recognitions, of communications. Here what is important is both the secret and the lie (but not the error). Here what is important is immodesty and insult, and the like. The dead thing does not exist at the limit, it is an abstract element (conditional); every whole (nature and all its phenomena, as a whole) is to some degree a personality. (TPBHum., 7)

Although the distinction between personality and thing is a bit unsteady in this passage—we can be forgiven for thinking that Bakhtin regards 'things' as, in the end, dispensable—the end in view is *knowledge* of personalities, in an emphatic sense. The disinterested relationship of revelation, recognition, and communication we maintain towards them is determined by epistemological considerations, rather than a desire to get on well. Hanging on to the distinction between knowing personalities and knowing things is critical, of course, but hanging on to the fact that both relationships are cognitive is just as important. For behind the passage lurks the fear of naturalism, which models all existence on that of the natural object and measures all knowledge by its success in approximating the knowledge of such objects. In such a 'theoreticized' world, to the extent that personalities refuse to act like things, we cannot know them. Bakhtin takes almost the opposite view, implying that knowledge of things is rather compromised by 'practical interestedness', and he does so by distinguishing the personality phenomenologically from the thing. The personality with whom we become acquainted in discourse (opening, revelation, recognition, and communication) is not a failed or fuzzy thing, but a different kind of object, irreducible in its mode of existence to a natural thing. It is constituted by a differing intention and has differing qualities—an inner, distanced kernel and a distance from use which reflect not some limit on what we can know about it, but what it is. Hence there is no need for scepticism here—Bakhtin still speaks of knowledge—only sensitivity to the necessarily different criteria which apply in the knowledge of personalities.

This is not a fine point of philosophy, for behind it lies the difference between the higher realism Bakhtin aspires to and the scepticism and liberal ethics with which it can be easily confused. We are naturally tempted to construe the distanced kernel which constitutes the essence of the personality as a limit on our knowledge of others, an inner sanctum of consciousness which we dare not intrude upon for fear of cramping the *other*'s freedom of thought. On this reading, the decision to treat others as personalities is a moral one: they may be 'things', with bodies and a brain, but we must value something inside them, and we do so by giving it room to move. But in fact the distanced kernel registers the very mode in which the personality exists in discourse with others, and precisely the fact that the personality *can only exist* in discourse with others. 'Expression', which is never fully itself, and always indicates something beyond and within, is what makes personality possible, which is to say that it is not an external-ization of subjective intentions, but always an intersubjective fact. Its indeterminacy is not *mystery*, but the indeterminacy characteristic of any act of discourse as such, its openness, which is indistinguishable from its public and historical character. Individuals can only come to be in inter-subjective discourse and they exist not as a substance in a fixed time and space, but in history, as something for which development and becoming are constitutive. These features of the personality ensure that our know-ledge of them has an analogously open and historical character: in isolation one would have not a yet-to-be-known individual, but a subject unable to fix its identity or claim its unique autonomy.

In no paragraph does Bakhtin's cited claim to be 'a neo-Kantian with emendations from Husserl's phenomenology' sound more plausible.[4] From the former he draws the essential distinction between personality and thing, from the latter a phenomenological manner and method. At the same time, something new is added to the mixture, transforming the end result: the phenomenological distinctions are rewritten in terms of differing kinds of discourse. In Husserl's phenomenology distinctions between kinds of object are distinctions within the structure of consciousness, which the philosopher can only approach via the tortuous procedures of phenomen-ological introspection. In Bakhtin, they are distinctions between forms of

---

[4] Bakhtin is quoted as having said this in conversation in Kaganskaia, 'Shutovskoi khorovod', 142.

language use, in which social relationships, beyond the reach of introspection, are implicated. In this crucial respect he differs from other writers who tried to establish the priority of the ethical in phenomenological terms, such as Scheler, from whom he otherwise drew so lavishly. Scheler also regards the personality as an absolutely distinct being, characterized by its moral bearing: 'As soon as we tend to "objectify" a human being in any way, the bearer of moral values disappears *of necessity*.'[5] Yet Scheler still describes knowledge of another person as the 'intuition' of that person's 'value-essence', that is, as something experienced by an individual within the bounds of consciousness rather than achieved via a certain form of discourse.[6] His 'values' will therefore retain a metaphysical air, ideal yet still thing-like.

Different kinds of language—different kinds of relationship. Having gone through the phenomenological side of the argument, we are prepared for the re-emergence of the ethical dimension 'in a higher sense'. It may be that apprehending the personality as such demands philosophical disinterestedness, embodied in dialogue, questioning, or prayer. But even in philosophy, it takes two to tango: disinterestedness is not an attitude struck by the philosopher, but a relationship from which 'the secret and the lie', 'immodesty and insult' have been expunged. In relationships between personalities the formal dividing-line between cognitive truth and ethical truth, questions of the true and questions of right or social appropriateness, fades. One only discovers true personalities where one creates love and solidarity, because it is the very activity of relating to the *other* as a personality which allows it to emerge as unique and responsible. The self-disclosure which the knower encourages is the very act whereby the personality is constituted as such.[7] We are no longer dealing, therefore, with knowledge which leaves the *other* untouched (like a thing), but with a form of knowledge with ethical effects and meaning. And once Bakhtin has let the ethical cat out of the bag, nothing can stop it from becoming a more political animal. The same principles which govern the self-disclosure of personalities could apply with equal force to citizens or comrades as well. One does not discover the latter by flushing out some inner truth (such as a 'class consciousness' lurking below the surface) but by striving for the intersubjectivity in which speaking and acting as citizens and comrades is possible. This, I think, is what Gramsci had in mind when he remarked that a party which asked 'the prior permission of the masses before acting'

---

[5] Scheler, *Formalism in Ethics*, 86.

[6] Ibid. 488.

[7] Habermas has described the self-consciousness through which an individual comes to be as the '*ethical self-assurance* of an accountable person', which takes place in dialogue; see 'Individuation through Socialization: On Mead's Theory of Intersubjectivity', in *Postmetaphysical Thinking*, 168.

(by means of formal votes) had already decided it was not a revolutionary party, no matter what the response to its enquiries. The style of its discourse already signalled that it chose not to instantiate the kinds of relations in which revolutionary comrades could exist.[8] So it is with every form of discourse in political life, from strikes to referenda: they are not different modes for ascertaining the convictions of those they address, but play a role in determining what a conviction (or belief, or whatever) *is* in the given circumstance, and the connection it might have with social action. Democracy is therefore not merely the free expression of beliefs or commitments, but the question of the very form those beliefs and commitments assume. 'Towards Philosophical Bases of the Human Sciences' claims to be concerned with something far more intimate, with the modesty, considerateness, sincerity, and so forth necessary for personality. Even a superficial acquaintance with the social and intellectual history of early twentieth-century Europe, however, reveals that personality was an ideal framed by the traumas and transformations of modern Europe, demanded not only by Bakhtin, but by secular and worldly intellectuals like Weber, Simmel, and Nietzsche.[9] The point of personalities was that one needed them at a particular moment in the history of modern Europe; they were to be a new kind of person with a new kind of dignity, suitable to the social forms and conflicts of the age. Modesty and sincerity would make the personality just as, in an earlier age, honour and propriety made the gentleman. What makes the democratic citizen? Not the mere opportunity for expression at any rate, but values corresponding to a new and appropriate *structure* of expression.

A structure which, arguably, ought to transcend the historical opposition of personality and thing so critical to Bakhtin's project. Gillian Rose has shrewdly argued that the ultimate origin of this neo-Kantian motif was not anything in the least philosophical, but the Roman law, which distinguished between the two in its pursuit of orderly property relations.[10]

---

[8] Antonio Gramsci, 'Political Capacity', *Selections from Political Writings, 1910–1920*, trans. John Matthews (London: Lawrence & Wishart, 1977), 348. He goes on to say: 'Similarly no revolutionary movement can be decreed by a workers' national assembly. To call such an assembly is to confess in advance one's disbelief in revolution; it amounts, therefore, to exercising a prejudicial pressure against it' (p. 349).

[9] On the idea of *Persönlichkeit* in German theorizing, see Liebersohn, *Fate and Utopia*, 88, 108–25. Liebersohn notes that one source for Weber's use of this concept is the Protestant theologian Adolf von Harnack who, interestingly enough, is also cited as an important source for Bakhtin's interpretation of Christianity (in the notes to 'Author and Hero', 408–9 n. 17/240–1 n. 73). Harnack believed that the essential Christian community consisted of a meeting of pure personalities, unencumbered by the merely 'Hellenistic' rituals of the established Church.

[10] Gillian Rose, *Dialectic of Nihilism: Post-Structuralism and Law* (Oxford: Basil Blackwell, 1984), 16–24. Her critique seems to me final: 'The kingdom of ends is, of course, strictly speaking, inconceivable: for it is intelligible, a practical principle (an ought), not a theoretical concept. This inconceivability itself arises from the attempt to make persons and things, conditioned by each

Bakhtin is clear on the fact that the distinction is not ontological ('thing and personality are *limits*, not absolute substances', TMHum., 387/164–5), but he nevertheless denigrates the thing in favour of the personality. The poor thing, all finitude and usefulness, appears as a sad technical necessity for creatures which really have their hearts set on entering the kingdom of ends. But the disparagement of technique and use, all too familiar in twentieth-century *Kulturkritik*, can only make redemption less likely and less worthwhile. The image of the technical as discourse in which the subject is already constituted, fully in control, and bent only on manipulation for subjective 'practical' ends is pure fantasy; it reassures us that entering the 'sphere of openings, of revelations' and so on, requires only detachment from the practical and the local, as if true dialogue demanded a certain abstraction from everyday cares. But matters are more complicated than that: dialogical relations are the rule, for which technique is no exception, and if our technical-practical activity depends upon the same open intersubjectivity as our relations with *others*, then it follows that 'practical interestedness'—the desire to 'use' finite objects—is not itself the problem. The opposition of the merely practical and the personality, like its ancestor, the Kantian contrast of natural desire and moral reason, is false, because our thing-like economic needs are more than a distraction, and our secular, calculative discourse on things is not reducible to mere manipulation. The 'practical interestedness' dismissed by Bakhtin is inextricable from the claim to justice in this world without which talk of redemption is just a plea for more time.[11]

Not surprisingly, the relative balance of philosophy and social science in the views of Bakhtin scholars tends to determine the weight they give to Bakhtin's interest in language. Those who would present Bakhtin as a moral philosopher regard language as a mere medium for relationships, the essential qualities of which are defined elsewhere. For them, the linguistic turn in the 1920s does not affect the core of his ethical position. By contrast, semioticians (Ivanov serves as a good example) see it as an essential scientific manoeuvre, without which Bakhtin might have languished in the empty wilderness of ontology. Ethics without language, language without ethics; these are the two extreme options open to an interpretation. They are also, however, the index of a larger issue, that of Bakhtin's relationship

other, into unconditioned values—from the attempt to idealize them. A life based on persons and things cannot be idealized, cannot be made into an Ideal of Reason, or the form of the intelligible, since the opposition which is thereby formalized is that of the bearers of the substance of Roman private law' (p. 23).

[11] Bakhtin occasionally seems to realize that things cannot serve as a mere foil for personalities. See his comment in the notes labelled 'Rhetoric, to the extent that it is something false . . .': 'The object wants to leap out of itself, it lives by faith in the miracle of its own sudden transformation' (Rhet., 67).

to the social sciences or, if you like, the relationship between his conception of the human sciences and the social sciences. For in turning to language, Bakhtin and his colleagues enter a field which is being claimed for social science at that very moment. Formal linguistics itself is part of the modernity and the modernization of world-views with which Bakhtin must come to terms.

LANGUAGE AS AESTHETIC

At the very outset of his career, Bakhtin focused on language for strikingly different reasons. In 'Towards a Philosophy of the Act', it appeared as the unique place in which the ethical force of actuality was still preserved and from which it could be exhumed by philosophy:

Language historically grew up in the service of participatory thinking and the act; it began to serve abstract thought only in the present day of its history. The full plenitude of the word is required for the expression of the act from within the unique being-event, in which the act is accomplished: its substantive-semantic aspect (word-concept), graphic-expressive aspect (word-image), and emotional-volitional aspect (the intonation of the word) in their unity. The single full word can be responsibly valid in all these moments, it can be true and not just subjectively contingent. (TPA 105/31)

The concreteness of an 'event-like' (*sobytiinyi*) ethical reality found itself reflected or enacted in the language which conceptual argument had to rely on for expression. As such, language could be the perfect medium for the reintegration of the worlds split apart by modern life, the sphere of objectified cultural meanings and the 'world of life' in which linguistic acts take place. In its lost depth and 'emotional-volitional' thickness one could recover the link between the word as an act and the word as an element of a culture.

Just how language preserves this link becomes clearer from the perspective of the 1940s than it would have been in the early 1920s, for it appears to depend upon the dialogical model of truth Bakhtin only articulated later. 'It is perfectly possible to admit and suppose', Bakhtin would argue in 1929, 'that a unified truth demands a multiplicity of consciousnesses, that it in principle cannot be fitted into the boundaries of a single consciousness, that it is, so to speak, by its nature social and event-like and is born at the point of contact of various consciousnesses' (*PDA* 78/81). Bakhtin had inherited from neo-Kantianism the conviction that while, on the one hand, truth could not be relative to a single consciousness, indeed, could not be a phenomenon of consciousness in the strict sense at all, on the other hand, it was nevertheless a product of human spirit alone. But

Bakhtin thought the neo-Kantians had 'theoreticized' that spirit by abstracting it from the intersubjective context of *I* and *other* which ensured that truth had the character of an event. It was only in dialogue that 'the elements of language . . . become a real assertion or negation, they acquire a relation to truth, good and beauty, a relation to reality, they become the position of an individual person, they acquire an event-historical character' (PrepMat., 257–8). But only when Bakhtin began to speak of dialogism could one see that he was making truth inseparable from the dialogical community maintained in its pursuit, for only at that point did inter-subjectivity appear as something like discussion between individuals.

This last point can be clarified by a comparison with the discourse theory of truth which Habermas eventually derived from his theory of the public sphere (discussed in the Introduction). As we saw earlier, for Habermas, claiming that something is true is claiming that one could, in an ideal situation, persuade others that it is the case through sheer force of argument alone.[12] Every claim to truth accepts that it is fallible (because an open argument by definition acknowledges the possibility of new evidence), but at the same time maintains it is objective in the only manner possible: by virtue of its willingness to be tested in discourse. If one wishes to criticize an existing consensus—whether it is a consensus of scientific theory, of morality, or of art criticism—one does so not from some Archimedean point outside communication, but by claiming that a more universal or future discussion will bear one out. One appeals, in short, to a discursive community—a public sphere—extending not only through space but also over time. And although truth is proved only in explicit argument, the claim to it is always implicit in what we say. 'It's really quite simple,' Habermas has insisted, 'whenever we mean what we say, we raise the claim that what is said is true, or right, or truthful. With this claim a small bit of ideality breaks into our everyday lives, because such validity claims can in the end be resolved only with arguments.'[13] Habermas therefore differentiates discursively established truth into theoretical, moral-practical, and aesthetic forms (as Kant had done philosophically and Weber sociologically), which are united only formally, that is, in so far as each depends upon the idea of the better argument. In this sense the validity of any particular case is always linked to a community in which arguments take place.

[12] The discourse theory of truth is systematically expounded in Habermas's essay 'What is Universal Pragmatics?', in *Communication and the Evolution of Society*, 1–68; his most recent and extended defence of his position is found in the essays comprising *Justification and Application: Remarks on Discourse Ethics*, trans. Ciaran P. Cronin (Cambridge, Mass. and London: MIT Press, 1993).

[13] Jürgen Habermas, 'What Theories Can Accomplish—and What They Can't', in *The Past as Future*, trans. and ed. Max Pensky (Cambridge: Polity Press, 1994), 102.

Bakhtin makes a similar, but symptomatically distinct, case. He sees truth as formally unified not by the notion of the 'better argument' but by virtue of the dialogical action—the taking of positions, the making of assertions, agreement and disagreement—which is its precondition in every sphere. Every truth argued for therefore functions, or ought to function, both as an element of a specific field of culture—science, art, politics, or whatever—and as the index of a higher ethico-religious truth, which is the 'truth' of our intersubjective condition. When, as in the discourse of 'theoreticized' modern science, law, and philosophy, the moment of 'openings, revelations, recognitions, and communications' is absent, one finds as a consequence 'an element of coldness and estrangement in truth. Elements of good and love, endearment and joy, are only smuggled into it as contraband' (Rhet., 67). The dialogical community instanced in every grasping towards truth should link the act of taking a position or making a claim to the validity of the claim itself, thus ensuring a relationship of responsibility between subjects and their 'objective' culture. But whereas in Habermas the dialogical community stretches into the future because the argument never ends, in Bakhtin the existence of this community points permanently at the possibility of a redeemed life—it is a value in itself in a way that Habermas's discursive community is not.

As dialogue, therefore, language could link the truth contents of culture to the very act of discourse. But at the time of 'Towards a Philosophy of the Act' and 'Author and Hero' Bakhtin lacked the concept of dialogue, and he therefore described this link as an attribute of language itself: 'One must further say that language, which to a significant degree is found in advance by the verbal artist, is profoundly aestheticized, mythological, and anthropomorphic, and it gravitates toward the value centre of the person: hence, aestheticism deeply penetrates all of our thinking . . .' (AH: FC 156/229–30). The link is experienced by us as an aesthetic thickening of language, an intonational overlay which gives form to the fact that language not only communicates but is also an act, the utterance of a speaker. Even 'the temporal process of the flow of human thought', Bakhtin tells us in the opening fragment of 'Author and Hero', 'is not contingent-psychological but aestheticized, rhythmic' (AH: FC 140/210). If the aesthetic work 'must reflect in itself the image of the finished *event* of its creation' (AH: FC 140/210), it follows that language itself will be full of such aesthetic traces, which the philosopher or critic can follow back to their source in 'event-like' ethical reality. There is only one problem. According to the principles of 'Author and Hero', aesthetic concreteness always relies on an author, who alone is able to endow discourse with the bodiliness which distinguishes art. If language in its entirety (and not just a particular expression of it) appears aesthetic, then there must be a corresponding author whose 'outsidedness' is sufficiently broad for this all-encompassing concreteness. Only God can play that role in this early work: the divine alone is in a position to see in language *tout court* a worldly plenitude.

It is not God, however, but Bakhtin who uncovers the intonational concreteness of language for us, and he relies not on a bird's-eye view of it, but on neo-Kantian 'value philosophy' and some deft phenomenology. The last reveals to him a residue in the language of *others* which, when comprehended, indicates something irreducible to the abstract semantics of the concept: 'Any kind of expression is too concrete for pure meaning, it distorts and muddies its validity and purity of meaning' (TPA 105/31). This residue, the 'emotional-volitional tone' or 'intonation' of language, Bakhtin interprets as an almost sensuous mark of the utterer's unique obligation for his or her statement: 'the word not only denotes the object as something present, but, by means of its intonation . . . it also expresses my value relation to the object' (TPA 106/32). It is this insistence that an existential commitment is inscribed in individual speech itself that lends a somewhat decisionistic character to this early philosophy, explicit in Bakhtin's comment that 'it is not the content of an obligation which obligates me, but my signature under it, the fact that I have acknowledged it at one point, that I have signed a given acknowledgement' (TPA 110–11/38; today's critic, having read his or her Derrida, knows all about the conventional character of the signature and the agreements which underlie its force).[14] Bakhtin may bond this insight into language to the doctrine of *I* and *other* elsewhere in the essay, but he still theorizes the linguistic utterance as the act of a subject, with a weight and density reflecting its specific position in an ethical world.

So although Bakhtin consistently argued that closer attention to language would reveal the ethical and event-like nature of the world, he at first attributed this to the *aesthetic* nature of language, and only later to the *dialogical* nature of language. But the first perspective was not merely a mistaken or imprecise version of the second; it lived on in Bakhtin's later writing as an independent and productive position. As a consequence, Bakhtin ended up maintaining that one could recover the 'concreteness' of language from two different directions. From the point of view of a *participant*, meanings are concrete in so far as they are the sediment of an intersubjective encounter; their validity is inseparable from the ethical act of confronting an *other* in discourse. From the point of view of an *observer/author*, meanings are concrete when endowed with an aesthetic thickness

---

[14] See Derrida's famous polemic with speech act theory, in which he persuasively contests the idea of the speech act as a moment of will, in which a self-possessed subject commits itself to action: 'Signature Event Context', in *Margins of Philosophy*, trans. Alan Bass (Chicago, Ill.: University of Chicago Press, 1982), 307–30.

and worldly bodiliness which reflect their origins in a particular social situation. In the first case, the world as a whole is rendered ethical in so far as its maintenance requires continued participation in the intersubjective network; in the second, in so far as language is suffused with the historically framed intentions of responsible subjects. To these differing accounts of language correspond the two different aspects of dialogism we examined in Chapter 2, which a modern novelistic writing ought to synthesize. The dialogical relation of person to person or hero to hero reflects the perspective of a participant, in which the symmetry of dialogue is an essential constituent of its meaning. The dialogical relation of author to hero, or author to 'socio-ideological language', reflects the perspective of the contextualizing observer, who makes language a worldly and historical object. At first glance, it appears that only the first of these has political significance. Grounding the validity of cultural meanings, whether moral or technical, in the dialogue of a community in which participants disclose themselves and are committed to a world without secret, lie, or hubris, is a gesture which places immediate demands on social relationships; it implies an ideal of intersubjectivity against which actual dialogues can be measured. But as we saw earlier, the authorial perspective sheds light on aspects of democratic life which a pure concept of dialogue would leave in darkness. In particular, it enforces the demand that we respond to the utterances and behaviour of *others* not by a knee-jerk application of Christian ethics, but by an aggressive interpretation of our social and historical situation. 'Pure dialogue' assumes we perceive the ethics of the situation at once, by virtue of our faith; the authorial view instructs us to build an image of the language, as part of our effort to devise a historically acute and appropriate norm of interaction. What the perspective of the author/observer lacks in symmetry, it makes up for in modernity, for in its characterization of the contexts of speech it creates the secular, historical, and differentiated world which gives actual intersubjectivity its shape.

When the time came to write about language as such, Voloshinov found himself anticipating this dual evocation of the concrete, albeit in a different register. This is sharply etched in the central concept of his philosophy of language, which is not the act or even the 'dialogue' but 'the utterance', or perhaps one should say 'the concrete utterance', because the adjective draws out what was supposed to be the critical difference separating utterances from those benighted creatures of formal linguistics and philosophy, sentences and propositions. As the 'real units' of language, utterances are determined by their social situation, but that situation itself bifurcates into two separable aspects, 'the given *situation* of the utterance and its *audience*' (MPL 115/96). On the one hand, the shape of the utterance depends on the social sphere in which it is located with its characteristic world-view, topos, style, and vocabulary. On the other hand, as 'a common territory between speaker and interlocutor' (*MPL* 102/86), discourse is made concrete by the fact of being part of a dialogue. It was in this text that the two-sidedness of the dialogical encounter became a decisive fact: '*Any utterance, no matter how significant and complete in itself, is only a moment in unbroken speech communication*' (*MPL* 112/95). Voloshinov thereby effectively secularizes the idea of concreteness. The emotional-volitional tone which tied language to life becomes what Voloshinov calls the 'accent' language acquires in a specific social and historical location; the ethical reality of language becomes the dialogical concreteness of utterances, 'itself, in its turn, only a moment in the unbroken, all-inclusive, *becoming* of a given social collective' (*MPL* 114/95), i.e. in its historical task, however differently conceived. It takes strong metaphysical convictions indeed to see in these transpositions a vulgarization of Bakhtin's ideas.

THE IDEAL OF A CONCRETE UTTERANCE

This fundamental duality in the meaning of the event or of the concrete is a legacy which Bakhtin will never disavow. The utterance and dialogism figure as the pivotal concepts in his further philosophy of language, but their definition is never made exact. The various disciplines—sociological stylistics, stylistics of genre, metalinguistics—with which Bakhtin proposes to replace linguistic formalism are distinguished by their analytical focus on concrete utterances, but the means by which one will distinguish the utterance remain unclear. While it may be expressed syntactically, it need not be; while it can occupy the same linguistic space as a statement or assertion, it cannot be confused with them. In 'The Problem of the Text', probably Bakhtin's most extended account of his philosophy of language, the utterance appears as at once unique and yet defined in relation to the most abstract of values: 'But at the same time every text (as an utterance) is something individual, unique and unrepeatable, and in this lies its entire meaning (its project, for which it was created). This is that in it which has a relation to truth, veracity, good, beauty, history' (PTxt, 308/105). 'Individual, unique and unrepeatable': these words have given rise to a great deal of confusion and misunderstanding. The immediate temptation is to take uniqueness to mean spatio-temporal uniqueness, as if the abstractly different 'moment' of every speech act was reflected in some infinitesimal difference of meaning. Not only, however, does such an interpretation make the reference to 'truth, veracity, good, beauty' and so forth inexplicable, it leaves us unable to comprehend how anyone could recognize the meaning of an utterance to begin with. That is, the crudely spatio-temporal or empirical specificity of the utterance does not entail a difference in meaning, for meaning is by definition an ideal moment, the identity of which depends on a certain reproducibility.

Bakhtin was prepared for this misunderstanding: he warned against it in his lecture on religion in 1924. Discussing the nature of religious consciousness, he distinguished its characteristic uniqueness from the spatio-temporal kind:

I am found in being, as in an event: I participate in a unique point of accomplishment; religious inscrutability is completely different from the physical kind; my ineffaceability, the indestructibility of my unique place in being; by means of an analogy with physical inscrutability, dogmatic metaphysics transforms it into something substantive, whereas it is only an *event-like* participation. And thus its consciousness is *conscience*: i.e. not moral but unique obligation: no one except myself in the entire world can accomplish that which I must accomplish. (Lec., 235)

One experiences the address of religious discourse as unique, because it is in the nature of such discourse to address its respondents as unique, irreplaceable, and therefore responsible persons (as in the case of the personality, uniqueness is not a property of the individual discovered by discourse, but an attribute of the individual created by the right kind of intersubjectivity). This distinguishes it from the discourse of law-like morality, for which the individual figures as an instance, an example or abstraction more or less identical with every other individual. Thus uniqueness is not a matter of distinct location or distinctness of person, but of whether one feels uniquely obligated to a norm rather than compelled 'on principle', as anyone else might be. By extension, 'utterances' are unique only in relation to values because it is in that context that they 'become a real assertion or negation', representing an irreducible moment of commitment or position-taking with intersubjective consequences: 'Every utterance moves life forward, not only communicates something new, but also introduces something new into the interrelations between people (of a more or less broad circle); every utterance is in this respect *historical*' (PrepMat., 253). Habermas has made the same point in a usefully different way: 'Every agreement, whether produced for the first time or reaffirmed, is based on (controvertible) grounds or reasons. Grounds have a special property: they force us into yes or no positions.'[15] The 'yes or no position', which we *cannot avoid*, is what makes the utterance unique and individually compelling for the speaker. Confusing it with the fact that one never steps into the same river twice reduces ethical uniqueness to its theoretical counterpart.[16]

---

[15] Habermas, 'Philosophy as Stand-In and Interpreter', 19.
[16] It may have been the case that the coincidence of spatio-temporal and moral uniqueness was, if not actual, the ideal aim. N. O. Lossky, one of the Petrograd philosophers by whom

This explains one of the recurring aporia of the Bakhtin circle. Having dismissed the concepts of linguistics and 'theoreticist' philosophy as hopelessly abstract, Bakhtin, Voloshinov, and Medvedev found themselves lumbered with the unhappy task of devising a means for apprehending the unique and unrepeatable. The 'concrete' objects put forward as alternatives—the utterance, intonation, genre—all fall at the same fence. For each attempts to objectify a dimension of meaning which is by its nature unformalizable, in so far as its units must be identified with both theoretical and ethical criteria. The metaphor of 'intonation' exemplifies the difficulty. It implies a concrete sensuousness, indicating a level of feeling and intentionality beyond words, yet it must also be a form which can be recognized if it is to have any meaning or force. Caught between the requirements of form and sensuous immediacy, intonation appears in the end to mark a problem rather than a solution. It signifies a domain of evaluation which Bakhtin admits may be 'only partially realized in the course of a reading (of a performance)' (TMHum., 389/166). Voloshinov himself makes the difficulty explicit terminologically when he divides the linguistic universe into 'inner speech', a kind of pure and formless evaluative force, and the 'outer speech' in which meaning acquires semiotic weight. The passage from one to the other is as mysterious as could be, a process of calcification or meltdown beyond conceptual or scientific explanation.

In order to make progress with this problem, we must disentangle the threads which have become twisted upon one another. In particular, we need to separate the distinction between abstract and concrete perspectives from the distinction between the theoretical or, as I want to call it here, representational point of view, and the ethical point of view. The call, repeated many times throughout Bakhtin's career, for a philosophy of language which would apprehend the concrete, conflates these two in the manner I have described. The move to the concrete on the one hand means a shift to a new kind of *representation* of language, a representation which, by sketching in details of occasion, social context, speaker, and addressee, reveals the unique connection of that language with a certain social sphere and certain forms of social action. But the move to the concrete also means a shift to the ethical point of view, that is, to the perspective of a participant in dialogue, where understanding what is said is indissociable from entering into the sphere 'of openings, of revelations, of recognitions, of communications', and from the ethical commitments which might follow from it. The utterance made concrete because

Bakhtin claimed to be taught, defined salvation as the establishment of a concrete totality in which no action could be repeated; by contrast the essence of egoistic action was its repeatability. See Lossky's *Tsennost' i bytie* [*Value and Being*] (Paris: YMCA Press, 1931), 65–6.

directed to an addressee immediately places itself beyond the theoretical world of states of affairs, because it is made in anticipation of a response, manifested either verbally or by an action of some kind. In this latter case philosophy of language is concrete to the extent that it addresses texts or language as a partner in dialogue. It embodies the intersubjective point of view, and defines the concrete utterance as the trigger for some kind of reciprocal activity. In short, to be concrete in Bakhtin's sense, philosophy of language has not only to represent contexts, but to respond to them.

Bakhtin's philosophy of language thereby straddles the same ambiguity that had defined the novel. In 'Discourse in the Novel' the genre was dialogical in two distinct senses: as a genre which presented a 'system of languages' refracted by the image-making power of the author, and as a set of texts each of which polemically opposed other texts as a whole. In entirely typical fashion, Bakhtin projects this theoretical ambiguity onto the history of the novel itself, which he accordingly divides into two stylistic lines of development. In the First Stylistic Line, the novel is itself 'single-languaged' but 'involves a sideways glance at the languages of others' (DN 187/376)—it is a participant in heteroglossia; the Second Stylistic Line 'introduces social heteroglossia into the composition of the novel, orchestrating its meaning through it' (DN 186/375)—it represents heteroglossia within itself. Both are, of course, novels, and the novelness of each depends upon an intimate relation with heteroglossia. But it is heteroglossia seen from two different angles.

SAUSSURE AND THE SOLUTION

Combining these two perspectives was possible, but only when it became clear that representing a language in all its density and situatedness was a part of the process of engaging in dialogue with it as a participant, or, to put it more bluntly, when the ethical relations possible in language could be liberated from the straitjacket of Christian ethics. Ironically, it was probably Saussure who provided the spur for this next move. It was the revolutionary merit of the linguist from Geneva that he wrested language from the self-enclosed history to which the comparative philologists had condemned it, and established contemporary intersubjectivity as its necessary medium. Saussure rightly discerned in the historical orientation of earlier linguists a tendency to separate language off from social life; in interpreting language as a sphere of autonomous historical development, lawlike or otherwise, Young Grammarians and their kin reified that which was only the sediment of intersubjective communication. Saussure's knockdown response to these accounts of language was that all such laws, historical tendencies, and comparative links have no relevance for the meaning linguistic signs have in ordinary communication, and that for linguistics the perspective of the contemporary native speaker must be absolutely decisive. His entire programme for a new science of language revolves around the need to reconstruct the structures of meaning created by the ceaseless activity of speakers and listeners. But this priority is only persuasive to those who have already agreed that the primary 'justification' of language itself is as a conduit for ordinary communication, rather than, say, as a means for the transmission of a valued cultural tradition, or to make possible the perception and articulation of a world. Saussure can make the agreement maintained by intersubjective communication the only and final court of what does and what does not belong to language, in so far as he is willing to make communication in itself the sole *telos* of language.

Other Russian intellectuals were more alive to the democratic possibilities of this theory than Bakhtin and Voloshinov. They saw Saussure as the figure who had disenchanted language and relieved it of burdensome links to logic, religion, or visions of a lost national past. A linguistic structure made valid only by the consent of its users, in need of no other legitimation, appeared as a more pliant means of social reconstruction, and a readier instrument for a people ready to remake their culture, than earlier models of language. Thus the linguist Grigory Vinokur, a contemporary of Bakhtin and Voloshinov (whose seminar at the Gorky Institute Bakhtin may have attended in 1940) saw in Saussurean theory the justification for a consciously conducted 'linguistic politics', an organized intervention into the means of communication.[17] Vinokur knew that Saussure had himself claimed that conscious intervention could not change the structure of language, but he nonetheless argued that knowledge of the laws of any social institution rendered it reconstructible for chosen social ends. Language being 'not an organism, but an organization', one could identify those constitutive elements 'on the basis of which it would be possible to rationalize this organization'.[18] The desired result—'the transformation of language from a means of instinctive usage to material of cultural construction, clarified in every aspect'[19]—was plausible precisely to the extent that Saussure and a certain kind of Soviet collectivism shared common ground. Common ground which Bakhtin and Voloshinov did not wish to share, however much they may have been devoted to some

[17] See Grigory Vinokur, 'Kul'tura iazyka (Zadachi sovremennogo iazykoznaniia)', *Pechat' i revoliutsiia*, 5 (1923), 100–11. The invitation to Vinokur's seminar on 'Language as the Object of a Science of Literature' is mentioned in *Con.*, 315 n. 27.
[18] Vinokur, 'Kul'tura iazyka', 106.
[19] Ibid.

kind of progressive cultural revival. It is therefore worth our while to briefly examine its contours.

That Soviet left avant-gardism (of which Vinokur was a theorist at the time he wrote the above) would identify socialist reconstruction with the prioritizing of the 'collective' should surprise no one.[20] But this collectivism had a distinctive character, for it inherited not only egalitarian tasks but also the business of disenchantment, left typically unfinished by Russia's weak bourgeoisie. In the West, the dispersal of mystery and tradition by reason had been assigned to the bourgeois individual of liberalism, sober and scientific, and confident that his rationality entitled him to sovereignty over his affairs. Russia had few such liberals, and no such liberalism, and as a consequence, collectivism found itself confronted with the whole panoply of feudal tradition. If the individual was not willing to bear the principle of rationality, then the collective would have to, and at this stage of European history the obvious form of the rational collective was the machine. So it was not the clear-headed calculating individual, but the team working in machine-like concert which embodied the principle of reason for Soviet avant-gardists. Conversely, the individual was condemned not as a selfish calculator, but as a mystic and a metaphysician, an ostentatiously backward creature for whom every sentiment pointed towards the heavens. And as we are talking about aesthetic ideologies in this case—Constructivism, Productivism, to a lesser extent, Futurism—the collective rationality of the machine would be a source not only of progress, but also of aesthetic pleasure.

The frequently parodied image of Stakhanovite workers, for whom collectivism meant a lack of sentiment bordering on the pathological, was thus grounded in more than the propaganda needs of the Soviet state. The Russian worker in factory or collective farm would work happily not only to the extent that material conditions improved, but because this new form of labour was rational and disenchanted. Collectivism therefore embodied

---

[20] A classic example is the introductory editorial, 'Our Verbal Work', of the journal of the Left Front in Arts, *LEF*. Polemicizing against the received distance of poetry and prose from 'practical speech, the jargon of the street, from the precise language of science', it characterizes the task of art in self-consciously industrial terms, in order to ensure that the artist thinks of him- or herself as a worker in a collective. Thus:

We do not want to recognize a distinction between poetry, prose, and practical language

We recognize a single material of discourse and we submit it to a contemporary reworking.

We work on the organization of the sounds of language, on the polyphony of rhythm, on the simplification of verbal structures, on the making precise of linguistic expressiveness, on the selection of new thematic devices.

All this is **work for us—not an aesthetic end in itself, but a laboratory for the best expression of the facts of contemporaneity**.

We are not priest-creators but master executors of the social task. (*LEF*, 1 (Mar. 1923), 40–1)

not just the dominance of the state, but a standard of the good life, in which the effective meshing of individuals became a virtue in itself, indissociable from aspirations to equality and freedom from unjustified authority. There was no reason why language should not be judged by the same standards. Its transformation from 'organism' to 'organization' would replace unreasoned and unjustified evolution with conscious coordination, and a theorist who claimed language was no more than what people made of it could only be an ally in this struggle. Vinokur (but not only Vinokur) saw the possibilities and drew the logical conclusions.

Saussure did not imagine language as a machine, but Vinokur was not unjustified in thinking that his theory embodied an adaptable collectivism. In common with other practitioners of neo-Kantian social science, Saussure endowed collective 'facts' with a new aura, by freeing them from the need to be justified by science or philosophy. Gillian Rose has lucidly described how neo-Kantians separated the question of the validity of categories from the question of their objectivity.[21] According to a sociology like Durkheim's, the objectivity of categories stems from the constraining power of collective representations, which act as a transcendental force in relation to the individual consciousness. The 'sociological *a priori*' is a brute and unreasoned source of objectivity, the categories of which neither require, nor are amenable to, philosophical justification. Saussure takes this into his theory of language: the object of linguistics is a language system, *langue*, the objectivity and constraining force of which is grounded by nothing other than collective agreement. The 'signs' which have linguistic *value* have nothing in the way of philosophical or scientific *validity*, nor do they need it to play their role in the facilitation of communication. As Saussure described it, the arbitrary nature of links between signifier and signified, sound-image and meaning, means that one can never even raise the question of the validity of this or that element of the language system for 'no reason can be given for preferring *sœur* to *sister*, *Ochs* to *bœuf*, etc.'.[22] The result, as Göran Therborn has argued of Durkheim's sociology, is the valorization of common ends or solidarity in themselves, i.e. without particular regard for their content.[23] The sociologist not only discovers, but promotes the sharing of representations in a 'collective consciousness', believing that the problems posed by modern, atomistic society should be solved by as much 'community' as possible. Saussure (who was certainly familiar with sociological debate, and Durkheim in particular) merely transposes this powerful motif into language: the value of language is the speech community erected and maintained through it; the arbitrariness of

[21] See Gillian Rose, *Hegel Contra Sociology* (London: Athlone Press, 1981), 2–13.
[22] Saussure, *Course*, 73.
[23] See Göran Therborn, *Science, Class and Society* (London: Verso, 1976), 240–70.

signs is but the flip side of the formalism of this valorization of the community.[24]

Vinokur was therefore half-right: as language did not have to be justified
by specialist discourses of science or philosophy, people could choose to
speak whatever language they wished, so long as they chose the same one.
But he was half-wrong, too. For Saussure had made 'passive citizens' of the
ordinary speakers he empowered, and had reduced the ethical possibilities
of discourse to the maintenance of the linguistic system—and thus the
speech community—itself. The ethics of speech in Saussurean theory
comes down to the need to *match* the speech of the other, either in the
system of language one carries around in the mind or when one speaks in
return. Innovation is, he claims, strictly a matter of *parole* or the vagaries of
performance; the language structure revolves around the need for identity
and commonality. Intersubjectivity therefore depends almost entirely on
the ability of language users to mimic and imitate with precision, for the
inflections of users lead not to subtle differences of relationship, but to
confusion and atomization.

By flattening discourse into a system of grammatical and lexical conventions, Saussure thought he could establish social usage as the arbiter
of linguistic propriety, while preserving the one-dimensional unity of
language itself. Even within his own system, however, there proved to be
a weak link—syntax, for which Saussure was unable to come up with a
separate account. Voloshinov shrewdly fastened onto this:

All the fundamental categories of contemporary linguistic thought, which were
worked out primarily on the basis of Indo-European comparative linguistics, are
thoroughly *phonetic* and *morphological* . . . Through these spectacles, it attempts to
view the problem of syntax, and this has led to its morphologization. (*MPL*
131/109)

As Françoise Gadet has pointed out, Saussure can never decide whether
syntax is systematizable, that is, whether it belongs to *langue* or *parole*.[25]
Bakhtin believed that this was precisely because the contortions of syntax
are markers of the intersubjective situation itself, which can never be
reduced to a shared 'collective consciousness': 'the internal politics of a
style (the combination of elements) is determined by its external politics

---

[24] See the addendum to Robert Godel, *Les Sources manuscrites du cours de linguistique générale de
F. de Saussure* (Geneva: Droz, 1969), 282, where he cites W. Doroszewski's claim (in 'Durkheim
et F. de Saussure', *Journal de Psychologie* (1933), 82–91) that Saussure 'followed the philosophical
debate between Durkheim and Tarde with profound interest', and mentions that the claim itself
derives ultimately from Saussure's student Sechehaye.

[25] Gadet, *Saussure and Contemporary Culture*, 71–2. Gadet cites the third version of Saussure's
course, where he is recorded as saying: 'In sum, it is only in *syntax* that there appears a waver-
ing between what is fixed by *langue* and what is left to individual freedom' (Godel, *Les Sources
manuscrites*, 169; translation by Gregory Elliott in Gadet).

(its relation to the discourse of an other)' (DN 97/284). In the end, Saussure's theory can find no principled reason for distinguishing between the kind of meaning instanced by a sentence and by a sign.[26] As a consequence, the pragmatic elements of linguistic meaning tend to be buried underneath the stark representationalism embodied by the sign. To the extent that meaning appears to be a matter of 'theoretical' representation, the ethical force of language recedes from view.

So while Saussure makes progress by recasting language as a 'social institution', he reduces the practical tasks of speaking subjects to the precise reproduction of a given system. If community is the all-important social end of language, then the most important task for the speaker is to speak correctly, i.e. as everyone else does. Voloshinov concurs with Saussure's social starting-point, but recognizes that the relations language can work through are both more variegated and more substantive: 'Normally, the criterion of linguistic correctness is absorbed by a purely ideological criterion: the correctness of an utterance is absorbed by its truthfulness or falsity, its poeticalness or banality, and so on' (MPL 84/70). Once taken seriously, Saussure's claims to ground his theory on the perspective of ordinary communication turn out to be quite weak. In *Marxism and the Philosophy of Language* Voloshinov shows that Saussure transforms the linguist's desire for a systematic object into a speaker's desire for a systematic language. As was pointed out in the Introduction, the *Course* offers two different justifications for the centrality of the language system (*langue*) to linguistics: first, that it is the only object orderly enough to serve as the focus for a linguistic science, and second, that it describes the appearance of language to the individual consciousness. These, however, are incommensurable perspectives:

The subjective consciousness of the speaker does not in the least work with language as a system of normatively identical forms. Such a system exists only as an abstraction arrived at with great effort and from a definite cognitive and practical orientation. The system of language is a product of reflection on language, created neither in the least bit by the consciousness of the speaker himself from a given language nor in the least bit with the goals of immediate speaking. (MPL 81/67)

What renders an element of language valid for the linguist is not what renders it valid for consciousness, for which systematicity and regularity in language have only a secondary, technical importance. The defining purpose of linguistic activity is not to create systems for the contemplation of linguists, but, as Bakhtin had put it, 'to push life forward', by creating

---

[26] '*Sign* and *sentence* are not mutually exclusive and there is no boundary between them' (Gadet, *Saussure and Contemporary Culture*, 73).

truth, regulating and coordinating action, and making beautiful works of verbal art, always in concert with others. The violation or reconstruction of linguistic norms in the service of these causes is as ineluctable a moment of language as its regularity.

In the end, Saussure empowers ordinary society, but at the price of casting it in the role of a new kind of 'popular' traditional authority: 'It is because the linguistic sign is arbitrary that it knows no other law than that of tradition, and because it is founded on tradition that it can be arbitrary.'[27] The everyday communicative practice which undergirds language turns out to be democratic and unjustified *habit*, both perfectly egalitarian and perfectly irrational. The modern speech community rests on a consent renewed in practice but never submitted to reflective argument, a disenchanted form of authority in which dull compulsion has replaced the prestige of the monarch, the divine, and the past. Killing the linguistic king is in the end only the beginning of the battle.

Nevertheless, Bakhtin and Voloshinov do not escape unscathed from their encounter with Saussure. The confrontation with this new 'social' linguistics obliges them to acknowledge the weight and relative autonomy of language itself, and the extent to which it contains forms of interaction which philosophy cannot predict on its own. Before this encounter language was granted a certain density, but its possibilities were restricted by Bakhtin's neo-Kantian division of forms of consciousness into science, ethics, art, and religion. Each of these might have been allowed some historical freedom of development, but only within the ideal form of intersubjectivity which set their boundaries. As language gradually occupies the high ground in the Bakhtin circle's theory, these ideal forms of intersubjective truth slowly but surely yield to the sober facts of social life offered up by semiotics. Voloshinov, while taking his distance from the greater part of Saussurean theory, nevertheless accepts that language in its social existence has a power to create values and intersubjective forms for which no philosophical licence is required. In his discussion of the relation between the individual consciousness and the categories of culture—his rewriting, if you like, of 'Towards a Philosophy of the Act'—in the pivotal chapter 3 of *Marxism and the Philosophy of Language*, he finds himself inventing a sphere of linguistic practice unbound from culture in the strict sense: the nether regions of 'worldly ideology' (*zhiteiskaia ideologiia*). Unlike the 'established ideological systems of social mores, science, art and religion' (*MPL* 108/91) these local patterns of interaction have no philosophical justification but are 'forms of living communication, to some degree stabilized and secured by everyday life and circumstances' (*MPL* 115/96–7). 'Village gatherings, urban festivities, workers' chitchat' (*MPL*

---

[27] Saussure, *Course*, 74.

116/97): the very modesty of the examples illustrates the degree to which kinds of discourse unsanctioned by philosophy have made a place for themselves. But it is also here, rather than in the self-sustaining culture of ethics and science, that ethical energies are expressed most powerfully, so much so that they become the energy source for the grand projects embodied in the great cultural spheres. Their vitality encompasses concreteness in both of its senses: they have the sociological thickness which science appears to lack and incarnate a practical dialogical world which will more directly make its mark on their linguistic terms:

> The established ideological systems of social mores, science, art and religion crystallize out of worldly ideology, and in their turn exert a powerful return influence upon it and, normally, set the tone of this worldly ideology. But at the same time, these established ideological products constantly preserve the most living organic contact with worldly ideology, they drink its juices and outside of it they are dead, just as, for example, a finished literary work or cognitive idea is dead without a living, evaluative perception of it. (*MPL* 108–9/91)

The need for constant commerce between scientific cultures and the everyday interactions of worldly ideology cannot hide the fact that Voloshinov has set the latter loose from philosophy. In effect, the first step from the neo-Kantian quadrivium to the wild world of the public sphere, where one meets the language 'of the student, the language of a generation, the language of the minor intellectual, the language of the Nietzschean' (DN 104/291) has been taken. Differentiation by philosophical means is giving way to differentiation by 'genres'.[28]

THE LAST GASP OF THE 'PURE VOICE'

Problems of Dostoevsky's Art, so neatly bisected into parts dealing with 'authors and heroes' and 'discourse' respectively, is proof that philosophy would not give way without a struggle. Nikolaev is right to point out that two different projects (or two different stages of the same project) coexist uneasily within its pages, one literary-philosophical, the other stained by the emergence of a sociological-linguistic approach. For while the discussions of single- and multi-directed discourse examine Dostoevsky

---

[28] Bakhtin's 'sociologization' of neo-Kantianism is in this respect quite different from that of Habermas. The latter takes his cue from Weber's analysis of the division of modern social life into spheres of moral-practical, economic, and aesthetic activity, each with its own rationality and its own 'expert culture'. In effect, Habermas does not replace the great Kantian values with sociological ones, but agrees to sociologize the Kantian critiques themselves: the value of theoretical truth is contextualized by the purposive-rational system of technology, the value of right by the system of communication, the value of beauty by the institutions of art. See *Knowledge and Human Interests*, 209–12.

stylistically, and find styles too varied for the Procrustean bed of neo-Kantianism, the chapters on author and hero cling to the idea of a pure ethical intersubjectivity. Dostoevsky's heroes do not concern themselves with the social world as such, but pass directly to a world-transcending space of 'ultimate questions', with the consequence that 'personal life becomes distinctively disinterested and principled, while higher ideological thought becomes intimately personal and passionate' (*PDA* 74/79). In the revised second edition Bakhtin emphasized the *homogeneity* of Dostoevsky's language, and castigated those who confused dialogism with the social characterization of speech. (A position which, of course, represented no more than a hasty covering of tracks: Bakhtin's work from 'Discourse in the Novel' onwards depended on the belief that the saturation of language by social forces was expressed precisely in 'linguistic changes in the markers of language (in the linguistic symbols)' (*DN* 106/293)). With Dostoevsky, Bakhtin grabbed at a last chance to concretize speech in, as it were, one dimension only. As pure decontextualized intersubjectivity, Dostoevsky's dialogism produced a language which is dialogical in the participatory sense only, apparently completely void of historical reference. Presented as the artist of the 'threshold', who 'is not able to work with great masses of (biographical and historical) time' (Rhet., 64), Dostoevsky is used by Bakhtin to make the case for a kind of absolute synchronicity, in which discourse figures as the distillate of confrontations between *I* and *other*. Voloshinov, as well as Medvedev in *The Formal Method*, had translated concreteness as observation into the language of social description; in his study of Dostoevsky Bakhtin attempted a final separation of the dialogical principle from the contingent objectivity of discourse, lingering for a final moment on what a pure dialogue might have to offer. And although this gave way to other conceptions of language in the 1930s, it lived on in the claim that only the 'radical violation' of everyday life was a truly historical, redemptive event. Bakhtin would never fully wake from the dream of a purely ethical dialogue, uncoloured by social and historical concreteness: responding later in life to a question about twentieth-century polyphonic novels, he names not Joyce or T. S. Eliot, the artists of linguistic variation, but Camus and Kafka.[29]

In seeking to separate Dostoevsky from the historical modernity to which he gives such striking expression, Bakhtin tried to have his cake and eat it too. The dialogism of the Dostoevskian novel invests personality with an orientation to the future it has earned only recently: 'Personality loses its gross external substantiality, its thing-like simplicity, from being it becomes event' (*PDA* 242). For the personality to come into its own, older

[29] M. M. Bakhtin, 'O polifonichnosti romanov Dostoevskogo' ['On the Polyphonicity of Dostoevsky's Novels'], in *Rossiia/Russia*, vol. ii (Torino: Einaudi, 1975), 193.

roles and identities had first to be stripped away; its transformation from being to event was a historical event in its own right. And one condition of this was the embodiment of the personality in language. Actual persons have life-spans with beginnings and ends, bodies and needs: in short, too much being for Dostoevsky's purposes. The reduction of every personality to language in the modern sense—'the hero in Dostoevsky is not an image but a fully-valued discourse, a *pure voice*' (*PDA* 63/53)—itself made possible the absolute indeterminacy which Bakhtin extracted from Dostoevsky's form. The hypothetical openness of every discourse, which extends beyond the biological life of the person ('the person has passed from life, having spoken his word, but the word itself remains in unconsummated dialogue' (N61, 360/300)) is what endowed the personality with a determining future orientation, and this openness was itself a historical achievement (and by no means a secure one, even today). But when dialogism is separated from its historical origins, the result is a strangely weightless and bodiless language, a language of pure justification, without objects to justify. Bakhtin portrayed Dostoevsky as the dialogizer of the older genre of monological confession, precisely because he hoped that Dostoevsky could produce in dialogical form that purity of spirit which had earlier been the aim of the endless self-negation of confessional discourse.

THE DELAYED SYNTHESIS

Saussure's account of language renders it 'mere being', historical sediment without justification; Dostoevsky renders it pure event, the forward force of argument and justification without material. An adequate account of language would have to balance these as two different strands of intersubjectivity. In dialogism the subject addresses a personality in an open process of discourse, but it always addresses a personality which it conceives of historically, in the context of a social life with its own institutions, objects, norms, and types of action. And the historical character of the personality, on which its freedom and responsibility depend, is defined both by a redemptive attitude towards the future and by the future orientation intrinsic to modern contexts. Or to put it differently, and perhaps more pointedly: the subject of dialogism finds itself in dialogue not with other persons but with other languages, and these languages are not the pure voices of which Bakhtin dreams in 1929, but the thicker and more resistant objects which Saussure outlines. Bakhtin nowhere explicitly combines these complementary arguments about language. Nowhere, that is, except in his description and analysis of the style of the novel. For this last embodies precisely a dialogue with languages of diverse origin, whose historical weight and limits have to be accepted as a matter of fact.

Both elements of intersubjectivity might be catered for in this account. The style of the novel renders language concrete by bonding it to a socio-ideological position and thereby making it an *other* with a 'distanced kernel'; but it also renders language concrete in the sense of providing it with a context of social and historical dimensions. In fact, in 'Discourse in the Novel' these two tasks are treated as one task: the representation of language as *other*, as an 'image', is at the same time the provision of a context. From the mass of actual language in any text, socio-ideological languages will emerge as they are hewn out and placed in relation to a context. For the true characters of the novel are its constituent styles and languages, and they are forced to cohere not by literally being attached to a character, but by unifying around some quasi-characterological function or meaning in the text.

Which is to say that discrete stylistic features do not signify on their own, but only receive meaning within an essentially narrative context:

The role of the context framing represented speech in the creation of an image of a language is of critical significance. The framing context, like the chisel of a sculptor, hews out the borders of alien speech, and carves the image of a language from the raw empirical being of speech life: it fuses and combines the internal tendency of the represented language itself with its external objective determinations. The authorial discourse representing and framing alien speech creates a perspective for it, it distributes light and shadow, it creates the situation and all the conditions for it to sound, finally, it penetrates it from within, it carries into it its own accents and its own expressions, it creates a dialogizing background for it. (DN 169–70/357–8)

If one takes this to be a description of modern, European language as a whole rather than of novelistic technique alone, then the crux of Bakhtin's critique of Saussure becomes clear. It is that in a democratized, modernized world, meaning emerges not from grammar in isolation, but from the narrative situation of an act of speech. For Saussure the 'framing context' grounding any particular meaning is the linguistic structure corresponding to the homogeneous speech community; for Bakhtin it is a narrative orientated to the future. To wit, the linguistic system, *langue*, which makes meaning possible, has the structure of a novel rather than that of a dictionary.

Gadet has pointed out the essentially passive nature of the linguistic system, figured by Saussure not only as a 'dictionary' but as a storehouse, or sum of impressions.[30] One could take the novelistic critique of Saussure

---

[30] Gadet, *Saussure and Contemporary Culture*, 69–70.

in a similar spirit. As Voloshinov commented earlier, the limits of formal linguistics appear to be the phoneme and the morpheme, and indeed, Saussure limits the structures of language to the structures of grammar. He thereby leaves out precisely narrative, which provides the conditions necessary for the local elements of grammar to acquire meaning of any kind. But then meaning itself must be something very different from what the impoverished concept of the signified implies. Different, because every grammatical or lexical element 'tastes of the context and contexts in which it has lived its socially charged life' (DN 106/293) and therefore preserves a historical reference or feel wholly alien to Saussure's conception.

Bakhtin did not make this argument about language *per se*, however, or at least, did not make it directly. He chose to discuss a literary form, the novel, although he made clear that this self-confessed 'system of languages' was in fact a model for the modern European vernaculars themselves. It is to this theory that we should now turn.

CHAPTER FIVE

The Novel

Although the novel is the dialogical genre, it is not, in Bakhtin's account, only a dialogical genre. It is also a narrative genre, the genre of chronotopes. Its antecedents, cited in detail in Bakhtin's various attempts at its prehistory, include not only the sceptical energy of parodic and satiric speech, but, just as importantly, the practice of ancient biography and autobiography, eulogy and apology, confession and self-accounting.[1] In short, the novel is responsible for telling the story of particular lives as much as for making possible dialogism with embodied voices.

Yet though the novel has two weapons, dialogism and chronotope, at its disposal, it seems constitutionally incapable of using them both at the same time. Whenever Bakhtin spoke of dialogism he was silent on narrative, and whenever he spoke of narrative, he forgot to mention dialogue, as if the flourishing of one principle entailed the reticence of the other. *Problems of Dostoevsky's Art*, while praising the discovery of dialogism, does not so much discuss problems of narrative as pause on them (for a mere eleven pages), and does so only to point out that Dostoevsky had found a way to free his characters from the straitjacket of ordinary plot. In the great texts on the novel of the 1930s, Bakhtin alternates with precision between works on the dialogical style of the genre, and studies of its narrative project. 'Discourse in the Novel' features no more than an excursus on narrative issues (at five pages, even shorter than the earlier one), while the extant texts from the *Bildungsroman* project (including all the material on the chronotope) hardly mention style and dialogism at all. When Bakhtin lectured at the Gorky Institute in 1940–41, there was perfect, but exclusive, balance: one lecture (later published as 'From the Prehistory of Novelistic Discourse') on style, another (later published as 'Epic and Novel') on narrative.[2]

---

[1] Craig Howes has noted that the essays of the 1930s articulate what are in fact two very different literary histories: on the one hand, a constant and unending struggle waged by the parodic and satiric genres against monologism; on the other hand, the gradual development of the basic formal structures of the novel out of various precursors (medieval satire, classical rhetoric and autobiography, etc.). See his 'Rhetorics of Attack: Bakhtin and the Aesthetics of Satire', *Genre*, 19: 3 (1986), 231–43.

[2] These papers originally had different titles. 'From the Prehistory of Novelistic Discourse' was read at the Gorky Institute on 14 Oct. 1940 under the title 'Discourse in the Novel'; 'Epic and Novel' was read at the Institute on 24 Mar. 1941 under the title 'The Novel as a Literary Genre'.

Symptomatically, even when dialogism is Bakhtin's chosen theme, narrative appears as a hazard and a danger to be mastered by the pitiless application of the dialogical principle. When he broaches the question of 'The Monological Discourse of the Hero and Narrative Discourse in Dostoevsky's Tales' in *Problems of Dostoevsky's Art*, narration as a syntactic or structural feature of the text is in effect swept aside. Rather than talk about narrative, and its relation to the hero enclosed by it, Bakhtin talks in terms of an authorial discourse which 'is orientated toward the hero as toward a discourse, and is therefore *dialogically addressed to him*' (*PDA* 70/63), that is, he talks about narration as if it were no more than a voice which has been placed on an equal level with the hero itself. No longer embodied as a structure of events or a meaningful chronology, narration is made equivalent to its objects by being cast as the discourse of a speaker thereby on a par with 'his' characters.[3] Narrative makes an appearance, but only after it has been robbed of its ontological dignity.

DIALOGUE AND NARRATIVE

At the same time, narrative remains central not only to Bakhtin's conception of the novel's project, but to the conception of dialogism itself, whatever slights it may endure along the way. In a different context, Alasdair MacIntyre has pointed out that the very concept of a dialogue includes an inevitable reference to narrative:

If I listen to a conversation between two people my ability to grasp the thread of the conversation will involve an ability to bring it under some one out of a set of descriptions in which the degree and kind of coherence in the conversation is brought out: 'a drunken, rambling quarrel', 'a serious intellectual disagreement', 'a tragic misunderstanding of each other', 'a comic, even farcical misconstrual of each other's motives', 'a penetrating interchange of views', 'a struggle to dominate each other', 'a trivial exchange of gossip'.

The use of such words as 'tragic', 'comic' and 'farcical' is not marginal to such evaluations. We allocate conversations to genres, just as we do literary narratives. Indeed a conversation is a dramatic event, even if a very short one, in which the participants are not only the actors, but also the joint authors, working out in agreement or disagreement the mode of their production. For it is not just that conversations belong to genres in just the way that plays and novels do; but they have beginnings, middles and endings just as do literary works. They embody reversals and recognitions; they move towards and away from climaxes. There

---

[3] Interestingly enough, before the novel itself became the focus of Bakhtin's historicizing concerns, it was defined as the architectonic form which realized in an aesthetic object 'the artistic consummation of the historical or social event . . .' (PCMF 19/269).

may within a longer conversation be digressions and subplots, indeed digressions within digressions and subplots within subplots.[4]

The very concept of dialogue 'narrativizes' language, in so far as it forces the flow of discourse into the shape of an argument, a segmented event with characters, actions (the statements seen as utterances), and a meaningful temporal succession. But not only for a third person or observer: as MacIntyre notes, the participants in dialogue are simultaneously the actors *and* the authors of their drama; in order to contribute to a dialogue one must grasp its narrative flow from within.

This returns us to the distinction between the participant's perspective and the observer's perspective with which we were forced to conclude the previous chapter. It dissolves when we understand that responding to the expressions of another person depends upon placing that expression within a narrative context. Dialogues do not stand suspended; they move, and the nature of their motion is part of the meaning of their constituent utterances. In conversation one is simultaneously 'author' and 'hero', and one takes the authorial perspective not only on the *other's* utterances but on the conversation *as a whole*. The God's-eye or novelistic view of language is, in fact, one more piece of the participant's dialogical equipment, which does not so much consummate the conversation as allow it to go forward. And supposing our two conversationalists have different ideas about the narrative form of their mutual discourse (something we have surely all experienced)? When narrative enters into the participant's viewpoint does it descend to the status of a psychological fact or opinion? Not at all, for the point is that since one is creating the narrative and not just following its course, the participants must agree not only on the meanings of words and syntax, but the meaning their utterances assume as part of a narrative. The narrative of a dialogue is not merely an interpretation of it from outside, but the fruit of a mutual effort, and without agreement on its course, conversation ceases to be possible (and this may include not only what one says, but what one does in the course of the dialogue). For sure, there are times when something so unexpected happens that it cannot be fitted into the narrative; but at those points, it is not only the narrative which breaks down, for the dialogue falls with it (of course, this misunderstanding may then be incorporated into a larger narrative).

Narrative is the key to the authorial perspective, and it is inseparable from dialogue itself. In an exceptionally intelligent article, Cesare Segre has argued that Bakhtin should not have confused these, for the dialectic of author and hero ('polyphony') belongs not to the representation of language as heteroglot (to dialogism) but to the mechanism of narrative:

[4] Alasdair MacIntyre, *After Virtue*, 2nd edn. (London: Duckworth, 1985), 211.

'Bakhtin, in separating the history of polyphonic procedures from that of narrative invention, brings together in the category of polyphony phenomena with very different origins and functions.'[5] As a result, two different projects are conflated: (1) the separation of the authorial voice from those of the characters, in fact an element of narrative technique; (2) the representation of the linguistic stratification of society. In conclusion, Segre calls for the regrouping of these elements: 'on the one hand is the history of narrative structures we call the *roman*; on the other hand is the development of a perspectival perception of reality whose decisive establishment Bakhtin rightly locates in the Renaissance'.[6] Segre has pinpointed what is essential to Bakhtin's concept of an author–hero dialogism, but he is critical of the very thing we might see as interesting.

For Bakhtin, while agreeing with MacIntyre's basic argument, would not have been terribly interested in the tragic or comic qualities of the dialogues he described, for they fall short of dramatizing the 'perspectival perception of reality'. They remain, in Bakhtin's terms, 'dramas', whereas he wants 'novels', and what distinguishes novels are their heroes, which are not persons but socio-ideological languages. But the novelist who strives to represent these socio-ideological languages must nevertheless shape them as actors in a narrative, precisely because their identity *as* socio-ideological languages depends upon their imbrication in 'historical becoming and social struggle'. In all of Bakhtin's writings, authors are compelled to gather together scattered elements to form narrative wholes, that is, heroes and languages, which change and develop by their very nature. 'Plot itself', Bakhtin comments, 'is subordinated to this task—the coordination and mutual exposure of languages' (DN 177/365), but this subordination turns out to be only temporary, for plot reappears in the form of the languages themselves, the dialogism of which 'cannot be essentially dramatized or dramatically consummated (authentically finished)' (DN 139/326), so ineluctable is their forward historical movement. Narrative is not a scaffolding for languages, but their truth.

To represent heteroglossia, one must therefore have narrative, and to have narrative: one must represent heteroglossia. 'Individual multi-voicedness, misunderstandings and contradictions' (DN 139/325) can give rise only to half-hearted narratives, from which genuine history somehow escapes. If one aims for modest heroes, whose problems can be framed and resolved within the bounds of a stable, existing lifeworld (a 'single language'), one ends up with a modest narrative and, so far as Bakhtin is

---

[5] Cesare Segre, 'What Bakhtin Left Unsaid: The Case of the Medieval Romance', in Kevin Brownlee and Marina Scordiles Brownlee (eds.), *Romance: Generic Transformations from Chrétien de Troyes to Cervantes* (Hanover, NH: University Press of New England, 1985), 26.

[6] Ibid. 28.

concerned, a modest narrative is no more than the counterfeit of a true one. For the point is to narrate, as Bakhtin said of Flaubert, 'not changes within the limits of a given life (progress, decline) but the possibility of a life different in principle, with different scales and dimensions' (Flau., 132). Only when the grammar of the world is heteroglot can we be sure that history, 'a time maximally focused on the future' (FTC 357/207), will leave no stone unturned or unturnable.

NARRATIVE AND THE CONSTITUTION OF THE SELF

By narrating profound historical change, the novel appears to do no more than be faithful to a profoundly changing history. But the fact of history is an ethical fact for Bakhtin, rather than a theoretical one, and narratives have to embody 'becoming' not in order to represent an external history, but to make possible an inner one. In the only extant essay in which Bakhtin discussed narration (*rasskazyvanie*) as such, it is a means for distancing the reader from the apparent solidity of things: 'Essential to narrative is a moment of notification ⟨,⟩ the communication of something new, unknown, unexpected, strange, curious, and so forth. The violation of taboo, of the norm, of the prohibition, crime, error, and so on—such are the objects of narration' (QuThNov., 48). Error and crime force the norms they violate to reveal themselves as values which must be justified, and with this small gesture narration changes everything. It shows us—or ought to show us, to accomplish all Bakhtin expects of it—that every routine and norm, every institution and law, in short, the symbolic structure of a whole life or a whole social world, has no substance other than meaning and value, and no force once it no longer appears justified. The motor of history—to use a metaphor which would have repelled Bakhtin—is therefore not technical or political, but the conviction or suspicion that one's life is no longer justifiably valuable (which is to say that the motor of history is not really a motor at all, and Bakhtin would have been right to reject the idea). But no subject will take the 'leap in the open air of history' (Benjamin's phrase) alone: it must be persuaded to trade a security based on fragile norms for the promise that its life may be transformed and justified anew in the history that follows it.[7] Only a world searching for its own justification, a world unsure of itself, so to speak (not 'given' but 'set as a task'), can make that promise. The subject that realizes that it has, as Bakhtin put it, 'no alibi in being', that is, no metaphysical or traditional given on which to steady itself, can think of itself in historical terms only

[7] The phrase is Walter Benjamin's—Thesis 14, 'Theses on the Philosophy of History', in *Illuminations*, trans. Harry Zohn (New York: Schocken Books, 1969), 261.

by entrusting its life to a future which may re-evaluate and revalorize it.[8] But in that sense the future exerts a pressure on the present not because time goes on and on, but because the need for meaning and justification constantly bears down on us.

Why should this essentially ethical task fall to the novel? Because moral self-reflection on its own cannot, according to Bakhtin, generate any kind of narrative at all. The ethical *I* is present to itself 'as a task', as a project of self-realization for which time figures as opportunity and demand rather than as an aspect of its existence. 'My unity for myself is a unity which is perpetually yet-to-be' (AH 117/126), and every attempt to construct the unity of the subject as a unity in time (as what Bakhtin calls 'the soul') appears to an ethically free subject as an attempt to entangle it in the morass of the already existent and determined. The hero's inner life as a whole with temporal extension, a beginning and end, progress and regress, is therefore 'transgredient to his directedness to meaning in life, to his self-consciousness' (AH 95/100) and available only from the perspective of the *other*. Only the *other* can grasp the self as a unique but finite personality which has value in itself, which means that 'the soul, as an inner whole that becomes *in time*, a *given, present-on-hand* whole, is constructed in aesthetic categories' (AH 95/100).

When *others* see our acts—particularly others who write novels—they can construe them as the meaningful *expression* of a self, and this makes possible the construction of a personality out of the events of a lifetime. But for the *I* whose deeds are guided by ethical norms, by 'only goals and values which direct it and give it meaning' (AH 129/139), everything which exists, including its own acts, will never be good enough and is stained by its location in a definite time and place. Constituting one's life as a coherent narrative therefore depends upon the existence of a context where you are forced to adopt the *other's* perspective. The practice of auto-biography provides Bakhtin with the genre he needs.

In autobiography, the doomed striving for ethical purity and perfect self-knowledge is replaced by a desire for the good opinion of others. When 'the possible other . . . who is with us when we look at ourselves in a mirror, when we dream of glory, when we make up external plans for life' (AH 141/152) writes our life history, then 'life' itself acquires a weight and value independent of ethical good and evil. Recognition by actual social others, conceived as descendants who will celebrate your glorious pursuits,

---

[8] See the oft-quoted section of 'Towards a Philosophy of the Act': 'That which can be accomplished by me, no one else can ever accomplish. The uniqueness of present-on-hand being is necessarily obligating. This fact of *my non-alibi in being*, on which the most concrete and unique obligatoriness of the act is based, is not known and not cognized by me, but recognized and affirmed by me in a unique manner' (TPA 112/40).

or contemporaries who have a good opinion of your behaviour as citizen, worker, or head of household, provides a necessary stability and a kind of secular equivalent of the aesthetically consummated soul. Where the demanding reflection of confession tortures the soul, the practice of biography celebrates it as a worldly and temporal string of achievements. But biographical forms of narration have their own problems as well.

For whether one celebrates life in the genre of 'adventure', or through what Bakhtin calls a 'social-quotidian' desire to observe and experience a loved world over and over again, one is depending entirely on values with no authority other than the mere fact of their prevalence. Biography relies on a 'proximate world (kin, nation, state, culture)' (AH 152–3/165) grounding the values shared by author and hero, but this proximate world has the character of Gillian Rose's 'sociological *a priori*': it establishes values by virtue of its collective weight, but it does not and cannot justify them in a reflective fashion. Unequipped with reasons which could convince anyone outside its charmed circle, the 'biographically valuable life hangs by a thread' (AH 153/165), vulnerable to the least scepticism. In 'Author and Hero' the complementary weaknesses of moral self-reflection and unreflective biography lead to a dialectic between life histories in the first and second persons, which passes through lyric, classical, and Romantic fiction, and the lives of the saints, with no obvious modern solution. 'To free the good from all naïvety, to sober up every aspect of the good' (Archive, 495) is a task passed on to the novel, now charged with the creation of a world in which modern subjects can act reflectively, yet feel at home.[9]

It applies itself to the job in a spirit every bit as modern as its subject-matter. In 'Author and Hero' time and space had been divided phenomenologically, into the medium of the *I-for-myself* and the sphere of the *other-for-me*, to wit, into 'ethical' time and space and 'aesthetic' time and space. In the 1930s the novel leaves all this to one side, and dedicates itself to the generation of ever more refined and more 'realistic' chronotopes with a Puritan patience and determination (the task takes 2,000 odd years to complete) which would have impressed even Weber. It starts, therefore, not with a point of view, *I-* or *other-* orientated, but with a particular historical location: in the public square of antiquity, where ancient autobiography has its roots.

The classical forms of autobiography and biography were not works of a literary-bookish character, cut off from the concrete socio-political event of their noisy publication. On the contrary, they were completely defined by this event, they were verbal civic-political acts of the public glorification or the public self-

[9] The quotation comes from notes on French realism found together with the notes which have been published as 'On Flaubert'.

accounting of real people . . . Precisely in the conditions of this real chronotope, in which one's own or an alien life was disclosed (made public), the boundaries of the image of a person and his life were formed, they were definitively brought to light. (FTC 282/131)

In the classical public square one constructs an image in front of and for the sake of the judgement of others, the self thereby acquiring a 'public unity'. Lacking any interiority, the classical hero can make a life story which is 'all surface' without sacrificing its own integrity. Bakhtin thereby sets himself up for a rerun of the familiar history he retold in 'Author and Hero', in which the substantial and mythological unity of the classical self gives way to the interiority so lovingly elaborated in Christianity, and both await their synthesis in modern life itself. This is also the narrative which Georg Misch follows, and it is his *Geschichte der Autobiographie* which is the source not only for the above, but for everything Bakhtin knows, or at least tells us, about ancient autobiography.[10] But this time Bakhtin avoids the familiar story.

Instead, he takes this opportunity to 'sociologize' the split in time and space which had at first appeared philosophically inescapable. The constitution of the task-orientated subjectivity of the *I-for-myself* is now explained by the emergence of a domain of private life, private space, and private time in Hellenistic and Roman society, while the perspective of the *other* is equated with the political life of the citizen in the public square. The subject then loses its unity not because self-reflection demands it, but because of the 'translation of whole spheres of being, both within and beyond the person, into a *mute register* and into a *principled invisibility*' (FTC 285/134), that is, spheres which are beyond the control of public-rhetorical politics. Bakhtin does not, therefore, take the obvious route of linking the emergence of this private self to the growing importance of Christianity in

---

[10] The section of 'Forms of Time and of the Chronotope' on ancient autobiography follows Misch in its choice of authors, in its description of practices, and, most strikingly, in its classification of types of autobiography. According to the editors of the *Collected Works*, Bakhtin had made a lengthy conspectus of the first volume of Misch's *Geschichte der Autobiographie* (Leipzig and Berlin: B. G. Teubner, 1907); English translation: *A History of Autobiography in Antiquity*, 2 vols., trans. E. W. Dickes (London: Routledge & Kegan Paul, 1950) on which he drew in several essays. They date the conspectus at 1940–41, but Bakhtin had clearly consulted the work well before then; Brian Poole has discovered that in the original typescript of 'Discourse in the Novel' Bakhtin 'drew special attention to Misch's chapter on "Self-Characterization in Realistic Forms of Literature"' (Poole, 'Bakhtin and Cassirer', 570 n. 10). So, for example, Bakhtin's discussion of the two types of classical Greek autobiography, 'Platonic' and 'rhetorical' (FTC 280–8/130–7), reproduces the classification offered in Misch's chapter on 'Classic Attic Literature' (*A History of Autobiography in Antiquity*, 96–175); his discussion of Aristotle's influence on Roman autobiography and on Cicero's letters (FTC 290–5/140–5) follows Misch's discussion of Aristotle's influence (pp. 292–5) and Cicero's letters (pp. 357–72), even to the point of naming precisely the same texts as Cicero's literary heirs. Most significantly, Misch's discussion of the 'realistic literature' of Lucian and Petronius (pp. 371–403), and the significance of satire for autobiography, is the source for the section of 'Forms of Time' on these two writers.

Roman life (which is how Misch ends his study of ancient autobiography). In fact, this new and secularized account leaves the phenomenological foundations of his Christian ethics in ruins. For the Roman distinction between *res publica* and *res privata*, though doubtless bound up with cultural and sociological features, was at bottom a legal–juridical one, and legal distinctions, unlike phenomenological ones, can be altered. One could therefore hypothetically 'solve' the problem of balancing the demands of the forward-directed *I* and the pacifying *other* by simply giving private subjectivity a foothold in public life.

At first glance, this is exactly the solution at which Bakhtin arrives, however unintentionally. Although the materials collected as 'Forms of Time and of the Chronotope' and those published explicitly as fragments of the book *The* Bildungsroman *and its Significance in the History of Realism* differ slightly in their chronology and emphasis, they both focus on the gradual constitution of an active and self-questioning subject, whose historical form then gradually infects its surrounding public world, in the following fashion. First, the hero exists as a mere motivation for plot adventures and changes of locale. Second, the hero becomes the focus of attention, but its unity is based on a 'rhetorical–juridical conception of the person', which 'transformed the novel into a kind of court of judgement for the hero' (*Bil.*, 201/12), determining its unchanged and unchangeable essence through a series of tests and trials. Third, the hero's life acquires a biographical depth and unity, on the one hand becoming more complex, with events being 'localized in the whole of this life process' (*Bil.*, 207/18), but, on the other hand, consisting of no more than the display of a set of pre-existing traits. Fourth, the hero becomes capable of change in response to conditions and events, and, as a result, time acquires an irreversible, unrepeatable character, but the change 'takes place against the stationary background of a world which is already made and fundamentally quite solid' (*Bil.*, 214/23). Finally, historical change spreads its wings, and we arrive at the ideal form embodied in different respects by Rabelais (who dominates the scene of 'Forms of Time') and Goethe (the key figure in the extant *Bildungsroman* materials).

In 'the novel of becoming' they perfected, the hero

becomes *together with the world*, he reflects within himself the historical becoming of the world itself. He is no longer within an epoch, but on the border of two epochs, at the point of transition from one to the other. This transition is achieved in him and through him. He is forced to become a new, unprecedented type of human being. The issue here is precisely the becoming of a new person; the organizing force of the future is therefore extraordinarily great and it is, of course, not a private-biographical future, but a historical future. It is the *foundations* of the world that change, and the person must change with them. (*Bil.*, 214/23–4)

Note: we witness the birth of a new kind of world, in order to make possible a new kind of person (in a letter written more than twenty years later, Bakhtin confirmed that the novel prepared the way for a 'new *being* of the person'[11]). The environment is thus forced to 'speak', so that the becoming of the personality may be a matter of historical transformation rather than adaptation to circumstances. Thus the solution to the antithesis of the merely worldly and the endless demand for meaning and justification turns out to be a modern, historical world, pliable to the change demanded of it by its subjects. When 'change in the hero itself acquires *plot [siuzhetnoe] significance*' (*Bil.*, 212/21) self-transcendence and transformation become possible within the bounds of the earthly.

AN AESTHETIC OF THE HISTORICAL

'The task is to find a *visible*, graphic, *historical space* for representation, a space with a new scale, with a new distribution of things and people' (Mayak., 55). In the period between 1937 and 1944, when European history was outdoing itself in the creation of inconceivable, unrepresentable horror, Bakhtin wrote of four different attempts to make history, in the strong sense he gives to the term, representable in verbal art. Mayakovsky had recourse to grand public forms like the ode, introduced rhythms and vocabulary with public resonance, and combined the individual with the machine and the collective.[12] Shakespeare had invented a 'topographical' drama, in which 'action, discourse, and gesture' on stage referred to the 'extremes' or 'limits' of the world, to life and death, hell and heaven, in short, to the metaphysical poles which made the physical world a meaningful place.[13] Rabelais had drawn from popular culture the idea of using visible *growth* as a figure for the future-orientation of the world and of using ambivalent images of organic life to symbolize the ever-present possibility of spiritual transformation. But Goethe had approached the matter directly. By looking always for the *'marks of the passage of time'* (*Bil.*, 216/25) in the world around him, even in the most apparently changeless natural formation, he had given temporality a physical embodiment and made movement through space a historical journey. Refusing the distinction between appearance and essence, Goethe insists that we look down the horizontal axis of history for the meaning of what we encounter in present space and time. Goethe's world is eternally 'at the point of transi-

---

[11] Letter to V. V. Kozhinov, 1 Apr. 1961, in 'Pis'ma M. M. Bakhtina', 147.

[12] In Bakhtin's sketch for the article 'On Mayakovsky' (Mayak., 50–62).

[13] As described in Bakhtin's lengthiest discussion of Shakespeare, in 'Additions and Amendments to "Rabelais"' (AddAmR, 85–99).

tion', and this transitoriness—which keeps alive the possibility of a 'life different in principle'—becomes a structural feature of all that he represents.

The object-world is thus, according to Bakhtin, transformed into a historical world. But the demand to give representable form to history requires more than marking the passage of time. The passage of time must be made meaningful, it must be justified, with movement from event to event following some kind of narrative logic. How can one represent this logic without dissolving the world itself into the forward movement of a goal-directed *I*? Bakhtin's account of Goethe's solution is revealing:

Necessity, as we have already pointed out, became the organizing centre of the Goethean sense of time. He wished to pull together and connect the present, past and future with the ring of necessity. This Goethean necessity was very distant both from the necessity of fate and from mechanical natural necessity (in the naturalistic sense). It was a visible, concrete, material, but materially creative, historical necessity. (*Bil.*, 233/39)

What kind of necessity can be both 'material' and creative? The answer was provided in Goethe's own time by Kant—the infamous 'purposiveness without purpose' which characterizes the aesthetic object. Every detail of the art object is, or should be, experienced as necessary, but it cannot be mechanically connected with a prior cause, nor is its role determined by the strict force of reason. The heroes of the mature novel of becoming, whose greatest exponent is Goethe, are therefore neither put on trial like their predecessors (because the point is no longer their goodness or badness), nor are their actions embedded in a naturalistically conceived causal series (because the point is also not to explain them). While the novel of becoming works hard to establish its protagonist as responsible for its acts and words, it does so not to sit in judgement, but to celebrate—i.e. aestheticize—the very fact of this responsibility. And though the heroes in question will no doubt have definite and precise reasons for wanting to change themselves and the worlds they inhabit, these will be but a moment in the larger scheme of the novel itself, which will focus not on a particular cause of action, but on the possibility of transformation itself. In his sketch for an article on Mayakovsky, Bakhtin asked himself the real question—'whether becoming can be beautiful' (Mayak., 61)—perhaps not realizing that he had already answered it by defining history itself in terms which made it beautiful. For if in Goethe's world 'everything is visible, everything is concrete, everything is bodily, everything is material in this world, and at the same time everything is intensive, meaningful, and creatively necessary' (*Bil.*, 236/42–3), then everything is, in short, part of an aesthetic whole, and beautiful by definition.

Fair enough, one might say: novels ought to be aesthetic wholes. But does human history have to follow suit? In his forthcoming book on Bakhtin, Graham Pechey shrewdly points out that chronotopicity does not signal an original but lost historical concreteness but the very means by which it becomes possible to distinguish literary concreteness from abstract conceptuality.[14] The 'authentic chronotope' of Goethe does not, *pace* Bakhtin, represent 'real historical time', but creates the kind of historical concreteness Bakhtin requires for his *ethical* project. But since chronotopes reveal this ethical world from a third-person perspective, they appear to achieve precisely that which Bakhtin would generally deem impossible: the representation of ethical reality from a point outside its architectonics.

We thus confront, once more, the ambiguity which structured Bakhtin's theory of dialogism and account of language. From a philosophical point of view—that represented best in 'Author and Hero', but audible in muffled form later on as well—narrative depends upon the presence of an *other*, a second person or 'thou', who can make whole the life of a symmetrical *I*; from a historical point of view, narrative depends on a gradual concretization of time and space, an aesthetic thickening of historical context which implies the supposedly impossible perspective of a third person. The symmetrical dialogue, and the participant's sense of language as concrete, find their equivalent in the former perspective; the asymmetrical dialogism of the novelist who makes images of language, and the observer's sense of language as innately aesthetic, finds its correlate in the latter. Given that the theory of dialogism hinged on the belief that the novelist's task was to render language part of 'historical becoming', there is good reason to think that this reprise of the old ambiguity in fact reveals its inner logic. The underlying source of Bakhtin's hesitation between models of language and models of dialogism is an uncertainty over the relationship of narrative—in fact, of *history* in its modern sense—to the ethical reality he so forcefully craves.

On the one hand, ethical reality means the unconditional distinction between *I* and *other*, and the faith to which its architectonics points. On the other hand, it means a world driven by the self-making energies of subjects, open because ruled by science and free experiment rather than myth. A historical world to which Rabelais and Goethe, in their different ways, have given expression:

The 'whole world' and its history, as the reality which faced the artist–novelist, had changed profoundly and essentially by Goethe's time. Even three centuries

---

[14] Graham Pechey, 'Chronotope, Concept, Carnival', unpublished MS, 34. This will be a chapter in Pechey's forthcoming book on Bakhtin. I am greatly indebted to Graham Pechey for kindly allowing me to read several chapters of what will doubtless be the most brilliant and incisive theoretical account of Bakhtin on record.

earlier the 'whole world' was a unique symbol, which could not be adequately grasped by any model, by any map or globe. In this symbol the visible and known, earthly-real 'whole world' was a small and cut-off piece of earthly space and a similarly minor and cut-off segment of real time; everything remaining dissolved into the mist, it was removed to and interwoven with worlds beyond, abstract-ideal, fantastic, and utopian worlds . . . The addition of the otherworldly broke down, decomposed, the real compactness of the world, it impeded the bringing together and rounding off of the real world and real history into a unified, compact and full whole. The otherworldly future, torn from the horizontal of earthly space and time, was raised up as an otherworldly vertical to the real flow of time, bleeding white the real future and earthly space as the arena of this real future, endowing everything with symbolic meaning, devaluing and rejecting everything that did not submit to symbolic interpretation.

In the epoch of the Renaissance the 'whole world' began to coalesce into a real and compact whole. (*Bil.*, 237/43)

A process which the eighteenth-century Enlightenment completes, rendering the world compact and historical.[15] When places become part of a determinate geographical reality ('part of *this*, utterly real and in principle observable world of human history') and events become part of an irreversible human history ('a moment which cannot be transferred in time') then the world and history undergo a qualitative change: 'they coalesced, were embodied and filled up by the creative possibilities of further endless *real* becoming and development' (*Bil.*, 245/50). The utopian and salvational energies of religion are reintegrated into, and thus transform, this world.

Bakhtin rightly sees that every eschatology or anticipation of the end of time will devalue the ethical substance of the present, but he frames the alternative as a different kind of faith rather than as the sceptical refusal of faith. 'Not faith (in the sense of a definite faith in Orthodoxy, in progress, in man, in revolution, and so on), but a *feeling of faith*, that is, an integral relation (of the whole person) to a higher and ultimate value' (N61, 352/294): this distinction, made in the course of a discussion of Dostoevsky, reflects an apparently continuing belief that the forward movement of history has to be grounded in an unredeemable anticipation of redemption. In the context of his philosophy of language this faith appears as the immanent orientation of every utterance to a 'higher superaddressee (a

[15] Although Bakhtin continuously and sharply condemns all rationalist philosophy, he interprets the Enlightenment as the Age of History rather than Reason. Further research may reveal the extent to which this simply reflected the growing influence of the work of Ernst Cassirer, whose *Philosophy of the Enlightenment* and *Goethe and the Historical World* argued a similar case (see Poole, '"Nazad k Kaganu"', 40–1). Later in the *Bildungsroman* materials, Bakhtin acknowledges that as a result of one side of Enlightenment criticism (presumably the 'mechanical materialist' wing) 'the world became poorer and drier. But this abstract negative critique of the Enlighteners, dissolving the remnants of otherworldly connections and mythical unity, helped reality collect itself and coalesce into the visible whole of the new world' (*Bil.*, 239/44–5).

third), an absolutely just answering understanding' (N61, 337/126) which, of course, never actually arrives (one might describe this as a desecularized version of the 'unavoidable idealization' which Habermas once called 'the ideal speech situation').[16] But in both cases Bakhtin assures us that the need for meaning and justification, the critical sense of the future which makes historical movement compelling, is based on faith in an ultimate value beyond history rather than the inner logic of cultural activity itself.

Could we not accept Bakhtin's description of the historical world, so compelling in its details, and lose the unnecessary metaphysical baggage? A tempting, *almost* workable, solution; but, unfortunately, faith inserts itself into the very conception of history and ethical life Bakhtin outlines, most strikingly in the fact that Bakhtin presents Goethe's texts not as pointers to a future historical culture but as realizations of an achieved one. For if it is essential to a historical world that the people within it labour creatively and not just 'technically', that it embodies the logic of self-transformation and responsibility, and not just the satisfaction of human needs, then the world of Goethe was not, and could not have been, historical. Bakhtin may not have been politically astute, but he would have known that what Goethe saw was not the evidence of a generalized human creativity, but the products of societies dominated by minority political and cultural power. Only some of the subjects of Goethe's time laboured 'creatively'; most of them worked technically, to satisfy immediate needs and the commands of their superiors. Although Goethe's world was for the most part pre-capitalist, making understandable, if not excusable, a certain degree of romanticism about the nature of its labour process, it was overwhelmingly the case that its subjects were not living in the historicized world of which Bakhtin was such an eloquent champion.[17]

If Bakhtin nevertheless thought this world was 'compact and historical' even on his own definition, it was not because he was indifferent to the fate of the majority of his fellow creatures, but because the criteria for being historically responsible had been set so low that the most down-trodden serf could meet them. An aesthetic model of 'real historical time' does not have to concern itself with political or economic power, because it has already decided that a narrative of one's life depends more on the

[16] See *Legitimation Crisis*, 110. Perhaps entirely understandably, some readers of Habermas persistently treated the 'ideal speech situation' precisely as a mythical image of a possible real future, and then proceeded to denounce it as such. Although it is clear from the outset that Habermas has nothing like this in mind, he later conceded that his choice of words was a hostage to fortune; see 'Discourse Ethics, Law and *Sittlichkeit*', in *Autonomy and Solidarity*, 260.

[17] Goethe's *Faust* has been described as an epic of capitalist effort, which establishes the very means by which capitalist expansion disavows the violence it entails. See Franco Moretti, *Modern Epic: The World System from Goethe to García Márquez*, trans. Quintin Hoare (London and New York: Verso, 1996), 22–34, and Marshall Berman, *All that is Solid Melts into Air: The Experience of Modernity* (New York: Simon & Schuster, 1982), 60–71.

other than on one's own achievements. Bakhtin assumes from the outset that factual control or lack of control over one's destiny does not matter, in so far as any attempt of the *I* to frame its own narrative is pointless. The terms of the argument conceal a calculated sacrifice: the subject's autonomy—its ability to direct its own life—is traded against the unity it might achieve by letting the *other* aestheticize it. Symptomatically, in 'Author and Hero', where this (un)holy bargain is struck, the origins of narration are placed in the activity of remembering: 'The aesthetic categories for giving form to the inner person (as well as the outer person) are born, essentially, of the emotional-volitional attitude of remembering the departed . . .' (AH 101/106–7). If narration is in principle a matter of memory, then the only work left for it is to redeem a finished life, for judging that life or any of its constituent moments in the present no longer serves any purpose.

AUTONOMY, NARRATIVE, AND JUDGEMENT

But can autonomy be exchanged for redemption so easily? Even within the terms of Bakhtin's argument, the answer is no. The responsible subject which the *other* will save 'in memory' cannot wait for its rescue: it has to unify itself as a precondition of being responsible to begin with. In his rush to appropriate phenomenological insights for Christian ethics, Bakhtin forgets that narration is necessary even for the autonomy of the *I-for-myself*: constituting one's actions *as* one's own actions requires asserting the continuity of one's self and with it, responsibility over time rather than only at a singular moment. The relentless orientation to the future, which Bakhtin thought narrative could cure, itself depends on an already accomplished knitting together of temporal experience. Far from being an endlessly postponed unity, the *I-for-myself* is a consequence of narrative unity, a subject which has successfully integrated its experience into a whole and which can act in the future because it has a past.

Narrative therefore serves two masters, ethics and aesthetics, rather than one. And its dual orientation suggests a dual origin, that it arrives not thanks to the beneficence of the *other*, but as the result of the joint work of first, second, and, as we shall see below, third persons in communication. Bakhtin's neat division of roles between an ethical *I* and an aestheticizing *other* ignores the role intersubjectivity must play both in ethical discourse (in the constitution of an autonomous subject) and in aesthetic discourse (in the constitution of satisfactory narratives). He establishes intersubjectivity, but on the basis of a dogmatic gap between the first and second persons, as if a distinction between forms or modes of intersubjectivity could be reduced to a difference between its participants.

Ironically, this account endorses the very liberal individualism Bakhtin elsewhere challenges (as the abstract 'idea of man', natural rights theory, and so on).[18] For in rejecting the ideal of autonomy on account of its individualist origins Bakhtin takes on faith the liberal, subjectivist explanation of the origins of autonomy itself. The Enlightenment may well have been a historical moment *par excellence*, but its achievement may be linked to ideas about autonomy which Bakhtin has found it convenient to ignore.

But if autonomy and personality are not 'gifts', but intersubjective accomplishments, then they enter inevitably into the process of judgement. The author or *other* does not have to be endowed with extraordinary Christian benevolence if the narrative identity of every personality or hero is something which must be agreed upon or recognized. Habermas has pinned down the inevitable consequences of a turn to actual intersubjectivity:

Once the vertical axis of the prayer has tipped into the horizontal axis of inter-human communication, the individual can no longer redeem the emphatic claim to individuality solely through the reconstructive appropriation of his life history; now the positions taken by others decide whether this reconstruction succeeds.[19]

Since Kant and Fichte, Habermas argues, individuality (the unique, irreplaceable personality) has not been a given property of particular persons, which could be acknowledged from on high, but has been indissolubly tied to the act of self-constitution and the claim to autonomy of an ego.[20] To be an individual or a unique personality means to be accountable—i.e. responsible—for one's own actions, and this self-accountability is a claim made in the first person within a community of other individuals. No one else can grant the continuity which comes from the desire to be autonomous, but it rests upon a claim made to, and ratified by, others.

Bakhtin acknowledges that personalities as such cannot exist outside of intersubjectivity. But he does not allow for the historical evolution of intersubjectivity itself. Although he claims to recognize that intersubjectivity has various forms—ethico-political, scientific, aesthetic, religious—all of these turn out to be variations on the fixed roles of *I* and *other*, which are themselves derived from an unashamedly religious model of intersubjectivity, and an unashamedly Christian one at that. The problem lies not in Bakhtin's shrewd articulation of the weakness of modern subjectivity, incarnate in the experience of the *I-for-myself*, or in his suggestion that the cure lay in the narrative power of others—the problem is that Bakhtin fails

---

[18] In 'Author and Hero', Bakhtin criticized the 'idea of the person' for abstracting personhood from the absolute distinction between *I* and *other*; see AH 52/52 and 57–8/58–9.

[19] Habermas, 'Individuation through Socialization', 167.

[20] Ibid. 158–70.

to recognize that the *Is* which he saw as so infinitely discontented were modern European *Is* living in generally capitalist societies, and that the idea of saving them through an aesthetic consummation of their life was the product of a long period of artistic effort and evolution, not a spontaneous gift of the *other*. By positing the religious form of intersubjectivity as, in effect, the origin of all others, Bakhtin puts to one side all those other forms of response—practical, political, sexual, scientific, strategic, and so on— which do not conform to the ideal of Christian mercy, even though they are simply other elements of a complex social life of which Christianity is but one part. More than that, the privileging of a Christian form of religious intersubjectivity condemns to second rank every kind of response which entails an act of judgement rather than mercy, even though it is these forms which are at the centre of the modern concept of a history which is made and valued rather than passively experienced.

Historical forms of intersubjectivity have historical limits: if the subject's ability to act responsibly, to accept or acknowledge its responsibility (its 'non-alibi in being'), depends upon an accountability recognized by others, then responsibility is an *achievement* rather than something which any subject can accomplish, irrespective of circumstances. In his earliest philosophy Bakhtin hoped that subjects might be persuaded to acknow- ledge a responsibility which was, in a sense, theirs already, but he did so in the conviction that this was no more than the God-given possibility of every Christian soul, was what made it a Christian soul. But responsibility can *fail*, and can fail not because its subject lacks the requisite devotion, but because the intersubjective community—more precisely, the distribution of authority and power within it—makes it impossible for it to act responsibly. If Bakhtin's subjects take no such risk, it is because he has stacked the deck in their favour, by subtly conflating two senses of the word 'responsibility'. One can be responsible as a minimal condition for the existence of a self or ego, in the sense that one can recognize the decisions one has to make as *one's own* decisions, no matter what the external circumstances. But if historical becoming means the ability to create 'a life different in principle, with different scales and dimensions', then it requires not only autonomous intentions, but the symbolic authority necessary to fulfil them; otherwise, responsibility is as other- worldly and invisible, as unlikely to make its mark in 'real space and time', as the mythical activities it is meant to displace. Responsibility in the latter sense means not only making decisions, but having the authority to take part in the particular decisions that shape a historical form of life.[21] 'Men make history', as the old nostrum goes, 'but not in circumstances of

[21] Though he may be very surprised to learn it, I owe knowledge of this distinction to Martin Bauer.

their own choosing.' And indeed, those who make history often do so by making others make it for them.

If the point of being responsible is to seek salvation or redemption, then whether one is 'in effect' responsible does not matter. Before God, one is a unique individual, and one whose responsibility transcends the particular position or roles one occupies in a given social formation. But if we do not want to stake all on redemptive possibilities, then responsibility cannot be disentangled from the roles we play in an actual social world, roles or positions which determine the depth and limits of our responsibilities. It was, of course, precisely this legal-juridical concept of responsibility, the basis for much neo-Kantian social thought, which Bakhtin sought to supplant.[22] He sought a responsibility 'with no excuses', knowing that the legal-juridical concept set limits to what a subject could be held responsible *for* (and thus, when it could be deemed negligent, for example). With his eye firmly on the weaknesses of the rational-bureaucratic attitude, Bakhtin sought to combine the belief in differentiation characteristic of neo-Kantian philosophy with a faith which would provide totalizing glue. 'There is not aesthetic, scientific, and then, next to them, ethical obligation; there is only that which is aesthetically, theoretically or socially valid, with which obligation can be united, and which is all technical in relation to it' (TPA 85/5). The last phrase is the giveaway: the norms attached to roles are only 'technical' because whether one believes in them (i.e. is convinced they are valid) is secondary; they are only values of this world, and the subject which places too much stock in their worth binds itself to the fate of the temporal and earthly.

Bound to a totalizing ethics, uninterested in consequences, brooking no compromise: Bakhtin is a textbook example of the Russian intellectual Weber had in mind when he attacked the 'ethics of conviction' in the essay 'Politics as a Vocation'.[23] Weber's 'ethics of responsibility', worldly and strategic, are the antithesis of Bakhtin's. For the sociologist who believes only in the validity of the here-and-now, responsible action must be constrained by a sense of possibilities and consequences, by knowledge of the limits of one's power, and by the calculation of potential allies and opponents, that is, by precisely those factors that Bakhtin regards as alibis for actual responsibility. But Weber did not intend to provide excuses, and the subject willing to meet him half-way, so to speak, does not trade in the ideal of a redeemed existence for the cheap but temporary thrills of the merely possible. Discharging its secular responsibilities entitles it to redemption's secular equivalent, the dignity afforded by communal recognition of its existence and achievements. In the partner essay 'Science as a

[22] See Nikolaev, introductory comments in 'Lektsii i vystupleniia', 226–7.
[23] In *From Max Weber*.

Vocation' (discussed in Chapter 2 above), Weber emphasized that the scholar who stuck to the requirements of his or her specialism (and, so the argument went, kept out of politics) would reap the reward of being grounded in an intersubjective community extending not only geographic-ally but also historically. Only such a subject, in such a manner, 'becomes *together with the world*' and so fulfils Bakhtin's requirements for a historical culture, because the differentiation of spheres *and the differentiation of 'ought-ness' with it* was constitutive of the modern world Bakhtin and Weber inhabited. Thus while Bakhtin may have been wrong to displace all responsibility into an absolute and religious form, he was right to claim that responsibility, and the achievement of personality, is its own reward. Subjects whose ability to act autonomously is acknowledged receive more than the direct pay-off of the desired end: they are recognized as competent subjects, and, by being so recognized, they become historical actors, whose achievements fit into a narrative which will transcend their own lives.

THE DEMAND FOR MEANING

If responsibility is not the prerogative of the *I-for-myself* alone, then, con-versely, the impulse to aestheticize may not be the sole property of the *other*. In his early critique of biography, Bakhtin openly warned against this form's tendency to confuse the roles of author and hero. The author of biography 'simply continues that which is already established in the life of the hero itself' (AH 151/163): the hero acts, possessed by the *other* and desirous of its good opinion, and the *other* plays along by celebrating a life that was lived with precisely this in view. Thus Bakhtin sees biography as inherently linked to an '*aesthetic of life*' (AH 141/152), in which an antici-pation of aesthetic pleasure determines the subject's practical conduct. While Bakhtin is surely right to recognize the role the aesthetic may play in the determination of practical acts, he is just as surely wrong to see in this a distortion of the purity of the ethical. Bakhtin insists that a moral consciousness can only be compromised by a sense of its own determi-nateness:

For the acting consciousness itself its act needs not a hero (that is, a determinate personality), but only goals and values which direct it and give it meaning. My acting consciousness as such only poses questions like: for what purpose? what for? how? is it correct or not? is it necessary or not? should one or shouldn't one? is it good or not? but never questions like: who am I? what am I? and of what sort am I? (AH 129/139)

To which one can respond: these are exactly the questions one asks, because the goals we pursue are inseparable from the contexts we occupy, the communities within which we act, and the kind of person we wish to be. In so far as every act is also a symbolic act, tied to the establishment or maintenance of an intersubjective network, it is endowed with a meaning transcending its particular location in time and space. Whenever one acts responsibly, one fulfils the requirements of a particular position or symbolic role—one acts in order to become the kind of person one wants to be, and to institute the kind of relations one wants to live within. But this means one is acting for motives which Bakhtin would deem aesthetic, in order to construct a life-story 'in the third person' with which one can be satisfied.

In recent writings, Habermas has warned of the danger of confusing what he calls ethical questions with strictly moral ones. Moral questions require a solution which is just and with which all possible participants in discussion could agree—they admit of universalist solutions; ethical questions, by contrast, are inextricable from the issue of 'Who am I and who would I like to be?'—they are bound to the particular traditions, conditions, and self-understanding of a concrete lifeworld.[24] What Habermas calls an ethical question, Bakhtin describes as an aesthetic one, and while Habermas recognizes the role such questions will productively play in the field of practical-moral decisions broadly conceived, he shares with Bakhtin a desire to separate off a sphere of 'pure' moral decision where such matters will have no relevance (this may in turn explain why Habermas has never really been able to integrate the aesthetic point of view into his system; it appears as a less than necessary adjunct to modern social life in his theory). Bakhtin is afraid that any aesthetic clouding of the issue will lead the subject to too great a concern with its status in this world; Habermas wants to ensure that there is a sphere in which questions can be settled on grounds not relative to a particular form of life. In both cases the subject is asked to abstract its action from any consideration of its life-story and the narrative of its social context. When moral life was orientated to an order which transcended earthly history, this may well have been the case. But for the modern personality the desire to act justly is inextricable from the desire to be a righteous or just person, to live in a just community, perhaps to fight for a just future, which is to say that it cannot comprehend moral action without thinking of it as a moment of a narrative. More to the point, subjects conceive of their failure to act morally in narrative terms also, and may conceive of their suffering and that experienced by their communities (whether national, class, sexual, ethnic, or geographic) as a denial of narrative satisfactions granted to others.

[24] See Habermas, 'On the Pragmatic, Ethical and Moral Employments of Practical Reason', in *Justification and Application*, 4–6.

Bakhtin would seem to have believed that a novelized culture could be constructed beyond the borders of politics, but the political nub of his argument is inescapable. It is that narrative has become another currency of social debate and conflict, a medium in which people become satisfied or dissatisfied, happy or unhappy, with the structures of social and political life. Besides, and often instead of, demands for rights, for just institutional arrangements, for the competent organization and regulation of social life, we find social and political demands for meaningful narratives and the intersubjective recognitions they entail. Discussions of democracy focus on the power granted to citizens at a point in time, or at a succession of points in time, without concern for their narrative coherence. But the subjects of democracy are people with bounded lives, whose efforts take place in the context of communities, institutions, and movements with a history and a future of their own. As sociable creatures, they are not just bearers of rights and duties, but also 'heroes' of narratives, and their desire for a good life embraces not only material goods, reasonable living conditions, pleasant relationships, peace and security, and so on, but also a narrative which endows all these features with a symbolic meaning which makes them 'something more' than just material goods, reasonable living conditions, and so on. One might say that twentieth-century political consciousness is inevitably a narrative consciousness and, taking this word in its broadest sense, a historical consciousness, in the sense that we identify power with the ability to make history, in however large or modest an arena. But making history means not just a string of disconnected accomplishments, but actions bound together as a coherent story, which inevitably depend upon some kind of connection between the interlocking plots of a nation-state, a class, a family, and an individual life.

The narratives Bakhtin first described as the 'adventurous-heroic' and 'social-quotidian' variants of the biographical life, orientated respectively towards 'glory' and 'love for extended residence with loved people, objects, situations and relations' (AH 149/161), are therefore great cultural achievements, in so far as they provide templates for a life worth living, a life as something extended in time, and not just a succession of individual moments. The subjects of any modern, secular polity, founded on the presumption that salvation in the next world is no alternative to a decent life in this one, depend on them to savour and enjoy their lives 'aesthetically'. And if these narratives—which today we find not just in novels, but in journalism, film, television—are also vehicles of disavowal, bad faith, and unacknowledged compromise, this does not mean we can dismiss them as mere stories. It means political conflict will be conflict over the kind of narrative we want, and political transformation will be a question not just of new institutions and values, but of a new aesthetic of narrative, providing us with a form of symbolic gratification we deem more just, reward-ing, or dignified. Struggles for national or ethnic self-determination, for political power among the disenfranchised, for an end to economic exploitation, for respect in public life, already depend upon narratives which justify them as moments of a larger and longer story.[25] 'Glory' may not be on the minds of most people, but 'respect', its egalitarian version, is; present circumstances are crucial, but interpreted against the backcloth of narrativized memories.[26] In a world which knows it is historical, the critique of social forms leads inexorably to the critique of social forms of narrative.

As a mode of interpreting social life, modern narrative has a unique feature: it can close up the gap between the ordinary and profane processes of social life and the values we use to justify them, the gap between the 'world of culture' and the 'world of life'. Only through narrative can one establish that 'sacredness of culture' of which Bakhtin's friend Kagan had spoken: only through this form of discourse can we show that the values which transcend our history and make its movement meaningful are rooted in that history itself. But it has to be the right kind of narrative. Kagan passed on to Bakhtin the insight that a sacred culture has to be a historical one, which sees justification and meaning as something located in the future rather than the past, and Bakhtin translated this insight into the distinction between novelistic and epic narration. For while epic narrative, devoted to commemoration and tradition, endows individual lives with meaning and significance, it is on the basis of a sphere of the heroic or ancestral utterly distant from them, and it thereby separates the sacred and transcendent from present history. To dignify our present, to endow it with the power to justify itself, it must be experienced as some-thing which 'by its whole essence demands continuation, it moves into the future' (EN 472/30), creating the very categories and values through which it can be reinterpreted and revalued. Which is to say that just as democracy demands a historical consciousness, which will narrativize the

[25] Although there is a rich literature on the narrative structures of formal history-writing, there is little on the narrative form taken by the political and economic demands of the population at large. A partial and unintentional exception is E. P. Thompson, who consistently polemicized against interpretations of popular social revolt as a quasi-biological reaction to changes in 'material' conditions, insisting that such uprisings could only be understood against the backcloth of morally informed world-views and popular historical conceptions. For his debate with the tendencies of economic historians see the chapter 'Exploitation' in *The Making of the English Working Class* (New York: Vintage, 1966), 189–212.

[26] On 'respect' as the egalitarian form of glory see Roberto Mangabeira Unger, *Knowledge and Politics* (New York: The Free Press, 1975), 66. There is now a substantial literature on the poli-tics of recognition. See Honneth, *The Struggle for Recognition*; Nancy Fraser, *Justice Interruptus: Critical Reflections on the 'Postsocialist' Condition* (London and New York: Routledge, 1997); Charles Taylor et al., *Multiculturalism: Examining the Politics of Recognition*, ed. Amy Gutmann (Princeton, NJ: Princeton University Press, 1994).

struggles of the present, so a true historical consciousness demands democracy. The orientation to the future depends on throwing all responsibility for what is back into the laps of autonomous subjects, who alone can set in motion a self-transcending historical movement.

Bakhtin contrasted change in material circumstances, or in the material 'facts' of the past with the meaning of the past, 'itself stronger than any force' (TMHum., 387/165). While the first was clearly beyond repair, the second was eternally revisable. Once our lives became objects of narration, they took up permanent residence in a sphere of meaning which could always be transformed. But his oft-quoted claim—'Nothing is absolutely dead—every meaning will have its festival of rebirth' (TMHum., 393/170)—is a promise only a god could keep. Ordinary mortals know that a happy life requires responsibility not only in the minimal sense but in the institutional sense (that it, the symbolic authority to accomplish things) as well, and that recognition of the former in past human beings can never undo the consequences of their having been denied the latter. Not everything can be made meaningful in the eyes of a later generation, because human history is shaped by human decisions, and human decisions must render some aspects of the past more interesting, more admirable, more regrettable than others. A past redeemed in all its moments, such as Walter Benjamin dreamt of, is a past redeemed by God rather than people. Once narrative becomes the business of democracy, decisions have to be made not only about the future, but also about the past.

Bakhtin sought to guard against the danger of making human decisions the final court of judgement, while at the same time celebrating the 'unconsummated present' which the finality of human decision made possible. But once he agreed that the novel had made the world compact and historical by virtue of its representational achievements, that is, from essentially a third-person perspective, he could not put the historical genie back into its bottle. If 'experience, knowledge, and practice (the future) determine the novel' (EN 459/15), then the symbolic roles and justifying values it tracks will come from the inventive force of social life rather than religious or philosophical insight into the nature of things. To fulfil the task assigned to it, the novel of becoming had to acknowledge not only those values handed down to it by Kantian philosophy and Christian ethics, but also those maintained or established by no more than the force of actual intersubjective agreement and practice. The roles, habits, relationships, and projects observed by the novel cannot be derived from the dialectic of *I* and *other*; like the forms of language abstracted by Saussure, they are philosophically ungrounded and provide, as it were, their own justification. In Bakhtin's world they are measured not against some final set of values, but against the demand that they get the historical ball rolling. And for this

Bakhtin's older wish that the *other* should merely 'make whole' the life of the subject is no longer enough.

By Bakhtin's own account the modern novel of becoming combined a passion for historical movement—movement we now realize is rooted in the autonomy of modern subjects—with an interest in particularities inherited from that glorification of finitude, the biographical novel. 'The conception of life (the idea of life) on which the biographical novel is based', Bakhtin complained, 'is defined either as its objective results (works, deserts, efforts, exploits) or by means of the category happiness/unhappiness (in all its variants)' (*Bil.*, 207/17). The point is surely not that objective results and happiness are unimportant, nor that the contingent particularities of life do not merit a certain respect, but that these particularities should not be isolated. Novelistic representation is defined in Bakhtin's texts as the dialogue which ensures that the merely private is not cut off from the narratives surrounding it and thereby lost to history. The given and the posited, the merely existent and the meaningful: these polarities, so central to Bakhtin's philosophical framework, are reflected again within the structure of the novel, where the given achieves a prestige and dignity which philosophy refused it. Once Bakhtin realizes that historical movement is 'chronotopic' rather than a matter of pure personalities, maintaining the spontaneity of an unconsummated present becomes a rather more complicated affair. One has to find it not by escaping from the specific responsibilities imposed by a particular present, but by going deeper into them. In the institutionalized responsibilities and reciprocal expectations of ordinary secular life lies the orientation to the future in which Bakhtin placed so much hope. And if this pattern of responsibilities and powers appears to lead not to the future but to more of the same, then perhaps it is the distribution of secular responsibilities which is the problem, not a lack of faith amongst its subjects.

CHAPTER SIX

The Public Square as Public Sphere

In one of the fragments dedicated to Goethe and the *Bildungsroman* Bakhtin wrote eloquently of the moment when 'the image of the becoming person begins to overcome its private character (of course, within certain limits) and to enter a completely different, *spacious* sphere of historical being' (*Bil.*, 214–15/24). Spacious, roomy, the Russian is *prostornyi*: the cognate therefore of the 'open spaces'—*prostory*—'of public squares and streets' which Bakhtin had earlier so graphically counterposed to the cramped quarters of the artist. A comparison which reminds us that the marvellously open expanses of the public square are not only literally but metaphorically spacious, allowing history a room for movement which it is denied in the bourgeois parlour or home. The early twentieth century is, of course, full of the latter: rooms, old houses, or offices which an external history enters only as an incomprehensible or destructive force. Whether it erupts into private life as a meaningless arrest and trial, or as a war which robs the home of its best and brightest, history again and again violates the privacy of the bourgeois until, like Bulgakov's Master, his ultimate desire is not to become 'world-historical', but to gain protection—'peace'—in a quiet home by the river.

Bakhtin thus had to turn back to Goethe for evidence of more Faustian ambitions, and to Rabelais and the Renaissance for models of individuals who see in open spaces opportunities to spread their wings rather than the threat of exposure. The proto-bourgeois confidence of Rabelais and Goethe, however, could provide only raw materials and inspiration for the person who wants to play a part in twentieth-century history. They wrote when cultured burghers were still hoping that enlightened monarchs might give history the forward push it needed, and before it became clear that capitalism would endow history with a volatile, *differentiated* motion no one could have imagined, and no one could master. Even more importantly, their public squares were still for markets rather than mass meetings, and at a time when communicating in print (never mind by the electronic media) was still a minority experience.

Above all, in Rabelais and Goethe making history is still a matter of culture rather than political revolution, and so far as Bakhtin is concerned, this is all to the good. Those who grilled Bakhtin at the defence of his dissertation were shocked that the French 'humanist' was being praised, not for delivering the *coup de grâce* to medieval obscurantism, but for providing access to the forgotten culture of the medieval public square.[1] But for Bakhtin Rabelais matters less as a prefiguration of the heroic and enlightened political bourgeois (the figure whose short life extends from 1789 to 1848) than as a writer who can link the progressive element of Renaissance humanism to a popular-festive interest in the cultivation of life rather than the acquisition of power. As we shall see in Chapter 7, in Bakhtin's eyes political power does not thrust you onto the historical stage, but merely allows you to make a fool of yourself. The class or person—it makes little difference in his theory—who occupies the political heights may impress its point of view on the world, but its essence remains as private as if it had never left the domestic hearth. Pragmatism or 'interestedness', whether economic or political, condemns its bearer to the contingency of a private, dissociated ego, no matter on what scale it pursues its goals.

Bakhtin's third hero, Dostoevsky, was, like Bakhtin himself, askew to the bourgeois political project merely by virtue of being Russian. *Problems of Dostoevsky's Art* accordingly argued for the enlargement of the individual perspective by skipping over historical life entirely. Dostoevsky's heroes become 'distinctively disinterested and principled' not as defenders of bourgeois legality or constitutionalism, but as members of a metaphysical community constructed out of 'purely human material' (*PDA* 241/281). Their ethical high-mindedness derives from a utopian, invented sociality rather than a historical one.

Thus the spectacular appearance of the public square and its linguistic expression, heteroglossia, indicates a significant change of tack. For heteroglossia is that moment at which linguistic distinctions match up with socio-ideological ones, when precipitation in linguistic form is a precondition for the existence of historical points of view, when history no longer lurks either beneath or above the surface of discourse, but is embodied in unique configurations of lexis, grammar, and style. Even in

---

[1] From Bakhtin's opening remarks at the defence: 'And as I wandered through this field, I came upon Rabelais, in whose work this world of unfinished, unconsummated being, the world of grotesque forms, was very thoroughly revealed, revealed at the junction of two epochs—our contemporary consciousness, and that past one of which his novel is the continuation, the development and the consummation. Therefore, to a certain degree, his novel may serve as a key to this world of grotesque form' ('Stenogramma', 56).

This refusal to consign medieval culture to the dustbin of history called forth an angry reply from one of those present, M. P. Teriaeva: 'When you speak of Rabelais, of his language, of his system of images, then, in the end, which Rabelais remains? In your work the Rabelais who remains is not the Rabelais whom we love and know best of all—Rabelais the humanist and fighter against all medieval obscurantism; instead there remains a Rabelais with his class essence emasculated' ('Stenogramma', 75).

the book on Dostoevsky, Bakhtin was having doubts—probably inspired by Voloshinov's work on Saussure—as to whether the pure voice was bodily enough an entity to carry the burden of historical becoming. But it is only when he asks the novel to bear the burden of historical becoming that acquiring sociological definition becomes a *sine qua non* of participation in unconsummated historical life. And at the same moment as Bakhtin finds the right genre for the task, he discovers the right community for it— the 'heteroglot' public square.

THE IMAGE OF THE PUBLIC SQUARE

We should immediately be suspicious. Can the language of a community so neatly correspond to the language of a particular genre? No one doubts that modern European societies, characterized by an unprecedented degree of social differentiation and mobility, generate a vast range of technical languages, jargons, social dialects, and the like. But stylistic details do not by definition have socio-ideological significance, and there is another way to interpret the fact of linguistic differentiation, deriving from Lukács rather than Bakhtin: that the multiplication of specialized languages is a symptom of reification, the separating off and technicization of human powers. Perhaps these developing languages and modes of discourse don't express anything as coherent, or even interesting, as a value or point of view? Conversely, ideological structures do not necessarily manifest themselves in the form of a recognizable language. One can accept the view of society as a field of endlessly, even randomly clashing interests, without assuming that heteroglossia will follow. The distinguishing feature of the latter is the assumption that socially distinct experiences will be articulated as *language* (i.e. by means of the creation of distinct, ideologically charged syntactic, grammatical, and lexical forms). But social pressures and conflicts are not always translated into coherent languages or ideologies; they may find expression by other means: as 'nonsensical' ruptures in normal language or social practice, or as a turning away from language altogether, to retreat into silence or resort to physical force.[2] Such eventualities are not covered by the concept of heteroglossia, which assumes that ideological distinctions play themselves out as a 'heteroglot conception of the world', confronting the ordinary speaker. But do we invariably interpret stylistic features as signs of social ideologies?

As for language in general, the answer is clearly no. But within the bounds of the novel . . . there things are as they should be, 'in the novel

---

[2] On the expression of class interests in the form of ruptures rather than articulate ideologies see Nicos Poulantzas, *State, Power, Socialism*, trans. Patrick Camiller (London: Verso, 1978), 152–7.

the formal markers of languages, manners and styles are symbols of social horizons' (DN 169/357). What is presented in heteroglossia as the natural state of affairs, 'the social ideologeme knit together with its own discourse, its own language' is, not coincidentally, the aesthetic project of the novel itself. All of which reminds us that the true function of 'novels' within Bakhtin's scheme is not to gather already existing styles from the marketplace, but to create them, by bonding social ideology tightly to identifiable linguistic form.

In a moment of Hegelian weakness, Bakhtin claimed that 'heteroglossia-in-itself becomes in the novel and thanks to the novel heteroglossia-for-itself' (DN 211/400). But the novel does not realize tendencies which flow spontaneously out of social life, for the novel is Bakhtin's word for these tendencies themselves. The distinction between the image of a language within the novel and a socio-ideological language outside the novel is, in Bakhtin's terms, meaningless, for the historical context that makes language into 'socio-ideological language' is dependent upon a novelistic (which is to say, narrative) intersubjectivity to begin with. In short, heteroglossia, if it existed, would constitute the 'novelization' of the social world. A desirable situation, perhaps, but not a neutral description of 'discourse in life', or even of latent properties of language, striving for expression.

Is the heteroglossia of the public square just an illusion, then? Not so much an illusion as a peculiar kind of double reflection. At the beginning of this study I argued that the novel denotes a form of modern intersubjectivity, which can be found outside printed texts as well as within them. Despite appearances, the public square is not the historical origin of that intersubjectivity: it is a sociological *image* of it, the reflection in an imagined form of social life of the 'images of language' whose actual origin is in the novel. Rather than fill his public square with a historically precise 'people', Bakhtin populates it with peasant Balzacs and merchant Dostoevskys, who speak with all the sophistication and modernity of proper novelists. Because the public square is presented as an image, we are tempted to think that speaking in socio-ideological languages comes naturally to them, but in fact it is the public square itself, as a kind of novel come to life, which must create this language. This explains the peculiar indeterminacy of public square heteroglossia, which appears at once as something historical and yet also something imagined, 'given' and 'set as a task' at one and the same time. As a concrete image derived from a philosophy of modern language, it reminds us of modern intersubjectivity but in a form which is, if you like, too immediate to be convincing. No one looks to Bakhtin's discussion of the public square for historical illumination—nor should they, however important public squares have been—but they nonetheless sense the pulse of something familiar.

The public square is an image of oral speech—everyday, informal language and conversation; the novel is, even in Bakhtin's philosophical account, written or printed, and thereby formalized communication. We may think that the first is concrete and ordinary, the latter abstract and secondary. But a public square in which people speak as novelists draws our attention to a central fact of discourse, which I want to call the *uneven structuring of language*. Language is unevenly structured in the sense that it is composed not of more or less equivalent utterances spoken by more or less equivalent individuals, but of a series of interacting forms of discourse and intersubjectivity, which vary according to the durability of the utterance, the size and nature of speaker and audience, the degree and kind of literacy required for participation, as well as the social context in which such discourse can take place.[3] Although the face-to-face conversation may appear as the most natural and spontaneous form of language, as in one sense it is, a theory of language which models itself on this kind of inter-subjectivity alone takes no account of the historical transformation of language itself. To use the putatively 'ordinary' dialogue as an analytical model for the television broadcast, the government directive, the religious service or cultic ceremony, the written record or literary text is mislead-ing, in so far as all these forms will appear somehow compromised—distant, indirect, or unbalanced—in comparison with the idealized speak-ing norm. Not only do such intersubjective forms often entail some kind of internal unevenness, such as a clear and irreversible distinction between speaker and listener, the relations among them are also uneven. Writing, then print, then the electronic media of the twentieth century, have endowed certain speech acts with a reach and force distinct from others, while oral conversation retains a flexibility and reciprocity which 'medi-ated' forms cannot always match. The unevenness runs along many different axes, and there is no single form of language which holds the trump card. But it is this uneven structuring which defines the physiog-nomy of our speech life, and it is the same structure which determines what politically significant access to a common language really means. To describe language as a vast ocean of utterances, speech acts, or undiffer-entiated *parole*, all more or less alike, is to homogenize a more complexly articulated process.

[3] While this argument has some similarities with the programme Foucault famously outlined in 'The Order of Discourse' (in Robert Young (ed.), *Untying the Text: A Post-Structuralist Reader* (Boston, Mass., London, and Henley: Routledge & Kegan Paul, 1981), 48–78), its general emphasis is different. First, my starting-point is a conception of language as the form of inter-subjectivity, rather than as a self-propelling process of discourse. Secondly, Foucault conceives of the ordering and rarefying procedures as instruments of control: they guard against the spontaneity of discourse itself; I do not assume that the unevenness in language is always a matter of control or repression.

If by 'language' we meant only grammar and vocabulary, then the presence of these plebeian novelists in the public square would have only curiosity value. But Bakhtin argued that one could not understand even simple formal structures outside of the intersubjective and narrative contexts which give them meaning. He used the term 'author' to refer both to the narrative structure of a certain kind of printed text *and* to a perspective available in everyday intersubjectivity. Apparently, he thought this would prove that the novel, or the work of prose art more generally, was the flowering of a tendency in ordinary speech; in the event, he demonstrated the opposite conclusion—that the modern verbal world he called 'the novel' has become a structural feature, though not the only feature, of our everyday, even oral, discourse. To the extent that novelistic discourse modernizes language, its effects are felt throughout the speech world. The historical consciousness of novelistic style, its national reach, its narrative conventions, its secular interest in everyday detail, its extended vocabulary, its new capacity for self-reflection, its 'sobriety and simplicity': all these modern linguistic innovations become *differentially* available to the members of a speech community, invading and restructuring existing speech forms. When Bakhtin insists we need a new philosophy of language to appreciate these innovations, he slips us the information that this image of the cultural past is simply his philosophy of language made flesh. But the philosophy of language is in turn the reflection of historical facts it does not acknowledge—cultural innovations like the modern press, the nineteenth-century university, the mass printed book, popular education, and, of course, the novel itself, which decisively altered the discourse of Europe. There are plebeian subjectivities endowed with novelistic verve and modern capabilities, but they owe these to history rather than the spontaneity of the public square. The latter's habitués have intersubjective capabilities which only a modernized uneven structure can generate.

Bakhtin did not draw this conclusion. He could not, given that his interest was in a community of unique individuals, made autonomous through discourse, but in some sense ultimately responsible before a deity rather than through one another. For this reason he ceaselessly conflated structures outside face-to-face dialogue—the novel being the obvious example—with face-to-face dialogue, as if the first were ultimately reducible to the second. The historical truth lying behind his insights is more in evidence when he describes what *opposes* the public square. When he can separate off the historical fact of modernity from those aspects of it he wishes to exploit, he feels free to describe uneven structures: to be exact, the uneven facts of a 'unified language' (*edinyi iazyk*).

THE 'UNIFIED LANGUAGE'

In 'Discourse in the Novel' Bakhtin described the 'unified language' as an idea and a fact which dominated European linguistic consciousness and which was specifically responsible for making it impossible to grasp the novel's aesthetic distinctiveness. His definition is revealing:

The category of unified language is the theoretical expression of historical processes of linguistic unification and centralization, the expression of the centripetal forces of language. A unified language is not given, but is, in essence, always set as a task [*zadan*] and in every moment of linguistic life it opposes actual heteroglossia. But at the same time it is real as a force overcoming this heteroglossia, setting defined borders for it, guaranteeing a certain maximum of mutual understanding and crystallizing in the real, though relative, unity of a ruling conversational (everyday) and literary language, 'correct language'. (DN 83–4/270)

Not given but set as a task, and, at the same time, a real force opposing 'actual' heteroglossia: what is this unified language? Bakhtin makes clear that it is not a question of 'a system of elementary forms (linguistic symbols) guaranteeing a *minimum* of understanding in practical communication' (DN 84/271): it is not the weak unity of a national language allowing variation within its bounds. But how can it be an actual constituent of the language world, a socio-ideological language in its own right, and at the same time a force throughout linguistic life as a whole? Despite Bakhtin's wild historical generalizations, the historical identity of the unified language is clear enough: it is not the Latin of medieval Europe, but the prestige or so-called standard form of a European vernacular ('a hard and stable linguistic kernel', as he describes it, within a 'heteroglot national language' (DN 84/271)). It is, of course, characteristic of such standard forms that most of the national population *does not use them* in ordinary speech, and, indeed, may not be able to use them at all (in England the prestige form is defined largely by accent—'received pronunciation'—and is consciously defined by the minority status— Oxbridge- or public school-educated, and the like—of its speakers). Yet it is true enough that 'every utterance participates in the "unified language"' (DN 85/272), like it or not.

Every utterance participates in it because it is part of its discursive world, one of the structures within it, even if it is not the one used for ordinary speech or writing. Standard forms of a national language dominate the discursive field by becoming the language of crucial institutions of political and cultural power: what constitutes them as standard is not the degree to which they are spoken, but their administrative and political reach. In this sense, the definition of a unified language is political rather than linguistic—it is language which needs to be unified because of the social institutions with which it is bound up. (The standard form of Italian, for example, was the national language of Italy, even though until 1982 less than half of all Italians used it as their first language. It was national not by virtue of common use, but because of when and where it was used, and by whom.)[4] But the power of such modern 'official' languages does not reside solely in their ability to maintain the coherence and exclusiveness of a ruling group (bureaucrats, a political class, army officers, and so on); it does not work only through efficient segregation. For although used by a minority, the unified language exercises pressure on the language world beyond it; its institution simultaneously marginalizes popular language by branding it 'common' or uneducated, and it accumulates resources systematically denied to other forms of the language.[5] You cannot force everyone to speak the standard or official language, nor do you usually want to. But the very existence of this language, and its relative position in political and cultural life, alters what is possible for every other kind of language. If dictionaries, literary expression, educational efforts, and media production are orientated to the development of one form, it affects all others, and affects the way we regard all others.[6] Every utterance participates in the unified language, because every utterance is affected by the fact of its existence.

From the perspective of formal linguistics, that is, of a linguistics concerned with formal structures of grammar and vocabulary alone, such heteroglot tensions are difficult to describe. There is, of course, an impressive socio-linguistic literature detailing the role of linguistic variation and substantial work on the operation of linguistic authority, but the idea of one form restructuring another, so to speak, is alien to any perspective which takes a unified linguistic system as its norm.[7] It is the uneven structuring of language which makes such otherwise bizarre phenomena comprehensible as language. We encounter unified 'standard' language in specific oral contexts and, denizens of the twentieth century as

[4] Information from Nigel Vincent, 'Italian', in Bernard Comrie (ed.), *The Major Languages of Western Europe* (London: Routledge, 1990), 271.

[5] A classic and theoretically sophisticated account of this process can be found in Étienne Balibar and Pierre Macherey, 'On Literature as an Ideological Form', in Young (ed.), *Untying the Text*, 79–99.

[6] On the role of 'standard English' and the cultural weaponry used to develop it, see Tony Crowley, *The Politics of Discourse: The Standard Language Question in British Cultural Debates* (Basingstoke: Macmillan, 1989).

[7] On linguistic variation, see William Labov, *Sociolinguistic Patterns* (Oxford: Basil Blackwell, 1978). On the operation of linguistic authority see James and Lesley Milroy, *Authority in Language: Investigating Language Prescription and Standardisation*, 2nd edn. (London: Routledge, 1991); Lesley Milroy, *Language and Social Networks*, 2nd edn. (Oxford: Basil Blackwell, 1987); and Renate Bartsch, *Norms of Language* (London and New York: Longman, 1987).

we are, in the reproduction of oral speech through the electronic media (first radio and the movies, then television, now video). We do not need to use it ourselves for it to exercise a structuring force on our everyday speech; encountering it in, say, formal educational contexts and the media is more than enough. But it depends for its force on its presence in specific regions of language use, for if it existed only as the language of a minority it would exclude, but not have any ideological or cultural significance for the rest of language. And regrettable as we may feel the existence of such official languages is, their existence calls our attention to the fact that the languages of the newspaper, or the radio broadcast, or the television programme, are something we participate in whether or not we want to—they are part of the structure of our linguistic world, which any kind of cultural politics has to bear in mind. In short, *Gesellschaft*—as modernity, differentiation, a society full of relatively autonomous levels and structures—is the order of the day, even in the human recesses of language, and any attempt to democratize it cannot get around this central historical fact.

Bakhtin certainly tried hard to do so. By opposing unified language to actual heteroglossia, monologism to dialogism, he sought to define the authoritarian as the destruction or repression of linguistic diversity from on high, the flattening of vibrant heteroglossia by central institutions. And yet even from his own description it is clear that 'poetic' texts, the unified language, monological discourse, and the rest do not ignore the fact of linguistic differentiation but depend upon it; they are, so to speak, the strategic reaction of the politically authoritarian to this inescapable circumstance. Conversely, dialogism and the novelistic are not spontaneous effects of life, but themselves the product of an unevenly structured social world, depending as much on cultural institutions, new technologies, and formalized skills like literacy, as their political opponents. From a theoretical point of view, official-poetic language and novelistic language are both 'dialogical', as both are strategies for dealing with the facts of linguistic diversity and modernity. Bakhtin's comment about the actuality of heteroglossia, with the reservations above, has therefore an element of historical truth in it. Modern language is heteroglot in the sense that mass politics and culture, differentiated societies, and a multi-levelled discursive world constitute the terrain on which all politics, including, naturally enough, 'cultural politics', takes place. When political authoritarianism takes root in modern European society, it has to take a recognizably modern form, which means not ignoring or setting to one side the speech of 'the people', and not discounting modernity's uneven restructuring of the linguistic world, but incorporating it into a cultural strategy. It was precisely these considerations which led Europe's most linguistically orientated revolutionary, Antonio Gramsci, to the conclusion that both Left and Right struggled not for absolute ideological domination, but for 'hegemony' within a field which was not of their own making.

The public square thus represents a response to the problems of a modern, partly democratized linguistic world; it is not that democratized world itself. It constitutes heteroglossia as a desirable end, it does not merely acknowledge its prior existence. Which ought to remind us, if we need reminding, that, despite appearances, Bakhtin's theory of language does not, and cannot, constitute a politics in itself, just as any theory of language cannot constitute a politics in itself. Bakhtin recognizes the democratization of language and, in his own way, urges it on, but this is on the basis of philosophical and social beliefs irreducible to ideas about language. Just as the values behind dialogism cannot be traced back to the bare fact of dialogue, so the public square does not derive its qualities from the 'historical becoming and social struggle' it plays host to, for it is responsible for the kind of social struggle and historical becoming we find in it. The apparently spontaneous force of the public square implies it is something we must either accept or reject in full, but its picture of a historical struggle of languages is in fact quite carefully drawn, and it is worth examining some of its features in detail. Here I want to look more carefully at three: its representative structure, its conception of historical 'becoming', and its institution of a form of responsibility based on roles rather than 'pure voice'.

REPRESENTATION

The language of the public square is heteroglot, but this heteroglossia orders rather than reflects the diversity of modern language. Diversity alone is too factual for Bakhtin, and demands a principle which will transform it into something meaningful:

Between all these 'languages' of heteroglossia there are the most profound methodological distinctions: at their basis there lie completely different principles of specification and formation (in some cases a functional principle, in others, a content-thematic one, in a third group, a strictly social-dialectological one). Therefore the languages do not exclude one another and intersect in a variety of ways (the Ukrainian language, the language of epic poetry, the language of early Symbolism, the language of the student, the language of a generation, the language of the minor intellectual, the language of the Nietzschean, and so on). It may seem that the very word 'language' loses all meaning in the face of this, for there is evidently no single plane on which all these 'languages' can be juxtaposed. But in actual fact, there is a common plane methodologically justifying our juxtaposition of them: all the languages of heteroglossia, no matter what principle their particularization is based on, are specific points of view on the world . . . (DN 104/291)

Or can be made into points of view, when necessary. This vision of heteroglossia has the advantage of levelling a linguistic field which is itself uneven. For the difference between a newspaper and a shout in the street is not a difference in point of view, and it takes some doing to make it appear that way. If every language is defined according to different criteria, then extracting a full-blooded ideology from each of them is going to depend on a new context, the formal principle of which will be the production of ideological positions as such. The public square is this new context.

Like a parody of the salon life it implicitly criticizes, in the public square one simply has to have an opinion. No linguistic element can pass itself off as merely functional or practical, as instrumental or accidental, for every element must participate in the articulation of an ideology or project transcending the here-and-now of the utterance. In other words, in the public square language is forced not only to express and refer, but also to represent; it serves not just as an instance of language, but as the image of a language drawn from beyond the bounds of the square itself. The student, Nietzschean, Ukrainian, or Symbolist may have arrived on private business, but once through the gate he or she must speak *as* a student, Nietzschean, Ukrainian, or Symbolist. Within the context of the square one's private world becomes a world-view, personal passion is transmuted into public conflict, and one has not only to make small talk, but to make history. However disparate the participants involved, they share an un-thematized, subtextual narrative of transformation, in which they leave their practical cares behind for the pure business of ideological dialogue and debate.

Perhaps the most concrete sociological observation Bakhtin ever made was that the catastrophic nature of Russian capitalism, its sudden intro-duction from outside civil society itself, was a condition of the emergence of Dostoevsky's polyphony: such a coexistence of discrete voices, he argued, could only arise when communities which had existed in a state of relative isolation were thrown together in a moment of sudden modernization (*PDA* 30/19–20). The implied geographical narrative—a journey from local context to urban metropolis, itself, of course, a great nineteenth-century theme—is arguably a metaphor for a different plot, that of the movement of interests across institutions from the local and private to the cosmopolitan and public. The word in the public square, like that of the novel, tastes of 'two contexts', a home from which it acquires energy and a purpose, and the public square itself, which forces it into the form of an ideology. Except that Bakhtin, however much he writes about this second context, refuses to recognize it as such: he would like to think of it as a place where people feel free to express themselves, rather than as an institution in which people are *compelled* to express themselves. David Lloyd and Paul Thomas have argued that the idea of culture as a sphere in which higher aspirations are represented depended on the belief that this was a function which had to be discharged by cultural specialists on behalf of a generally disenfranchised populace. 'Its transcendence of specialization and division in order to provide a space of reconciliation', they write, 'nonetheless depends itself on a differentiating specialization of function.'[8] As an instrument of culture, the public square is precisely such a specialized 'representative' institution, a definite context rather than the truth of all contexts.

It is first and foremost a national context, the place where a 'heteroglot national language' can take shape. The market square of medieval times had, of course, a constituency both smaller and bigger than the nation: smaller, because it served a local agricultural community or parish, bigger because it could be host to merchants or traders travelling from faraway lands. But Bakhtin is not describing a medieval public square, he is describing a modern discursive space as a medieval public square. The making public of ideologies and positions, the assumed legitimacy of popular points of view, the conception of society as a differentiated arena of conflicting values—these are features of a national public discourse, premised on the identity of people and nation, and on a secular conception of the structure of society.

It is not, however, identical with what political theory might call 'civil society', that is, the ordinary social and economic life of the nation. For what is strictly impermissible in the public square is, in fact, precisely the business of medieval, Renaissance, and modern public squares—trade and bargaining, buying and selling, the pursuit of earthly satisfactions and private profit. To the extent that it screens out every motive unconnected with the cultivation of a pure, disinterested ideological position, a position orientated to the ultimate, not the usual, questions, it declares itself an exceptional cultural space, dedicated to the extraordinary cultivation of ideologies which lie dormant in everyday 'practically interested' discourse. And however deep and passionate the populism which animates a text like 'Discourse in the Novel', to the extent that the cultivation of ideologies is deemed an extraordinary pursuit, distinct from everyday life, it will require a cadre of extraordinary specialists—to wit, the intellectuals.

National intellectuals in modern Europe spend a great deal of time talking—in coffee houses, cafés, learned societies, and universities—but their

[8] *Culture and the State* (New York and London: Routledge, 1997), 65.

principal medium has been the printed word. Historically, it was the printing press which brought national languages into being as 'print-languages'
(to use Benedict Anderson's phrase), and it was publications like the newspaper, the monthly or weekly journal, and the book which created an
effectively national discursive space.[9] The image of the public square
implies open oral interchange, but the features of its language depend on a
secular and vernacular print culture. The languages of heteroglossia meet—
Bakhtin knows this perfectly well—not outside the artist's study, but in the
pages of printed texts.

HISTORICAL 'BECOMING'

Having willed this 'struggle among socio-linguistic points of view' into
being, however, Bakhtin is strikingly averse to taking what, in any liberal
democracy, would be the obvious next step: resolving the struggle or
deciding amongst its constituent points of view. Unlike the public sphere,
the public square does not encourage discourse in order to produce a
rational outcome, freed from local prejudice, but in order to produce a
'historical becoming' which Bakhtin has freed from the burden of making
decisions. Making a decision, in the sense of judging one perspective
closer to the truth than others, is, in fact, not only unnecessary, but
dangerous to the public square. Dialogue which succumbs to the desire for
ordinary cognitive truth ends up selling its birthright for the pleasures of
mere 'rhetoric': 'In rhetoric there are the unconditionally innocent and the
unconditionally guilty, there is complete victory and there is annihilation
of the opponent. In dialogue the annihilation of an opponent also annihi-
lates the dialogical sphere of the life of the word itself' (N70–71, 375/150).
This presumably calculated affront to rhetoric—the very art of which was
central to the public square of classical democracy—tells us more about
Bakhtin's project than he probably intended. The practice of classical
rhetoric is central to the social life of antiquity precisely to the extent that
politics is central to it. In a context where the latter is deemed an
ennobling and fulfilling pursuit, an argument with winners and losers is not
a catastrophe for social relations. But Bakhtin downgrades politics, and
with it, rhetoric, because in the background of his public square lie
Christian values which, in his case at least, force the logic of political
decisions and consequences into second place. A Christian public square:
the idea is not in the least bit strange, for many of the public squares of
medieval and Renaissance Europe are organized around cathedrals or
churches. Yet Bakhtin has no interest in these actual historical spaces, for

[9] Benedict Anderson, *Imagined Communities*, 37–46.

their focus was not vibrant popular discourse, but the commanding presence of the building itself, which, as Sitte pointed out, was sited so that it could dominate the visual space of the square.[10] When Bakhtin comes to discuss the public square as a historical phenomenon he will therefore focus on a different, 'popular-festive' religiosity, orientated not to the Church but to the streets and square just beyond it, as if this represented a liberation from its authority.

Dispute and social struggle are fine, so long as they never end. This apparently unchristian belief in the virtues of permanent conflict makes Bakhtin less rather than more pertinent as a social or political thinker. For it stems from the conviction that historical becoming is not articulated by decision and action, but by the *autocriticism of discourse* (DN 223/412) embodied in the novelistic voice. The languages of the public square do not strive to convince, but to maintain a constant pressure on one another, so that each and every ideology will be reminded of its necessarily unfinished character. Social struggle is therefore not the cause of historical becoming in Bakhtin's schema, but the index of it. And it is *social* rather than the individual struggle so beloved of liberalism and bourgeois civil society which counts, precisely because the latter ends (in victory for one or the other side, or in compromise), while the former is inexhaustible. When individuals struggle with one another, it can only be for goals articulated within a form of life (or so at least Bakhtin assumes); only when they can narrate that form of life from the outside, when they can represent a social language as a historical style of intersubjectivity, do they sense the fragility of the values and structures they work within, and their need for justification in the future. At the point when they see their language as the structure of a kind of intersubjectivity rather than as a tool, their activity becomes 'immersed in social heteroglossia, reinterpreted through it' (DN 139/326) and is borne aloft by the powerful forward-moving flow of historical culture.

But this willingness to stand on the sidelines of social struggle and admire the view depends on Bakhtin's dogmatic distinction between *I* and *other*. If, as argued in Chapter 5, the narrative integrity of voices, and their corresponding forms of life, depends on autonomy and judgement as much as aesthetics and love, then the balance between struggle and decision begins to look a little different. Bakhtin assumes that what he calls voices or socio-ideological languages are made whole when the ethical impulses of subjects

---

[10] On the medieval public square in its architectural aspect, see Camillo Sitte, *City Planning according to Artistic Principles* [1889], trans. in George R. Collins and Christiane Crasemann Collins, *Camillo Sitte: The Birth of Modern City Planning* (New York: Rizzoli, 1986). In this polemic with modern architectural style, Sitte defended the medieval practice of building squares as a gathering space for the Church, and opposed this to the practice of designing squares with the flow of pedestrians and vehicles in mind.

are narratively aestheticized by an author or an *other*, and that subjects can only represent their discourse to themselves by means of a certain inner irony or distance. Styles of language or intersubjectivity, however, with their mix of ethical and aesthetic features, are elaborated cooperatively among subjects, and the roles assigned to the *I* or the *other* in this process are not fixed. The element in them which endows a form of life with a sense of justification or narrative meaning is therefore not a gift bestowed or withheld according to the charity of the *other*, but the product of judgements or decisions made in the course of intersubjective language practice itself. Sometimes these decisions, which are decisions about symbolic roles and authority, the meaning of our actions, and the shape our linguistic and social interchange should take, are the product of open and explicit discussion; more often they depend on implicit consent to, or refusal of, innovations offered to the users of a language. In the end, however—and here Saussure was right—some kind of decision is made, for a language undergirding a form of life is maintained by nothing else besides the agreement of those who participate in it.

An intersubjectivity with these options is one which makes history in a discriminating fashion. It does not endorse every claim to symbolic authority, no matter what its substance, nor does it accept every narrative shaping of words or actions which subjects have to offer. It picks and chooses, and often says no. And, as we all know too well, the picking and choosing of language forms takes place not on a level playing field, but in an unevenly structured linguistic world, in which some speakers and institutions have a great deal more influence than others. And that is why historical becoming, in actuality as opposed to Bakhtin's philosophy, consists of violent struggle as much as verbal give-and-take: because its narratives, *pace* Bakhtin, are made by turning-points and decisions which are often enforced on *others* by fiat rather than presented to them as a gift.

The endless development of Bakhtin's public square stems from the fact that, within its bounds, no one says no: it represents the utopia of a differentiated society in which every socio-ideological language develops spontaneously, and no story conflicts with another. It is a context without narrative substance of its own, which nevertheless allows every language within it to acquire a narrative movement and shape. All of which is designed to convince us that language acquires historical momentum by virtue of a simple and certain self-reflexivity. It can begin to 'become' by becoming aware of its historical position, and all that stands in its way is non-reflexive, 'serious', monologism. But that is not all that stands in the way of a language developing historically: other languages stand in the way. For historical becoming means that some languages develop at the expense of others, not in the sense that the latter are extinguished (though that happens too), but in the sense that any narrative contextualization of languages places them in unequal and different relations—some advance and develop, others are marginalized, or merely stand still. This is obviously true not only of any particular literary novel one cares to name, but of the social world itself, the arrangements of which cater for all manner of socially distinct styles, but always in a form which establishes definite relations of power and authority among them. This means more than that certain languages are perceived as having relative prestige; it means that certain forms have access to institutional contexts (media, educational institutions, dictionaries, publishers, and so on) which encourage them to develop as others do not. Neither is this a sign of the wretched state of the world: wretched it may be, but the condition of historical change in the linguistic world is the making of decisions about what sort of language one wants to use, and decisions inevitably have consequences for the 'lives' of those languages one chooses not to use.

But had Bakhtin admitted that a struggle amongst socio-linguistic points of view entails winners and losers, and constant hard choices, he could not have claimed that a language with a sense of its context is by virtue of that fact alone an active participant in historical life. In *any* dialogue speakers have to adopt an authorial position on their conversation as a whole, in order to coordinate their utterances: language consists not just of what one says, but of the narrative which makes this a move in the social world, thereby endowing one's utterance with a concrete intersubjective significance. But in most cases this authorial context is not something the speakers invent, but something they must accept merely to engage in successful social discourse. Whether or not a particular style of language or intersubjectivity becomes, in Bakhtin's sense, historical, therefore depends on the power speakers have in shaping narrative contexts, and this in turn depends on the situation of particular dialogues within the uneven structuring of language as a whole. The very category of 'reported speech' so central first to Voloshinov, then to Bakhtin, illustrates this. For it depended on the intersection of new printed forms of language, having a distinctive social physiognomy and origin, with oral and written speech which could come from very different social and political spaces. You could not call the printed 'reporting' form the self-reflection of all the oral or written 'reported' forms, unless you imagined language as one vast homogeneous entity. A concrete, narratively meaningful utterance arises not from the self-awareness of discourse itself, but from a collision of elements from different places in the unevenly structured linguistic world.

If the dual role of author and actor is one we have to play merely to speak at all, then the decisive issue is not whether one speaks 'culturally' or instrumentally, as a socially orientated author or as a practically interested actor, but how this metalinguistic relation is articulated across the existing structures of communication. Bakhtin's hostility to the grasping, forward-moving *I* masks a deeper analysis of the problem. Although he often echoed the hostility of fellow cultural critics and philosophers to the vulgar interestedness of bourgeois civil society and its means-orientated actors, at other times he implied that he did not believe in the possibility of a compromised, purely practical, means-orientated intersubjectivity. A sphere in which ideal values did not determine conduct would be a sphere beyond language itself, and this, on his account, is nonsensical:

The rift between real everyday life [*byt*] and symbolic ritual. The unnaturalness of this rift. Their false opposition. People say: in those days everyone travelled in troikas with bells, that was real life [*byt*]. But in everyday life there remains a carnival overtone, and in literature this can become the fundamental tone. Pure everyday life is a fiction, an invention of intellectuals. Human everyday life is always endowed with form, and this endowment with form always has an element of ritual (even if only 'aesthetic'). (N70–71, 379/154)

Meaningless, endless, probably repetitive everyday life is therefore not so much a product of modernity as one of its leading fictions. Bakhtin thus parts company with the line of cultural criticism with which he otherwise has a great deal in common—the critique of instrumental reason. According to the line of cultural argument which extends from early sociology through to Habermas, the sin of capitalist civilization is that it introduces a means-orientated, instrumental rationality which worries only about how to be efficient, rather than about the values of one's actions. Whether this is expressed in Weber's idea of 'purposive-rational action', the Frankfurt School's idea of instrumental reason, or Habermas's concept of strategic action, it expresses the belief in the possibility of a mode of conduct where unrationalized interests drive one forward. The strategic actor aims to manipulate others, or maximize profits, or maintain power, and he (one may as well let it remain a he in this case) *uses* language to achieve the desired result. The obvious question is whether such a thing is, in fact, possible, or whether the strategic actor is merely a useful fiction for those who hope that culture or language in themselves are a source of cooperative and unselfish human effort. One could hardly deny that people act instrumentally—that they manipulate others, make cost-benefit calculations, seek to maximize their power and wealth, or just react in self-defence. But whether one can explain this by recourse to the political-economic category of 'interest' (class or personal), the ethico-religious idea of the selfish, or belief in an ego which can effectively isolate itself from intersubjective considerations, is another matter. Whenever Bakhtin reduces the contrast between dialogism and monologism to the distinction

between a relation to personalities and a relation to things (as in his philosophical notes from the 1940s) he joins forces with this Romantic camp.
But at those points where he admits 'the general dialogicity of all speech
genres (all forms of verbal intercourse) and the relative difference between
dialogue and monologue' (D-II, 223), he is compelled to find a different
explanation for this oddly self-possessed mode of action.

If instrumental or monological speech cannot be explained and condemned as uncultured speech, authorless speech, speech without a sense of
its own narrative frame or its necessarily intersubjective situation, then the
issue is no longer whether speech is framed or narrativized but how speech
is framed or narrativized (and the public square is no longer the place
where you discover that it is framed, but a particular kind of frame). In his
early attempts at a 'first philosophy', Bakhtin had argued that 'elementary
biological and economic motivation' became the impulse for social action
when culture became too distant from 'life'. But the turn to language and
literary forms rendered the idea of a primitive, uncultured kind of action
nonsensical, and from the 1930s onwards Bakhtin contrasted not culture
and mere biological life, but different forms of culture, embodied in
different types of narrative. In his study of Rabelais, the essay 'Epic and
Novel', and his fragments on the *Bildungsroman* Bakhtin demonstrated that
official culture depended on an epic or serious kind of narrativization,
which soaked up meaning and gave it a mythic, substantial form, leaving
everyday life shattered and bled white. Its aim was not to prevent the
emergence of other languages or the private activity of subjects, but to
dominate them narratively, to determine the shape and meaning of their
quasi-independent efforts. The epic narrative, for example, embodied all
value in the heroic figures of an unreachable national past, who could only
be approached by the reverential act of recounting their already known
stories. By making this the central narrative act, epic ensured that the
historical significance of present activity would be measured by its closeness to or distance from acts and figures who literally embodied everything
virtuous and admirable. The naturally public activities of the state would
thereby be in a position to present themselves as modern equivalents of
history's past glories, while stories beyond the public world, however well
functioning, would find themselves condemned to the sphere of the contingent and the historically insignificant.

Social conflict therefore takes the form not of a struggle between
languages which are developing over time, but of a struggle over the
context, narrative or otherwise, which will embody the development of
some languages at the expense of others. But modern societies are over-
producers of language and narrative, and, rather than throw all their efforts
into one arena, they spread them around the various levels and institutions

of the social structure. Competing languages thus do not struggle on the level surface of the city square, as Bakhtin imagined, but in the urban maze of an unevenly structured linguistic world. Some occupy positions in the great public buildings, others have their strongholds in the streets or underground, and their weapons are as various and as specialized as those of a modern army: media broadcasts (on television, film, radio), audio recordings, newspapers and magazines, dictionaries, novels, public meetings and parliamentary sessions, software programs, not to mention the house-to-house weapons used so casually in oral speech. And just as armies have subjective as well as objective resources (such as discipline and fighting experience), so the ability of speakers to advance their linguistic cause depends on education (formal and informal), expertise, and the qualities Benjamin once summarized as 'courage, humour, cunning and fortitude'. In the 1960s Hans Magnus Enzensberger shrewdly observed that Western societies had to train the very intellectuals they hoped would maintain traditional hegemonies, and that this entailed creating reflexive and scientific powers which could not necessarily be kept in check.[11] He was right, and his observation reminds us not only that linguistic and cultural resources are unequally distributed, but that in the end languages and their narrative forms can only 'become' in the mouths of those they have to persuade.

Social conflict does not therefore prove that historical becoming is alive and well, precisely because it is among other things a conflict over what will historically become, and what will not. Bakhtin could not envisage the public square as a *specific* narrative context, in which historical movement was given not just a shove but a direction. While recognizing that language became historical in a number of different narrative contexts (biographical, novelistic, epic, and so on), he could not bring himself to give the secular screw a final turn, and acknowledge that historical becoming was not an absolute value, but itself the product of linguistic argument and struggle. A democratic intersubjectivity has to endow its constituent languages with a sense of historical movement and relevance, but it cannot appeal to this historical movement as a metaphysically sanctioned value. Cultural democracy in the strict sense, as open and equal access to cultural resources, never mattered much to Bakhtin, because he assumed that the historical becoming which led to heteroglossia had already been perfected in Goethe, Rabelais, Dostoevsky, and the modern European vernaculars. He ignored the fact that once the people acquired the right to be authors, they might exercise their power in genres previously beyond their reach, and

[11] Hans Magnus Enzensberger, 'The Industrialization of the Mind', in *Critical Essays* (New York: Continuum, 1982), 3–14.

that a secular and knowledgeable citizenry might have its own ideas about what a meaningful history should look like.

ROLES AND RESPONSIBILITIES

At the same time, one cannot help but be struck by how secular and modern Bakhtin's public square creatures are. Not least because their participation in historical becoming is bound so tightly to the stratification and differentiation of language. Heteroglossia describes not merely the condition of the public square; it is also applied to the divided modern consciousness of speakers themselves. In an infamous passage Bakhtin selected a peasant as his emblem of the consciousness condemned to live in separate worlds:

Thus an illiterate peasant, far away from any centre, naïvely immersed in a still inert and unshakeable everyday life, lived in several language systems: he prayed to God in one language (Church Slavonic), sang songs in another, spoke to the family in a third, and, when starting to dictate a petition for the district authority to someone who could write, tried to speak in a fourth (the official-written language of documents). These are all *different languages* even from the point of view of abstract social-dialectological markers. But these languages were not *dialogically related* in the linguistic consciousness of the peasant; he passed from one to the other without thinking, automatically: each was beyond dispute in its own place, and the place of each was beyond dispute. He still was not able to look at one language (and the verbal world corresponding to it) through the eyes of another language (at the language of everyday and the everyday world through the language of prayer or song, or vice versa). (DN 108/295–6)

In this and the following paragraphs—in which, lo and behold, our peasant learns to think like a modern novelist—we find a characteristic mix of insight and naïvety. For while the illiterate peasant doubtless lives in a variety of linguistic spheres, his problem is not an inability to see one through the eyes of another. For the language of prayer probably does frame his experience of the language of everyday life, excluding in its very structure any hint of modern relativization. It is the hierarchy of languages, and the substance of those on top, which prevents 'critical inter-illumination', not the distance between them. And the hierarchy between languages is connected to the hierarchies within them: the illiterate peasant can speak Church Slavonic but cannot read or write it (at most he probably has so-called phonetic literacy—he can pronounce, but not understand the written language); his subordination in the face of official-literate language requires no comment, and as for home, we might assume that there are hierarchies in place there which work in his favour, but to the disadvantage of his family. If these are his problems, then there is no overarching historicizing force which can deliver him from his naïvety (in fact, Bakhtin hints, in a moment of realism, that his move to the city is what prompts some change); he cannot become modern by a simple levelling of languages, for the very levelling of languages requires modernity, not only as ideology, but as political and cultural rights as well.

Nevertheless, with this strange example of differentiation Bakhtin reminds us that a democratic language is not an undifferentiated one. The characters of all his essays enter into history through the gate of specific tasks and specific forms of discourse, each with its own pattern of development. In this sense, the responsibility which engagement with history entails is a responsibility tied to roles and historical patterns of relationship. The peasant would become a more responsible historical actor not by dispensing with his separate roles, but by rearranging the intersubjectivities within them and the relations between them. Even in his most philosophically inclined moments Bakhtin acknowledged that the separate spheres of activity had their own forms of responsibility, and that they alone could provide the content for the generalized form he sought to implant. If a life without responsibility was like a 'document without a signature', a life with only responsibility would be a signature in search of documents.

But disciplines and spheres of activity define and delimit responsibility, in a manner which Bakhtin might have thought compromised it. Participation in historical becoming requires responsibility in the secular sense, and sometimes in the legal–juridical sense as well. Although modern forms of intersubjectivity differ in the degree to which their constituent roles are reversible, certain kinds of organization demand a definition of roles distinct from the individuals who fill them, and even the most intimate relationship has to include a sense of the limits of responsibility as well. The potential for individual spheres to dictate different forms of reciprocity and responsibility is essential to them: no modern democrat can argue that every intersubjectivity, from financial planning to the one-night stand, requires reciprocity and responsibility in the same sense. By making Christian ethics *primus inter pares* in the world of responsibilities, Bakhtin thought he could establish an individuality separate from the world of social roles. But it is not another sphere of responsibility, where an ethics of conviction rules, but our ability to reflect on the pattern of existing responsibilities which guarantees our faithful effort. Only a process of reflection on our own languages, which satisfies both the need for autonomy and the need for a meaningful narrative, could guarantee that we do not, like Bakhtin's peasant, become naïvely immersed in our existing social world. But that reflection depends not upon the inner dialogical tendencies of language, but on the mastery of language's uneven structures, in the name of values irreducible to language itself.

In the public square the 'rogue, clown and fool' occupy a special position: the 'intermediate chronotope of the theatrical stage' (FTC 312/163). Intermediate because these exemplary public figures occupy two spaces at the same time: the chronotope of the life they represent in their playing, where their identity, responsibility, and project are clear and unambiguous, and the chronotope of the performance itself, from which actors and audience gain an external vantage-point on the activity represented. Bakhtin does not regard this as mere play, but as an idealized form of ethical life: 'A form of being was found where the person is a non-participating participant in life, its eternal spy and reflector, and specific forms were found for its reflection, a making public' (FTC 311/161). The right of these figures 'to be *other* in this world' (FTC 309/159) is the right to be an author in this world, to play one's role while evaluating it from a critical distance at the same time. This critical distance or other space is intrinsic to our social activities, but the ability to occupy it, that is, to reflect on a particular pattern of intersubjectivity from outside, is not granted as a general right. Bakhtin said more than he knew when he claimed that the rogue, clown, and fool were paradigmatically public figures, for the public context may be defined as precisely the intermediate space in which we see our language whilst inhabiting it.

Sometimes that second 'public' space has formal contours, with precise times for meetings, rules of discussion, and rooms or halls reserved for the occasion; at other times it is hastily improvised; perhaps most often of all it exists as a rupture in the ordinary chronotope of an established form of intersubjectivity, a moment when the need for justification suddenly emerges from the future. The novel incarnates this ambiguity in its very form; it must constantly negotiate the relationship between the author as a third person observing the events of the text and the author as a person speaking in a contemporary public world. For this reason, in the novel the question of 'personal authorship' 'arises not only on the same plane as for other genres, but on a formal-generic plane as well' (FTC 311/161). With the advent of novels in the strict sense any of the materials of everyday life (particularly the intimate materials of a private life—letters, diaries, and so on) could become an occasion for public reflection, and this dignifying of hitherto hidden, invisible space has been an essential element in movements for democratization since. But there is no settled position from which to make public linguistic and intersubjective arrangements: the public square has to be invented again and again, and anyone with experience of the Left knows that those unhappy with an existing critical space will feel free to invent new ones, more receptive to their needs. There is no set formula for the dialectic of institutionalization and fluidity which defines the idea of the public square. No set formula, but plenty of limits: limits prescribed by the need for time and space, for unharassed discussion, for the information necessary for reflection, and, last but not least, for freedom from fear. The public square required an element of boldness, to which our final chapter is devoted.

CHAPTER SEVEN

Fear and Democracy

Bakhtin must have known a thing or two about fear. He had been arrested in December 1928, and sentenced, first to a term in the labour camps (which, given his health, would have killed him), then to six years in exile. And having completed the term of exile, he had been shrewd enough to take a job at a pedagogical institute not in one of the major cities, but in the provincial city of Saransk, out of sight and mind. So when in the spring of 1937 the institute's Party Committee condemned the man who had hired him for having brought a former exile into their 'revolutionary' midst, Bakhtin knew there was plenty to be afraid of.[1] With uncharacteristic decisiveness, he requested permission to give up his post, and left with his wife as soon as it was granted, moving to a friend's house in Moscow even though he lacked the necessary residence permit. Presumably Bakhtin took with him the research on Rabelais which he had begun a few years earlier, and which would eventually lead to his doctoral dissertation, essays on the popular, 'unofficial' roots of the novel, and several notebooks' worth of jottings. In these texts Bakhtin drew a detailed picture of the 'popular-festive culture' of medieval and early Renaissance Europe, the culture of fairs and markets, feasts and mystery plays, which he claimed as a new source for the novel's sense of history. But all the attention showered on the idea of a culture of laughter should not distract us from the fact that it operated in the shadow of an official culture of fear and 'gloomy seriousness'. For roughly a decade, Bakhtin distinguished between laughter and fear rather than dialogism and monologism, and focused on the 'tonality' rather than the style of discourse, as if the technical distinctions he had first drawn between kinds of speech could not convey the experiential power of official Europe.

The obvious hypothesis—that the fear which suffused Soviet society during the great purges prompted this change of tack—is irresistible, even though Russian scholars have pointed out carnival activity and interests in a younger Bakhtin.[2] But the obvious hypothesis is misleading, for although

---

[1] Information from V. Laptun, 'M. M. Bakhtin v Saranske (1936–37, 1945–69 gg.)', in [Proceedings of] The Seventh International Bakhtin Conference, Book II (Moscow: Moscow State Pedagogical University, 1995), 401–2, and Laptun, 'Pervyi priezd M. M. Bakhtina v Saransk (1936–1937)'.

[2] Nikolaev has suggested that Bakhtin's theory of carnival and belief in the priority of the

the official fear Bakhtin wrote about and the fear he himself experienced are related, the former cannot be reduced to a mere transcription of the latter. The very genre of biography would lead us to think of the fear generated by Stalinism as a fear *in* the world, a local occasion with a specific cause. But, as always in his writing, Bakhtin went to extremes, claiming to have disclosed not a specific fear, but a world-constituting fear, not a fear with historical causes and effects, but a fear which made possible the consistency and texture of a certain kind of history itself. One could call it without exaggeration a phenomenological or philosophical fear, for this fear had no particular objects, but determined the value and meaning of objects in general. Or perhaps an anthropological fear, rooted in the sublime experiences of early humankind:

We must bear in mind the enormous role of *cosmic fear*—fear in the face of the immeasurably great and the immeasurably powerful: in the face of the starry heavens, of the material mass of mountains, of the sea, and fear in the face of cosmic upheavals and elemental disasters—in ancient mythologemes, worldviews, systems of images, in languages themselves and the forms of thinking bound up with them. *At the very foundation of human thought, discourse, and imagery there has been deposited a kind of dark memory of the cosmic upheavals of the past and a kind of vague fear of future cosmic shocks.* This cosmic fear, fundamentally not mystical in the strict sense (being a fear in the face of the materially great and in the face of a materially insurmountable force), is used by all religious systems for the suppression of the person and his consciousness. (*Rab.*, 371/335)

A dark and ineradicable memory of cosmic upheavals, which leaves a permanent imprint in our world. And yet in Bakhtin's work on Rabelais and medieval culture, fear is also a cultural fact, rooted in the structures of European absolutism and ecclesiastical power. When Bakhtin wrote as a cultural historian, he did not surrender his essentially philosophical manner of looking at things, and if this leaves us with historical constructions too neat to be convincing, it is because Bakhtin was peculiarly unwilling to sacrifice the 'ultimate question' of what historical change *means*. To interpret official fear as determining the phenomenological structure of a given world was to ask not only what subjects were scared of, but how fear might

culture of laughter dates back to his time in Nevel' and to his work with Pumpiansky, whose articles on the comic and Gogol Nikolaev regards as direct sources. If this is the case, then carnival cannot be a response to Stalinism in the 1930s; see Nikolaev, '*Dostoevsky i antichnost'* L. V. Pumpianskogo (1922) i M. M. Bakhtina (1963)', 8–10. Support for this view comes from Bakhtin himself, when he described the serious joking, composition of parodies and scholarly clowning which dominated his schoolday group 'Omphalos' (see Ch. 3 above).

Mikhail K. Ryklin has suggested nearly the opposite: that Bakhtin wrote on carnival as a means of neutralizing the violence of the period. See his 'Tela terrora: Tezisi k logike nasiliia', in *Bakhtinskii sbornik*, vol. i (Moscow: Prometei, 1990), 60–76; English translation 'Bodies of Terror: Theses towards a Logic of Violence', *New Literary History*, 24: 1 (1993), 51–74.

constitute what, in a certain society, it meant to be a subject to begin with, and why such a subject might be suitably docile even when there was nothing in particular to fear. As with so much of his work, Mikhail Bakhtin was ready to learn from historical experience, but only if he was allowed to radicalize his enquiry to the point at which the very concept of historical experience was itself the issue.

Do we have anything to learn from such an extreme concept of fear? I think we do, despite the nagging feeling that a secular Left has better things to do than rummage around in metaphysics and phenomenology. For citizens nurtured on modernity expect historical change and experience to mean *something*, and time and again they have shown that if permanent fear is the price of a meaningful history, it is one they are willing to pay. So while we can analyse Stalinism as a source of 'empirical fear', Bakhtin's implicit claim is that we fail to comprehend its power, or that of any other political formation, until we grasp it as a kind of historical world, a framework in which events acquire a meaning and significance transcending their immediacy. For while Bakhtin believed in a decisive shift to modernity, he did not accept the self-understanding of modernity as enlightenment and scientific disenchantment, as individualism and the priority of the drily empirical. He saw modernity as a struggle between two cultural forms, based on fear and laughter respectively, which competed for the right to create a meaningful history well into the twentieth century.

Not the least important implication of this argument will be that actually existing democracy, which ought to signal the end of fear, is in fact founded on it. Bakhtin chose Rabelais as his privileged object because 'there is no doubt that he is the most *democratic* of the founders of modern literature' (*Rab.*, 6/2; emphasis Bakhtin's). Most democratic? Bakhtin was virtually worthless as a political thinker in the strict sense, but his disdain for the ordinary business of politics, the distribution and mechanisms of political power, has a certain virtue, for it led him to think of democracy not as a political category, but as a cultural-aesthetic one, as the promise not so much of a society in which the people are sovereign as of a society with a historical experience worth having. And while no one should think democracy could ever be just a kind of culture, it may turn out that a democratic culture and a democratic politics proceed hand in hand or not at all. For if democracy has an inner connection to fearlessness then a more democratic world will be a less anxious one as well, and anxiety may have more to do with democracy's failures than we think. We have learned many times that a society which is democratic but unhappy or democratic and anxiety-ridden can be less appealing than we would hope, and that the provision of democratic rights and procedures can coexist with a fear which undermines their meaning.[3] Democracy may have to be more than politics in the strict sense to succeed as politics in the strict sense.

If official fear was capable of constituting a world, then only a principle of equal depth could counter it—the principle of carnival laughter and the public square. And if each of these cultures is capable of constituting a fundamental ethical reality itself, then it becomes pointless to try to describe their struggle within a world encompassing them both. We know the solution Bakhtin arrived at—make official seriousness and festive laughter not competing principles within a social world, but two worlds, in which medieval humanity could dwell simultaneously:

All of these ritual-spectacular forms, organized on the principle of *laughter*, were distinguished extraordinarily sharply—one could say, in principle—from *serious* official (ecclesiastical and feudal-state) cultic forms and ceremonies. They provided a completely different, emphatically unofficial, extra-ecclesiastical and extra-state aspect of the world, of the person, and of human relations; it is as if they constructed a *second world* and a *second life* beyond everything official, in which all medieval people participated to a greater or lesser degree, in which they *lived* for definite periods. This is a special kind of *double-worldness*, without taking account of which neither the cultural consciousness of the Middle Ages, nor the culture of the Renaissance can be correctly understood. (*Rab.*, 10/5–6)

A number of medievalists and Renaissance scholars have rightly questioned this extreme claim, or wondered at the description of a purely universalistic and benevolent carnival world which it implies.[4] Supposing that 'unofficial popular culture in the Middle Ages and even in the Renaissance had its own special territory, the public square, and its own special time, feast and fair days' (*Rab.*, 170/154) provides a useful ideal type, but no sense of how one makes the journey from official fear to carnival liberation, or of how the reach of the public square might be extended (although Peter Stallybrass and Allon White have provided an excellent history of its suppression[5]). Nevertheless, the abstraction of the culture of laughter and the culture of fear from their common social world provides clues for explaining why societies with formally democratic political systems can still, in the

[3] Jürgen Habermas has discussed the possibility of a 'meaningless emancipation' in the concluding remarks to his study of another unworldly critic; see 'Walter Benjamin: Consciousness-Raising or Rescuing Critique' [1972], in *Philosophical-Political Profiles*, trans. Frederick G. Lawrence (Cambridge: Polity Press, 1986), 157–9.

[4] See e.g. the early review of *Rabelais and His World* by Frances Yates, *New York Review of Books*, 13: 6 (9 Oct. 1969), 16–21. Russian medievalists have tended to be kinder, although Sergei Averintsev has suggested that Bakhtin's over-estimation of carnival's subversive power is a tactical gesture: see the reviews by A. Gurevich and L. Pinsky in *Voprosy literatury*, 6 (1966), 200–13 and Sergei S. Averintsev, 'Bakhtin and the Russian Attitude to Laughter', *Critical Studies*, 3: 2/4: 1–2 (1993), 13–19.

[5] Peter Stallybrass and Allon White, *The Politics and Poetics of Transgression* (London: Methuen, 1986).

end, succumb to official fear, and why democratic feeling may emerge in the midst of a heavily policed political world.

DIMENSIONS OF SERIOUSNESS

Seriousness was not originally a separate concern of Bakhtin's, even when working on Rabelais. According to the available evidence, Rabelais first figured in Bakhtin's canon as a radical practitioner of literary parody, then had his works dissected under the rubric of the chronotope, and only in 1940 or so emerged as the literary representative of a distinctive popular-festive culture.[6] 'The problem of seriousness' is announced as a topic in its own right in the middle of the short text 'Towards Philosophical Bases of the Human Sciences', and it receives its most elaborate treatment in the notes Bakhtin prepared when revising *Rabelais* for possible publication in 1944. Contrary to the usual belief, seriousness in itself is not a problem for Bakhtin; the problem lay in the corruption of an original, presumably classical, seriousness by what he describes as 'officialdom'. The latter's attachment to earthly power forces the serious genres to forgo their attachment to history, and as a consequence they become 'saturated with falseness, foolish conventionality, hypocrisy and fraudulence' (FTC 385/236). That this is not fatal to seriousness as such is indicated by a note from Bakhtin's archive, which makes clear that laughter is not for pleasure or play, but for keeping alive the ideal of historical becoming which seriousness has abandoned: 'The gloomy character of providentialism and pre-destination. The joyful character of time and historical process. This is a necessary stage in the path to a new (not, however, gloomy) historical seriousness' (Archive, 481). Over the next twenty years Bakhtin will therefore think about both official seriousness and the two forms of unofficial seriousness mentioned earlier: tragic seriousness, which continues the unfinished business of the ancients, and the seriousness of sentimentalism, which Bakhtin deems a genuinely modern invention, expressed most compellingly in (where else?) the works of Dostoevsky. The latter, the 'unofficial seriousness of suffering, of fear, of fright, of weakness, the

---

[6] See Gogotishvili, commentary to 'Towards Philosophical Bases of the Human Sciences' (*SS5*, 387), where she designates this passage as the first independent examination of the idea of seriousness (apparently, neither seriousness, nor the notion of a 'culture of laughter' figure in the 1940 version of the dissertation). Rabelais's distinctive 'philosophy of discourse' is discussed in 'Discourse in the Novel' at 122–4/309–10, and his work is analysed 'chronotopically' in 'Forms of Time and of the Chronotope in the Novel' at 316–55/167–206. According to Poole ('Bakhtin and Cassirer', 590 n. 9), a notebook of materials from 1938 devoted to the Rabelais project uses the term 'chronotope' but not 'carnival' to analyse the substance of popular-festive culture in Rabelais.

seriousness of the slave and the seriousness of the sacrificial victim', expresses 'the ultimate protest of individuality (bodily and spiritual) yearning for immortality, against change and absolute renewal, the protest of the part against its dissolution in the whole' (AddAmR, 81). The former differs in the character of its hero, who does not so much yearn for immortality as struggle for it, but is, of course, ultimately subdued by the tide of historical change. Nevertheless, to the extent that tragedy avoids any false reconciliation between the individual and historical life, it, like laughter, can be said to 'look being in the eye'. The '*serious* courage of tragedy' evokes the historical process from, as it were, the point of view of an individual fate: the tragic hero learns a sober historical lesson, and the spectacle of it frees us from our narrow and local fears and hopes.

What unites these admirable forms of seriousness to their corrupt official cousin is the individual point of view; what separates them is the official's use of political power to inflate it. For official seriousness seeks to make the individual more than merely individual—it wants to help the individual transcend its earthly limits, whilst retaining the essential changeless attributes of the singular person. Its promise is therefore not transformation, but immortality, in the form of ascension into heaven for the many, and an eternal presence on earth, embodied in memory and monuments, for the powerful few. It is therefore animated by 'the thirst for glory and immortality in the memory of one's descendants, for one's *proper name* (and not nickname) in people's mouths . . .' (AddAmR, 84). One of Bakhtin's most intriguing arguments was that the desire for immortality was not a wish for life but a denial of death, and that death was feared not as an end to life, but as the moment of possible transformation and self-transcendence.[7] The desire for official immortality is therefore above all a desire to prolong what exists and it is for this reason a kind of false history, time as continuation rather than becoming. It uses earthly power—the power to build monuments and to make oneself greater than others—as a substitute for the knowledge that one participates in history through a social network which transcends and outlasts one's own life.

For official seriousness time therefore exists in the form of tradition, and it is the substitution of tradition for history which constitutes one of its principal ideological tasks. This it accomplishes through the practice of epic, which embodies what from a Bakhtinian point of view must seem contradictory: a public space in which the difference between the context which represents and the context represented leads not to reflection, but to obedience, where it is the instrument for the strengthening, rather than

---

[7] 'One of the great and unnoticed themes in the discourses and images of the world is doubt in death; this theme has been disguised by the reactive, substitute theme of hope for immortality' (AddAmR, 114–15).

the questioning, of norms. '*In the epic everything better* is in the field represented' (Rhet., 63) and every act of representation is a reminder that the
present of the author and the audience is ineluctably impoverished. The
absolute distinction between a glorious distant past (with appropriately
ominous ancestors, national struggles, legendary exploits, and so on) and an
anaemic contemporaneity demands an author who is, as Bakhtin says,
'immanent' to the genre, unable or unwilling to assume the autonomy
necessary to 'personal authorship':

Epic discourse is a discourse according to tradition. By its very nature the epic
world of the absolute past is inaccessible to personal experience and does not allow
an individually personal point of view and evaluation. One cannot glimpse it,
probe it, touch it; one cannot look at it from just any point of view; one
cannot experience it, analyse it, take it apart, penetrate into its core. It is given
solely as tradition, sacred and inviolable, involving a common evaluation and
demanding a pious relationship with it. (EN 460/16)

The teller of epic stories does not appear as an autonomous person when
he or she relates a narrative which is already a common social possession.
In so far as time has lost its historical character, the epic storyteller gains
nothing by coming later; epic is what narrative looks like when its link to
the ideals of autonomy, progressive scientific knowledge, and the historic
authority of intersubjective judgement has been broken.

The epic Bakhtin describes has classical antecedents, of course, but the
official type Bakhtin describes is a thoroughly modern achievement. This
becomes clearer once we recognize that its distinguishing features—its
distance from the everyday present, and the unconditional nature of its
authority ('The epic world can only be accepted with reverence', EN
460/17)—are in fact the same feature. For the epic Bakhtin has analysed
defines its distance from the present as a distance from the place where the
'personal point of view and evaluation' reign supreme. The present from
which epic stays absolutely remote is the present as confusion, condition-
ality, opinion, and subjective decision—the cut and thrust of a democratic
public sphere. The epic past is thus almost a reverse image of this modern
present, but only almost, because its point is to present the past as a fount
of authority which will attract the 'spontaneous' popular agreement of
those who are its audience, to allow the public (for epic, too, requires a
public) to make its decisions without appearing to decide anything. In
short, epic seriousness is the seriousness of *populism* which, on this interpretation, appeals to the people not as a historic people in Bakhtin's sense,
but as descendants and inheritors responsible for the maintenance of a
tradition.

As Slavoj Žižek has argued in another context, the evocation of a law or regime ontologically superior to one's present, which is what an 'absolute past' amounts to, is a phenomenon in which pleasure and fear work to each other's advantage.[8] While the epic represents a world better than that of the present in which it is told, what is better about it is has to do not with the content or substance of its norms, but their absolute, irrational, and 'unrealistic' form. Where the present is uncertain and difficult, the past is unconditional and utterly authoritative. For the modern citizen, living in a world of imperfect decisions, this state must thus appear ideal but also terrifying, in so far as it has no need for his or her moral exertions or, indeed, moral commitments of any kind. In the light of this irrational, 'superegoic' state, the actual present, where one has to strive to establish or maintain these same values, is experienced as a relief. Epic is therefore both ideal and terrible, and it leaves the actual political subject with the pleasurable task of being able to emulate its world while being thankful he or she does not live in it.

This absolute authority is made possible by 'pure praise', which, by definition, has an 'official character' (AddAmR, 80). Contemporaneity is marked by the fact that all its objects must be 'ambivalent', mixing praise and abuse, and always in the process of self-transformation. Therefore 'to make an image serious means to remove ambivalence and ambiguousness from it . . . it means to stop the movement of the wheel, its turning . . . to separate praise from abuse . . .' (AddAmR, 83). The most characteristic expression of this praise is the official obsession with the proper name, which, as Bakhtin describes it, 'is the most profound and essential expression . . . of the glorifying, praising, purely blessing-giving, crowning (immortalizing) principles of language' (AddAmR, 100). The authority of the absolute ruler is summed up by the proper name itself, which signifies an intention to prolong an identity over time, without regard for specific qualities or achievements: 'to name is to establish for centuries beyond, to secure something in being forever, inherent in it is a tendency to ineradicability, for it cannot be washed away, it wants to be cut as deeply as possible in the hardest and most solid possible material, and so on' (AddAmR, 100). In this respect its clear antithesis is the formal title characteristic of democracy ('Prime Minister', 'Senator', and so on) which in its generality signifies not a particular person, but the 'empty place of power' which Claude Lefort has argued constitutes the originality of the democratic form of organization.[9]

To interpret the self-glorification of rulers as mere propagandistic exaggeration is therefore to miss the ontological point, the sense in which

[8] Žižek, *For they know not what they do*, 229–45.

[9] Claude Lefort, 'The Image of the Body and Totalitarianism', in *The Political Forms of Modern Society*, trans. Alan Sheridan (Cambridge: Polity Press, 1986), 292–306.

pure praise qualitatively restructures the social world around it. Modern European tyrants are not *too* great, but transform greatness into a contemporary equivalent of the sublime attitude characteristic of past fear. But despite its apparent roots in prehistory, pure praise should be understood as part of the modern assault on the 'uncertainty' of democratic politics. It is the systematic refusal of the very riskiness which a politics based on experience and its reflection entails, the modern constitutional form of which has been described by Habermas: 'The fallibility essential to the historical realization of universal constitutional principles—a fallibility from which the elected and appointed representatives of the state are not exempt—finds its counterweight in the non-institutionalizable suspicious nature of the citizens of a mature political culture.'[10] Modern ethics and politics assume that people make mistakes, and that the opinions of subjects will differ and will be imperfect; pure praise rules this out in principle. In the absolutism of the Rabelais book pure praise is an element of the spectacular displays of power by Church and court, which served to confirm their ontological privileges. But in Bakhtin's own time, such praise was used to mobilize a population against the 'petty wrangling' and 'vacillations' of a liberal state or the limits legality would place on a Communist one. And although the natural home of such metaphysics is the Right and, in particular, mass right-wing politics, it makes its appearance on the Left whenever the contrast between corruption and devotion to the cause replaces the difference between right and wrong arguments, and whenever the critical, reflective spirit necessary for democratic politics is condemned as indecisiveness or weakness.[11]

Seriousness and the Everyday

The official culture of seriousness, however, cannot and does not depend completely on the displays it can muster in public space. According to the most usual versions of the recent European past, economic or political crises, by virtue of the real fear they instil in citizens, can instigate a kind of popular regression, leading to the collapse of those properly modern, constitutional arrangements which ought to be the fate of European nations. On this account, fear leads citizens to surrender the modern, sober, calculating rationality that is their historical birthright in exchange for the more or less infantile security guaranteed by 'strong leaders'. But Bakhtin does not oppose official fear to disenchanted modernity: on the contrary, he interprets the sober individualism of civil society as the every-

[10] Habermas, 'On Right and Violence: A German Trauma', 136.
[11] A paradigmatic statement of the association of reflexivity with indecisiveness is Carl Schmitt's *The Crisis of Parliamentary Democracy*.

day correlate of official fear, as the behaviour of a subject scared out of its wits. In his writing the public displays of official power and the private experience of modern individualism form a constellation. Official seriousness may appear in dramatic form on the heights of the social formation, but it wreaks its most lasting damage in the culture of everyday life which it provides for its subjects.

In the everyday world official fear makes itself felt as the 'seriousness and importance of the *impending*' (QuLaugh., 49), which expresses itself paradigmatically in a relentless forward gaze, an anxiety about one's prospects in the most literal sense. The serious subject concentrates, in the sense of both directing and narrowing its energies and intentions. Ironically enough, although this seriousness entails complete hostility to any kind of game (the celebration of which therefore became central for Rabelais), one of Bakhtin's most persuasive descriptions of it is found in a brief section of 'Author and Hero' devoted to, of all things, sport (one of the few spheres of life which apparently held no interest for Bakhtin): 'The first rule of any sport: look directly ahead of yourself, not at yourself. During a difficult and dangerous action, I compress my entire self into a pure inner unity, I cease to hear and see anything external to me, I reduce all of myself and my world to pure self-sensation' (AH 45/45). For the athlete, every act is measured by its contribution to success or failure, and all his or her energy is focused on winning; when this is not the case, we get not sport but comedy (and tragedy, too, as any sports fan knows). The athlete's gaze is resolute, focusing on both the space in front of her and on the future before her. And if we think of the other firm and resolute gazes we are likely to run across in our culture—on the faces of far-seeing political leaders, army generals, or the moral heroes scattered across our cinema and television screens—we can't help but notice that this modern seriousness demands that we weather the distractions of the present for the sake of the future. The politician with vision (the metaphor is, of course, itself revealing) ignores the petty political calculation of immediate consequences, the courageous soldier the immediate danger he or she is placed in, as if an aesthetic dwelling on the present were a decadent luxury. Concentration and seriousness are therefore not extraordinary acts which lead you out of the everyday, but the very means by which everyday habit is prolonged. The subject's forward gaze carves out the narrow channel which will define his or her pseudo-future, like the runner whose determination leads her round and round the track.

If what is impending demands one's entire attention, then there is neither time nor point in looking side to side, or, even worse, at oneself. The essential feature of everyday seriousness is the privacy it assumes for everyday activity, privacy in the sense that every act is comprehended as the act of an individual, made meaningful in the frame of an individual life and, by extension, the fact of individual death. The actor afflicted by seriousness is endlessly trying to make what he or she does important and valuable, often by making it a symbol of something eternal, and endlessly failing, for no act can withstand the ravages of time. And those acts which relate to his or her bodily existence are the most precarious of all, and therefore the critical focus of carnival culture and Rabelais's text. As the body is the site of an inevitable mutability, it can serve as an index for a culture's interpretation of the fact of change. An official culture renders the bodily functions private, and thereby determines the meaning of physical pains and pleasures. In a serious culture, for example, eating and drinking

are the expression of a *present* satisfaction and the satiation of an individual-egoistic person, the expression of individual *enjoyment* rather than the *celebration* of the people as a whole. They are divorced from the process of labour and struggle; they are separated from the popular public square and shut up within the limits of the home and the private room ('domestic plenty'). (*Rab.*, 333/301–2)

Privacy means not only hostility to public spaces of representation, but also a refusal to cultivate the facts of one's bodily existence and, by extension, a refusal to integrate one's life into a larger aesthetic narrative. The Puritan capitalist of Weberian history is thus not strictly egoistic, but private, staking all on the renunciation of aesthetic satisfaction in favour of the strictly regulated, and, in that sense, utterly ethical and principled, pursuit of ideal yet historically finite values.

Bakhtin was hardly alone in fearing the triumph of the habitual, the routine, and the everyday, for this was perceived as the central sin of civilization by a range of writers contemporary with him, from the Russian Formalists to T. S. Eliot and the Surrealists. Modernist art understood itself as a pre-eminently shocking, distancing art, which would inject meaning into the deadened, repetitive world of the everyday, whether this was by making its subjects see anew (*à la* Russian Formalism) or by converting the hordes crossing London Bridge to religion. But for these modernists only a *dramatic* intervention could upset the steady rhythm of the everyday, a sudden irruption of meaning analogous to the thunder in Eliot's waste land or the happy accidents so beloved of Surrealism. And while prose writers and poets looked to sources outside (either historically or geographically) modern Europe to renew or revive meaning, social theorists were busy explaining why lives rich with meaning and symbol were simply no longer on the agenda. According to the line of social thought running from Weber to Foucault, in the modern world the oppressiveness of dramatic and tyrannical power inevitably gives way to the dull compulsion of ordinary existence and legal-rational regulation. For the sociologically minded, the grand, terrifying gesture, the expression of spectacular, charismatic power, is a thing of the past, and any meaning the present has must come from the micropolitics of the everyday or the undramatic but rational progress of science and politics.

For Bakhtin, however, the flat and rationalized landscape of Western civilization is not territory liberated from absolute power but the sign of its complete hegemony. Its aversion to meaning, its methodical seriousness and dedication to progress, are the index not of freedom but of its abject surrender to 'the eternal threat of *the present day* to everything that wishes to go beyond its limits: everything that is inopportune, unnecessary, which does not correspond to the tasks at hand' (Rhet., 65). Seriousness maps out its future according to definitions of success and failure locked into the present, fearing change as a threat to its careful calculation of appropriate behaviours. Time appears as a danger to it, as something for which it should prepare and something which preparation can help it master. And while this everyday life appears to align itself with those literary forms—biography and the historical novel—which are most concerned with time, it has in fact selected those which are least concerned with it, or rather, are only concerned with what we should think of literally as the passing of time, a time made aesthetically heavy and substantial. Though biography and historical writing appear to chart the fate of those who look into the future, in fact they flesh out 'the future as continuation, as the continuity of oppression, but not the way out to freedom, not transformation' (Rhet., 66). For this very reason Bakhtin will congratulate Dostoevsky on his inability 'to work with great masses of (biographical and historical) time' (Rhet., 64) and his penchant for scandal (the antithesis of the everyday) and crisis.

THE CARNIVAL 'ALTERNATIVE'

The Renaissance's other culture—the popular-festive culture of laughter—therefore presents itself as the one in which time is welcomed, treasured, and celebrated, and where miraculous transformation does not awaken dim memories of catastrophe, but is a reminder of the value of historical time itself:

In the previous chapter we saw how cosmic fear, and the images of world catastrophe and eschatological theories bound up with it, cultivated in the systems of the official world-view, found a laughing equivalent in the images of carnival catastrophes, parodic prophecies, and the like, which freed people from fear, brought the world closer to the person, lightened the burden of time and its path and transformed it into the festive path of the joyful time of changes and renewals. (*Rab.*, 436–7/394)

Such transformations depended upon the eruption of the public square into the chronotope of ordinary life; they took place in the 'intermediate sphere' whose paradigmatic inhabitants were the rogue, clown, and fool. In *Rabelais* we learn that these figures were in fact visitors from another world altogether, 'as if [they were] the constant bearers of the carnival principle, trapped in everyday (i.e. non-carnival) life' (*Rab.*, 13/8). Popular-festive culture is therefore a world in which everyone is a clown and fool, where 'there are no footlights', where there is no distinction between art and life, and where, accordingly, one is absorbed not with the performance of one's role—as with our paradigmatic sportsperson—but with the spectacle of historical change itself.

Carnival is free to devote itself to historical becoming, and it does so with a singlemindedness at odds with the ambivalence otherwise so central to it. Being essentially pre-modern, it does not see time as an opportunity for change but as the means of change itself. By refunctioning the cyclical imagery of natural mutation it arrives at a picture of historical movement over time, in which every image 'is profoundly *ambivalent*, it assumes the most essential relation to life–death–birth' (*Rab.*, 166/149). Nature, deaf to the hubris of human desire and intention, knows that 'death . . . is followed by rebirth, by the new year, new youth, a new spring' (*Rab.*, 220/198). But to make this strategy work, every fact of human life, no matter how lofty, must be 'debased', made part of a natural ambivalence which mixes up birth and death, eating and defecation, growth and destruction.

What from the perspective of the individual would appear as tragedy acquires a different meaning in the context of this ceaseless natural history. Nature provides the imagery, the people provide the longer view, and their combination provides the necessary corrective to the narrowness of the serious world-view and its hostility to the historical future. Brian Poole has argued that Bakhtin took the contrast of the mortal individual and the immortal people from later neo-Kantian writing.[12] Hermann Cohen, and then Matvei Kagan after him, claimed that the individual could participate in history only through the mediation of a historical people, and Kagan (in the article 'Judaism and the Crisis of Culture') distinguished the Jews as the first people to think of their identity in terms of a historical project.[13] In so far as Bakhtin believes that only a maximum of disinterest makes possible

---

[12] Poole, '"Nazad k Kaganu"', 38–40.
[13] M. I. Kagan, 'Evreistvo v krizise kul'tury', 231.

the representation of history, he idealizes a popular 'carnival' literature which is as anonymous, as removed from individual vanities, as possible, its individualist edges smoothed down by the steady erosion of popular usage.

This popular-festive 'voice of the whole' represents time as possibility and transformation. But for Rabelais, and for Bakhtin as well, it serves as a resource rather than an end in itself, as the means by which the movement of history, and, by extension, the practice of responsibility, can establish itself as the sole measure of value:

The material-bodily principle, earth and real time become the relative centre of a new picture of the world. Not the ascent of the individual soul along an extra-temporal vertical into the higher spheres, but the forward movement of all humanity along the horizontal of historical time becomes the fundamental criterion of all evaluations. The individual soul, having finished its business, grows old and dies together with the individual body, but the body of the people and of humanity, fertilized by those who have died, is eternally renewed and goes steadfastly forward along the path of historical perfection. (*Rab.*, 447/403–4)

While there are Stalinist touches here—'steadfastly forward'?—which should be safely put to one side, the sharp intersection between natural and social history defines the core of Bakhtin's argument. The earthly and the material-bodily stand for a life-substance which incarnates historical movement without being aware of it. Just as the novel always had to work from the concrete history represented in different, specific languages, Rabelais's new picture of the world works on the substance represented by natural history. But the assimilation of the history of a people to a natural history of continual metamorphosis, though it makes an admirable break with traditional nationalism, nevertheless is not without its own problems.

A HISTORY WITHOUT POLITICS

Not the least of these is the ease with which such an image of historical movement can dispense with the role of politics. While the life of peoples obviously depends upon many factors, some beyond human control entirely, politics is central whenever we speak of socio-historical change. The historic tasks undertaken by peoples, whether conceived religiously, nationally, or universalistically, depend upon the ability to articulate and shape their activity, and the classic expression of this in public form is politics. The movement of carnival time, however, bypasses politics completely, as if its positions, projects, and movements were mere extensions of individual conceits. Time may be the medium of earthly history, but it is the enemy of temporal power:

This old power and old truth come forward with pretensions to absoluteness, to extratemporal importance. Therefore all the representatives of the old truth and the old power are gloomily serious; they cannot and do not want to laugh (they are agelasts); they step forward majestically, in their enemies they see enemies of eternal truth and therefore they threaten them with eternal destruction. The ruling power and the ruling truth cannot see themselves in the mirror of time, therefore they do not see their own beginnings, boundaries, and ends either, they do not see their old and ridiculous face, the comic character of their pretensions to eternity and immutability. And the representatives of the old power and the old truth, with their very serious faces and in serious tones, finish playing their roles, after their audience has been laughing for a long time already. They continue to speak in the serious, majestic, threatening, terrible tone of kings or heralds of 'eternal truths', not noticing that time has already rendered this tone ridiculous in their mouths and transformed the old power and truth into a carnival Shrovetide dummy, into a comic scarecrow which the people tear to pieces to the sound of laughter in the public square. (*Rab.*, 236/212–13)

Passages such as this have made carnival the darling of many critics on the Left, even though its argument is little more than a popular rewrite of *sic transit gloria mundi*. But while it may reassure us to learn that the people know the emperor has only clothes, the victory time wins over political power is a cheap one. Bakhtin does not describe the 'non-institutionalizable suspicion of a mature political culture', but a generalized sense of the falsity of social and political roles. Such a sense will lead not to historic change but to the syndrome that Žižek has described as 'I know, but nevertheless . . .'.[14] 'I know that the old power is nothing, that its claims to eternity are absurd, etc., but nevertheless . . . I will obey it': Bakhtin's people in the public square can establish a distance between roles and actuality only by denying the reality of the symbolic network itself, as if the web of intersubjectivity—the roles, responsibilities, and conventions that shape social action—was not itself the condition of a historical existence.

This vision of historical change without politics—and by extension, historical change without law, without norms, and without states or peoples—runs up against the fact that the very responsibility which must exist for history to go forward is tied to the social roles which history renders inauthentic. Once Bakhtin has radicalized the clown and fool by designing a culture in their image, he destroys the intermediate space between life and art, the non-participating participation, that gave these figures a point. The clown, rogue, and fool reflected on the symbolic network of feudal society, but as supporting characters in a spectacle which revolved around kingship and political action. To take the most familiar

---

[14] Žižek, *For they know not what they do*, 241–53.

English-language examples, the fool in *King Lear* and the rogue Falstaff in
1 Henry IV certainly recontextualize the ethico-political world around
them, and they may represent an alternative form of being, but they themselves cannot drive the dramatic narrative forward: this depends on the
political sphere they reflect upon. Once Bakhtin begins to think of them
as visitors from a theatrical world of their own, the way is open for a conception of history which is entirely aesthetic. Once loosed from the actions
and responsibilities on the other side of the footlights, historical becoming
becomes an abstract force sweeping all before it, but making no real
difference.

And yet the simple identification of politics with official fear may have
a historical point. Bakhtin describes official fear as the heir to a cosmic,
mythico-religious fear at work since the (equally mythic) dawn of
humanity. But Bakhtin's focus on the Renaissance is historically shrewder
than we might think. In his narrative, official fear makes its appearance on
the historical stage at the very moment of Absolutism, that is, the moment
of the modern state. As is often the case, one has to throw Bakhtin's
historiography into reverse in order to grasp the real point. The politics of
the modern state is not an adaptation of some older cosmic fear, but its
birthplace, the origin of a *political fear* intrinsic to the very idea of the state.
In the notes published as 'Additions and Amendments to "Rabelais"'
Bakhtin describes the tragedy of usurpation so central to Shakespeare's
dramas as the enactment of a deeper logic:

Macbeth is not a criminal, the logic of all his acts is the necessary iron logic of self-
coronation (and more broadly, the logic of all coronation, of the Crown and of
power, and still more broadly, the logic of all life which is self-asserting and thus
hostile to change and renewal). Macbeth begins by murdering his father (Duncan
is the substitute for the father, he is a relative, a greybeard, and so on), here he is
the heir, he welcomes change; he finishes by murdering children (a substitute for
his son), here he is the father who does not accept change and renewal (dis-
crowning). This is the suprajuridical crime of all self-asserting life . . . the suprajuridical crime of a link in the chain of generations . . . this is the profound tragedy
of *individual* life itself, condemned to birth and death . . . But this tragedy (and
crime) of individual life itself is enclosed in the potentializing form of the tragedy
of the Crown/power (the sovereign, the king crowned, is the limit and triumph
of individuality, its crown, realizing all its possibilities); and here all the acts of
Macbeth are determined by the iron logic of all coronation and all power (hostile
to change), its constitutive moment is violence, suppression, falsehood, the trepi-
dation and fear of the subjected, as well as the complementary, converse fear of
the sovereign before those who are subjected. This is the suprajuridical crime of
all power. (AddAmR, 85–6)

The political fear Bakhtin describes is not a matter of the balance of forces, nor is it a fear based on particular calculations of the probability of injury: it is absolute. For the essence of political fear is the sense of one's absolute vulnerability to the *other*, rather than worry over a specific threat or danger. One is fearful not on account of any particular threat, but because political power as such institutionalizes a distance between the government and its subjects, between sovereign power and absolute vulnerability. Modern political theory is, in large part, the rationalization of this distance: since Hobbes and Rousseau, it has tried to explain how accidental advantage or brute force can be converted into the fact of sovereignty, into a power which subjects recognize and obey in general and as a matter of right.

From Bakhtin's perspective, all such attempts are doomed. In so far as the state is by definition a coercive mechanism, its essence is force, and force (together with its necessary correlate, fear) relieves subjects of their responsibility and, with it, the possibility of a coherent life-story. If the institution which expresses the public will is devoted to power rather than the creation and narration of historical life, then the narrative possibilities for its subjects will be drastically curtailed. Faced with the force of the state, subjects (or perhaps it would be better to say 'citizens') are left with two possible fates—to mimic this force, by following in the path of the state's own self-assertion, or to fight fear with fear (to coin a phrase), by counter-posing their own individuality and self-assertion to that of the state. These are not mere logical types, in fact; they appear to me to represent the strategies adopted in this century by populist nationalism on the one hand, and liberal democracy on the other.

At first glance, both the ethnically based nationalisms of the twentieth century and the project of historical Communism, which mixed class and national definitions together, appear to incarnate the notion of a historical people. Although typically premissed on a national or class-based heroic past, their focus, in so far as they are specifically ideologies of *mobilization*, is on the creation of a glorious future. The vision of a collective 'people', heroically marching into the future, seems not only to transcend the 'profound tragedy of the *individual* life', but also to promise the individual a way into a trans-individual history. Yet from Bakhtin's argument it is clear that such 'peoples' magnify, rather than transcend, the self-assertion of the individual. As he commented in 'Epic and Novel', the future they strive for is in reality the 'future memory of a past' (EN 462/19), that is, a future in which the nation can transcend the present by being an object of commemoration and epic memory. The ethical substance of such nation-peoples—the norms, values, and cultural forms by which they are notion-ally defined—is itself unchanging, and its extension through time is merely the prolongation of a finite 'positive' culture, a prolongation which amounts to the same thing as Macbeth's crime of self-assertion. A people unwilling to change cannot be, in Bakhtin's sense, historical.

The model for the assertive, epic state was no doubt the Soviet Union of the 1930s. The values incarnate in its official language—cult of the collective interest, belief in absolute work discipline (Stakhanovite propaganda), repression of sexuality and the intimate as weak and indulgent, the overriding importance of national mobilization—counterposed the grand tasks of a collective and forceful people to everyday concerns deemed petty and distracting. Only an everyday life structured as mimicry of the official language could have meaning (and much of the novel-writing of the time showed how such mimicry was possible); all else was false by definition (explained as a deviation, as identification with an alien class, as evidence of a conspiracy, and so forth). The individual wrapped up in an unofficial language was therefore forced to organize its life around values which had been, so to speak, ontologically demoted. It would be a 'contingent, isolated subject' not in the sense that its behaviour was random or disordered, but in the sense that it could not 'become *together with the world*', as its world had for all intents and purposes abandoned the ideal of becoming.

Recent events in that region have demonstrated, however, that claims to represent the historical future are always somewhat fragile. While an epic narrative may roll along apparently unhindered, other languages may grow to fill the need for meaning—in the interstices of institutions, in an increasingly internationalized media, in structures of everyday life designed to defend citizens against the predations of their own state. The smoothness of 1989, the velvetness of the eastern European 'revolutions' is testimony to how effectively new socio-ideological languages can take over the burden of providing a meaningful history (though just how new they are is a good question) without a major conflict erupting, and with old forms sloughed off like so much dead skin. But we should not underestimate the degree to which the development of alternative languages and narratives depended upon the modern structures of historical Communism itself: a high degree of literacy combined with the existence of well-developed print media (including the so-called samizdat), where flexible and critical narratives could develop, even given the existence of censorship; awareness of the alternative narrative of Western capitalism, whose postwar rise provided a model for certain Communist managers and intellectuals; the advent of television, which, once the reforms were under way, made possible the rallying of mass support; a cultural modernity which made narratives based on tradition increasingly hard to credit. Explanations of the very changes which made possible the publication of Bakhtin's work have focused on the inability of actually existing socialisms to deliver the economic goods. But the historic changes of regime were neither initiated nor led by the impoverished, and they depended critically on a communicative world which had grown up beside the epic tale of historical Communism.

And the liberal state, which, in so far as it remains liberal, hands over historical initiative to the private efforts of its citizens? Here the sovereignty of the people is enshrined by the guarantee of their rights. But such individual rights are but the mirror image of the power they supposedly limit; they are the means by which individuals can assert themselves within a space beyond public control; they can therefore only institute a mutual fear, can make fear the basis of social relationships throughout the polity. When democracy appears as the practical and logical consequence of individual rights which pre-exist it, it is no more than a generalization of the logic of self-assertion and the facts of political fear. Democracy as a doctrine of the state therefore held little interest for Bakhtin, as it would have appeared to accomplish no more than the generalization of the fear essential to political power. The universalism of the public square was intended to draw all into history and out of themselves, and so was the antithesis of the universal rights and mutual fear we might confuse with it.

Political fear thus makes time the enemy of the subject–citizen. Like a character caught in a bad novel, it cannot avoid feeling the pressure of the plot, and must pick its way carefully through a world at once senseless and hackneyed. If it goes along with the plot, and grounds its life-story on the value embedded in existing conventions, it does so in the secret knowledge that history may deal them a fatal blow, which it will experience as a meaningless catastrophe. 'Biographical life', as Bakhtin called such an existence, is 'always enveloped by a naïve faith' that existing values and conventions will simply continue under their own steam (AH 153/165). If, on the other hand, the subject-citizen strikes out on its own, and tries to construct a narrative with an original and self-sustaining integrity, it becomes an eccentric secondary character, its every act a mere historical parenthesis. Dull convention or spectacular isolation: either way, the subject finds the way to a historical life, which would satisfy both its need for freedom and for a meaningful history, blocked by the force of the state.

FEAR AND SCIENCE

Politics is therefore, to Bakhtin's mind, no solution, for it depends, even in its most liberal form, on the very fear one wishes to abolish. How, then, to cross the line from official life to the public square (even if only in our minds)? Could one argue one's way to it?

One of Bakhtin's most surprising, and least cited, claims is that laughter establishes 'that presupposition of fearlessness without which a realistic grasp of the world is impossible' (EN 466/23). Laughter was to break down not only the divide between art and life, but also that between science and life. In the supplementary notes to the study of Rabelais, Shakespeare figures, but Galileo as well, because the latter's ability to laugh was inseparable from his capacity for discovery. Just as art removes you from the demands of the ethical, science draws you out of the immediate by virtue of its inherently conceptual nature. True to Kant to the last, Bakhtin believes the free person is above all the disinterested person. Arguing against the view that Rabelais appealed to our erotic, sensual impulses, he claimed that:

their aim [the images in Rabelais] is the *sobriefication* of the person, his liberation from any kind of possession (including sensual), the raising of the person to the highest sphere of disinterested, absolutely sober and free being, to such heights of *fearless* consciousness where he is least of all liable to be muddied by any kind of sensual arousal. (AddAmR, 115)

Bakhtin could bring together science and art, ritually contrasted in the work of otherwise similar philosophers, because he did not equate science, even natural science, with use and technique but with the other disciplines which were historical in their structure and ready to countenance the inopportune and the unnecessary. Science was as critical as the novel to a democratic life, because science would render the world itself open, endowing it with the structure of something 'set as a task' rather than something we could take or leave (it was, of course, science, physics and mathematics in particular, which provided the original and definitive model for the neo-Kantians who established this distinction). And a world set as a task was the objective correlate of responsible subjects. If the phenomenological structure of the world remained closed, then no amount of democracy could make for an ethical life. As politics alone, democracy remained within the closed circle of fear and the present day, and only a culture which could grasp the world realistically would provide the critical difference.

But Bakhtin insisted that laughter had to come first: having established this distance from the immediate, one could grasp the world as a historical whole, but not vice versa. The emphasis on laughter has a certain populist appeal, and Bakhtin himself could imply that things were not so bad so long as people laughed and swore, mocked and refused to take things seriously. But just as miracles never really convince the positivist who sees them—he or she always has a scientific explanation on hand—laughter and festivity in themselves do not make for fearless people. Why does laughter abolish fear absolutely, and why can we not be *convinced* that there is nothing to be afraid of? The reason is that Bakhtin uses laughter as an equivalent of faith: the moment when one laughs is the moment when one gives up the immediate in favour of the work of history, and it is not at all an accident that even in Bakhtin's work this moment inhabits a separate place, with separate rules, and separate times. But in a truly novelized, secular world, one does not suddenly cross over into fearlessness, as if by a miracle, and one does not abandon immediate tasks and social identities in favour of pure history and responsibility. One has to be convinced, bit by bit, case by case, that there is nothing to fear. The sobriety and democracy which Bakhtin thought had overwhelmed modern discourse applies reflexively to the so-called culture of laughter itself. Although a democratic movement has to offer a culture which renders life meaningful as well as a politics which transforms public decision, those movements have to persuade their constituencies that they have a chance of success, that is, they have to have recourse to the very categories of seriousness that Bakhtin condemned out of hand. People do not give up their fears willingly: they surrender a consistent and predictable world only when convinced that a possible future will offer dignity, prosperity, or fulfilment unavailable in their present. Belief in the importance of calculable success is, in its own way, one of the most democratic achievements of recent times.

A DEMOCRATIC CULTURE, A CULTURED DEMOCRACY

Although Bakhtin described carnival's struggle with the old world at length, he did everything he could to ensure that they never had to share the same space. Had they confronted one another face to face, there would have been something to struggle over, and the democratic, plebeian life of carnival would have been tainted by an interest in mortal and this-worldly achievement. Historically, of course, struggles for a more democratic order have not only been tainted by grossly secular concerns, they have been defined by them. It is not the least irony of Bakhtin's work that the freedom, egalitarianism, democracy, and sobriety of which he dreamt were less the precondition of history than the yield of its costly struggles.

This is the price any theory pays when it tries to imagine history as a purely cultural fact. When Bakhtin defined the world as 'history and culture, objectivity and unbroken objectification in cultural labour', he papered over the unfortunate truth that not all labour has been or will be an item of cultural creation—nor should it be—and that history is moved by meaningless natural accidents and the contingent results of violent struggle as much as the conscious projects of cultural actors. For all his apparent interest in nature, Bakhtin refused to acknowledge its separateness from human designs (occasionally he would even try to make it speak),[15] and all his polemics with violence could not change the fact that historical transformations are imposed as much as created. The first refusal reminds us that Bakhtin could not say much about economics, the second that he would not entertain the facts and values of politics.

These calculated exclusions, however, saved Bakhtin from a different illusion. Because the violence and contingency of actual historical life were allowed no place within a history dominated by culture, they reappeared within culture itself, and thus put paid to any lingering belief that culture could be relied on to save humankind from its barbaric tendencies. However often Bakhtin sought to ground his cultural distinctions (between dialogism and monologism, novel and poetry, carnival and the official) in a broader distinction between action that was cultivated and action that was merely instrumental or manipulative, he could not avoid the existence of culture that was violent, culture that was epic rather than historical, and culture that made a home for the 'contingent, isolated subject'. The violence and fear which ran through history did not represent a withdrawal from culture, but a form of it, in the end every bit as reliant on the dialogism of language, the metalinguistic capacities of discourse, and the inevitability of public squares as its novelized antithesis. Every time Bakhtin's texts reveal, wittingly or not, that monologism, too, assumes a multiplicity of languages, that the epic is nevertheless a kind of historical narrative, and that, for all its faults, rhetorical discourse is a form of inter-subjectivity, they do some justice to Benjamin's reminder that 'there is no cultural document that is not at the same time a record of barbarism'.[16]

The ethical reality Bakhtin spent a lifetime formulating could not spring fully formed from the concept of culture itself, or from an axiomatic ideal of intersubjectivity—it bore the marks, or perhaps the scars, of its history too brazenly. 'Free and democratized language' is no doubt a fine thing, but it cannot be derived from language alone or the bare facts of *I* and *other*. But it is equally important to recognize that a free and democratized language cannot be derived from the bare institutional fact of democracy. For just as there is language which is dialogical, but somehow not quite dialogical enough, and narratives which are chronotopic, but somehow not authentically chronotopic, so we have social orders which are democratized, and yet not democratic. Every time a critic from the Left chokes on the words 'liberal democracy' or 'liberal-capitalist democracy' (never

---

[15] See the well-known 'witness and judge' section of 'From the Notes of 1970–71', which opens: 'The witness and the judge. With the appearance of consciousness in the world (in being), and perhaps, even with the appearance of biological life (perhaps not only animals, but also trees and grass bear witness and judge), the world (being) radically changes' (N70–71, 360/137).

[16] Walter Benjamin, 'Edward Fuchs, Collector and Historian', in *One-Way Street and Other Writings*, trans. Edmund Jephcott and Kingsley Shorter (London: New Left Books, 1979), 359.

mind its historical antagonist, the 'people's democracy'), he or she acknowledges this awkward fact. Democracy is no longer an unequivocal ideal, it is also a historical fact, not just the prize but the battleground on which social struggles take place. Like dialogism and the chronotope, it is perched on the divide between fact and value, both the name of a historical aspiration and a political reality with which actors from all over the political spectrum must come to terms. Both Left and Right work the terrain of democracy, and though the ground ought to favour the former, it is from the latter that some of the most successful and inventive thrusts have come.

The democratization of social life is more than ideology; it cannot be reduced to the homage that every secular political movement pays to the authority of the people. A national vernacular, a mass electronic communications network, a system of population-wide formal education, and techniques for the mobilization of crowds in public spaces are facts embedded in modern ethical life, not mere constraints or tools, but realities which shape contemporary social relations. They may be politically mobile, and they are by no means either universal realities or ones destined to last forever, but for a large part of the world they represent a level of popular mobilization and power no political movement can ignore. When Bakhtin describes the language of modern Europe as dialogical and heteroglot, he acknowledges that these democratizing transformations have changed the rules of the game. Dialogism, a sense of history, and heteroglossia in themselves could not deliver the novelistic historical world Bakhtin hoped for, but they articulated the terrain on which a democratic culture would have to be fought for and won in any reasonably modern society.

Conversely, poetic monologism and epic are not merely regressive; they are modern too, and, in their way, depend on democracy just as nationalism and fascism do. Had they been no more than dust on history's shoes, Bakhtin would not have had to work so hard to distinguish them from their dialogical and novelistic antitheses. But although he could see the forces of monologism, he could only explain the fact of their existence as a misrecognition of an underlying ethical reality which only philosophy could disclose. This led to an underestimation of their historical power, to be sure, but it wreaked greater damage on the understanding of dialogism and the novel. For if the novel represented an ethical reality underneath historical life, which could be grasped but not demonstrated, it followed that historical facts themselves were of secondary importance. The privileging of the meaning of the past over the facticity of the past, of the pure concept of responsibility over the power to discharge specific, historically defined, responsibilities, meant the novel could only figure an ideal of historical movement which its definition betrayed. Autonomy, as the power to be guided by one's own will, was essential to the historical world Bakhtin envisaged, but ruled out of bounds as the mere illusion of the *I-for-myself.*

The historical and novelized culture Bakhtin desired could thus only be delivered by recourse to the very political ideals he hoped to sidestep. The responsibility he defined as the 'logical condition of ethical reality' was possible only on the basis of a claim to autonomy and the ratification of specific responsibilities by a social network. What Bakhtin could not, or did not, want to acknowledge was that subjects did not assume their responsibilities as a matter of faith, but rested their claims to particular roles or identities on the recognition afforded them within the intersecting networks of social life. The latter, of course, vary in nature and extent, and struggles over identities and roles, responsibilities and their corresponding expectations, are the rule rather than the exception. But what knits the world of life and the world of culture together is judgement and agreement over the contours of particular social forms. Bakhtin did not want inter-subjectivity to be negotiable in this way, but he set his sights on a histori-cal becoming which could issue from nothing less.

One has to agree to the distribution of roles; one has the opportunity to comment on them, judge them, suggest others: this means democracy. When responsibilities and identities are something we can reflect upon, and when their concatenation is something we narrate with *others*, we have passed over the threshold of the novel. The novel and strictly political democracy differ, however, in their definition of the context which makes it possible to reflect upon particular roles and actions: for the democrat, it is a political community of equals; for the novelist, historical becoming. History is the framing context which brings a language out of itself and dialogizes it, introducing that element of self-distance necessary for critical judgement; history, because the point of responsible action is not only the satisfaction of needs and the enactment of justice, but the creation of a meaningful narrative. We read novels, in the ordinary sense of the term, and witness other narratives precisely because they supply the conviction that our actions lead somewhere, and that our lives or parts of our lives can constitute wholes which we can enjoy aesthetically. But as we have seen above, at the very point where Bakhtin apparently decided that, in the famous words of Schiller, world history is the ultimate court of judgement, he found a way to avoid the secular hazards of his conclusion. For Bakhtin the history which served as the context of reflection was not the history made by the fallible judgements and efforts of ordinary humans, but the story of the world as it would be seen by one willing to redeem it as a whole. The super-addressee who could judge all fairly would presumably judge with tools more reliable than the ones endlessly improvised and improved upon by humanity itself. Such a historical perspective is not only unlikely, it is also unnecessary, and runs counter to the political ideals intrinsic to the dream of a historical culture itself. Worst of all, it promises meaning as a substitute for prosperity and justice rather than as their elaboration.

Ironically, in this respect Bakhtin shares ground with the liberal philosophy he otherwise took exception to. For liberal democracies also preach responsibility in the absence of earthly power, and they celebrate a freedom which depends not on particular roles but on the bare fact of personal decision. The 'negative liberty' of the liberal society guarantees an autonomy founded not on the agreement and judgement of *others* to a proposed narrative, but on decisions made in the idiom of the *I-for-myself*. Liberal democracy would also have us abstract the making and judging of narratives from the intersubjective community, but with the difference that it makes no promise of redemption. In theory, liberal democracies assume that they should do no more than regulate the competitive pursuit of private stories, and that history as a larger narrative is none of their concern. In practice, the political classes know they cannot leave narrative to chance, or allow their societies to be reduced to an agglomerate of competing individuals. They therefore have characteristically supplied resources for narrative—the waging of war, national ceremony, the invention of traditions, the scripts of social mobility—in abundance. But although they are capable of epic sentiment, particularly when in the business of making war, in general liberal states have deferred to essentially private forms of narrative, modern versions of the social-quotidian biography which emerge from civil society. The key histories of these societies are those which place and contextualize the individual life through families, work (whether as career or means of familial betterment), communities, romantic life, and, of course, the endless soap opera of consumption—all private rather than state concerns. So although their directive functions in relation to the economy have grown, and their welfare provision has increased dramatically, liberal capitalist states for the most part continue to function as aids to, rather than direct producers of, languages and narratives which properly belong to civil society.

Bakhtin's theory has to make its peace with secular democratic politics. But the example of populism shows us what the idea of democracy would get out of this reconciliation. A democracy without novelistic culture, or, to be exact, a democracy with an epic culture, is determined to give 'the people' a narrative without giving them, in Bakhtin's sense, a history. Particularly in its nationalistic variant, populism is ready to supply the meaningful national narrative which liberalism deems below itself. But there is no *risk* in populism, no risk and no future, because populist citizens know themselves already, and know that there is nothing more to know about themselves. They abjure precisely the sphere of 'experience, knowledge, and practice (the future)' which defines the novel, and are no more interested in a history constituted by the communication and judgements of a community than Bakhtin was. From the perspective of history in a populist key, an open, experimental history is a threat to the meaningfulness of history itself.

Bakhtin defended his concept of a historical culture in the wake of a history gone populist, counterposing a novelized and carnivalesque people to the staid creatures of the Stalinist imaginary. By insisting that the people only made history in the public square and endowing them with the consciousness of novelists he made them less believable as a people, but more realistic as an image of democracy. For the novelistic consciousness knows that modern and uneven communicative structures are facts of ethical reality, and every democracy must not only adapt to them, but exploit them to the hilt. For at every turn it will face an opponent as modern as itself and as willing to play the democratic game. Populism may absorb everyday life into the tasks of the nation, make a substance of values and throw them into an unfathomable past, impose a hierarchy on the diversity of linguistic forms, but it does so in a modern manner and with a willingness to cater to the citizenry's need for *some* kind of language and culture which will implant them in a larger and grander history.

In recent history, populism has meant not just particular regimes or particular historical moments, but a tendency at work in every partly democratized society. As the reaction of the Right to the fact of democracy, populism is a unique, albeit uniquely regrettable, contribution to democratic life.[17] But populism infects the Left as well, whenever we try to separate the ideals of a historical culture—scientific and experimental in character, differentiated in form—from the aspiration to democracy, whenever, that is, we seek a democracy without culture. A democracy which has surrendered the orientation to the future and the ethical advantages of an unevenly structured communicative life demeans its

[17] I therefore do not regard populism as a politically mobile discourse, as Ernesto Laclau argued in his early essays, 'Fascism and Ideology' and 'Towards a Theory of Populism', in *Politics and Ideology in Marxist Theory* (London: Verso, 1979), 81–198. Laclau claimed that populism depended on the opposition between people and state, and that in capitalist societies this division could be articulated in different political directions (essentially, a theoretical justification for politics of the Popular Front variety). I differ because I think the opposition was always more concrete than Laclau allows, whether it was articulated from the Left or Right. Populism depends not only on belief in 'the people' but also on a certain construction of 'the people', as a repository of naturally given virtue or instinct in opposition to the artificial excrescence of the state. But just as people are fallible, so 'the people' are fallible, and a political movement which does not include this in its self-understanding is unlikely to lead to anything very progressive.

citizens, as if they were not up to the burden of a modern historical existence. It assumes that democracy is a matter of subjective dispositions allied to state power, rather than communicative structures irreducible to the workings of a single consciousness. But when Bakhtin described the democratization of life in the following bookish terms, he was not merely reflecting the prejudices of a scholar:

The issue is not the quantity of great discoveries, new voyages and knowledge acquired, but a new *quality* in the comprehension of the real world which appeared as a result of all this: the new, *real* unity and integrity of the world went from being a fact of abstract consciousness, theoretical constructions and *rare books* to being a fact of concrete (ordinary) consciousness and practical orientations, a fact of ordinary books and everyday reflections . . . (*Bil.*, 238/44)

Bakhtin recognized that the concreteness and accessibility of the historical world depended on mobilizing all the resources of modern culture; while for the populist, democracy means no books at all, for they can only confuse an idealized people's naturally concrete and practical sense of the world. Debate and discussion, experiment and evidence, and all the communicative means for them would imply the people had a right and an obligation to determine the course of their history, not just an opportunity to tag along to a narrative already in place. But what Benjamin claimed of fascism is true of populism as a whole: it wishes to give the masses 'not their right, but instead a chance to express themselves'.[18]

Although Bakhtin was willing to give the masses their history, he was afraid it would be devalued if given in the language of rights. Doing so would have meant recognizing the ultimate authority of a secular humanity, and with it the secular truths that not everything can or should be redeemed, that sometimes one eats to live and not the reverse, and that we become responsible in specific situations and for specific tasks; that is, sometimes we have an alibi. Public squares and novels are critical to our historical sense of responsibility: they ensure that the roles and tasks, and the possible guilt we may assume, do not become limited to that which lies straight ahead. But a world which is only a novel gives us at once too much responsibility (there are never alibis) and too little (our immediate responsibilities will pass away, just as the old power will). Bakhtin could never square these requirements. But they seized his imagination, and forced him to dream of dialogues and spaces both unrealistic and utterly necessary. He has now bequeathed his dream to us, but when the day's residues are Europe and its violent modernity, the need to wake up is all the more compelling.

---

[18] Walter Benjamin, 'The Work of Art in the Age of Mechanical Reproduction', in *Illuminations*, 241.

Bibliography

M. M. BAKHTIN

Bakhtin's works (essays, books, sets of notes, fragments, his dissertation) are listed below not in the order in which they were published, but according to our best estimate of their date of composition. Many of the essays and fragments were published in full in the collections which have become the standard texts for Bakhtin scholars and readers; publication details for these follows the chronological list of works.

Essays and Fragments, 1919–1927

'Isskustvo i otvetstvennost" ['Art and Responsibility'], 1919. First published in *Den' iskusstva* (Nevel'), 3 Sept. 1919, 3–4. Reprinted in *Estetika slovesnogo tvorchestva*, 7–8. English translation in *Art and Answerability*, 1–3.

'K filosofii postupka' ['Towards a Philosophy of the Act'], *c*.1920–27. In *Filosofiia i sotsiologiia nauki i tekhniki* (Moscow: Nauka, 1986), 80–138. English translation: *Towards a Philosophy of the Act*, trans. Vadim Liapunov (Austin, Tex.: University of Texas Press, 1994).

'Avtor i geroi v esteticheskoi deiat'elnosti (Fragment pervoi glavy)' ['Author and Hero in Aesthetic Activity (Fragment of the First Chapter)'], *c*.1924–27. In *Filosofiia i sotsiologiia nauki i tekhniki* (Moscow: Nauka, 1986), 138–57. English translation in *Art and Answerability*, 208–31.

'Avtor i geroi v esteticheskoi deiat'elnosti' ['Author and Hero in Aesthetic Activity'], *c*.1924–27. In *Estetika slovesnogo tvorchestva*, 9–191. English translation in *Art and Answerability*, 4–208.

'Problema soderzhaniia, materiala i formy v slovesnom khudozhestvennom tvorchestve' ['The Problem of Content, Material, and Form in Verbal Artistic Creation'], *c*.1924. In *Voprosy literatury i estetiki*, 6–71. English translation in *Art and Answerability*, 257–325.

Notes from the Philosophical Seminar, 1924–1925

'Lektsii i vystupleniia M. M. Bakhtina 1924–1925 gg. v zapisiakh L. V. Pumpianskogo' ['Lectures and Interventions by M. M. Bakhtin in 1924–1925, from notes by L. V. Pumpiansky']. Bakhtin's contributions to the Leningrad philosophy seminar. Ed. N. I. Nikolaev, in L. A. Gogotishvili and P. S. Gurevich (eds.), *M. M. Bakhtin kak filosof* (Moscow: Nauka, 1992), 221–52.

Notes from Bakhtin's Lectures on Russian Literature, 1920s (taken by R. M. Mirkina)

'Iz lektsii po istorii russkoi literatury: Viacheslav Ivanov' ['From Lectures on the History of Russian Literature: Viacheslav Ivanov'], 1920s. In *Estetika slovesnogo tvorchestva*, 394–403.

'Konspekty lekstii M. M. Bakhtina' ['Conspectuses of M. M. Bakhtin's Lectures'], 1922–23. Notes from lectures on Tolstoy. In *Prometei: Istoriko-biograficheskii al'manakh*, 12 (Moscow, 1980), 257–68.

'Lektsii ob A. Belom, F. Sologube, A. Bloke, S. Esenine (v zapisi R. M. Mirkinoi)' ['Lectures on Andrei Bely, F. Sologub, A. Blok, S. Esenin (from the notes of R. M. Mirkina)'], 1920s, ed. and introd. S. G. Bocharov, *Dialog Karnaval Khronotop*, 2–3 (1993), 135–74.

'Lektsii M. M. Bakhtina po russkoi literature 1922–1927 gg.: Zapis' R. M. Mirkinoi' ['Lectures on Russian Literature by M. M. Bakhtin, 1922–1927: Notes of R. M. Mirkina']. Includes lectures on Leonov, Fedin, Erenburg, Tynianov, and Zoshchenko. *Dialog Karnaval Khronotop*, 1 (1993), 97–104.

'Lektsiia o Maiakovskom' ['A Lecture on Mayakovsky'], c.1926–27, *Dialog Karnaval Khronotop*, 2 (1995), 111–23.

Books, Articles, and Essays, 1929–1940

Problemy tvorchestva Dostoevskogo [*Problems of Dostoevsky's Art*] (Leningrad: Priboi, 1929). English translation: the text of the revised *Problemy poetiki Dostoevskogo* (1963) was translated in full; three fragments of the parts of the 1929 text which did not survive revision were translated as an appendix. See *Problems of Dostoevsky's Poetics*, trans. Caryl Emerson (Manchester: Manchester University Press, 1984): the appendix is found on pp. 275–82.

'Predislovie' ['Preface']. In L. N. Tolstoy, *Polnoe sobranie khudozhestvennykh proizvedenii* [*Collected Artistic Works*], vol. xi: *Dramatic Works*, ed. K. Khalabaev and B. Eikhenbaum (Moscow and Leningrad: Gosizdat, 1929), pp. iii–x. Repr. in *Literaturno-kriticheskie stat'i*, 90–9. English translation by Caryl Emerson in Gary Saul Morson and Caryl Emerson (eds.), *Rethinking Bakhtin: Extensions and Challenges* (Evanston, Ill.: Northwestern University Press, 1989), 227–36.

'Predislovie' ['Preface']. In L. N. Tolstoy, *Polnoe sobranie khudozhestvennykh proizvedenii* [*Collected Artistic Works*], vol. xiii: *Resurrection*, ed. K. Khalabaev and B. Eikhenbaum (Moscow and Leningrad: Gosizdat, 1929), pp. iv–x. Repr. in *Literaturno-kriticheskie stat'i*, 100–20. English translation by Caryl Emerson in *Rethinking Bakhtin: Extensions and Challenges*, 237–57.

'Slovo v romane' ['Discourse in the Novel'], 1934–35. In *Voprosy literatury i estetiki*, 72–233. English translation in *The Dialogic Imagination*, 259–422.

'Roman vospitaniia i ego znachenie v istorii realizma' ['The *Bildungsroman* and its Significance in the History of Realism'], 1936–38. Fragments from a book-length work of the same title, apparently never completed . In *Estetika slovesnogo tvorchestva*, 199–249. English translation in *Speech Genres and Other Late Essays*, 10–59.

'Formy vremeni i khronotopa v romane: Ocherki po istoricheskoi poetike' ['Forms of Time and of the Chronotope in the Novel: Notes for a Historical Poetics'], 1937–38 (Concluding Remarks in 1973). These are fragments from the *Bildungsroman* project described above, brought together editorially in a single essay. In *Voprosy literatury i estetiki*, 234–407. English translation in *The Dialogic Imagination*, 84–258.

'Rable v istorii realizma' ['Rabelais in the History of Realism'], 1940–46. Two copies, one in the Bakhtin Archive, another in the Manuscript Section of the Gorky Institute of World Literature, Moscow. This book was submitted as a doctoral dissertation to the Gorky Institute in 1946. A somewhat revised version was prepared by Bakhtin in 1949–50 for the Higher Attestation Commission; a copy of it exists in the Bakhtin Archive. A transcription of the original defence was published in 'Stenogramma zasedaniia Uchenogo soveta Instituta mirovoi literatury im. A. M. Gorkogo: Zashchita dissertatsii tov. Bakhtinym na temu "Rable v istorii realizma", 15 noiabria 1946 g.', *Dialog Karnaval Khronotop*, 2–3 (1993), 55–119. An abridged and revised edition of the first (1940) variant of the dissertation was published in 1965 (see below). A fragment of the dissertation entitled 'Rabelais and Gogol' was published in 1970 (see below).

Notebooks and Essays, 1940–1950

'Iz predystorii romannogo slova' ['From the Prehistory of Novelistic Discourse'], 1940. In *Voprosy literatury i estetiki*, 408–46. English translation in *The Dialogic Imagination*, 41–83.

'Mnogoiazychie, kak predposylka razvitiia romannogo slova' ['Multilanguagedness as a Precondition of the Development of Novelistic Discourse'], *c*.1940. In *Sobranie sochinenii*, vol. 5, 157–8.

'Satira' ['Satire'], an article for the never published tenth volume of the *Literary Encyclopedia*, 1940. In *Sobranie sochinenii*, vol. 5, 11–38.

'"Slovo o polku Igoreve" v istorii epopei' ['"The Lay of Prince Igor" in the History of Epic'], *c*.1940–41. In *Sobranie sochinenii*, vol. 5, 39–42.

'K istorii tipa (zhanrovoi raznovidnosti) romana Dostoevskogo' ['On the History of the Type (Generic Variety) of the Novel of Dostoevsky'], *c*.1940–41. In *Sobranie sochinenii*, vol. 5, 42–4.

'K filosofskim osnovam gumanitarnykh nauk' ['Towards Philosophical Bases of the Human Sciences'], *c*.1940–43. In *Sobranie sochinenii*, vol. 5, 7–10.

'K voprosam ob istoricheskoi traditsii i o narodnykh istochnikakh Gogolevskogo smekha' ['On Questions of the Historical Tradition and the Popular Sources of Gogolian Laughter'], *c*.1940–45. In *Sobranie sochinenii*, vol. 5, 45–7.

'K voprosam teorii romana. K voprosam teorii smekha. O Maiakovskom' ['On Questions of the Theory of the Novel. On Questions of the Theory of Laughter. On Mayakovsky'], *c*.1940–45. In *Sobranie sochinenii*, vol. 5, 48–62.

'Epos i roman: O metodologii issledovaniia romana' ['Epic and Novel: On the Methodology of the Investigation of the Novel'], 1941. In *Voprosy literatury i estetiki*, 447–83. English translation in *The Dialogic Imagination*, 3–40.

'Ritorika, v meru svoei lzhivosti . . .' ['Rhetoric, to the extent that it is something false . . .'], 1943. In *Sobranie sochinenii*, vol. 5, 63–70.

'"Chelovek u zerkala"' ['"The Man in the Mirror"'], 1943. In *Sobranie sochinenii*, vol. 5, 71.

'K voprosam samosoznaniia i samootsenki' ['On Questions of Self-Consciousness and Self-Evaluation'], *c*.1943–46. In *Sobranie sochinenii*, vol. 5, 72–9.

'Dopolneniia i izmeneniia k "Rable"' ['Additions and Amendments to "Rabelais"'], 1944. In *Sobranie sochinenii*, vol. 5, 80–129.

'O Flobere' ['On Flaubert'], *c*.1944–45. In *Sobranie sochinenii*, vol. 5, 130–7.

'K stilistike romana' ['On the Stylistics of the Novel'], *c*.1944–45. In *Sobranie sochinenii*, vol. 5, 138–40.

'Voprosy stilistiki na urokakh russkogo iazyka v srednei shkole' ['Questions of Stylistics for Russian-language Classes in Secondary School'] , *c*.1944–45. In *Sobranie sochinenii*, vol. 5, 141–56.

Notes and Unfinished Articles, 1950–1960

'Osobennosti kitaiskoi literatury i ee istoriia', 'Kitaiskaia literatura', 'Kitaiskii iazyk' ['The Peculiarities of Chinese Literature and its History'; 'Chinese Literature'; 'Chinese Language'], in note form, early 1950s. In A. F. Eremeev (ed.), *M. M. Bakhtin: Esteticheskoe nasledie i sovremennost'*, vol. i (Saransk: Izdatel'stvo Mordovskogo universiteta, 1992), 5–12.

'Problema rechevykh zhanrov' ['The Problem of Speech Genres'], 1953. In *Sobranie sochinenii*, vol. 5, 159–206. English translation in *Speech Genres and Other Late Essays*, 60–102. Preparatory notes and materials for this article: 'Dialog', 1952. In *Sobranie sochinenii*, vol. 5, 207–9. 'Dialog I', 1952. In *Sobranie sochinenii*, vol. 5, 209–18. 'Dialog II', 1952. In *Sobranie sochinenii*, vol. 5, 218–40. 'Podgotovitel'nye materialy' ['Preparatory Materials'], 1952–53. In *Sobranie sochinenii*, vol. 5, 240–86.

'Mariia Tiudor' (review of local production of Victor Hugo's *Mary Tudor*), 1954. In *Sobranie sochinenii*, vol. 5, 298–303.

'Iazyk v khudozhestvennoi literature' ['Language in Artistic Literature'], 1954–55. In *Sobranie sochinenii*, vol. 5, 287–97.

'Problema sentimentalizma' ['The Problem of Sentimentalism'], 1958–59. In *Sobranie sochinenii*, vol. 5, 304–5.

'Problema teksta' ['The Problem of the Text'], 1959–60. In *Sobranie sochinenii*, vol. 5, 306–28. English translation in *Speech Genres and Other Late Essays*, 103–18. NB: the existing English translation is of the originally published version of this text, entitled 'The Problem of the Text in Linguistics, Philology and the other Human Sciences: An Experiment in Philosophical Analysis', and found in *Estetika slovesnogo tvorchestva*, 297–325. The editors of the *Sobranie sochinenii* have now revealed that this first version of the text included, as its second half, the first part of the text listed below as '1961 god. Zametki' ['Notes from 1961'].

Notes and Revised Books, 1961–1975

'1961 god. Zametki' ['Notes from 1961'], 1961. In *Sobranie sochinenii*, vol. 5, 329–63. This text, which is effectively the publication of a notebook with this title on its cover, was previously published as two separate texts: the first section as the latter half of the 'The Problem of the Text in Linguistics, Philosophy and the other Human Sciences' (see above) and the second section as 'K pererabotke knigi o Dostoevskom' ['Towards a Reworking of the Book on Dostoevsky'], in *Estetika slovesnogo tvorchestva*, 326–46. English translation: first section in *Speech Genres and Other Late Essays*, 118–28; second section as appendix to *Problems of Dostoevsky's Poetics*, trans. Emerson, 283–302.

'Dostoevsky. 1961g.', 1961. In *Sobranie sochinenii*, vol. 5, 364–74.

'K Dostoevskomu' ['On Dostoevsky'], 1962. In 'Iz chernovykh tetradei', *Literaturnaia ucheba*, 5–6 (1992), 165.

'Zametki 1962 g.–1963 g.' ['Notes from 1962–1963']. In *Sobranie sochinenii*, vol. 5, 375–8.

Problemy poetiki Dostoevskogo [*Problems of Dostoevsky's Poetics*] (Moscow: Sovetskaia Rossiia, 1963). English translation: *Problems of Dostoevsky's Poetics*, ed. and trans. Caryl Emerson (Manchester: Manchester University Press, 1984).

Tvorchestvo Fransua Rable i narodnaia kul'tura srednevekov'ia i renessansa [*The Art of François Rabelais and the Popular Culture of the Middle Ages and the Renaissance*] (Moscow: Khudozhestvennaia literatura, 1965; repr. with new pagination in 1990). Revision of the book on Rabelais first written in 1940–46. All citations are taken from the 1990 edition. English translation: *Rabelais and His World*, trans. Hélène Iswolsky (Cambridge, Mass.: MIT Press, 1968).

'Rable i Gogol: Isskustvo slova i narodnaia smekhovaia kul'tura' ['Rabelais and Gogol: The Art of the Word and the Popular Culture of Laughter']. Fragment of the 1940 Rabelais text revised for publication. In *Voprosy literaturi i estetiki*, 484–94. English translation: 'The Art of the Word and the Culture of Folk Humour (Rabelais and Gogol)', trans. Henryk Baran, in Henryk Baran (ed.), *Structuralism and Semiotics: Readings from the Soviet Union* (White Plains, NY: International Arts and Sciences Press, 1976), 284–96.

'Otvet na vopros redaktsii *Novogo mira*' ['Response to a Question from the Editors of *Novyi mir*']. *Novyi mir*, 11 (1970), 237–40. Repr. in *Estetika slovesnogo tvorchestva*, 347–54. English translation in *Speech Genres and Other Late Essays*, 1–9.

Internal review of L. E. Pinsky's *Shekspir*, 1970. In *Estetika slovesnogo tvorchestva*, 431–2.

'Iz zapisei 1970–1971 godov' ['From the Notes of 1970–1971']. In *Estetika slovesnogo tvorchestva*, 355–80. English translation in *Speech Genres and Other Late Essays*, 132–58.

Review of A. M. Polamishev's play 'Ach, Nevsky, vsemogushchii Nevsky! . . .', 1971. *Dialog Karnaval Khronotop*, 4 (1997), 124–5.

'K metodologii gumanitarnykh nauk' ['Towards a Methodology of the Human Sciences'], 1974. Revised version of 'K filosofskim osnovam gumanitarnykh nauk', *c*.1940–43. In *Estetika slovesnogo tvorchestva*, 381–93. English translation in *Speech Genres and Other Late Essays*, 159–72.

Other Works

'Zametki' ['Notes'], undated. The majority, though not all, of these notes were later published with editorial apparatus elsewhere. In *Literaturno-kriticheskie stat'i*, 509–31.

Collections of Essays in Russian and English

Voprosy literatury i estetiki: Issledovaniia raznykh let [*Questions of Literature and Aesthetics: Investigations from Various Years*] (Moscow: Khudozhestvennaia literatura, 1975).

The Dialogic Imagination: Four Essays by M. M. Bakhtin, ed. Michael Holquist, trans. Caryl Emerson and Michael Holquist (Austin, Tex.: University of Texas Press, 1981).

Bakhtin School Papers, ed. Ann Shukman, Russian Poetics in Translation 10 (Somerton: RPT Publications, 1983).

Estetika slovesnogo tvorchestva [*The Aesthetics of Verbal Creation*], 2nd edn., ed. S. G. Bocharov (Moscow: Isskustvo, 1986).

Literaturno-kriticheskie stat'i [*Literary-Critical Articles*], ed. S. G. Bocharov and V. V. Kozhinov (Moscow: Khudozhestvennaia literatura, 1986).

Speech Genres and Other Late Essays, ed. Caryl Emerson and Michael Holquist, trans. Vern W. McGee (Austin, Tex.: University of Texas Press, 1986).

Art and Answerability: Early Philosophical Essays by M. M. Bakhtin, ed. Michael Holquist and Vadim Liapunov, trans. Vadim Liapunov and Kenneth Brostrom (Austin, Tex.: University of Texas Press, 1990).

Sobranie sochinenii v semi tomakh, vol. 5: *Raboty 1940-kh–nachala 1960-kh godov* [*Collected Works in Seven Volumes*, vol. v: *Works from the 1940s to the Beginning of the 1960s*], ed. S. G. Bocharov and L. A. Gogotishvili (Moscow: Russkie slovari, 1996).

Letters from Bakhtin

TO M. I. KAGAN. Eight letters, 1921–22. Published in Iu. M. Kagan, 'O starykh bumagakh iz semeinogo arkhiva (M. M. Bakhtin i M. I. Kagan)', *Dialog Karnaval Khronotop*, 1 (1992), 60–88.

TO M. V. IUDINA. Published in 'Iz perepiski M. V. Iudinoi i M. M. Bakhtin', *Dialog Karnaval Khronotop*, 4 (1993), 41–85.

TO V. V. KOZHINOV. Extracts from eighteen letters, 1961–65. Published as 'Pis'ma M. M. Bakhtina', *Literaturnaia ucheba*, 5–6 (1992), 144–52.

TO I. I. KANAEV. Two letters, 1962, 1969. Published in *Estetika slovesnogo tvorchestva*, 416–17.

TO V. N. TURBIN.

28 Dec. 1962. Published in Turbin, 'Po povodu odnogo pis'ma M. M. Bakhtina', *Dialog Karnaval Khronotop* 1 (1992), 53–9.

19 Jan. 1963. Published as '"Ni proizvedenii, ni obrazov Dostoevskogo . . . i v pomine net"', in *Bakhtinskii sbornik*, vol. ii (Moscow: published by editors, 1991), 371–3.

6 and 31 Mar. 1964. Published as '". . .I zakhvatite s soboi masla i sakharu" (Dva pis'ma M. M. Bakhtina: publikatsiia i primechaniia', in K. G. Isupov (ed.), *M. M. Bakhtin i filosofskaia kul'tura XX veka*, vol. ii (St Petersburg: Obrazovanie, 1991), 99–106.

Interviews

'U Bakhtina v Maleevke' ['With Bakhtin in Maleevka'], interview with A. Z. Vulis, 1966. In Abram Zinovevich Vulis, *Ser'eznost' neser'eznykh situatsii: Satira, prikliucheniia, detektiv* (Tashkent: Gafur Guiama, 1984). Repr. in *Dialog Karnaval Khronotop*, 2–3 (1993), 175–89.

'O polifonichnosti romanov Dostoevskogo' ['On the Polyphonicity of Dostoevsky's Novels'], interview with Zbigniew Podgórzec, 1971. In *Rossiia/Russia*, vol. ii (Torino: Einaudi, 1975), 189–98.

Besedy V. D. Duvakina s M. M. Bakhtinym [*Conversations between V. D. Duvakin and M. M. Bakhtin*], interviews from 1973, ed. V. B. Kuznetsova, M. B. Radzishevskaia, and V. F. Teider (Moscow: Progress, 1996).

Reminiscences

BOCHAROV, S. G., 'Ob odnom razgovore i vokrug nego', *Novoe literaturnoe obozrenie*, 2 (1993), 70–89; abr. trans. by Vadim Liapunov and Stephen Blackwell, 'Conversations with Bakhtin', *PMLA* 109: 5 (1994), 1009–24.

—— 'Primechanie k memuaru', *Novoe literaturnoe obozrenie*, 3 (1993), 209–10.

BROITMAN, S. N., 'Dve besedy s Bakhtinym', in S. N. Broitman and N. Gorbanov (eds.), *Khronotop* (Dagestan: Dagestanskii gosudarstvennyi universitet, 1990).

ESTIFEEVA, V. B., 'Vospominaniia o Bakhtine', *Strannik* (1995), 1: 37–45; 2: 110–16; 3: 25–32; 4: 71–90.

GACHEV, GEORGY, '"Tak, sobstevenno, zaviazalas' uzhe tselaia istoriia . . ." (Georgy Gachev vspominaet i razdumyvaet o M. M. Bakhtine)', *Dialog Karnaval Khronotop*, 1 (1993), 105–8.

KAGANSKAIA, MAIIA, 'Shutovskoi khorovod', *Sintaksis*, 12 (1984), 139–96.

KOZHINOV, V. V., '"Tak eto bylo . . ."', *Don*, 10 (1988), 156–60.

—— 'Kak pishut trudy, ili Proiskhozhdenie nesozdannogo avantiurnogo romana', *Dialog Karnaval Khronotop*, 1 (1992), 109–22.

—— 'Bakhtin i ego chitateli: Razmyshleniia i otchasti vospominaniia', *Dialog Karnaval Khronotop*, 2–3 (1993), 120–34.

—— '"Ia prosto blagodariu svoiu sud'bu . . ." (Vadim Kozhinov vspominaet o tom, kak udalos' pereizdat' *Problemy tvorchestva Dostoevskogo*)', *Dialog Karnaval Khronotop*, 1 (1994), 104–10.

KOZHINOV, V. V., 'Kozhinov on Bakhtin' (interview with Nicholas Rzhevsky), *New Literary History*, 25: 2 (1994), 429–44.

—— 'Ob odnom "obstoiatel'stve" zhizni M. M. Bakhtina', *Dialog Karnaval Khronotop*, 1 (1995), 151–60.

—— 'Bakhtin v zhivom dialoge', in *Besedy V. D. Duvakina s M. M. Bakhtinym*, ed. V. B. Kuznetsova, M. B. Radzishevskaia, and V. F. Teider (Moscow: Progress, 1996), 272–81.

LEIBOVICH, S. L., 'Tridtsat' let spustia: Redaktor "Rabelais" S. L. Leibovich vspominaet o podgotovke knigi k izdaniiu', *Dialog Karnaval Khronotop*, 1 (1997), 140–86.

LIKHACHEV, D. S., 'Vospominaniia', *Dialog Karnaval Khronotop*, 1 (1995), 143–4.

MIRKINA, R. M., 'Bakhtin, kakim Ia ego znala (Molodoi Bakhtin)', *Dialog Karnaval Khronotop*, 1 (1993), 92–6.

POLAMISHEV, A. M., 'A. M. Polamishev vspominaet dva razgovora s M. M. Bakhtinym o "karnaval'noi chushi bytiia"', *Dialog Karnaval Khronotop*, 4 (1997), 118–23.

PONOMAREVA, G. B., 'Vyskazannoe i nevyskazannoe . . .', *Dialog Karnaval Khronotop*, 3 (1995), 59–77.

TURBIN, V. N., 'Iz neopublikovannogo o M. M. Bakhtine', Book I [Proceedings of] The Seventh International Bakhtin Conference (Moscow: Moscow State Pedagogical University, 1995), 169–79.

—— 'Emigratsiia v MACCP', *Dialog Karnaval Khronotop*, 4 (1997), 92–113.

VASIL'EV, L. G., 'Takim Ia ego pomniu . . .', *Dialog Karnaval Khronotop*, 4 (1994), 109–15.

ZHUKOV, N. A., '"Oni ub'iut . . .! Oni nepremenno ub'iut ego! . . ." (iz vospominanii o M. M. Bakhtine)', *Dialog Karnaval Khronotop*, 3 (1994), 98–129.

ZHURAVLEVA, A. I., 'M. M. Bakhtin (vpechatleniia)', *Dialog Karnaval Khronotop*, 2 (1996), 78–81.

M. I. KAGAN

'O lichnosti v sotsiologii' ['On the Personality in Sociology'], *c.*1918–19. Unpublished transcription of MS by Brian Poole; forthcoming in M. I. Kagan, *Filosofiia dolzhenstvovaniia* [The Philosophy of the Ought], ed. Brian Poole (Moscow: Agraf).

'Kak vozmozhna istoriia?' ['How is History Possible?'], 1919. *Zapiski Orlovskogo gosudarstvennogo universiteta, seriia obshchestvennykh nauk*, 1 (Orel: Gosizdat Orlovskoe gubernevskoe otdelenie, 1921), 137–92. A new version will appear in *Filosofiia dolzhenstvovaniia*.

'O khode istorii: iz problem filosofii istorii' ['On the Course of History: A Problem in the Philosophy of History'], 1920. Unpublished transcription of MS by Brian Poole; forthcoming in *Filosofiia dolzhenstvovaniia*.

'German Kogen (4 Iulia 1842g.–4 Aprelia 1918g.)', 1920. *Nauchnye izvestiia, akademicheskii tsentr Narkomprosa*, 2 (Moscow: Gosizdat, 1922), 110–24.

'Filosofiia kak filosofiia istorii' ['Philosophy as Philosophy of History'], c.1921–23. Unpublished transcription of MS by Brian Poole; forthcoming in *Filosofiia dolzhenstvovaniia*.

'Paul Natorp i krizis kul'tury' ['Paul Natorp and the Crisis of Culture'], 1922. *Dialog Karnaval Khronotop*, 1 (1995), 49–54.

'Evreistvo v krizise kul'tury' ['Judaism in the Crisis of Culture'], 1923. *Minuvshee*, 6 (1981), 229–36.

'Filosofiia i istoriia' ['Philosophy and History'], c.1923–24. Unpublished transcription of MS by Brian Poole; forthcoming in *Filosofiia dolzhenstvovaniia*.

I. I. KANAEV

'Sovremennyi vitalizm' ['Contemporary Vitalism'], *Chelovek i priroda*, 1 and 2 (1926), 33–42 and 9–22.

P. N. MEDVEDEV

'Uchenyi sal'erizm: O formal'nom (morfologicheskom) metode' ['Scholarly Salierism: On the Formal (Morphological) Method'], *Zvezda*, 3 (1925), 264–76. English translation by Ann Shukman in *Bakhtin School Papers*, 51–64.

'Sotsiologizm bez sotsiologii: O metodologicheskikh rabotakh P. N. Sakulina' ['Sociologism without Sociology: On the Methodological Works of P. N. Sakulin'], *Zvezda*, 2 (1926), 267–71. English translation by C. R. Pike in *Bakhtin School Papers*, 67–74.

Formal'nyi metod v literaturovedenii: Kriticheskoe vvedenie v sotsiologicheskuiu poetiku [*The Formal Method in Literary Scholarship: A Critical Introduction to Sociological Poetics*] (Leningrad: Priboi, 1928). Repr. New York: Serebrianyi vek, 1982 (with Mikhail Bakhtin named as author). English translation: M. M. Bakhtin/ P. N. Medvedev, *The Formal Method in Literary Scholarship: A Critical Introduction to Sociological Poetics*, trans. Albert J. Wehrle (Cambridge, Mass. and London: Harvard University Press, 1985).

Formalizm i formalisty [*Formalism and Formalists*] (Leningrad: Izd. pisatelei v Leningrade, 1934).

L. V. PUMPIANSKY

Dostoevsky i antichnost' [*Dostoevsky and Antiquity*] (Petersburg: Zamysly, 1922).

'Gogol', 1922. *Trudy po znakovym sistemam*, 18 (1984), 125–37.

'Ob ode Pushkina "Pamiatnik"' ['On Pushkin's Ode, "Monument"'], 1923. *Voprosy literatury*, 8 (1977), 135–51.

I. I. SOLLERTINSKY

Gustav Maler (Leningrad: Gosmuzizdat, 1932).
Arnold Shenberg (Leningrad: Leningradskaia filarmonia, 1934).
Muzykal'no-istoricheskie etiudy [Musical-Historical Studies] (Leningrad: Muzgiz, 1956).

V. N. VOLOSHINOV

'Po tu storonu sotsialnogo: O freudizme' ['Beyond the Social: On Freudianism'], *Zvezda*, 5 (1925), 186–214.
'Slovo v zhizni i slovo v poezii: K voprosam sotsiologicheskoi poetiki' ['Discourse in Life and Discourse in Poetry: On Problems of Sociological Poetics'], *Zvezda*, 6 (1926), 244–67. English translation by John Richmond in *Bakhtin School Papers*, 5–30.
Freidizm: Kriticheskii ocherk [*Freudianism: A Critical Sketch*] (Moscow and Leningrad: Gosizdat, 1927). Reprints: 'Bakhtin pod maskoi, mask pervaia: V. N. Voloshinov' ['Bakhtin Under a Mask, First Mask: V. N. Voloshinov'], *Freidizm* [*sic*] (Moscow: Labirint, 1993); Valentin Voloshinov, *Filosofiia i sotsiologiia gumanitarnykh nauk* [includes *Freidizm* and *Marksizm i filosofiia iazyka*] (St Petersburg: Asta Press, 1995); M. M. Bakhtin and V. N. Voloshinov, *Freidizm: Kritischeskii ocherk* (New York: Chalidze Publications, 1983). English translation: *Freudianism: A Marxist Critique*, ed. and trans. I. R. Titunik in collaboration with Neal H. Bruss (New York: Academic Press, 1976).
'Noveishie techeniia lingvisticheskoi mysli na zapade' ['The Latest Trends in Linguistic Thought in the West'], *Literatura i Marksizm*, 5 (1928), 115–49. English translation by Noel Owen in *Bakhtin School Papers*, 31–49.
Marksizm i filosofiia iazyka: Osnovnye problemy sotsiologicheskogo metoda v nauke o iazyke [*Marxism and the Philosophy of Language: Fundamental Problems of Sociological Method in the Science of Language*] (Leningrad: Priboi, 1929). English translation: *Marxism and the Philosophy of Language*, trans. Ladislav Matejka and I. R. Titunik (Cambridge, Mass. and London: Harvard University Press, 1986).
'Stilistika khudozhestvennoi rechi' ['The Stylistics of Artistic Speech'], *Literaturnaia ucheba* (1930), 2: 48–66; 3: 65–87; 5: 43–59. English translation by Noel Owen and Joe Andrew in *Bakhtin School Papers*, 93–152.

BIOGRAPHICAL MATERIALS ON BAKHTIN AND MEMBERS OF THE BAKHTIN CIRCLE (INCLUDING DISCUSSIONS OF THE AUTHORSHIP DISPUTE)

ALPATOV, V. M., 'K istorii knigi V. N. Voloshinova *Marksizm i filosofiia iazyka*', *Izvestiia Akademii Nauk, seriia literatury i iazyka*, 54: 3 (1995), 63–76.
——'Zametki na poliakh stenogrammmy zashchity dissertatsii M. M. Bakhtina', *Dialog Karnaval Khronotop*, 1 (1997), 70–97.

Anon., 'Rable v istorii realizma', *Vestnik Akademii Nauk SSSR* 5 (1947), 123.

Anon., 'Pamiati M. M. Bakhtina', *Sintaksis*, 7 (1980), 102–5.

Anon., 'Ot izdatel'stva', in Bakhtin [*sic*], *Formal'nyi metod v literaturovedenii* (New York: Serebrianyi vek, 1982), 3–7.

BOCHAROV, S., 'Sobytie bytiia' [introduction to Bakhtin's interviews with Duvakin], *Chelovek*, 4 (1993), 137–40.

CHUDAKOV, A., 'Ia sprashivaiu Shklovskogo', *Literaturnoe obozrenie*, 6 (1990), 93–103.

EDGERTON, WILLIAM, 'Iu. G. Oksman, M. I. Lopatto, N. M. Bakhtin i vopros o knigoizdatel'stve "Omphalos"', in *Piatye Tynianovskie chteniia* (Riga, 1990), 211–37.

'Gazeta *Molot* (1918–1920)', *Nevel'skii sbornik*, vol. i (St Petersburg: Akropol', 1996), 147–57.

IANEVICH, I., 'Institut mirovoi literatury v 1930-e–1970-e gody', in *Pamiat': Istoricheskii sbornik*, vol. v (Paris, 1982), 83–162.

IUDINA, M. V., *Mariia Veniaminovna Iudina: Stat'i, vospominaniia, materialy* (Moscow: Vsesoiuznoe izd. sovetskii kompozitor, 1978).

IVANOV, V. V., 'Ob avtorstve knig V. N. Voloshinova i P. N. Medvedeva', *Dialog Karnaval Khronotop*, 4 (1995), 134–9.

KAGAN, IU. M., 'O starykh bumagakh semeinogo arkhiva (M. M. Bakhtin i M. I. Kagan)', *Dialog Karnaval Khronotop*, 1 (1992), 60–88.

——and KAGAN, S. I., 'O pamiatnom, o vazhnom, o bylom . . . (ustnye vospominaniia S. I. Kagan i Iu. M. Kagan)', *Dialog Karnaval Khronotop*, 2 (1995), 165–81.

KAGAN, S., 'Est' li pravo prostit' sistemu' (Letter to the Editor), *Literaturnaia gazeta*, 25, 25 June 1991.

KONKIN, S. S., 'Arest i prigovor', *Sovetskaia Mordoviia*, 26 Mar. 1991, 3.

——'Pora zakryt' vopros o rodoslovnoi M. M. Bakhtina', *Dialog Karnaval Khronotop*, 2 (1994), 119–23.

——'Posleslovie k stat'e "Pora zakryt' vopros o rodoslovnoi M. M. Bakhtina"', *Dialog Karnaval Khronotop*, 3 (1994), 135–7.

——'Esli obratit'sia k pervoistochnikam . . . (k rodoslovnoi M. M. Bakhtina)', [Proceedings of] The Seventh International Bakhtin Conference, Book II (Moscow: Moscow State Pedagogical University, 1995), 244–50.

——'O M. Bakhtine i ego soavtorakh', *Literaturnoe obozrenie*, 2 (1995), 45–8.

——and KONKINA, L. S., *Mikhail Bakhtin: Stranitsy zhizni i tvorchestva* (Saransk: Mordovskoe knizhnoe izdatel'stvo, 1993).

KOZHINOV, VADIM, 'Kniga, vokrug kotoroi ne umolkaiut spory', *Dialog Karnaval Khronotop*, 4 (1995), 140–7.

——and KONKIN, S., 'Mikhail Mikhailovich Bakhtin: Kratkii ocherk zhizni i deiatel'nosti', in S. Konkin (ed.), *Problemy poetiki i istorii literatury* (Saransk: Mordovskii gosudarstvennyi universitet, 1973), 5–15.

KRAFT, JOSEPH, 'Letter from Moscow', *The New Yorker*, 31 Jan. 1983, 104–19.

LAPTUN, V. I., 'K "Biografii M. M. Bakhtina"', *Dialog Karnaval Khronotop*, 1 (1993), 67–73.

LAPTUN, V. I., 'K biografii M. M. Bakhtina', *Dialog Karnaval Khronotop*, 3 (1994), 72–9.

——'M. M. Bakhtin v Saranske (1936–1937, 1945–1969 gg.)', [Proceedings of] The Seventh International Bakhtin Conference, Book II (Moscow: Moscow State Pedagogical University, 1995), 401–2.

——'Arkhivnie materialy o prepodavatel'skoi rabote M. M. Bakhtina v Mordovskom pedinstitute', *Dialog Karnaval Khronotop*, 1 (1996), 63–78.

——'Pervyi priezd M. M. Bakhtina v Saransk (1936–1937gg.)', *Nevel'skii sbornik*, vol. i (St Petersburg: Akropol, 1996), 61–74.

——and KUKLIN, V. N., 'K biografii M. M. Bakhtina', in *Bakhtinskii sbornik*, vol. iii (Moscow: Labirint, 1997), 368–72.

LISOV, A. G., and TRUSOVA, E. G., 'Repliki po povodu avtobiograficheskogo mifotvorchestva M. M. Bakhtina', *Dialog Karnaval Khronotop*, 3 (1996), 161–6.

MEDVEDEV, IU. P., '"Nas bylo mnogo na chelne. . ."', *Dialog Karnaval Khronotop*, 1 (1992), 89–108.

——Letter to the Editors, *Dialog Karnaval Khronotop*, 4 (1995), 148–56.

——'Vitebskii period zhizni P. N. Medvedeva', in *Bakhtinskie chteniia*, vol. i (Vitebsk: N. A. Pan'kov, 1996), 63–86.

——'Na puti k sozdaniiu sotsiologicheskoi poetiki', *Dialog Karnaval Khronotop*, 2 (1998), 5–57.

——and AKIMOV, VLADIMIR, 'Ne maski, a litsa', *Sevodnia*, 4 May 1994.

MIKHEEVA, L., *I. I. Sollertinsky: Zhizn' i nasledie* (Leningrad: Sovetskii pisatel', 1988)

NIKOLAEV, N. I., 'M. M. Bakhtin v Nevele letom 1919', in *Nevel'skii sbornik*, vol. i (St Petersburg: Akropol', 1996), 96–101.

OSOVSKY, O. E., '"Neslyshnyi dialog": Biograficheskie i nauchnye sozvuchiia v sud'bakh Nikolaia i Mikhaila Bakhtinykh', in K. G. Isupov (ed.), *M. M. Bakhtin i filosofskaia kul'tura XX veka*, vol. ii (St Petersburg: Obrazovanie, 1991), 43–51.

PAN'KOV, N. A., 'Zagadki rannego perioda (Eshche neskol'ko shtrikhov k "Biografii M. M. Bakhtina")', *Dialog Karnaval Khronotop*, 1 (1993), 74–89.

——'"Ot khoda etogo dela zavisit vse dal'neishee . . ." (zashchita dissertatsii M. M. Bakhtina kak real'noe sobytie, vysokaia drama i nauchnaia komediia)', *Dialog Karnaval Khronotop*, 2–3 (1993), 29–54.

——'Predislovie k zapozdavshemu "Poslesloviiu . . ." S. S. Konkina', *Dialog Karnaval Khronotop*, 3 (1994), 130–4.

——'Mifologema Voloshinova (neskol'ko zamechanii kak by na poliakh arkhivnykh materialov)', *Dialog Karnaval Khronotop*, 2 (1995), 66–9.

——'"No my Istorii ne pishem . . ."', *Dialog Karnaval Khronotop*, 1 (1997), 98–139.

——'Archive Material on Bakhtin's Nevel Period', *South Atlantic Quarterly*, 97: 3/4 (1998), 733–52.

PASTERNAK, B., 'Boris Pasternak–Pavel Medvedev' [Twelve letters from Pasternak to Medvedev, 1929–1930], in *Literaturnoe nasledstvo*, vol. xciii (Moscow: Nauka, 1983), 702–17.

PERLINA, NINA, 'Bakhtin–Medvedev–Voloshinov: An Apple of Discourse',

University of Ottawa Quarterly, 53: 1 (1983), 35–47.

——'Funny Things are Happening on the Way to the Bakhtin Forum', Kennan Institute Occasional Papers 231 (Kennan Institute for Advanced Russian Studies, 1989).

REVZIN, O. G. [account of meeting in honour of Bakhtin's seventy-fifth birthday], *Voprosy iazykoznaniia*, 2 (1971), 160–2.

SAVKIN, I. A., 'Delo o Voskresenii', in K. G. Isupov (ed.), *M. M. Bakhtin i filosofskaia kul'tura XX veka*, vol. ii (St Petersburg: Obrazovanie, 1991), 106–21.

STRADA, VITTORIO, Letter to the Editors, in *Bakhtinskii sbornik*, vol. iii (Moscow: Labirint, 1997), 373–9.

TITUNIK, I. R., 'Bakhtin &/or Voloˇinov &/or Medvedev: Dialogue &/or Doubletalk', in Benjamin A. Stolz, Lubomir Doložel, and I. R. Titunik (eds.), *Language and Literary Theory* (Ann Arbor, Mich.: University of Michigan, 1984), 535–64.

VASIL'EV, N., 'M. M. Bakhtin ili V. N. Voloshinov', *Literaturnoe obozrenie*, 9 (1991), 38–43.

——'V. N. Voloshinov—biograficheskii ocherk', in Valentin Voloshinov, *Filosofiia i sotsiologiia gumanitarnykh nauk* (St Petersburg: Asta Press, 1995), 5–22.

——'M. M. Bakhtin i V. N. Voloshinov', [Proceedings of] The Seventh International Bakhtin Conference, Book II (Moscow: Moscow State Pedagogical University, 1995), 396–400.

——'Kommentarii k kommentariiam biografov M. M. Bakhtina', *Dialog Karnaval Khronotop*, 4 (1995), 157–70.

[Voloshinov], 'Lichnoe delo V. N. Voloshinova', *Dialog Karnaval Khronotop*, 2 (1995), 70–99.

CRITICAL STUDIES OF BAKHTIN AND THE CIRCLE

ALEXANDROV, DANIEL, and STRUCHKOV, ANTON, 'Bakhtin's Legacy and the History of Science and Culture: An Interview with Anatolii Akhutin and Vladimir Bibler', *Configurations*, 1: 3 (1993), 335–86.

Anon., Review of *Problemy poetiki Dostoevskogo*, *Oktiabr*, 11 (1929), 195–7.

ARONOWITZ, STANLEY, 'Notes From Underground: Mikhail Bakhtin Changes the Face of Criticism', *Village Voice Literary Supplement*, 72 (1989), 22–4.

AUCOUTURIER, MICHEL, 'The Theory of the Novel in Russia in the 1930s: Lukács and Bakhtin', in John Garrard (ed.), *The Russian Novel from Pushkin to Pasternak* (New Haven and London: Yale University Press, 1983), 227–40.

AVERINSTEV, SERGEI, 'Lichnost' i talant uchenogo', *Literaturnoe obozrenie*, 10 (1976), 58–61.

——[Untitled], *Soviet Literature*, 1 (1977), 145–51.

——'Mikhail Bakhtin: Retrospektiva i perspektiva' [Review of Bakhtin, *Literaturno-kriticheskie stat'i*], *Druzhba narodov*, 3 (1988), 256–9.

——'Bakhtin and the Russian Attitude to Laughter', *Critical Studies*, 3: 2/4: 1–2 (1993), 13–19.

BAGBY, LEWIS, 'Mikhail Bakhtin's Discourse Typologies: Theoretical and Practical Considerations', *Slavic Review*, 41: 1 (1982), 35–58.

BARSHT, K. A., 'Etiko-esteticheskie vzgliady rannego Bakhtina', in L. V. Gorshkóva (ed.), *Problemy nauchnogo naslediia M. M. Bakhtina* (Saransk: Mordovskii gosudarstvennyi universitet, 1985), 105–15.

BARSKY, ROBERT, and HOLQUIST, MICHAEL (eds.), *Bakhtin and Otherness*, special issue of *Discours social/Social Discourse*, 3: 1–2 (1990).

BATKIN, LEONID, 'Smekh Panurga i filosofiia kul'tury', *Voprosy filosofii*, 12 (1967), 114–23.

BAUER, DALE, *Feminist Dialogics: A Theory of Failed Community* (Albany, NY: State University of New York Press, 1988).

BENNETT, TONY, *Formalism and Marxism* (London: Methuen, 1979).

BERKOVSKY, N., Review of *Problemy tvorchestva Dostoevskogo*, *Zvezda*, 7 (1929).

BERNARD-DONALS, MICHAEL F., *Mikhail Bakhtin: Between Phenomenology and Marxism* (Cambridge: Cambridge University Press, 1994).

BERNSTEIN, MICHAEL ANDRÉ, 'The Poetics of *Ressentiment*', in Gary Saul Morson and Caryl Emerson (eds.), *Rethinking Bakhtin: Extensions and Challenges* (Evanston, Ill.: Northwestern University Press, 1989), 197–223.

—— 'When the Carnival Turns Bitter: Preliminary Reflections upon the Abject Hero', *Critical Inquiry*, 10: 2 (1983), 283–306.

BERRONG, RICHARD M., *Rabelais and Bakhtin: Popular Culture in Gargantua and Pantagruel* (Lincoln, Nebr. and London: University of Nebraska Press, 1986).

BIBLER, V. S., *Myshlenie kak tvorchestvo: Vvedenie k logiku myshlennogo dialoga* (Moscow: Izd. politicheskoi literatury, 1975).

—— *M. M. Bakhtin, ili poetika kul'tury* (Moscow: Progress–Gnozis, 1991).

BOCHAROV, SERGEI, 'Sobytie bytiia: O Mikhaile Mikhailoviche Bakhtine', *Novyi mir*, 11 (1995), 211–21.

BONETSKAIA, N. K., 'M. M. Bakhtin i traditsii russkoi filosofii', *Voprosy filosofii*, 1 (1993), 83–93.

—— 'K sopostavleniiu dvukh redaktsii knigi M. Bakhtina o Dostoevskom', in *Bakhtinskie chteniia*, vol. i (Vitebsk: N. A. Pan'kov, 1996), 26–32.

—— 'Bakhtin's Aesthetics as a Logic of Form', in David Shepherd (ed.), *The Contexts of Bakhtin: Philosophy, Authorship, Aesthetics* (New York: Harwood Academic Press, 1998), 83–94.

—— 'Bakhtin glazami metafizika', *Dialog Karnaval Khronotop*, 1 (1998), 103–55.

BRANDIST, CRAIG, 'Bakhtin, Cassirer and Symbolic Forms', *Radical Philosophy*, 85 (1997), 20–7.

CHUDAKOV, A. P., 'V. V. Vinogradov i teoriia khudozhestvennoi rechi pervoi treti XX veka', in V. V. Vinogradov, *O iazyke khudozhestvennoi prozy* (Moscow: Nauka, 1980), 285–315.

CLARK, KATERINA, and HOLQUIST, MICHAEL, *Mikhail Bakhtin* (Cambridge, Mass. and London: Harvard University Press, 1985).

—— 'A Continuing Dialogue', *Slavic and East European Journal*, 30: 1 (1986), 96–102.

CLIFFORD, JAMES, 'On Ethnographic Authority', *Representations*, 1: 2 (1983), 118–46.

CURTIS, JAMES M. 'Michael [*sic*] Bakhtin, Nietzsche, and Russian Pre-Revolutionary Thought', in Bernice Glatzer Rosenthal (ed.), *Nietzsche in Russia* (Princeton, NJ: Princeton University Press, 1986), 331–54.

DE MAN, PAUL, 'Dialogue and Dialogism', *Poetics Today*, 4: 1 (1983), 99–107.

DYMSHITS, A., 'Monologi i dialogi', *Literaturnaia gazeta*, 82, 11 July 1964.

EMERSON, CARYL, *The First Hundred Years of Mikhail Bakhtin* (Princeton, NJ: Princeton University Press, 1997).

FRIDLENDER, G., 'Real'noe soderzhanie poiska', *Literaturnoe obozrenie*, 10 (1976), 61–4.

GARDINER, MICHAEL, *The Dialogics of Critique: M. M. Bakhtin and the Theory of Ideology* (London: Routledge, 1992).

GASPAROV, M. L., 'M. M. Bakhtin in Russian Culture of the Twentieth Century', trans. Ann Shukman, *Studies in 20th Century Literature*, 9: 1 (1984), 169–76.

GODZICH, WLAD, 'Foreword', in M. M. Bakhtin/P. N. Medvedev, *The Formal Method in Literary Scholarship*, trans. Albert J. Wehrle (Cambridge, Mass. and London: Harvard University Press, 1985), pp. vii–xiv.

——'Correcting Kant: Bakhtin and Intercultural Interactions', *boundary 2*, 18: 1 (1991), 5–17.

GOGOTISHVILI, L. A., 'Varianty i invarianty M. M. Bakhtina', *Voprosy filosofii*, 1 (1992), 115–33.

GOSSMAN, LIONEL, 'Mikhail Bakhtin', *Comparative Literature*, 38: 4 (1986), 337–49.

GROSSMAN-ROSHCHIN, I., 'Dni nashei zhizni. O poznavaemosti khudozhestva proshlogo. O "sotsiologizme" M. N. [*sic*] Bakhtina, avtora *Problemy tvorchestva Dostoevskogo*', *Na literaturnom postu*, 18 (1929), 5–10.

GÜNTHER, HANS, 'M. Bakhtin i "Rozhdenie tragedii" F. Nitsshe [F. Nietzsche]', *Dialog Karnaval Khronotop*, 1 (1992), 27–34.

GUREVICH, A., 'Smekh v narodnoi kul'ture srednevekov'ia', *Voprosy literatury*, 6 (1966), 206–13.

HALE, DOROTHY J., 'Bakhtin in African American Literary Theory', *ELH* 61 (1994), 445–71.

—— *Social Formalism: The Novel in Theory from Henry James to the Present* (Stanford, Ca.: Stanford University Press, 1998).

HIRSCHKOP, KEN, 'Bakhtin, Discourse and Democracy', *New Left Review*, 160 (1986), 92–113.

——'Is Dialogism for Real?', *Social Text*, 30 (1992), 102–13.

——and SHEPHERD, DAVID, 'Bakhtin and the Politics of Criticism' (Letter to the Editor), *PMLA* 109: 1 (1994), 116–18.

————(eds.), *Bakhtin and Cultural Theory* (Manchester: Manchester University Press, 1989).

HITCHCOCK, PETER (ed.), *Bakhtin/'Bakhtin': Studies in the Archive and Beyond*, special issue of *South Atlantic Quarterly*, 97: 3/4 (1998).

HOLQUIST, MICHAEL, *Dialogism: Bakhtin and his World* (London and New York: Routledge, 1990).

HOWES, CRAIG, 'Rhetorics of Attack: Bakhtin and the Aesthetics of Satire', *Genre*, 19: 3 (1986), 231–43.

IVANOV, V. V., 'Znachenie idei M. M. Bakhtina o znake, vyskazyvanii i dialoge dlia sovremennoi semiotiki', *Trudy po znakovym sistemam*, 6 (Tartu: Tartu gosudarstvennyi universitet, 1973), 5–45; trans. into English in Henryk Baran (ed.), *Structuralism and Semiotics* (White Plains, NY: International Arts and Sciences Press, 1976), 186–243.

—— 'O Bakhtine i semiotike', *Rossiia/Russia*, vol. ii (Torino: Einaudi, 1975), 284–97.

LUNACHARSKY, A. V., 'O "mnogogolosti" Dostoevskogo', *Novyi mir*, 10 (1929), 195–209.

MAKHLIN, V. L., *Mikhail Bakhtin: Filosofiia postupka*, Znanie 6 (1990).

—— 'Bakhtin i Zapad (opyt obzornoi orientatsii)', *Voprosy filosofii*, 1 (1993), 94–114, and 2 (1993), 134–50.

—— *Ia i Drugoi: istoki filosofii 'dialoga' XX veka* (St Petersburg: Russkii khristianskii gumanitarnyi institut, 1995).

MALCUZYNSKI, M.-PIERRETTE, 'Mikhail Bakhtin and Contemporary Narrative Theory', *University of Ottawa Quarterly*, 53: 1 (1983), 51–65.

MATEJKA, LADISLAV, 'On the First Russian Prolegomena to Semiotics', in V. N. Voloshinov, *Marxism and the Philosophy of Language*, trans. Ladislav Matejka and I. R. Titunik (Cambridge, Mass. and London: Harvard University Press, 1986), 161–74.

MIHAILOVIC, ALEXANDER, 'With Influence and Without Separation: Bakhtin and the Chalcedonian Ideal', [Proceedings of] The Seventh International Bakhtin Conference, Book II (Moscow: Moscow State Pedagogical University, 1995), 351–5.

MORSON, GARY SAUL, 'Two Voices in Every Head', *New York Times Book Review*, 10 Feb. 1985.

—— 'The Baxtin Industry', *Slavic and East European Journal*, 30: 1 (1986), 81–90.

—— 'Bakhtin and the Present Moment', *American Scholar*, 60: 2 (1991), 201–22.

—— 'Introduction' to the Russian Cluster, *PMLA* 107: 2 (1992).

—— and EMERSON, CARYL, *Mikhail Bakhtin: Creation of a Prosaics* (Stanford, Ca.: Stanford University Press, 1990).

NIKOLAEV, N. I. (ed.), 'Lektsii i vystupleniia M. M. Bakhtina 1924–25 v zapisiakh L. V. Pumpianskogo', in L. A. Gogotishvili and P. S. Gurevich (eds.), *M. M. Bakhtin kak filosof* (Moscow: Nauka, 1992), 221–32.

—— '*Dostoevsky i antichnost'* L. V. Pumpianskogo (1922) i M. M. Bakhtina (1963)', [Proceedings of] The Seventh International Bakhtin Conference, Book I (Moscow: Moscow State Pedagogical University, 1995), 1–10.

PARROTT, RAY, '(Re)Capitulation, Parody or Polemic?', in Benjamin A. Stolz, Lubomir Doložel and I. R. Titunik (eds.), *Language and Literary Theory* (Ann Arbor, Mich.: University of Michigan, 1984), 463–88.

PECHEY, GRAHAM, 'Chronotope, Concept, Carnival'; 'Avantgarde Projects and the Vanguard Party'; 'Eternity and Modernity; or, Bakhtin and the Theoretical Sublime'; 'Speech within Speech: Writing as Hearing' (unpublished MSS).

—— 'Boundaries versus Binaries: Bakhtin in/against the History of Ideas', *Radical Philosophy*, 54 (1990), 23–31.

—— 'Modernity and Chronotopicity in Bakhtin', in David Shepherd (ed.), *The Contexts of Bakhtin: Philosophy, Authorship, Aesthetics* (New York: Harwood Academic Publishers, 1998), 173–82.

—— 'Philosophy and Theology in "Aesthetic Activity"', *Dialogism*, 1 (1998), 57–73.

PINSKY, L., review of *Rabelais*, *Voprosy literatury*, 6 (1966), 200–6.

PIROG, GERALD, 'The Bakhtin Circle's Freud: From Positivism to Hermeneutics', *Poetics Today*, 8: 3–4 (1987), 591–610.

POLAN, DANA, 'Bakhtin, Benjamin, Sartre: Toward a Typology of the Intellectual Cultural Critic', in Catriona Kelly, Michael Makin, and David Shepherd (eds.), *Discontinuous Discourses in Modern Russian Literature* (Basingstoke: Macmillan, 1989), 3–18.

POOLE, BRIAN, 'Mikhail Bakhtin i teoriia romana vospitaniia', in V. L. Makhlin (ed.), *M. M. Bakhtin i perspektivy gumanitarnykh nauk* (Vitebsk: N. A. Pan'kov, 1994), 62–72.

—— '"Nazad k Kaganu"', *Dialog Karnaval Khronotop*, 1 (1995), 38–48.

—— 'Rol' M. I. Kagana v stanovlenii filosofii M. M. Bakhtina', in *Bakhtinskii sbornik*, vol. iii (Moscow: Labirint, 1997), 162–81.

—— 'From Phenomenology to Dialogue: Max Scheler's Phenomenological Tradition and Mikhail Bakhtin's Development from *Towards a Philosophy of the Act* to his Study of Dostoevsky', forthcoming in Ken Hirschkop and David Shepherd (eds.), *Bakhtin and Cultural Theory*, 2nd rev. edn. (Manchester: Manchester University Press).

—— 'Bakhtin and Cassirer: The Philosophical Origins of Bakhtin's Carnival Messianism', *South Atlantic Quarterly*, 97: 3/4 (1998), 537–78.

RYKLIN, MIKHAIL K., 'Tela terorra: Tezisi k logike nasiliia', in *Bakhtinskii sbornik*, vol. i (Moscow: Prometei, 1990), 60–76; English translation: 'Bodies of Terror: Theses towards a Logic of Violence', *New Literary History*, 24: 1 (1993), 51–74.

SEGRE, CESARE, 'What Bakhtin Left Unsaid: The Case of the Medieval Romance', in Kevin Brownlee and Marina Scordiles Brownlee (eds.), *Romance: Generic Transformations from Chrétien de Troyes to Cervantes* (Hanover, NH: University Press of New England, 1985), 23–46.

SHEPHERD, DAVID, 'Recent Work on Bakhtin: "Homecoming" and "Domestication"', *Scottish Slavonic Review*, 18 (1992), 61–79.

—— (ed.), *The Contexts of Bakhtin: Philosophy, Authorship, Aesthetics* (New York: Harwood Academic Publishers 1998).

SHUKMAN, ANN, 'M. M. Bakhtin: Notes on his Philosophy of Man', in William Harrison and Avril Pyman (eds.), *Poetry, Prose and Public Opinion: Aspects of Russia 1850–1970* (Letchworth: Avebury, 1984), 241–50.

—— 'Bakhtin's Tolstoy Prefaces', in Gary Saul Morson and Caryl Emerson (eds.), *Rethinking Bakhtin: Extensions and Challenges* (Evanston, Ill.: Northwestern University Press, 1989), 137–48.

STALLYBRASS, PETER, and WHITE, ALLON, *The Politics and Poetics of Transgression* (London: Methuen, 1986).

STAM, ROBERT, *Subversive Pleasures: Bakhtin, Cultural Criticism, and Film* (Baltimore, Md. and London: Johns Hopkins University Press, 1989).

THOMSON, CLIVE, 'The Semiotics of M. M. Bakhtin', *University of Ottawa Quarterly*, 53: 1 (1983), 11–21.

—— and DUA, HANS RAJ (eds.), *Dialogism and Cultural Criticism* (London, Canada: Mestengo Press, 1995).

—— and WALL, ANTONY, 'Cleaning Up Bakhtin's Carnival Act', *Diacritics*, 23: 2 (1993), 47–70.

TIHANOV, GALEN, 'Bakhtin, Lukács and German Romanticism: The Case of Epic and Irony', in Carol Adlam *et al.* (eds.), *Face to Face: Bakhtin in Russia and the West* (Sheffield: Sheffield Academic Press, 1997), 273–98.

—— 'Bakhtin's Essays on the Novel (1935–41): A Study of their Intellectual Background and Innovativeness', *Dialogism*, 1 (1998), 30–56.

TITUNIK, I. R., 'The Baxtin Problem: Concerning Katerina Clark's and Michael Holquist's *Mikhail Bakhtin*', *Slavic and East European Journal*, 30: 1 (1986), 91–5.

TODOROV, TZVETAN, *Mikhail Bakhtin: The Dialogical Principle*, trans. Wlad Godzich (Manchester: Manchester University Press, 1984).

USPENSKY, BORIS, *A Poetics of Composition: The Structure of the Artistic Text and Typology of a Compositional Form*, trans. Valentina Zavarin and Susan Wittig (Berkeley, Ca.: University of California Press, 1973).

WEHRLE, ALBERT, 'Introduction M. M. Bakhtin/P. N. Medvedev', in Bakhtin/Medvedev [*sic*], *The Formal Method in Literary Scholarship* (Cambridge, Mass. and London: Harvard University Press, 1985), pp. xv–xxix.

WHITE, ALLON, 'The Struggle over Bakhtin: Fraternal Reply to Robert Young', *Cultural Critique*, 8 (1987–88), 217–41.

WILLIAMS, RAYMOND, 'The Uses of Cultural Theory', *New Left Review*, 158 (1986), 19–31.

YATES, FRANCES, review of *Rabelais*, *New York Review of Books*, 13: 6 (9 Oct. 1969), 16–21.

YOUNG, ROBERT, 'Back to Bakhtin', *Cultural Critique*, 2 (1985), 71–92.

ZIMA, PETER, 'Text and Context: The Socio-linguistic Nexus', in id. (ed.), *Semiotics and Dialectics: Ideology and the Text* (Amsterdam: John Benjamins, 1981).

HISTORY, SOCIAL THEORY, AND PHILOSOPHY

ADORNO, THEODOR, *Minima Moralia*, trans. E. F. N. Jephcott (London: Verso, 1974).

ANDERSON, BENEDICT, *Imagined Communities: Reflections on the Origin and Spread of Nationalism* (London: Verso, 1983).

ANDERSON, PERRY, 'Max Weber and Ernest Gellner: Science, Politics, Enchantment', in *Zones of Engagement* (London: Verso, 1992), 182–206.

ASKOL'DOV, S., 'Vnutrennyi krizis trantsendental'nogo ideializma', *Voprosy filosofii i psikhologii*, 125 (1914), 781–98.

BALIBAR, ÉTIENNE, and MACHEREY, PIERRE, 'On Literature as an Ideological Form', in Robert Young (ed.), *Untying the Text: A Post-Structuralist Reader*

(Boston, Mass., London, and Henley: Routledge & Kegan Paul, 1981), 79–99.

BARTHES, ROLAND, 'Saussure, the Sign, Democracy', in *The Semiotic Challenge*, trans. Richard Howard (Oxford: Basil Blackwell, 1988), 151–6.

BARTSCH, RENATE, *Norms of Language* (London and New York: Longman, 1987).

BELY, ANDREI, *Mezhdu dvukh revoliutsii* (Moscow: Khudozhestvennaia literatura, 1990).

BENJAMIN, WALTER, *Illuminations*, trans. Harry Zohn (New York: Schocken Books, 1969).

——'Edward Fuchs, Collector and Historian', in *One-Way Street and Other Writings*, trans. Edmund Jephcott and Kingsley Shorter (London: New Left Books, 1979), 349–86.

——'On the Programme for a Coming Philosophy' [1917–18], trans. Mark Ritter, in Gary Smith (ed.), *Benjamin: Philosophy, Aesthetics, History* (Chicago, Ill.: University of Chicago Press, 1989), 1–12.

BERMAN, MARSHALL, *All that is Solid Melts into Air: The Experience of Modernity* (New York: Simon & Schuster, 1982).

BERNSTEIN, J. M., *Recovering Ethical Life: Jürgen Habermas and the Future of Critical Theory* (London and New York: Routledge, 1995).

BROWN, E. J., *The Proletarian Episode in Soviet Literature, 1928–1932* (New York: Octagon, 1971).

CALHOUN, CRAIG (ed.), *Habermas and the Public Sphere* (Cambridge, Mass. and London: MIT Press, 1992).

CAMERON, DEBORAH, 'Demythologizing Sociolinguistics: Why Language Does Not Reflect Society', in John E. Joseph and Talbot J. Taylor (eds.), *Ideologies of Language* (London: Routledge, 1990), 79–93.

—— *Verbal Hygiene* (London and New York: Routledge, 1995).

CASSIRER, ERNST, *The Philosophy of Symbolic Forms* [1923–29], 3 vols., trans. Ralph Manheim (New Haven and London: Yale University Press, 1955).

—— *The Individual and the Cosmos in Renaissance Philosophy* [1927], trans. Mario Domandi (Philadelphia: University of Pennsylvania Press, 1963).

—— *The Philosophy of the Enlightenment* [1932], trans. Fritz C. A. Koelln and James P. Pettegrove (Princeton, NJ: Princeton University Press, 1951).

CHARTIER, ROGER (ed.), *The Culture of Print: Power and the Uses of Print in Early Modern Europe*, trans. Lydia G. Cochrane (Cambridge: Polity Press, 1989).

CHOMSKY, NOAM, *Language and Responsibility*, trans. John Viertel (Sussex: Harvester Press, 1979).

CHUDAKOVA, M. O., and TODDES, E. A., 'Tynianov v vospominaniiakh sovremennika', in *Tynianovskii sbornik: Pervye Tynianovskie chteniia* (Riga: Zinatne, 1984).

COLLETTI, LUCIO, 'Rousseau as Critic of "Civil Society"', in *From Rousseau to Lenin: Studies in Ideology and Society*, trans. John Merrington and Judith White (New York and London: Monthly Review Press, 1974), 143–93.

COMRIE, BERNARD (ed.), *The Major Languages of Western Europe* (London: Routledge, 1990).

CROWLEY, TONY, *The Politics of Discourse: The Standard Language Question in British Cultural Debates* (Basingstoke: Macmillan, 1989).

—— 'That Obscure Object of Desire: A Science of Language', in John E. Joseph and Talbot J. Taylor (eds.), *Ideologies of Language* (London: Routledge, 1990), 27–50.

—— *Language in History: Theories and Texts* (London: Routledge, 1996).

DERRIDA, JACQUES, 'Genesis and Structure of the *Essay on the Origin of Languages*', in *Of Grammatology*, trans. Gayatri Chakravorty Spivak (Baltimore, Md.: Johns Hopkins University Press, 1976), 167–71.

—— 'Signature Event Context', in *Margins of Philosophy*, trans. Alan Bass (Chicago, Ill.: University of Chicago Press, 1982), 307–30.

—— 'The Force of Law: The "Mystical Foundation of Authority"', *Cardozo Law Review*, 11: 5–6 (1990), 919–1045.

EDER, KLAUS, 'Politics and Culture: On the Sociocultural Analysis of Political Participation', in Axel Honneth, Thomas McCarthy, Claus Offe, and Albrecht Wellmer (eds.), *Cultural–Political Interventions in the Unfinished Project of Enlightenment*, trans. Barbara Fultner (Cambridge, Mass. and London: MIT Press, 1992), 95–120.

EISENSTEIN, ELIZABETH L., *Print as an Agent of Change*, 2 vols. (Cambridge: Cambridge University Press, 1979).

ELEY, GEOFF, 'Nations, Publics, and Political Cultures: Placing Habermas in the Nineteenth Century', in Nicholas B. Dirks *et al.* (eds.), *Culture/Power/History: A Reader* (Princeton, NJ: Princeton University Press, 1991), 297–335.

ENZENSBERGER, HANS MAGNUS, 'Constituents of a Theory of the Media', *New Left Review*, 64 (1970), 13–36.

—— 'The Industrialization of the Mind', in *Critical Essays* (New York: Continuum, 1982), 3–14.

ERMOLAEV, HERMANN, *Soviet Literary Theories, 1917–1934* (Berkeley, Ca.: University of California Publications, 1963).

FEBVRE, LUCIEN, and MARTIN, HENRI-JEAN, *The Culture of the Book: The Impact of Printing, 1450–1500*, ed. Geoffrey Nowell-Smith and David Wootton, trans. David Gerard (London: Verso, 1984).

FITZPATRICK, SHEILA (ed.), *Cultural Revolution in Russia, 1928–1931* (Bloomington, Ind.: Indiana University Press, 1978).

—— *The Cultural Front: Power and Culture in Revolutionary Russia* (Ithaca and New York: Cornell University Press, 1992).

FOUCAULT, MICHEL, 'The Order of Discourse', in Robert Young (ed.), *Untying the Text: A Post-Structuralist Reader* (Boston, Mass., London, and Henley: Routledge & Kegan Paul, 1981), 48–78.

FRASER, NANCY, *Unruly Practices: Power, Discourse and Gender in Contemporary Social Theory* (Cambridge: Polity Press, 1989).

—— *Justice Interruptus: Critical Reflections on the 'Postsocialist' Condition* (London and New York: Routledge, 1997).

GADET, FRANÇOISE, *Saussure and Contemporary Culture*, trans. Gregory Elliott (London: Hutchinson Radius, 1989).

GODEL, ROBERT, *Les Sources manuscrites du cours de linguistique générale de F. de Saussure* (Geneva: Droz, 1969).

GRAMSCI, ANTONIO, *Selections from Political Writings, 1910–1920*, trans. John Matthews (London: Lawrence & Wishart, 1977).

——*Selections from Cultural Writings*, trans. William Boelhower (London: Lawrence & Wishart, 1985).

HABERMAS, JÜRGEN, 'The Classical Doctrine of Politics in Relation to Social Philosophy', in id., *Theory and Practice*, trans. John Viertel (Boston, Mass.: Beacon Press, 1973), 41–81.

——*Legitimation Crisis*, trans. Thomas McCarthy (London: Heinemann, 1976).

——*Communication and the Evolution of Society*, trans. Thomas McCarthy (London: Heinemann, 1979).

——'On Right and Violence: A German Trauma', *Cultural Critique*, 1 (1985), 125–39.

——'Walter Benjamin: Consciousness-Raising or Rescuing Critique' [1972], in *Philosophical-Political Profiles*, trans. Frederick G. Lawrence (Cambridge: Polity Press, 1986).

——*Knowledge and Human Interests*, trans. Jeremy J. Shapiro (Cambridge: Polity Press, 1986).

——*The Philosophical Discourse of Modernity*, trans. Frederick Lawrence (Cambridge: Polity Press, 1987).

——*On the Logic of the Social Sciences*, trans. Shierry Weber Nicholsen and Jerry A. Stark (Cambridge, Mass. and London: MIT Press, 1988).

——*The Structural Transformation of the Public Sphere: An Inquiry into a Category of Bourgeois Society*, trans. Thomas Burger and Frederick Lawrence (Cambridge, Mass. and London: MIT Press, 1989).

——*Moral Consciousness and Communicative Action*, trans. Christian Lenhardt and Shierry Weber Nicholsen (Cambridge, Mass. and London: MIT Press, 1990).

——*Autonomy and Solidarity: Interviews with Jürgen Habermas*, rev. edn., ed. Peter Dews (London: Verso, 1992).

——'Further Reflections on the Public Sphere', in Craig Calhoun (ed.), *Habermas and the Public Sphere*, 421–61.

——*Postmetaphysical Thinking*, trans. William Mark Hohengarten (Cambridge: Polity Press, 1992).

——*Justification and Application: Remarks on Discourse Ethics*, trans. Ciaran P. Cronin (Cambridge, Mass. and London: MIT Press, 1993).

——*The Past as Future*, trans. and ed. Max Pensky (Cambridge: Polity Press, 1994).

HELLER, AGNES, *Everyday Life* (London: Routledge & Kegan Paul, 1984).

HIRSCHKOP, KEN, 'A Complex Populism: The Politics of Raymond Williams', *News from Nowhere*, 6 (1989), 12–22.

——'Short-Cuts to the Long Revolution: The Russian Avant-garde and the Modernization of Language', *Textual Practice*, 4: 3 (1990), 428–41.

HOBSBAWM, ERIC, *Age of Extremes: The Short Twentieth Century* (London: Michael Joseph, 1994).

HOGGART, RICHARD, *The Uses of Literacy* (London: Chatto & Windus, 1957).

HONNETH, AXEL, 'Critical Theory in Germany Today: An Interview with Axel Honneth', *Radical Philosophy*, 65 (1993), 33–41.

—— *The Struggle for Recognition: The Moral Grammar of Social Conflicts*, trans. Joel Anderson (Cambridge: Polity Press, 1995).

HUSSERL, EDMUND, *Logical Investigations*, trans. J. N. Findlay (London and Henley: Routledge & Kegan Paul, 1970).

—— 'Philosophy as Rigorous Science', in *Husserl: Shorter Works*, ed. Peter McCormick and Frederick Elliston (Brighton: Harvester Press, 1981), 166–97.

IAKOVENKO, B., 'O teoreticheskoi filosofii Germana Kogena', *Logos*, 1 (1910), 199–249.

JAMES, C. VAUGHAN, *Soviet Socialist Realism: Origins and Theory* (London: Macmillan, 1973).

JAMESON, FREDRIC, *The Prison-House of Language: A Critical Account of Structuralism and Formalism* (Princeton, NJ: Princeton University Press, 1972).

—— *Fables of Aggression: Wyndham Lewis, the Modernist as Fascist* (Berkeley, Ca.: University of California Press, 1981).

KEMP-WELCH, A., *Stalin and the Literary Intelligentsia, 1928–1939* (Basingstoke: Macmillan, 1991).

KLUBACK, WILLIAM, *The Legacy of Hermann Cohen*, Brown Judaic Studies 167 (Atlanta, Ga.: Scholars Press, 1989).

KÖHNKE, KLAUS CHRISTIAN, *The Rise of Neo-Kantianism: German Academic Philosophy between Idealism and Positivism*, trans. R. J. Hollingdale (Cambridge: Cambridge University Press, 1991).

KOSELLECK, REINHART, *Futures Past: On the Semantics of Historical Time*, trans. Keith Tribe (Cambridge, Mass. and London: MIT Press, 1985).

—— *Critique and Crisis: Enlightenment and the Pathogenesis of Modern Society* (Cambridge, Mass.: MIT Press, 1988).

KOSIK, KAREL, 'Metaphysics of Everyday Life', in *Dialectics of the Concrete*, trans. K. Kovanda and J. Schmidt (Dordrecht: D. Reidel, 1976).

KRISTEVA, JULIA, 'The Ethics of Linguistics', in *Desire in Language,* ed. Leon S. Roudiez, trans. Thomas Gora, Alice Jardine, and Leon S. Roudiez (Oxford: Basil Blackwell, 1980), 23–35.

LABOV, WILLIAM, *Sociolinguistic Patterns* (Oxford: Basil Blackwell, 1978).

LACLAU, ERNESTO, *Politics and Ideology in Marxist Theory* (London: Verso, 1979).

LEFEBVRE, HENRI, *The Critique of Everyday Life*, vol i: *Introduction*, trans. John Moore (London: Verso, 1991).

LEFORT, CLAUDE, *The Political Forms of Modern Society*, trans. Alan Sheridan (Cambridge: Polity Press, 1986).

LEPENIES, WOLF, *Between Literature and Science: The Rise of Sociology*, trans. R. J. Hollingdale (Cambridge: Cambridge University Press, 1988).

LEVINAS, EMMANUEL, *The Theory of Intuition in Husserl's Phenomenology*, trans. André Orianne (Evanston, Ill.: Northwestern University Press, 1973).

LIEBERSOHN, HARRY, *Fate and Utopia in German Sociology, 1870–1923* (Cambridge, Mass. and London: MIT Press, 1988).

LLOYD, DAVID, and THOMAS, PAUL, *Culture and the State* (New York and London: Routledge, 1997).

Logos (1910–14, 1925), Tübingen and Moscow.

LOSSKY, N., *Vvedenie v filosofiiu*, vol. i (St Petersburg: Stasiulevich, 1911).

—— 'Novaia forma filosofskogo krititsizma', *Voprosy filosofii i psikhologii*, 23: 3 (1912), 118–67.

—— *Tsennost' i bytie* (Paris: YMCA Press, 1931).

LUKÁCS, GEORG, *The Theory of the Novel*, trans. Anna Bostock (Cambridge, Mass.: MIT Press, 1971).

MacINTYRE, ALASDAIR, *After Virtue*, 2nd edn. (London: Duckworth, 1985).

MAGUIRE, ROBERT, *Red Virgin Soil: Soviet Literature in the 1920s* (Princeton, NJ: Princeton University Press, 1968).

MARX, KARL, *Early Writings*, trans. Rodney Livingstone and Gregor Benton (Harmondsworth: Penguin Books, 1975).

MATEJKA, LADISLAV, and POMORSKA, KRYSTYNA (eds.), *Readings in Russian Poetics* (Cambridge, Mass.: MIT Press, 1971).

MILROY, JAMES, and MILROY, LESLEY, *Authority in Language: Investigating Language Prescription and Standardisation*, 2nd edn. (London: Routledge, 1991).

MILROY, LESLEY, *Language and Social Networks*, 2nd edn. (Oxford: Basil Blackwell, 1987).

MISCH, GEORG, *Geschichte der Autobiographie* (Leipzig and Berlin: B. E. Teuber, 1907); English translation: *A History of Autobiography in Antiquity*, 2 vols., trans. E. W. Dickes (London: Routledge & Kegan Paul, 1950).

MOMMSEN, WOLFGANG J., *The Political and Social Theory of Max Weber: Collected Essays* (Cambridge: Polity Press, 1989).

MORETTI, FRANCO, *The Way of the World: The* Bildungsroman *in European Culture*, trans. Albert Sbragia (London: Verso, 1987).

—— *Signs Taken for Wonders*, 2nd edn., trans. Susan Fischer, David Forgacs, and David Miller (London: Verso, 1988).

—— *Modern Epic: The World System from Goethe to García Márquez*, trans. Quintin Hoare (London and New York: Verso, 1996).

NAUEN, FRANZ, 'Hermann Cohen's Concept of the State and the Problem of Anti-Semitism (1867–1907)', in *Jahrbuch des Instituts für deutsche Geschichte*, vol. viii (Tel Aviv: University of Tel Aviv, 1979), 257–82.

NGŨGĨ WA THION'GO, 'The Language of African Literature', *New Left Review*, 150 (1985), 109–27.

OAKES, GUY, *Weber and Rickert: Concept Formation in the Cultural Sciences* (Cambridge, Mass.: MIT Press, 1988).

'Our Verbal Work', *LEF*, 1 (Mar. 1923), 40–1.

PASTERNAK, BORIS, *Doctor Zhivago*, trans. Max Hayward and Manya Harari (New York: Pantheon, 1958).

—— *Safe Conduct: An Autobiography and Other Writings* (New York: New Directions, 1958).

PAULIN, TOM, 'A New Look at the Language Question', in Field Day Theatre Company, *Ireland's Field Day* (London: Hutchinson, 1985), 3–17.

PIERCE, CHARLES SANDERS, 'The Scientific Attitude and Fallibilism', in *Philosophical Writings of Pierce* (New York: Dover, 1955), 42–59.

PITKIN, HANNAH FENICHEL, 'Representation', in Terence Ball, James Farr, and Russell L. Hanson (eds.), *Political Innovation and Conceptual Change* (Cambridge: Cambridge University Press, 1989), 132–54.

PIVEN, FRANCES FOX, and CLOWARD, RICHARD, *Why Americans Don't Vote* (New York: Pantheon, 1989).

POULANTZAS, NICOS, *State, Power, Socialism*, trans. Patrick Camiller (London: Verso, 1978).

'Problema teorii romana', *Literaturnyi kritik*, 2 (1935), 214–49, and 3 (1935), 231–54.

RAEFF, MARC, *Origins of the Russian Intelligentsia: The Eighteenth-Century Nobility* (New York and London: Harcourt Brace, 1966).

RAWLS, JOHN, *A Theory of Justice* (Oxford: Clarendon Press, 1972).

RIASANOVSKY, NICHOLAS V., *A Parting of Ways: Government and the Educated Public in Russia, 1801–1855* (Oxford: Clarendon Press, 1976).

ROBBINS, BRUCE (ed.), *The Phantom Public Sphere* (Minneapolis, Minn.: University of Minnesota Press, 1993).

ROSE, GILLIAN, *Hegel Contra Sociology* (London: Athlone Press, 1981). ·

—— *Dialectic of Nihilism: Post-Structuralism and Law* (Oxford: Basil Blackwell, 1984).

ROUSSEAU, JEAN-JACQUES, *The Social Contract and Discourses*, trans. G. D. H. Cole (London and Melbourne: J. M. Dent & Sons, 1973).

—— *Essay on the Origin of Languages*, trans. John H. Moran (Chicago, Ill.: University of Chicago Press, 1986).

SALTZMAN, JUDY DEANE, *Paul Natorp's Philosophy of Religion within the Marburg Neo-Kantian Tradition* (New York: Georg Olms Verlag Hildesheim, 1981).

SAUSSURE, FERDINAND DE, *Course in General Linguistics*, ed. Charles Bally and Albert Sechehaye, trans. Roy Harris (London: Duckworth, 1983).

SCHELER, MAX, *Formalism in Ethics and Non-Formal Ethics of Values*, trans. Manfred S. Frings and Roger L. Funk (Evanston, Ill.: Northwestern University Press, 1973).

SCHMITT, CARL, *The Crisis of Parliamentary Democracy*, trans. Ellen Kennedy (Cambridge, Mass.: MIT Press, 1985).

SCHNÄDELBACH, HERBERT, *Philosophy in Germany, 1831–1933*, trans. Eric Matthews (Cambridge: Cambridge University Press, 1984).

SENNETT, RICHARD, *The Fall of Public Man: On the Social Psychology of Capitalism* (New York: Vintage, 1976).

SEYFFERT, PETER, *Soviet Literary Structuralism: Background—Debate—Issues* (Columbus, Oh.: Slavica, 1985).

SHEIN, LOUIS J., *Readings in Russian Philosophical Thought* (The Hague: Mouton, 1968).

SHPET, GUSTAV, *Iavlenie i smysl': Fenomenologiia kak osnovnaia nauka i ee problemy* (Moscow: Germes, 1914).

—— *Vnutrennaia forma slova: Etiudy i variiatsii na temu Gumbol'ta* (Moscow: Gosudarstvennaia Akademiia khudozhestvennykh nauk, 1927).

SITTE, CAMILLO, *City Planning According to Artistic Principles* [1889], trans. in George R. Collins and Christiane Crasemann Collins, *Camillo Sitte: The Birth of Modern City Planning* (New York: Rizzoli, 1986).

STEINER, PETER, *Russian Formalism: A Metapoetics* (Ithaca, NY and London: Cornell University Press, 1984).

STRIEDTER, JURIJ, *Literary Structure, Evolution and Value: Russian Formalism and Czech Structuralism Reconsidered* (Cambridge, Mass. and London: Harvard University Press, 1989).

TAYLOR, CHARLES, *Hegel* (Cambridge: Cambridge University Press, 1975).

——, APPIAH, K. ANTHONY, HABERMAS, JÜRGEN, *et al.*, *Multiculturalism: Examining the Politics of Recognition*, ed. Amy Gutmann (Princeton, NJ: Princeton University Press, 1994).

TAYLOR, TALBOT J., *Mutual Misunderstanding: Scepticism and the Theorizing of Language and Interpretation* (London: Routledge, 1992).

THERBORN, GÖRAN, *Science, Class and Society* (London: Verso, 1976).

——'The Rule of Capital and the Rise of Democracy', *New Left Review*, 103 (1977), 3–41.

THEUNISSEN, MICHAEL, *The Other: Studies in the Social Ontology of Husserl, Heidegger, Sartre and Buber*, trans. Christopher Macann (Cambridge, Mass. and London: MIT Press, 1986).

THOMPSON, E. P., *The Making of the English Working Class* (New York: Vintage, 1966).

TIMPANARO, SEBASTIANO, 'Structuralism and its Successors', in *On Materialism*, trans. Lawrence Garner (London: Verso, 1976), 135–219.

TODD, WILLIAM MILLS III, *Fiction and Society in the Age of Pushkin: Ideology, Institutions, and Narrative* (Cambridge, Mass. and London: Harvard University Press, 1986).

UNGER, ROBERTO MANGABEIRA, *Knowledge and Politics* (New York: The Free Press, 1975).

VAN DER LINDEN, HARRY, *Kantian Ethics and Socialism* (Indianapolis and Cambridge: Hackett, 1988).

VENTURI, FRANCO, *Roots of Revolution: Populist and Socialist Movements in Nineteenth-century Russia*, trans. Francis Haskell (Chicago, Ill.: University of Chicago Press, 1960).

VINOKUR, GRIGORY, 'Kul'tura iazyka (Zadachi sovremennogo iazykoznaniia)', *Pechat' i revoliutsiia*, 5 (1923), 100–11.

VVEDENSKY, A. I., *Psikhologiia bez vsiakoi metafiziki*, 2nd edn. (Petrograd: Stoeiulevich, 1915).

——*Filosofskie ocherki* (Prague, 1924).

WEBER, MAX, *Economy and Society*, 2 vols., ed. Guenther Roth and Claus Wittrich (Berkeley, Ca.: University of California Press, 1978).

——'Science as a Vocation', and 'Politics as a Vocation', in *From Max Weber*, ed. H. H. Gerth and C. Wright Mills (London: Routledge & Kegan Paul, 1991).

WILLETT, JOHN, *The New Sobriety: Art and Politics in the Weimar Period, 1917–33* (London: Thames & Hudson, 1978).

WILLEY, THOMAS E., *Back to Kant: The Revival of Kantianism in German Social and Historical Thought, 1860–1914* (Detroit, Mich.: Wayne State University Press, 1978).

WILLIAMS, RAYMOND, *Resources of Hope*, ed. Robin Gable (London: Verso, 1989).

—— and SAID, EDWARD, 'Media, Margins and Modernity', in Raymond Williams, *The Politics of Modernism: Against the New Conformists* (London: Verso, 1989), 177-97.

WITTGENSTEIN, LUDWIG, *Philosophical Investigations*, trans. G. E. M. Anscombe (Oxford: Basil Blackwell, 1981).

ŽIŽEK, SLAVOJ, *The Sublime Object of Ideology* (London: Verso, 1989).

—— *For they know not what they do: Enjoyment as a Political Factor* (London: Verso, 1991).

Index

act, and oughtness 50–1
Adorno, Theodor 89, 155, 178
aesthetic form:
  and ideology 41–3
  of language 207–10
  and modernity 72–82, 95–108
  and narrative 177–9, 243–8
  and the novel 90–2
  and representation of history 235–9
  as type of intersubjectivity 58–67, 161–3
aesthetic love 60, 67
aesthetics:
  and collectivism 215
  and democracy 40–3, 105–8, 292–8
  role of 156
Alpatov, V. M. 139, 185 n. 137
Anderson, Benedict 261
  Imagined Communities 22 n. 31
Andropov, Iuri 191
Antonov, A. F. 175 n. 125
Aragon, Louis 184
author, role of:
  in aesthetic activity 60–7
  in epic 278
  in novel 69, 71, 78–81, 85–6, 192
author/observer, perspective of, in dialogue
  208–9, 227–8, 236, 264
authoritarianism, and heteroglossia 40, 101,
  257–8
  see also official culture; seriousness
authority:
  absolute, and official seriousness 278–80
  in language 19, 87–9, 219, 263–4
  see also power, political
authorship dispute 126–40, 162
autonomy 239–43, 278, 295–6
Averintsev, Sergei 120–1, 275 n. 4

Bakhtin, Mikhail:
  attitude of, towards politics 3, 145
  biography, construction of 111–14, 115,
  124–6
  career, shape of 11, 52–8, 148–9
  death of 193
  education of 140–4
  employment of 158, 175
  family 111–12, 140
  friendships 124–6, 144–5, 146–8

  and Marxism 131–3
  osteomyletis 168–9, 176
  as philosophical personality 120–1, 125–6,
  129–30, 133–8
  publication of works by 112–13, 115–24,
  140
  rehabilitation of 114–26, 190–1
  and Soviet intellectual life 158, 176, 184–5,
  189
  and Stalinist repression 168–9, 171, 175–6,
  272–3

BAKHTIN, MIKHAIL (WORKS)
  'Additions and Amendments to "Rabelais"'
  182, 276, 287, 291
  'Art and Responsibility' 61, 112, 147
  'Author and Hero' 11–12, 52, 54–67,
  69–82 *passim*, 96, 97–8, 108, 134–5, 149,
  162–3, 167, 178, 207, 231, 232, 236,
  239, 281
  'Author and Hero: First Chapter' 122
  Bildungsroman project 113, 176–9, 225,
  233–4, 266
  Collected Works 86, 113 n. 5, 122–4, 137, 140
  The Dialogic Imagination 119, 120, 122 n. 30
  'Dialogue – II' 84, 123 n. 32, 187–8
  'Discourse in the Novel' 54–7, 62, 67–93,
  96, 123, 170, 174–5, 178, 187, 213, 221,
  223, 225, 255
  'Epic and Novel' 96, 266, 288
  Estetika slovesnogo tvorchestva 121–2, 123, 138
  'On Flaubert' 86–7, 176, 183
  'Forms of Time and of the Chronotope in
  the Novel' 176, 179, 193, 233
  'Language in Artistic Literature' 187–8
  'Lectures and Interventions' (from 1924 to
  1925 seminar) 211
  'On Mayakovsky' 176, 183
  'Notes from 1961' 124
  'Notes from 1970–71' 55 n. 9, 191–2
  'The Problem of Content, Material and
  Form' 52, 112, 119, 149, 161–2
  'The Problem of Speech Genres' 84, 123,
  137, 187, 188–9
  'The Problem of the Text' 123, 187, 210
  Problems of Dostoevsky's Art 12, 14, 61–2,
  74–6, 88, 101, 112, 115–17, 136, 137,
  167–8, 174, 178, 189, 190, 220–2, 225,
  226, 250

BAKHTIN, MIKHAIL (WORKS) (cont.):
  Problems of Dostoevsky's Poetics 116–17,
    120 n. 25
  'On Questions of Self-Consciousness' 182
  'On Questions of the Theory of the
    Novel' 182–3
  Rabelais (dissertation and book) 114, 117,
    120 n. 25, 136, 176, 180–5, 191, 249–50,
    266, 284–5
  'Rhetoric' 182
  'Satire' 113, 176
  Tolstoy prefaces 112–13, 169
  'Towards a Methodology of the Human
    Sciences' 55 n. 9, 193
  'Towards Philosophical Bases of the
    Human Sciences' 123, 186, 193, 200–3,
    276
  'Towards a Philosophy of the Act' 34, 52,
    91, 122, 134–5, 149–56, 163, 205, 207
  'Towards a Reworking of the Dostoevsky
    Book' 116, 123–4
  Voprosy literatury i estetiki 119–20, 138

Bakhtin, Nikolai 111–12, 140, 141, 142, 144,
  145–6
becoming, see historical becoming
Bely, Andrei 142
Benjamin, Walter viii, 100 n. 43, 191, 247,
  267, 293, 298
Bergson, Henri 52 n. 5, 99, 151, 163
Bernstein, J. M. 41 n. 64
biography, genre of 230–1, 243, 283
Bocharov, S. G.:
  on Bakhtin circle 135, 147
  as Bakhtin's executor 119, 122 n. 30
  on disputed texts 128–9, 133, 137, 138
  as editor 121, 123
  and rehabilitation of Bakhtin 15, 116, 117
body 282
Bonetskaia, N. K. 6, 8, 55 n. 9, 133, 134
Buber, Martin:
  The Dialogical Principle 5
  I and Thou 5
Bühler, Karl 167
Bulgakov, Mikhail 128, 249

Camus, Albert 221
carnival, see popular-festive culture
Cassirer, Ernst 123, 142, 144
  Goethe and the Historical World 237 n. 15
  The Individual and the Cosmos in Renaissance
    Philosophy 114
  Philosophy of the Enlightenment 237 n. 15
  Philosophy of Symbolic Forms 143 n. 76, 167,
    178 n. 128
Chomsky, Noam 17 n. 21

Christianity:
  and aesthetic intersubjectivity 65–7, 82–3,
    162–3, 239–41
  and collectivism 165–6
  and ethical reality 154–5
  and interiority 232–3
  and the public square 261–2
  and structure of language 197–8
chronotopes 177–9, 225, 236, 270, 276
  see also narrative
circle(s):
  'Bakhtin' 133–5, 144–5, 146–8, 156–68,
    175–6
  as form of intellectual work 125–6, 158–60
Clark, Katerina 50, 111 n. 2, 122 n. 30, 127,
  174
Cohen, Hermann 25, 52 n. 5, 60, 102, 142,
  143 n. 76, 154, 161, 284
collectivism 165–6, 214–16
Colletti, Lucio 46
Communism 288–90
community:
  dialogical, and truth 207
  speech, as value 216–19
concreteness:
  and chronotopicity 236
  of language 208–13, 220–1, 223
confession 154, 166, 222
conflict, social 78–9, 90–1, 261–7
consummation, as aesthetic 58, 71–2, 74,
  95–8, 162
contemporaneity 12, 13 n. 17, 16
  see also modernity
context, public square as 259–60, 264–7
conversation 78–9
culture:
  fear and violence in 293
  as historical 101–3, 143–4, 164–5
  and obligation 50–1
  sacredness of 103, 246
  see also democratic culture; history

democracy viii–ix
  and decisions 261, 267–8
  and fear 274–6, 290
  as form of intersubjectivity 203
  and historical culture 293–8
  and language 17–18, 21, 26–49, 219
  and legitimacy 38 n. 58
  and modernity 56–7, 105–8
  and narrative 245–8
  and science 291–2
  uncertainty of, and authoritarianism
    278–80
democratic culture, idea of 27, 30–7, 42–5,
  274–5, 292–8

Den' isskustva 147
Derrida, Jacques 47, 48, 208
dialogism 67–108, 208–12, 221–3, 236
  contrasted with dialogue 3–10, 48–9, 54–8,
    76, 209, 221–3
  and ethical reality 167–8, 191–3
  historical content of 15–16, 21–2
  and the human sciences 188, 193
  and linguistic diversity 257
  and narrative 225–8, 264–6
  and politics 15–16, 77, 106–8
  and redemption 41–2
  and truth 205–7
  as truth of language 174–5, 204
Dilthey, Wilhelm 123 n. 32
disinterestedness 104–5, 202, 285, 291
disputed texts, *see* authorship dispute
Dostoevsky, Fedor:
  and Bakhtin circle 156, 161
  and carnival 190–1
  and dialogism 11, 191, 220–2, 259
  as figure of modernity 73–6
  as innovator 14, 267
  realism of 177, 198, 199
  and religion 128, 250
  and sentimentalism 276
double-voiced discourse 79–81, 87, 93, 95,
  175
  see also voice, concept of
Durkheim, Émile 18 n. 23, 155, 165, 216
Duvakin, V. D. 111, 112, 125
Dymshits, A. 117 n. 16

Eder, Klaus 30 n. 47
Eikhenbaum, Boris 142 n. 70
Eliot, T. S. 221, 282
embodiment 82–6
Emerson, Caryl 7–8, 130, 182
  The First Hundred Years of Mikhail Bakhtin
    99 n. 42, 115
  Mikhail Bakhtin 99 n. 42, 122 n. 30
Enlightenment 237
Enzensberger, Hans Magnus 37, 267
epic 246, 266, 277–9, 288–90
Ermilov, V. 118
ethical life:
  and language 35–6, 84, 86–90
  and narrative 229–48
  and theatrical space 270
ethical philosophy, project for 148–56, 173,
  197–8
ethical reality:
  and history 236, 293
  and the human sciences 163–6, 186–8
  and language 166–8, 173, 197–224
  and the novel 89, 104–5, 294–5

and philosophy 51–3, 147, 149–50
as source of obligation 152–6
see also I and *other*, architectonics of
Europe:
  cultural crisis of 50–2
  democracy in 34–5, 106
  political philosophy in 38–40
everyday language 265
everyday life 107, 191, 281–3
  epic distance from 278–9, 289

faith 154 n. 94, 155, 191, 237–8, 292
fear, culture of 272–6, 280–3, 287–92, 293
Fichte, J. G. 240
Ficino, Marsilio 114
Flaubert, Gustave 229
Formalism, Russian 83, 118, 119–20, 161–2,
  282
Foucault, Michel 253 n. 3, 282
Freud, Sigmund 155, 161, 163
Fridlender, G. 118, 120
future, orientation to 25, 96–7, 103, 108,
  178, 239, 246–8
  and seriousness 281, 288–9

Gachev, G. 15 n. 18
Gadet, Françoise 217, 223
Galileo 291
genre, concept of 10, 22, 188–9, 220
Goethe, J. W. 177, 179, 180, 233, 234–8 *pas-
  sim*, 249, 267
  Faust 238 n. 17
Gogol, Nikolai 156, 191
Gogotishvili, L. A. 6, 55 n. 9, 133, 187
Gorky, Maxim 169, 174
Gramsci, Antonio 202–3, 257–8
  Prison Notebooks 27

Habermas, Jürgen:
  on emancipation 275 n. 3
  on individuality 240
  Knowledge and Human Interests 166 n. 111
  on language 84, 105, 238
  on legitimacy 32 n. 51, 38, 40–1, 43
  On the Logic of the Social Sciences 173 n. 121
  on morality 244
  on the public sphere 30–3, 45, 47–8, 158,
    280
  on rationality 107, 220 n. 28, 265
  on role of philosophy 13, 97
  on truth 206, 207, 211
Hale, Dorothy 81 n. 25
Harnack, Adolf von 203 n. 9
Hegel, G. W. V. 51 n. 3, 70, 103 n. 52, 104,
  151, 161
Heidegger, Martin 100 n. 45

Hessen, Sergei 100 n. 45
heteroglossia 22–3, 68, 250–71
  and dialogism 77–9, 85–6, 90, 92, 213
  and narrative 228
historical becoming:
  as aesthetic substance of the novel 72,
    98–105, 177–84, 228–30, 233–9
  and democracy 295–8
  and philosophy 24–5
  and the public square 249–51, 258, 261–71
  and responsibility 241–3
  and seriousness 276–83, 287–92
history:
  and Bakhtin's theory of language 21–6
  as cultural creation 25, 89–95, 103–4, 156,
    245–8, 292–3
  and fear 273
  and modernity 13, 96–8
  and philosophy, in Bakhtin's work 10–15,
    23–5, 53–4
  see also literary history; modernity
Hobbes, Thomas 198, 288
Hoggart, Richard 62 n. 11
Holmes, Oliver Wendell 28 n. 43
Holquist, Michael 50, 111 n. 2, 119–20 n. 22,
  122 n. 30, 127, 174
Honneth, Axel 42 n. 66
Howes, Craig 225 n. 1
humanism, and Rabelais 184–5
Humboldt, Wilhelm von 173
Hume, David 198
Husserl, Edmund 65, 83, 100 n. 45, 161, 201

I and *other*, architectonics of:
  and aesthetics 59, 63–4, 243
  and Dostoevsky 75–6, 221
  and modernity 96–8
  and narrative 230, 236, 238–41, 262–3
  and philosophy 51–2
  sociologizing of 232–3
  see also ethical reality; individual horizon
Iakovenko, B. 103 n. 52
Iakubinsky, Lev 166
  'On Dialogic Speech' 123
immortality, desire for 277
individual horizon 59, 156
  and seriousness 277, 280–2
  transcendence of, by the novel 86–93,
    181–4, 262, 284–5
  transcendence of, by science 98–103,
    291–2
individuality, constitution of 240
inner and outer speech 212
instrumental reason, critique of 265
intellectual life, models of 129–30, 133–8
intention, concept of 117

interests:
  representability of 91–3
  and social movements 104–5
  see also practical interestedness
intersubjectivity 4–5, 59–69
  historical development of 13–15, 48–9,
    239–48, 262–4
  and language 18–20, 69, 80, 83–93, 197–8,
    201, 209, 213–24, 253–4
  and legitimacy 37–45, 153–6
  and politics 31–4, 77, 106–8, 202–3
  and responsibility 269–71, 286
  and truth 206–7
  see also ethical reality
intonation 208, 212
irony 80
Iudina, M. V. 135 n. 58, 147, 160
Ivanov, Viacheslav (Symbolist poet) 141 n. 69
Ivanov, Viacheslav (semiotician) 118, 119,
  125, 126, 127, 204

Jakobson, Roman 16 n. 19, 83 n. 28, 125 n. 36,
  189
Jameson, Fredric 78 n. 23
Jones, Ernest 161
Joyce, James 221
judgement, role of 240–1, 262–4, 295
justice, morality of 38–45
justification, and history 97–8, 229, 238,
  246–8, 263–4

Kafka, Franz 221
Kagan, M. I. 160, 171 n. 119, 176
  and Bakhtin circle 74 n. 21, 134, 135 n. 58,
    147, 148, 157, 161
  and historical consciousness 24, 25,
    102 n. 49, 103, 246
  'How is History Possible?' 156
  'Judaism in the Crisis of Culture' 156, 284
  and neo-Kantianism 142, 143, 144
Kanaev, I. I. 160
Kant, Immanuel:
  aesthetics of 58, 59, 235
  Bakhtin on 100, 160–1
  image of redemption in 155, 192, 291
  moral theory of 31, 32, 34, 51 n. 3, 151,
    153, 198–9
  neo-Kantian reading of 102, 103 n. 52
  and truth 206
Kartsevsky, Sergei 16 n. 19
Khrushchev, Nikita 115
kingdom of ends 192, 197
Konkin, S. S. 111, 115 n. 8, 127, 176
Kontekst 119
Koselleck, Reinhart 97, 158
Kozhinov, V. V.:

on Bakhtin 121 n. 28, 125 n. 36
and Bakhtin's biography 111 n. 2, 115 n. 8
as Bakhtin's executor 119
correspondence with Bakhtin 129
on disputed texts 127, 135, 138
and rehabilitation of Bakhtin 15 n. 18,
  116–18, 189
Kuhn, Helmut 94

Laclau, Ernesto 297 n. 17
language:
  and ethical life 35–6, 166–8, 173, 175,
    197–224
  and heteroglossia 250–70
  and metalinguistics 188–9
  and politics 15–21, 26–49, 258
  as transformed in the novel 78–93, 251–4
  turn to, in Bakhtin's work 11, 21–5, 69,
    166–8, 197–9, 204–5, 219–24
laughter 182–3, 290–2
  see also popular-festive culture
law 151–3
Lefort, Claude 279
Left Front in Arts 165
legitimacy 31–2, 32 n. 51, 37–45, 151–2
  see also oughtness/obligation
Leibovich, S. L. 117 n. 15
Lenin, V. I. 26
Liapunov, Vadim 25
liberal democracy, see democracy
liberalism:
  and autonomy 240, 296
  and dialogism 8–10, 92–3
  and disenchantment 215
  and individualism 184, 290
  and language 27–35
  and legitimacy 151–2
life, as value category 72, 92–3, 230–1
linguistic diversity, see heteroglossia
linguistics, concept of language in 16–21,
  23–4, 34–5, 213–19, 223–4
The Literary Critic 174
Literary Encyclopedia (Soviet) 174, 176
literary history, role of 97–8, 175, 176–7,
  213, 225 n. 1
Lloyd, David 260
Logos 100–1, 142–3
Lossky, N. O. 100 n. 45, 141, 211–12 n. 16
Lotman, Iuri 119
Lukács, Georg 86, 93, 174, 251
  History and Class Consciousness 132
  Theory of the Novel 73, 80, 174 n. 123
Lunacharsky, A. V. 169

MacIntyre, Alasdair 226–7
Makhlin, Vitaly 55 n. 9

Malevich, Kasimir 148
Marr, N. 123 n. 32
Marx, Karl 155, 164, 165
Marxism 8 n. 10, 129–33, 164–5, 169
Matejka, Ladislav 122 n. 30
Matijašević, Radovan 128 n. 42
Mayakovsky, Vladimir 234
meaning:
  concept of 4–5, 223–4
  demand for 282–3, 289
medium, and language 19–20
Medvedev, Iuri 127
Medvedev, P. N.:
  and authorship dispute 126–39, 162
  and Bakhtin circle 146, 148, 156, 158, 160,
    175, 176
  on concreteness 212, 221
  The Formal Method 62, 126–31, 134–5, 161,
    163–4, 221
  and neo-Kantianism 100, 165
Meier, A. A. 135 n. 58, 136, 155 n. 95,
  160 n. 105
Meillet, Antoine 20
Merezhkovsky, Dmitri 101
metalinguistic discourse 20
metalinguistics 187, 188, 191–2, 197
Metner, E. K. 100 n. 45
Mihailovic, Alexander 155 n. 95
Misch, Georg 123
  Geschichte der Autobiographie 232, 233
modernism 282
modernity:
  and aesthetic form 72–7, 93–105
  and democracy 105–8, 293–4, 297–8
  and fear 274, 280–3
  and legitimacy 32 n. 51, 152
  and the novel 12–14, 70, 192
  and politics 15, 38–45, 48–9, 56
  and Stalinism 172–3
  and voice 93–5
monologism 294
  see also authoritarianism; official culture;
    seriousness; unified language
Moretti, Franco:
  Signs Taken for Wonders 42
  The Way of the World 42, 78 n. 23
Morson, Gary Saul 7–8, 122 n. 30, 130, 133,
  182
  Mikhail Bakhtin 99 n. 42, 122 n. 30
multilanguagedness 19
  see also heteroglossia
myth 178–9

narrative 177–9, 223–48, 262–8
  as form of ideology 42
  and the modern state 288–90, 295–6

national language(s) 22–3, 26–7, 260–1
    standard forms within 255–8
nationalism 288, 296–7
Natorp, Paul 142
neo-Kantianism:
    and history 284–5, 291
    influence of, on Bakhtin 117–18 n. 17,
        141–4, 205–6
    and language 167, 216
    and moral theory 52 n. 5, 152–3
    and Marxism 130–1, 132, 164–5
    and personality 203
    and role of philosophy 24–5, 100–3, 160–1
Nevel' school 133–4
Nietzsche, Friedrich 52 n. 5, 99, 132, 151,
        163, 203
Nikolaev, N. I. 6, 133–4 149, 162,
        272–3 n. 2
    on Dostoevsky book 74 n. 20, 137, 168,
        220
novel:
    and democracy 106–8, 270, 294–8
    as dialogical 4–5, 48–9, 67–108, 213,
        222–8
    and heteroglossia 251–4
    and modernity 12–13, 23
    and narrative 222–38
    significance of theory of 170–86, 189,
        225–6
novel of becoming 233, 235, 247–8
Nusinov, N. M. 185 n. 137

official culture 70, 105–6, 163
    and epic 266
    fear and seriousness in 272–83, 287–90
    and individual horizon 183–4
    see also authoritarianism; seriousness; unified
        language
Omphalos 144–5, 273 n. 2
Orwell, George 26
Osokin, P. M. 160 n. 105
oughtness/obligation 50–2, 150–2, 242
    in communication 84–5
    and uniqueness 208, 211

Pan'kov, Nikolai 112 n. 3, 139
participant's perspective, in dialogue 208–9,
        212–13, 221, 227, 236
past, epic 278–9
Pasternak, Boris 130
    Doctor Zhivago 103, 116
Pechey, Graham 236
'the people', as category 45–6, 71, 288–9,
        297 n. 17
person and structure, dialectic of 21–2

personality:
    and language 200–4, 221–2
    and narrative 230–4, 239–45
phenomenology 65–7, 83, 96, 153–5, 201–2
philosophy:
    as cure to social crisis 50–6, 160–5
    and popular-festive culture 181–2
    role of, in Bakhtin's work 11–15, 23–5,
        50–6, 99–103, 108, 120–4, 186–7
    and sociology 131–8, 156–7, 219–20
Pico della Mirandola 114
Pierce, C. S. 95 n. 38
political fear 287–90
politics:
    Bakhtin's attitude towards 3, 108, 145,
        274, 290
    and culture 162–3, 274–6
    and historical change 285–98
    and language 15–49, 69–70, 258
    and modernity 38–45
    and narrative 245–8
    and theory of the novel 171–3
    value of dialogue within 74–5, 261
polyphony 167, 227–8, 259
Pompanazzi, Pietro 114
Poole, Brian:
    on Bakhtin's sources 25, 63, 114, 167,
        178 n. 128, 284
    on Bildungsroman project 113 n. 5, 276 n. 6
    and dating and editing of Bakhtin's texts
        123 n. 32, 135
Popova, I. L. 6
popular-festive culture:
    in Bakhtin's writing 171, 272, 275–6
    and Dostoevsky 190–1
    and historical becoming 180–2, 282, 283–7
    see also rogue, clown and fool
populism 68, 70–1, 107, 171, 278, 296–7
power, political:
    as individualistic 183–4, 250, 277, 285–90
    and responsibility 238–9, 241–2, 286
    see also authority
practical interestedness 90, 94–5, 180, 204,
        250, 260, 265
    see also interests
praise, pure 279–80
print culture 22–3, 260–1, 264
proceduralism 28–33
proper name 279
psychoanalysis 139, 154 n. 94, 161, 163
psychologism, struggle against 160–6
public sphere 30–2, 44–5, 158–60, 206
public square 231–2, 249–71, 284
Pumpiansky, L. V.:
    and Bakhtin circle 133–4, 135 n. 58, 144–9
        passim, 158, 160, 161, 174 n. 123, 176,

273 n. 2
Dostoevsky and Antiquity 73, 74 nn. 21–2, 156
Pushkin, Aleksandr 161
'Parting' 149

Rabelais, François:
  as exemplary novelist 177, 179, 233, 234, 236, 249–50, 267
  Gargantua and Pantagruel 181
  and popular-festive culture 272, 274, 276, 281, 282, 285, 291
Ranke, Otto 161
Rawls, John, *A Theory of Justice* 29 n. 44
realism:
  of the average 183
  and ethics 198–201
  and popular-festive culture 180–1
recognition, value of 242–3, 245–6
redemption:
  and democracy 43
  and the dialogical novel 41–2, 89–90, 108
  and history 155, 191, 192–3, 237
  and narrative 177–8, 229–30
  and practical interestedness 204
  and responsibility 242–3
religion:
  and Bakhtin interpretation 6–7
  and nature of obligation 211
  see also Christianity
reported speech 264
representation:
  artistic, of the *I-for-myself* 75–6
  artistic, of language 81–93, 212–13, 223, 227–8
  and democracy 47, 106–7
  epic 277–8
  and the public square 258–61
responsibility:
  aestheticization of 235, 238
  and communication 84–5
  crisis of, in Europe 34, 51
  and ethical life 147, 153–4, 165
  and historical becoming 247–8, 269–71, 286–8
  as intersubjective achievement 239–43, 295, 296, 298
  and the modern state 288
Revelation, significance of 84–5, 153
rhetoric 261
Rickert, Heinrich 100 n. 45, 142, 161
rights 290, 298
risk, and democratic politics 107, 280, 296–7
rogue, clown and fool 270, 284, 286–7
roles:
  and aesthetic satisfaction 244, 247–8

and responsibilities 242–3, 269–71, 286–7, 295
Rose, Gillian 203, 216, 231
Rousseau, J. J. 32, 45–9, 288
  Essay on the Origin of Languages 46, 47
  The Social Contract 45–6
Rozanov, V. V. 101
Rugevich, A. S. 160, 176
Russia:
  intellectuals in 158–60
  modernization of 215
Russkii sovremennik 112
Ryklin, Mikhail K. 273 n. 2

Saussure, F. de:
  concept of language 34, 35, 44, 155, 222, 247, 263
  Course in General Linguistics 16–21, 24
  influence of, on Bakhtin 173, 213–19
  and Voloshinov 16, 23, 131, 164, 214–15, 217–20, 223–4
Scheler, Max 161, 166, 198–9, 202
  The Essence and Forms of Sympathy 63
Schelling, F. W. 161
Schiller, Friedrich 295
Schmitt, Carl 43, 280 n. 11
science:
  and historical becoming 99–103, 180–1
  and language, *see* linguistics
  and metalinguistics 187–8
  and the novel 108, 291–2
  and philosophy 23–4, 118, 120–1, 160–5
  and theoreticism 150–1, 153
Segre, Cesare 227–8
Sennett, Richard 107
sentimentalism 183, 276–7
seriousness 183–4, 276–83
  see also authoritarianism; official culture
Shakespeare, William 234, 291
  1 Henry IV 287
  King Lear 287
  Macbeth 287
Shestov, Lev 101
Shklovsky, Viktor 118, 142 n. 70, 189
Shpet, Gustav 83 n. 28, 173
  Appearance and Meaning 50 n. 1
Simmel, Georg 100 n. 45, 163, 203
Siniavsky, Andrei 125 n. 36
Sitte, Camillo 262
socialist realism 172, 174
socio-ideological languages 77–95, 250–4, 262–4
sociology, role of 131, 133, 136, 137, 165
Sollertinsky, I. I. 139, 148, 158, 161 n. 106
Spengler, Oswald 163
Spitzer, Leo 123

sport 281
Stalin, Josef 39, 184
    'Marxism and Questions of Linguistics'
        187, 189
Stalinism 169, 171–4, 184, 272–4
Stallybrass, Peter 275
state:
    Bakhtin's concept of 70
    and fear 287–90
    and individualism 183–4
    see also power, political
Stepun, Fedor 100 n. 45
Strada, Vittorio 116–17
Struve, Peter 100 n. 45
style:
    dialogism as 79–81, 89
    and politics 16, 17, 21, 26–7, 36–7, 43–5
stylistics of genre 14
Sukhanov, N. N., Notes on the Revolution 174
superaddressee, concept of 237–8, 295–6
syntax, problem of 217–18

Taylor, Charles 184 n. 134
Teriaeva, M. P. 250
theoretical reason/theoreticism 50–2, 150–1,
        164, 171, 172, 186–7
Therborn, Göran 216
Thomas, Paul 260
Thompson, E. P. 246 n. 25
Tihanov, Galen 174 n. 123
time, see historical becoming
Titunik, I. R. 122 n. 30, 130
Todorov, Tzvetan 11, 55 n. 9, 173
    Mikhail Bakhtin: The Dialogical Principle 5
Tolstoy, A. N. 169
totalitarianism, concept of 39–40
tradition, and epic 277–8
tragedy:
    and individualism 182–3, 276–7
    and politics 287
truth:
    and authority 88
    dialogical model of 205–7
    and modernity 101
Tubiansky, M. I. 160, 176
Turbin, V. N. 124, 145, 191
Tynianov, Iuri 142 n. 70

understanding, as intersubjective 4–5, 82–5
uneven structuring of language 253–8,
        263–4, 266–70, 297–8
unified language 254–8
uniqueness, meaning of 210–12
Uspensky, Boris 118 n. 19, 119
utterance, concept of 209–13

Vaginov, K. K. 135 n. 58, 160
value:
    biographical 231
    and modernity 93–5
    and narrative 246–8
    and validity 216
Vinokur, Grigory 214–17
visibility, of history 179–80, 234–5
voice(s), concept of 80–2, 90–5, 105–8, 226
    see also socio-ideological languages
Voloshinov, V. N.:
    and authorship dispute 126–40
    and Bakhtin circle 146, 147, 148, 160, 161,
        162, 176
    'Discourse in Life and Discourse in Poetry'
        167, 197
    Freudianism 140, 163, 166
    influence of, on Bakhtin 53, 69, 133, 135,
        136, 166–8, 251, 264
    'The Latest Trends in Linguistic Thought'
        23
    and Logos 100
    Marxism and the Philosophy of Language
        122 n. 30, 126–40, 163–4, 165, 167, 218,
        219
    rehabilitation of 189
    and Saussure 16, 23, 164, 213, 217–20,
        223–4
    on the utterance 209–10, 212, 221
Voloshinova, N. A. 128 n. 42
Voprosy literatury 119
Vossler, Karl 100 n. 45
Vulis, A. Z. 53
Vvedensky, A. I. 141
    Psychology Without Any Metaphysics 143

Walzel, Oskar 123
Weber, Max:
    on legitimacy 37–8, 41, 43, 151, 155
    and modernity 101, 206, 265, 282
    and neo-Kantianism 100 n. 45, 165,
        220 n. 28
    and personality 203
    'Politics as a Vocation' 242
    'Science as a Vocation' 94–5, 242–3
White, Allon 275
Williams, Raymond ix, 3, 47, 61 n. 10,
        62 n. 11, 134
Windelband, Wilhelm 142
Wittgenstein, Ludwig 84
worldly ideology 219–20

Zelinsky, F. F. 100 n. 45, 113, 141
Žižek, Slavoj 88, 278–9
Zubakin, B. M. 147, 160, 176